PRAXIS I PPST: PRE-PROFESSIONAL SKILLS TEST

Third Edition

LEARNINGEXPRESS®

NEW YORK

Library of Congress Cataloging-in-Publication Data:

PPST : Praxis, Pre-Professional Skills Test / LearningExpress.—3rd ed.
    p.   cm.
  ISBN 978-1-57685-653-6
  1. Pre-Professional Skills Tests—Study guides.   I. LearningExpress (Organization).
LB2367.75.P677 2008
378.1'662—dc22

                                                      2008036929

Printed in the United States of America

9 8 7 6 5 4 3 2 1

Third Edition

For more information or to place an order, contact LearningExpress at:
  2 Rector Street
  26th Floor
  New York, NY 10006

Or visit us at:
  www.learnatest.com

PRAXIS I PPST: PRE-PROFESSIONAL SKILLS TEST

Contents

PRAXIS I PPST: PRE-PROFESSIONAL SKILLS TEST

How to Use▶
This Book

If you are applying to a teacher training or certification program in one of the many states, schools, or agencies that require testing for admission, chances are you will have to attain passing scores on the Praxis I®: Academic Skills Assessments. Most states choose the Praxis I because of its proven capability for determining scholastic aptitudes of applicants. Scores from the Praxis I help to ensure that those entering a teacher-training program—and ultimately the teaching workforce—are proficient in reading, math, and writing. These three exams of the Praxis I are known individually as Pre-Professional Skills Tests (PPST®). The purpose of the PPSTs is to ensure that you are qualified, and LearningExpress's goal is to ensure that you pass the tests!

THIS BOOK IS designed to give you the test-taking skills you need to tackle each of the PPSTs, whether you decided to take the paper-based tests or the computer-based tests. *Praxis I, Third Edition* contains all the information you need to improve your score in the shortest amount of time possible. This chapter serves as a guide for using this book (and the CD-ROM) effectively, so you get the most out of your time and effort.

▶ The Book

This book includes:

- a chapter explaining all about the Praxis I
- three review chapters covering the three subjects of the PPST tests
- three full-length Praxis I practice exams, complete with answers and explanations
- instructions on how to use the free CD-ROM that comes with this book

You may want to start with Chapter 1, "Praxis I." This chapter tells you how to register for the exam and where to find testing sites. It also gives you an overview of the test content and format. Even if you are already familiar with this information, it's still a good idea to review this chapter.

Next, read Chapter 2, "The LearningExpress Test Preparation System." As the title suggests, this chapter teaches you how to prepare for any test effectively using LearningExpress's proven test-taking strategies. You will learn to

- set up a personalized study plan, utilizing the lessons and tests in this book
- use your study time efficiently
- make educated guesses when you are unsure of an answer
- overcome test anxiety

After you have mastered these skills, try taking the first full-length practice exam in Chapter 3 before moving on to the reading, math, and writing reviews in Chapters 4, 5, and 6. This way, you can better assess your personal strengths and weaknesses, allowing you to focus your time where you need it most.

Once you have taken the first practice exam and read through the answer explanations, you are ready to get started with your study plan and move on to the review chapters. All three of the review chapters are great tools for studying for each of the PPSTs, and each includes examples and explanations so you can practice as you learn. You should read all of the review chapters, putting more emphasis on the subjects that were problematic for you on the first practice exam.

Chapter 4, the "Reading Test Review," is designed to review the reading skills you will need to pass the PPST Reading test. Since you will be timed on test day, you will learn how to be an active reader. In other words, this chapter shows you how to read passages to quickly spot the differences between the main ideas and supporting ideas and to pinpoint key concepts in a reading passage. Also, you will learn to skim through the less important information, so that unnecessary and irrelevant information will not bog you down.

The reading review also demonstrates how to make logical inferences, draw likely conclusions, and gauge an author's attitude based on the information given in a reading passage. And like each of the review chapters in this book, there are several practice questions allowing you to apply what you have just learned. There's nothing like having a lot of practice under your belt to make you feel confident when you go into the real exam.

Chapter 5 is the "Mathematics Test Review." Most test takers are intimidated by math questions, so the review is designed to be as clear and concise as possible to bolster your confidence. All of the basics are covered, including: mathematical terms, arithmetic, algebraic foundations and equations, percentages, ratios, measurement, and geometry. Plus, you will learn strategies for solving word problems, analyzing data, interpreting graphs and tables, spotting trends and patterns, and recognizing various ways for solving problems. Since many problems you will face on the PPST Mathematics test will require a combination of math skills to get the correct answer, you should review the examples throughout the chapter.

The "Writing Test Review" in Chapter 6 is an efficient crash course in writing. You will learn how to tackle the two separate sections of the writing exam: the multiple-choice questions and the essay-writing section. The writing multiple-choice review covers the basics in the areas of grammar, mechanics, word usage, and sentence structure. For the essay portion, you will find useful writing strategies so that you can compose a clear, well-organized essay, effectively stating your objective. Whether you choose to write your essay on paper or on the computer, you (or a trusted friend) should score it using the scoring criteria included in the lesson.

Chapter 7, "Praxis I Practice Exam 2," measures your improvement since your first practice exam. Check your answers and read the answer explanations for any questions that you may have guessed on or answered incorrectly. At this point, you should go through the review chapters again (if needed), fine-tuning any areas that still require improvement.

In Chapter 8, you will find the final full-length practice exam. By taking this test, you will practice your test-taking skills, continue to diagnose your weakest areas, and discover where you might still need improvement. Try taking this test under timed conditions—just like the real exam.

▶ The CD-ROM

Do not forget about the free CD-ROM included with this book. The CD-ROM allows you the option of taking a complete test, or just selecting some practice questions in any of the three subjects. In addition, the CD-ROM scores the tests for you and (like the book) offers detailed answer explanations.

If you are going to take the computer-based exam, the CD-ROM provides you with extra practice on the computer. Though the tests on our CD-ROM are not in the same format as the actual computer-based exam, working with this program will help familiarize you with the process of taking a test on a computer. Your actual testing computer at the exam site will go through a step-by-step tutorial on computer-based testing.

Our CD-ROM is designed to be user-friendly; however, please consult the "How to Use the CD-ROM" appendix in the back of this book before you use the program.

▶ You

You already have two valuable tools for passing the test—this book and the free CD-ROM; now the rest is up to you. Ultimately, you will have to rely on yourself to succeed. Remain disciplined, follow your study schedule, and do not give up. Most important—practice, practice, practice. Plenty of practice will improve your skills and build your confidence.

Good luck!

1 ▶ Praxis I

CHAPTER SUMMARY

Most teaching certification programs require that you demonstrate a certain level of academic aptitude in order to be admitted into their credential program. In addition, states that do not require teachers to have a degree in education to be considered for a job do require a passing score on a basic skills test. Of all the states in the country that require standardized testing as a form of measuring basic academic skills, the majority use the Praxis I: Academic Skills Assessments. This chapter will familiarize you with the Praxis I, which is administered by the Educational Testing Service (ETS). This chapter also discusses all of the pertinent information about the Praxis I, including: contact information, the registration process, examination fees, and test format and content. Additionally, you will learn about Praxis I scoring, what the scores are used for, and how they are reported.

ALL OF THE EXAMS in the Praxis Series are designed to measure the scholastic capability of teachers at different stages of their careers. The first exam in the Praxis Series, the Praxis I, is taken early in a student's college career in order to enter into a teaching credential program. It is also taken by prospective teachers to be considered for a license in states not requiring education degrees. The Praxis I is comprised of three individual tests called the Pre-Professional Skills Tests (PPSTs), which are in reading, mathematics, and writing.

The PPSTs are administered in both a paper- and computer-based format. This chapter will discuss both in detail. Although both forms of the test cover the same content, the procedures for registering and taking the tests are very different; therefore, these steps will be discussed separately in this chapter.

The Praxis Series

Praxis I is generally taken to gain entry into a teaching credential program and for state licensing.
Praxis II is taken by would-be teachers who are applying for state licensure as a teacher.*
Praxis III is taken in a classroom setting by beginning teachers.

*For more information on Praxis II, see Appendix A on page 377.

▶ States Using the Praxis I

Currently, the following states and United States territories require passing PPST scores as a component of their teacher certification process:

Alaska	Nevada
Arkansas	New Hampshire
California	New Jersey
Colorado	New Mexico
Connecticut	North Carolina
Delaware	North Dakota
District of Columbia	Ohio
Georgia	Oklahoma
Guam	Oregon
Hawaii	Pennsylvania
Idaho	Rhode Island
Indiana	South Carolina
Kansas	Tennessee
Kentucky	Texas
Louisiana	U.S. Virgin Islands
Maine	Utah
Maryland	Vermont
Minnesota	Virginia
Mississippi	Washington
Missouri	West Virginia
Nebraska	Wisconsin

Not Simply Certification

Some educational organizations require that you achieve passing PPST scores to gain membership. These organizations include: the American Speech-Language-Hearing Association (ASHA), the Council for Exceptional Children (CEC), the Department of Defense Education Activity (DODEA), and the National Association of School Psychologists (NASP).

All states and agencies using the Praxis Series require that examinees possess a high school diploma, a GED, or another high school equivalency form. Information regarding specific state or organization requirements may change from time to time. For more information, refer to the Praxis website at www.ets.org/praxis/.
Note: Although some of the information for the requirements of California is included on the Praxis website, those interested in meeting requirements for California should contact:

California Commission on Teacher Credentialing (CTC)
Information Services Unit
P.O. Box 944270
1900 Capitol Avenue
Sacramento, CA 94233-2700
Phone: 888-921-2682 or 916-445-7254, 12:00 P.M. to 4:45 P.M. (PST)
E-mail: credentials@ctc.ca.gov (include a postal address in e-mail)

Important Contact Information

ETS—The Praxis Series
P.O. Box 6051
Princeton, NJ 08541-6051
Phone: 609-771-7395, M–F 8 A.M. to 7:45 P.M. (EST)
Phone for the Hearing Impaired: 609-771-7714
Fax: 609-530-0581 or 609-771-7906
E-mail: praxis@ets.org
Website: www.ets.org/praxis/

▶ What Is the Praxis I Like?

All of the questions on the Praxis I, with the exception of the essay portion of the PPST Writing test, are in multiple-choice format. Each multiple-choice question has five answer choices. Because test scoring is based only on the number of items answered correctly, you are not penalized for guessing on the PPSTs—so be sure to fill in all of the answer blanks rather than leaving difficult questions unanswered.

Each of the three sections of the Praxis I is designed to test one of the following skills:

- Reading
- Math
- Writing

▶ Reading

The PPST Reading test measures your ability to comprehend and analyze written information. You will be asked to read a number of passages (which may vary in length from 100 to 200 words) and then answer questions that test your ability to comprehend what you have read. You will be tested only on your ability to understand and analyze the selection; you will not be required to have specific knowledge about the topics discussed in the passages. Chapter 4, "Reading Test Review," provides more detailed coverage of the question types you will face. The following are general types of questions that you may be asked:

Literal Comprehension
- main idea questions
- supporting idea questions
- organization questions ·
- vocabulary questions

Critical and Inferential Comprehension
- argument evaluation questions
- inferential reasoning questions
- generalization questions

▶ Mathematics

The PPST Mathematics test measures your proficiency in math. Generally speaking, the test requires a competency at the high school or first-year college level. The lessons in Chapter 5, "Mathematics Test Review," will give you more in-depth coverage of test content. Here are the four main math skills that will be tested:

Numbers and Operations
- order
- equivalence
- numeration and place value
- number properties
- operation properties
- computation
- estimation
- ratio, proportion, and percent
- numerical reasoning

Algebra
- equations and inequalities
- algorithmic thinking
- patterns
- algebraic representations
- algebraic reasoning

Geometry and Measurement
- geometric properties
- the *xy*-coordinate plane
- geometric reasoning
- systems of measurement

Data Analysis and Probability
- data interpretation
- data representation
- trends and inferences
- measures of central tendency
- probability

▶ Writing

The PPST Writing test is divided into two sections: The first section consists of multiple-choice questions that require you to find and/or correct errors in standard English; the second part asks you to write a 30-minute essay on an assigned topic, which will represent 50% of your total writing test score. The "Writing Test Review" (Chapter 6) provides detailed information on how to approach both sections of the writing test.

The multiple-choice section of the writing test is designed to measure your ability to use standard English correctly and effectively and is divided into two parts: usage and sentence correction.

Usage questions test your knowledge of:

- structural and grammatical relationships
- mechanics
- idiom or word choice

Usage questions also test your ability to identify error-free sentences.

Sentence Correction questions test your ability to:

- select the best way to state a given phrase or sentence
- correct sentences with errors in grammar, mechanics, idioms, or word choice

The essay portion of the PPST Writing test is designed to evaluate your ability to express ideas clearly and effectively in standard written English. You will be presented with a topic and asked to state an opinion in essay form. The given topics present situations that are generally familiar to all educated people and do not require any specialized knowledge in a particular field. Although you will be posing an argument and drawing conclusions based on examples from personal experience or observation, you will not be graded on your opinion—you will be scored only on how effectively you are able to get your ideas across.

The following qualities will be taken into consideration when your essay is scored:

- *Appropriateness:* whether or not your essay was written appropriately for the task and intended audience
- *Organization:* your ability to organize and develop the essay logically, and make clear connections between ideas
- *Unity and focus:* your ability to devise and sustain a clear thesis throughout the essay
- *Development:* the ability to develop your essay through examples and details that clearly and logically support the ideas presented in your essay
- *Mechanical conventions:* demonstration of a proficient use of the English language and ability to use proper syntax
- *Sentence structure:* the ability to effectively construct sentences, free from error, in standard written English

Nonscorable Questions

From time to time, the ETS needs to try out new questions to see if they are suitable to be used in future editions of the test. These questions will not be identified, because the ETS is trying to determinine how examinees will respond under real testing conditions. The questions are unscored, meaning that they do not count toward or against your score. Not all tests include unscored questions.

▶ What about Scores?

The ETS will mail your official score report about four weeks after your test date for the paper-based test and approximately two to three weeks after computer-based testing. If you take the computer-based test, you can (in most cases) view your reading and math scores at the end of your test session. Your score report will also be sent to the recipients (for example, schools) you designated on your registration form. The report shows a separate test score for each PPST subject that you take. Reading and math test scores are based on the number of items answered correctly. There is no penalty for answering a question incorrectly. The writing test score is based on the number of multiple-choice questions answered correctly combined with the essay score, which is scored on a scale of 1 to 6.

▶ Can I Cancel My Scores?

For the paper-based test, you may cancel your scores for a particular test by submitting a *Request for Score Cancellation* form to the ETS within one week after the test date. If you take a computer-based test, you are given the option to cancel your scores at the end of your test session before viewing the scores (once you have viewed your computerized scores, you cannot cancel them). All score cancellations are permanent, and refunds are not given.

▶ Passing Scores

Each state or institution determines its own passing score. The first thing you will want to do with your scores is to compare them to the passing scores set by your state. Along with your test scores, you will receive the *Understanding Your Praxis Scores* booklet that gives the passing scores for each state. The Praxis Series website (www.ets.org/praxis/) also has a complete state-by-state listing of required tests and passing scores.

▶ Retaking the Tests

If you don't pass one or more PPST tests, you will be allowed to take them again. How many times or how often you may retake each PPST is determined by the policies of individual states or institutions. The ETS does not limit how many times you can take the paper-based tests. However, the ETS does mandate that you may take each of the computer-based tests only once per 30-day period and no more than six times in one year. Individual states may have further restrictions.

► What to Bring to the Test

If you are taking the paper-based test, you will need to bring valid photo identification, your admittance ticket (which is mailed to you following registration or printed after online registration), several #2 pencils, and (if you are taking the writing test) blue or black ink pens. You may also choose to bring a watch, as long as it does not have calculator or keyboard functions. For the computer-based test, you will need your photo identification and your Social Security number.

You may not bring calculators, cell phones, pagers, books, bags, or other people into the test room with you. The test administrator will designate an area where you may keep your personal belongings during the test.

► Time Allowed

Paper-Based Tests

For each paper-based test, you will have 60 minutes of actual testing time. The test administrator will begin timing after all test booklets and Scantron sheets have been handed out and the instructions have been given. You should allow about one and a half hours (90 minutes) for each individual test or four and a half hours if you are taking all three tests on the same day.

Computer-Based Tests

You will be allowed two hours for each individual computer-based test or four and a half hours for the combined computer-based tests. This allows time for tutorials and the collection of background information. Please see "The Computer-Based Test at a Glance" box on page 16 for the time allotted for each individual test.

On test day, allow plenty of time in the morning to get to your test location, especially if you are unfamiliar with the area where the test is given. You should arrive at least 30 minutes before your test in order to sign in, present your identification, and get yourself settled.

► The Paper-Based Test

The paper-based test is offered approximately four times during a testing year at testing centers around the country. Questions are presented in multiple-choice format in a test booklet, and answers are entered onto a Scantron form. The essay portion of the PPST Writing test must be handwritten in blue or black ink.

The Paper-Based Test at a Glance

PPST	Test Code	Number of Questions	Time Allowed
Reading	0710	40 multiple-choice	60 minutes
Mathematics	0730	40 multiple-choice	60 minutes
Writing	0720	38 multiple-choice	30 minutes
		1 essay	30 minutes

Breakdown of Paper-Based Tests

The following table provides the approximate number and percentage of each question type on the paper-based PPSTs:

QUESTION TYPE	NUMBER OF QUESTIONS	PERCENTAGE OF TEST
PPST Reading		
Literal Comprehension	18	45%
Critical and Inferential Comprehension	22	55%
PPST Math		
Numbers and Operations	13	32.5%
Algebra	8	20%
Geometry and Measurement	9	22.5%
Data Analysis and Probability	10	25%
PPST Writing		
Grammatical Relationships	13	17%
Structural Relationships	14	18.5%
Word Choice and Mechanics	11	14.5%
Essay	1	50%

Fees for the Paper-Based Test

PPST Reading:	$40
PPST Math:	$40
PPST Writing:	$40
Registration fee:	$50 (charged once per testing year)
Special Service Fees	
Late registration:	$45
Test, test center, or test date change:	$45
Emergency registration:	$75
Telephone reregistration:	$35
File correction:	$35
Scores by phone:	$30
Additional score reports:	$40 (per report)

▶ Payment Options

You may pay using a Visa, MasterCard, American Express, Discover, or JCB credit card. You can also use a debit card or an authorized voucher. Checks and money orders are also accepted and should be made payable to: ETS—*Praxis*. Cash is never accepted. Fee waivers are available to applicants with financial need.

▶ How Do I Register?

Usually you will need to register at least four weeks prior to the test date. First-time applicants for the paper-based test **must** register by mail or online.

To register by mail you must download and complete the Praxis Registration Form. Approximately one week before your test date, you will receive a testing admission ticket, which you will need to bring for entrance into the test.

You can also register online at www.ets.org/praxis/. Online registration is available Monday through Friday, 7 A.M. to 10 P.M. (EST), and Saturday 7 A.M. through Sunday 8 P.M. (EST). To register online, you will need a valid e-mail address, mailing address, and phone number. Order confirmations and test admission tickets will be e-mailed to your e-mail address—you will not be sent a paper admission ticket by postal mail when you register online. Online registration is available only to those not needing special accommodations such as considerations for disabilities or Monday testing.

If you have taken a Praxis Series test previously, you can register by phone with a credit card. There will be a nonrefundable $35 service fee for the transaction, in addition to the standard registration and test fees. To register by phone, call 800-772-9476, 8 A.M. to 7:45 P.M. (EST), Monday through Friday.

Special arrangements may be available for individuals with documented disabilities or for test takers whose primary language is not English (PLNE). Monday test dates are available to those who cannot test on a Saturday test date due to religious convictions or military orders. These accommodations may vary from state to state. You should contact the ETS long before the test date to make inquiries.

▶ Emergency Registration

Those trying to register for a desired test date after the regular and late registration deadlines may still be able to take the test on that date by using the emergency registration service for an additional $75 fee. This service guarantees a seat at a test center. Emergency registration is not available for individuals needing special accommodations.

▶ Changing Your Test, Test Center, or Test Date

You may add or change a test or change your test center or test date by submitting a completed *Test, Center and Date Change Request* form with the $45 fee to the ETS. Please see the website to download the form and to learn more about deadlines and restrictions associated with your specific request.

To change your test and/or test center, the request form must be received by the emergency registration deadline. To change your test date, you need to submit your request form within two weeks of your original test date. Also, you can change your test date only to a future test date in the same testing year.

▶ To Cancel Your Test Date

You may cancel a test date if your written request is received by the ETS by the late registration deadline. To cancel a test date, you must download and complete the *Refund Request Form*, available online. Then, mail the form to:

Praxis, Registration Refund
P.O. Box 6051
Princeton, NJ 08541-6051

You will receive a refund of your test fees, but not registration or service fees. Refunds will not be given for requests received after the late registration deadline or if you are absent on the test date. Registration deadlines are updated and posted on the website. Refunds are mailed approximately four to six weeks after receipt of your request. If you used a credit card to make a payment, the refund will be credited to your credit card account.

▶ The Computer-Based Test

The Praxis I: Academic Skills Assessments are also available as computer-based tests in over 300 locations throughout the United States. In many ways, the computer-based test is more convenient than the paper-based version. It is given more frequently and provides faster score reporting. You don't have to know much about computers to take the computer-based version—each test begins with a tutorial on the use of the computer. You are encouraged to spend as much time as needed on the tutorial.

▶ About the Computer-Based PPST (CPPST)

With the exception of the essay portion of the writing test, all questions are in multiple-choice format. The questions are presented on the computer screen, and you choose your answers by selecting one choice or highlighting a section. The computer-based tests now have a special "mark" function, which allows you to "mark" a question that you would like to temporarily skip and come back to at a later time during the same section on the test. Test takers will have a review screen to see if a question has been answered, not seen yet, or "marked." The computer-based test is designed to ensure fairness, because each test taker receives:

- the same distribution of content
- the same amount of testing time
- the same test directions
- the same tutorials on computer use

The Computer-Based Test at a Glance (CPPST)

CPPST	Test Code	Number of Questions	Time Allotted
Reading	5710	46 multiple-choice	75 minutes
Mathematics	5730	46 multiple-choice	75 minutes
Writing	5720	44 multiple-choice	38 minutes
		1 essay	30 minutes

Breakdown of Computer-Based Tests

The following table provides the approximate number and percentage of each question type on the CPPSTs:

QUESTION TYPE	NUMBER OF QUESTIONS	PERCENTAGE OF TEST
CPPST Reading		
Literal Comprehension	21	45%
Critical and Inferential Comprehension	25	55%
CPPST Math		
Numbers and Operations	15	32.5%
Algebra	9	20%
Geometry and Measurement	10	22.5%
Data Analysis and Probability	12	25%
CPPST Writing		
Grammatical Relationships	15	17%
Structural Relationships	16	18.5%
Word Choice and Mechanics	13	14.5%
Essay	1	50%

Fees for the Computer-Based Test

One test:	$80
Two tests:	$120
Three tests:	$160
Combined test:	$130

Special Service Fees

File correction:	$35
Scores by phone:	$30
Additional score reports:	$40 (per report)

▶ How Do I Register?

In order to register for the CPPSTs of the Praxis I: Academic Skills Assessments, you need to contact the test center where you would like to take the test, or call Prometric Candidate Services (800-853-6773). Hearing-impaired registrants can call Prometric's TTY phone line (800-529-3590) to register. A list of computer-based testing centers and phone numbers is available at www.ets.org/praxis. For the computer-based tests, you do NOT register using the mail-in form included in the bulletin.

Reminder

Again, you may take the computer-based test only once a month, and no more than six times over the course of a year. This even applies to situations where you may have canceled your scores. If you violate this rule, your retest scores will not be reported and your fees will not be refunded.

▶ To Cancel a Computer-Based Test

You may cancel or reschedule an appointment by calling Prometric Candidate Services (800-853-6773) at least three *business* days prior to your first test date. You can receive a refund of $20 per test or $60 for the combined test as long as you have canceled the test at least three business days before the first scheduled test date. Refund requests must be made in writing and mailed to:

The Praxis Series
CBT Refund
P.O. Box 6051
Princeton, NJ 08541-6051

The ETS will mail your refund in the form of a check or refund your credit card account within eight weeks from the time the request was received.

Nonstandard Testing Accommodations

If you have a documented disability, you may be able to receive nonstandard testing accommodations. Online, you will find the *2007–08 Bulletin Supplement for Test Takers with Disabilities*, which contains contact information, registration procedures, and special registration forms.

If you are requesting accommodations, you cannot register online. Instead, send your completed requests for testing accommodations to:

ETS Disability Services
P.O. Box 6054
Princeton, NJ 08541-6054

► Where Do I Begin?

You have already taken the first step by reading this chapter and familiarizing yourself with the Praxis I. Perhaps you have even started researching to see which PPSTs you need to take, when the tests are offered, and where you would like to take them. Now you should begin your study program: Start with "The LearningExpress Test Preparation System" (Chapter 2). This exclusive system gives you valuable test-taking techniques and will help you devise a study schedule that works best for you. If you stick with your study plan and concentrate on improving the areas in which you need help, you are sure to succeed. Good luck!

CHAPTER

2 ▶ The LearningExpress Test Preparation System

CHAPTER SUMMARY

Taking the Praxis I can be tough. It demands a lot of preparation if you want to achieve a top score. Your future depends on your passing the exam. The LearningExpress Test Preparation System, developed exclusively for LearningExpress by leading test experts, gives you the discipline and attitude you need to be successful.

FACT: TAKING THE PRAXIS I is not easy, and neither is getting ready for it. Your future career as a teacher depends on your getting a passing score, but there are all sorts of pitfalls that can keep you from doing your best on this exam. Here are some of the obstacles that can stand in the way of your success:

- being unfamiliar with the format of the exam
- being paralyzed by test anxiety
- leaving your preparation to the last minute
- not preparing at all!
- not knowing vital test-taking skills: how to pace yourself through the exam, how to use the process of elimination, and when to guess
- not being in tip-top mental and physical shape
- messing up on test day by arriving late at the test site, having to work on an empty stomach, or feeling uncomfortable during the exam because the room is too hot or cold

What's the common denominator in all these test-taking pitfalls? One word: control. Who's in control, you or the exam?

Here's some good news: The LearningExpress Test Preparation System puts you in control. In nine easy-to-follow steps, you will learn everything you need to know to make sure that you are in charge of your preparation and your performance on the exam. Other test takers may let the test get the better of them; other test takers may be unprepared or out of shape, but not you. You will have taken all the steps you need to take to get a high score on the Praxis I.

Here's how the LearningExpress Test Preparation System works: Nine easy steps lead you through everything you need to know and do to get ready to master your exam. Each of the steps listed below includes both reading about the step and one or more activities. It's important that you do the activities along with the reading, or you won't be getting the full benefit of the system. Each step tells you approximately how much time that step will take you to complete.

Step 1: Get Information	50 minutes
Step 2: Conquer Test Anxiety	20 minutes
Step 3: Make a Plan	30 minutes
Step 4: Learn to Manage Your Time	10 minutes
Step 5: Learn to Use the Process of Elimination	20 minutes
Step 6: Know When to Guess	20 minutes
Step 7: Reach Your Peak Performance Zone	10 minutes
Step 8: Get Your Act Together	10 minutes
Step 9: Do It!	10 minutes
Total	**3 hours**

We estimate that working through the entire system will take you approximately three hours, though it's perfectly okay if you work faster or slower. If you take an afternoon or evening, you can work through the whole LearningExpress Test Preparation System in one sitting. Otherwise, you can break it up, and do just one or two steps a day for the next several days. It's up to you—remember, you are in control.

▶ Step 1: Get Information

Time to complete: 50 minutes
Activity: Read Chapter 1, "Praxis I."

Knowledge is power. The first step in the LearningExpress Test Preparation System is finding out everything you can about the Praxis I. Once you have your information, the next steps in the LearningExpress Test Preparation System will show you what to do about it.

Part A: Straight Talk about the Praxis I

Why do you have to take a rigorous exam, anyway? It's simply an attempt to be sure you have the knowledge and skills necessary for a teacher.

It's important for you to remember that your score on the Praxis I does not determine how smart you are or even whether you will make a good teacher. There are all kinds of things an exam like this can't test, like whether you have the drive, determination, and dedication to be a teacher. Those kinds of things are hard to evaluate, while a test is easy to evaluate.

This is not to say that the exam is not important! The knowledge tested on the exam is knowledge you will need to do your job. And your ability to enter the profession you've trained for depends on your passing this exam. And that's why you are here—using the LearningExpress Test Preparation System to achieve control over the exam.

Part B: What's on the Test

If you haven't already done so, stop here and read Chapter 1 of this book, which gives you an overview of the exam. Then, go to the Internet and read the most up-to-date information about your exam directly from the test developers.

► Step 2: Conquer Test Anxiety

Time to complete: 20 minutes
Activity: Take the Test Anxiety Test.

Having complete information about the exam is the first step in getting control of the exam. Next, you have to overcome one of the biggest obstacles to test success: test anxiety. Test anxiety not only impairs your performance on the exam itself, but also keeps you from preparing! In Step 2, you will learn stress management techniques that will help you succeed on your exam. Learn these strategies now, and practice them as you work through the exams in this book, so they will be second nature to you by exam day.

Combating Test Anxiety

The first thing you need to know is that a little test anxiety is a good thing. Everyone gets nervous before a big exam—and if that nervousness motivates you to prepare thoroughly, so much the better. It's said that Sir Laurence Olivier, one of the foremost British actors of the twentieth century, felt ill before every performance. His stage fright didn't impair his performance; in fact, it probably gave him a little extra edge—just the kind of edge you need to do well, whether on a stage or in an examination room.

On page 24 is the Test Anxiety Test. Stop and answer the questions, to find out whether your level of test anxiety is something you should worry about.

Test Anxiety Test

You don't need to worry about test anxiety unless it is extreme enough to impair your performance. The following questionnaire will provide a diagnosis of your level of test anxiety. In the blank before each statement, write the number that most accurately describes your experience.

0 = Never   1 = Once or twice   2 = Sometimes   3 = Often

_____ I have gotten so nervous before an exam that I simply put down the books and didn't study for it.

_____ I have experienced disabling physical symptoms such as vomiting and severe headaches because I was nervous about an exam.

_____ I have simply not shown up for an exam because I was scared to take it.

_____ I have experienced dizziness and disorientation while taking an exam.

_____ I have had trouble filling in the little circles because my hands were shaking too hard.

_____ I have failed an exam because I was too nervous to complete it.

_____ **Total: Add up the numbers in the blanks above.**

Your Test Anxiety Score

Here are the steps you should take, depending on your score. If you scored:

- **Below 3,** your level of test anxiety is nothing to worry about; it's probably just enough to give you that little extra edge.
- **Between 3 and 6,** your test anxiety may be enough to impair your performance, and you should practice the stress management techniques listed in this section to try to bring your test anxiety down to manageable levels.
- **Above 6,** your level of test anxiety is a serious concern. In addition to practicing the stress management techniques listed in this section, you may want to seek additional, personal help by contacting your academic counselor. Tell the counselor that you have a level of test anxiety that sometimes keeps you from being able to take the exam. The counselor may be willing to help you or may suggest someone else you should talk to.

Stress Management before the Test

If you feel your level of anxiety getting the best of you in the weeks before the test, here is what you need to do to bring the level down again:

- **Get prepared.** There's nothing like knowing what to expect and being prepared for it to put you in control of test anxiety. That's why you are reading this book. Use it faithfully, and remind yourself that you are better prepared than most of the people taking the test.
- **Practice self-confidence.** A positive attitude is a great way to combat test anxiety. This is no time to be humble or shy. Stand in front of the mirror and say to your reflection, "I am prepared. I am full of self-confidence. I am going to ace this test. I know I can do it." Record it and play it back once a day. If you hear it often enough, you will believe it.

- **Fight negative messages.** Every time someone starts telling you how hard the exam is or how it's almost impossible to get a high score, start telling them your self-confidence messages you learned about on the previous page. Don't listen to the negative messages. Turn on your recorder and listen to your self-confidence messages.
- **Visualize.** Imagine yourself reporting for duty on your first day as a teacher or in your teacher training program. Visualizing success can help make it happen—and it reminds you of why you are going to all this work in preparing for the exam.
- **Exercise.** Physical activity helps calm your body down and focus your mind. Besides, being in good physical shape can actually help you do well on the exam. Go for a run, lift weights, go swimming—and do it regularly.

Stress Management on Test Day

There are several ways you can bring down your level of test anxiety on test day. They will work best if you practice them in the weeks before the test, so you know which ones work best for you.

- **Practice deep breathing.** Take a deep breath while you count to five. Hold it for a count of one, then let it out on a count of five. Repeat several times.
- **Move your body.** Try rolling your head in a circle. Rotate your shoulders. Shake your hands from the wrist. Many people find these movements very relaxing.
- **Visualize again.** Think of the place where you are most relaxed: lying on the beach in the sun, walking through the park, or whatever. Now close your eyes and imagine you are actually there. If you practice in advance, you will find that you only need a few seconds of this exercise to experience a significant increase in your sense of well-being.

When anxiety threatens to overwhelm you right there during the exam, there are still things you can do to manage the stress level:

- **Repeat your self-confidence messages.** You should have them memorized by now. Say them quietly to yourself, and believe them!
- **Visualize one more time.** This time, visualize yourself moving smoothly and quickly through the test answering every question right and finishing just before time is up. Like most visualization techniques, this one works best if you have practiced it ahead of time.
- **Find an easy question.** Find an easy question, and answer it. Getting even one question finished gets you into the test-taking groove.
- **Take a mental break.** Everyone loses concentration once in a while during a long test. It's normal, so you shouldn't worry about it. Instead, accept what has happened. Say to yourself, "Hey, I lost it there for a minute. My brain is taking a break." Put down your pencil, close your eyes, and do some deep breathing for a few seconds. Then you are ready to go back to work.

Try these techniques ahead of time, and see if they don't work for you!

▶ Step 3: Make a Plan

Time to complete: 30 minutes
Activity: Construct a study plan.

Maybe the most important thing you can do to get control of yourself and your exam is to make a study plan. Too many people fail to prepare simply because they fail to plan. Spending hours on the day before the exam poring over sample test questions not only raises your level of test anxiety, it also is simply no substitute for careful preparation and practice over time.

Don't fall into the cram trap. Take control of your preparation time by mapping out a study schedule. On the following pages are two sample schedules, based on the amount of time you have before you take the Praxis I. If you are the kind of person who needs deadlines and assignments to motivate you for a project, here they are. If you are the kind of person who doesn't like to follow other people's plans, you can use the suggested schedules here to construct your own.

Even more important than making a plan is making a commitment. You have to set aside some time every day for study and practice. Try for at least 20 minutes a day. Twenty minutes daily will do you much more good than two hours on Saturday.

Don't put off your study until the day before the exam. Start now. A few minutes a day, with half an hour or more on weekends, can make a big difference in your score.

Schedule A: The 30-Day Plan

If you have at least a month before you take the Praxis I, you have plenty of time to prepare—as long as you don't waste it! If you have less than a month, turn to Schedule B.

TIME	PREPARATION
Days 1–4	Skim over any other study materials you may have. Make a note of areas you expect to be emphasized on the exam and areas you don't feel confident in. On Day 4, concentrate on those areas.
Day 5	Take the first practice exam in Chapter 3.
Day 6	Score the first practice exam. Identify two areas that you will concentrate on before you take the second practice exam.
Days 7–10	Study one of the areas you identified as your weak point. Don't forget, there is a Reading Test Review in Chapter 4, a Mathematics Test Review in Chapter 5, and a Writing Test Review in Chapter 6. Review one of these chapters in detail to improve your score on the next practice test.
Days 11–14	Study the other area you identified as your weak point. Don't forget, there is a Reading Test Review in Chapter 4, a Mathematics Test Review in Chapter 5, and a Writing Test Review in Chapter 6. Review one of these chapters in detail to improve your score on the next practice test.
Day 15	Take the second practice exam in Chapter 7.
Day 16	Score the second practice exam. Identify one area to concentrate on before you take the third practice exam.
Days 17–21	Study the one area you identified for review. Again, use the Reading, Mathematics, and Writing Test Reviews for help.
Day 22	Take the last practice exam in Chapter 8.
Day 23	Score the test. Note how much you have improved!
Days 24–28	Study any remaining topics you still need to review. Use the review chapters for help.
Day 29	Take an overview of all your study materials, consolidating your strengths and improving on your weaknesses.
Day before the exam	Relax. Do something unrelated to the exam and go to bed at a reasonable hour.

Schedule B: The Ten-Day Plan

If you have two weeks or less before you take the exam, use this ten-day schedule to help you make the most of your time.

TIME	PREPARATION
Day 1	Take the first practice exam in Chapter 3 and score it using the answer key at the end. Note which topics you need to review most.
Day 2	Review one area that gave you trouble on the first practice exam. Use the Reading Test Review in Chapter 4, the Mathematics Test Review in Chapter 5, and the Writing Test Review in Chapter 6. Review one of these chapters in detail to improve your score on the next practice test.
Day 3	Review another area that gave you trouble on the first practice exam. Again, use the Reading Test Review in Chapter 4, the Mathematics Test Review in Chapter 5, and the Writing Test Review in Chapter 6.
Day 4	Take the second practice exam in Chapter 7 and score it.
Day 5	If your score on the second practice exam doesn't show improvement on the two areas you studied, review them. If you did improve in those areas, choose a new weak area to study today.
Days 6–7	Continue to use the review chapters to improve some skills and reinforce others.
Day 8	Take the third practice exam in Chapter 8 and score it.
Day 9	Choose your weakest area from the third practice exam to review.
Day 10	Use your last study day to brush up on any areas that are still giving you trouble. Use the review chapters.
Day before the exam	Relax. Do something unrelated to the exam and go to bed at a reasonable hour.

▶ Step 4: Learn to Manage Your Time

Time to complete: 10 minutes to read, many hours of practice!
Activity: Practice these strategies as you take the sample tests in this book.

Steps 4, 5, and 6 of the LearningExpress Test Preparation System put you in charge of your exam by showing you test-taking strategies that work. Practice these strategies as you take the sample tests in this book, and then you will be ready to use them on test day.

First, you will take control of your time on the exam. It's a terrible feeling to know there are only five minutes left when you are only three-quarters of the way through the test. Here are some tips to keep that from happening to *you*:

- **Follow directions.** You may choose to take the computer-based Praxis exam. You should take your time taking the computer tutorial before the exam. Read the directions carefully and ask questions before the exam begins if there's anything you don't understand.
- **Pace yourself.** If there is a timer on the screen as you take the exam, keep an eye on it. This will help you pace yourself. For example, when one-quarter of the time has elapsed, you should be a quarter of the way through the test, and so on. If you are falling behind, pick up the pace a bit. If you do not take your exam on a computer, use your watch or the clock in the testing room to keep track of the time you have left.
- **Keep moving.** Don't waste time on one question. If you don't know the answer, skip the question and move on. You can always go back to it later.
- **Don't rush.** Though you should keep moving, rushing won't help. Try to keep calm and work methodically and quickly.

▶ Step 5: Learn to Use the Process of Elimination

Time to complete: 20 minutes
Activity: Complete the worksheet on Using the Process of Elimination.

After time management, your next most important tool for taking control of your exam is using the process of elimination wisely. It's standard test-taking wisdom that you should always read all the answer choices before choosing your answer. This helps you find the right answer by eliminating wrong answer choices. And, sure enough, that standard wisdom applies to your exam, too.

You should always use the process of elimination on tough questions, even if the right answer jumps out at you. Sometimes the answer that jumps out isn't right after all. You should always proceed through the answer choices in order. You can start with answer choice **a** and eliminate any choices that are clearly incorrect.

If you are taking the test on paper, like the practice exams in this book, it's good to have a system for marking good, bad, and maybe answers. We're recommending this one:

X = bad
✔ = good
? = maybe

If you don't like these marks, devise your own system. Just make sure you do it long before test day—while you're working through the practice exams in this book—so you won't have to worry about it just before the exam.

Even when you think you are absolutely clueless about a question, you can often use the process of elimination to get rid of one answer choice. If so, you are better prepared to make an educated guess, as you will see in Step 6. More often, the process of elimination allows you to get down to only two possibly right answers. Then you are in a strong position to guess. And sometimes, even though you don't know the right answer, you find it simply by getting rid of the wrong ones.

Try using your powers of elimination on the questions in the worksheet Using the Process of Elimination beginning below. The questions aren't about teaching; they're just designed to show you how the process of elimination works. The answer explanations for this worksheet show one possible way you might use the process to arrive at the right answer.

The process of elimination is your tool for the next step, which is knowing when to guess.

Using the Process of Elimination

Use the process of elimination to answer the following questions.

1. Ilsa is as old as Meghan will be in five years. The difference between Ed's age and Meghan's age is twice the difference between Ilsa's age and Meghan's age. Ed is 29. How old is Ilsa?
   a. 4
   b. 10
   c. 19
   d. 24

2. "All drivers of commercial vehicles must carry a valid commercial driver's license whenever operating a commercial vehicle." According to this sentence, which of the following people need NOT carry a commercial driver's license?
   a. a truck driver idling his engine while waiting to be directed to a loading dock
   b. a bus operator backing her bus out of the way of another bus in the bus lot
   c. a taxi driver driving his personal car to the grocery store
   d. a limousine driver taking the limousine to her home after dropping off her last passenger of the evening

3. Smoking tobacco has been linked to
   a. increased risk of stroke and heart attack.
   b. all forms of respiratory disease.
   c. increasing mortality rates over the past ten years.
   d. juvenile delinquency.

4. Which of the following words is spelled correctly?
   a. incorrigible
   b. outragous
   c. domestickated
   d. understandible

Here are the answers, as well as some suggestions as to how you might have used the process of elimination to find them.

1. **d.** You should have eliminated answer **a** right off the bat. Ilsa can't be four years old if Meghan is going to be Ilsa's age in five years. The best way to eliminate other answer choices is to try plugging them in to the information given in the problem. For instance, for answer **b**, if Ilsa is 10, then Meghan must be 5. The difference in their ages is 5. The difference between Ed's age, 29, and Meghan's age, 5, is 24. Is 24 two times 5? No. Then answer **b** is wrong. You could eliminate answer **c** in the same way and be left with answer **d**.

2. **c.** Note the word *not* in the question, and go through the answers one by one. Is the truck driver in choice **a** "operating a commercial vehicle"? Yes, idling counts as "operating," so he needs to have a commercial driver's license. Likewise, the bus operator in answer **b** is operating a commercial vehicle; the question doesn't say the operator has to be on the street. The limo driver in **d** is operating a commercial vehicle, even if it doesn't have passenger in it. However, the cabbie in answer **c** is *not* operating a commercial vehicle, but his own private car.

3. **a.** You could eliminate answer **b** simply because of the presence of the word *all*. Such absolutes hardly ever appear in correct answer choices. Choice **c** looks attractive until you think a little about what you know—aren't *fewer* people smoking these days, rather than more? So how could smoking be responsible for a higher mortality rate? (If you didn't know that *mortality rate* means the rate at which people die, you might keep this choice as a possibility, but you would still be able to eliminate two answers and have only two to choose from.) And choice **d** is not logical, so you could eliminate that one, too. And you are left with the correct choice, **a**.

4. **a.** How you used the process of elimination here depends on which words you recognized as being spelled incorrectly. If you knew that the correct spellings were *outrageous*, *domesticated*, and *understandable*, then you were home free. You probably knew that at least one of those words was wrong!

▶ Step 6: Know When to Guess

Time to complete: 20 minutes
Activity: Complete the worksheet on Your Guessing Ability.

Armed with the process of elimination, you are ready to take control of one of the big questions in test taking: Should I guess? The answer is: *Yes*. Some exams have what's called a "guessing penalty," in which a fraction of your wrong answers is subtracted from your right answers—the Praxis I does NOT work like that. The number of questions you answer correctly yields your raw score. So you have nothing to lose and everything to gain by guessing.

Your Guessing Ability

The following are ten really hard questions. You are not supposed to know the answers. Rather, this is an assessment of your ability to guess when you don't have a clue. Read each question carefully, just as if you did expect to answer it. If you have any knowledge at all of the subject of the question, use that knowledge to help you eliminate wrong answer choices.

1. September 7 is Independence Day in
   a. India.
   b. Costa Rica.
   c. Brazil.
   d. Australia.

2. Which of the following is the formula for determining the momentum of an object?
   a. $p = mv$
   b. $F = ma$
   c. $P = IV$
   d. $E = mc^2$

3. Because of the expansion of the universe, the stars and other celestial bodies are all moving away from each other. This phenomenon is known as
   a. Newton's first law.
   b. the big bang.
   c. gravitational collapse.
   d. Hubble flow.

4. American author Gertrude Stein was born in
   a. 1713.
   b. 1830.
   c. 1874.
   d. 1901.

5. Which of the following is NOT one of the Five Classics attributed to Confucius?
   a. the *I Ching*
   b. the *Book of Holiness*
   c. the *Spring and Autumn Annals*
   d. the *Book of History*

6. The religious and philosophical doctrine that holds that the universe is constantly in a struggle between good and evil is known as
   a. Pelagianism.
   b. Manichaeanism.
   c. Neo-Hegelianism.
   d. Epicureanism.

7. The third chief justice of the U.S. Supreme Court was
   a. John Blair.
   b. William Cushing.
   c. James Wilson.
   d. John Jay.

8. Which of the following is the poisonous portion of a daffodil?
   a. the bulb
   b. the leaves
   c. the stem
   d. the flowers

9. The winner of the Masters golf tournament in 1953 was
   a. Sam Snead.
   b. Cary Middlecoff.
   c. Arnold Palmer.
   d. Ben Hogan.

10. The state with the highest per capita personal income in 1980 was
    a. Alaska.
    b. Connecticut.
    c. New York.
    d. Texas.

Check your answers against the correct answers below.

1. c.
2. a.
3. d.
4. c.
5. b.
6. b.
7. b.
8. a.
9. d.
10. a.

► How Did You Do?

You may have simply gotten lucky and actually known the answer to one or two questions. In addition, your guessing was more successful if you were able to use the process of elimination on any of the questions. Maybe you didn't know who the third chief justice was (question 7), but you knew that John Jay was the first. In that case, you would have eliminated answer **d** and therefore improved your odds of guessing right from one in four to one in three.

According to probability, you should get $2\frac{1}{2}$ answers correct, so getting either two or three right would be average. If you got four or more right, you may be a really terrific guesser. If you got one or none right, you may be a really bad guesser.

Keep in mind, though, that this is only a small sample. You should continue to keep track of your guessing ability as you work through the sample questions in this book. Circle the numbers of questions you guess on as you make your guess; or, if you don't have time while you take the practice exams, go back afterward and try to remember which questions you guessed at. Remember, on an exam with four answer choices, your chances of getting a right answer is one in four. So keep a separate "guessing" score for each exam. How many questions did you guess on? How many did you get right? If the number you got right is at least one-fourth of the number of questions you guessed on, you are at least an average guesser, maybe better—and you should always go ahead and guess on the real exam. If the number you got right is significantly lower than one-fourth of the number you guessed on, you would, frankly, be safe in guessing anyway, but maybe you would feel more comfortable if you guessed only selectively, when you can eliminate a wrong answer or at least have a good feeling about one of the answer choices.

▶ Step 7: Reach Your Peak Performance Zone

Time to complete: 10 minutes to read; weeks to complete!
Activity: Complete the Physical Preparation Checklist.

To get ready for a challenge like a big exam, you have to take control of your physical, as well as your mental, state. Exercise, proper diet, and rest will ensure that your body works with, rather than against, your mind on test day, as well as during your preparation.

Exercise

If you don't already have a regular exercise program going, the time during which you are preparing for an exam is actually an excellent time to start one. And if you are already keeping fit—or trying to get that way— don't let the pressure of preparing for an exam fool you into quitting now. Exercise helps reduce stress by pumping wonderful good-feeling hormones called *endorphins* into your system. It also increases the oxygen supply throughout your body, including your brain, so you will be at peak performance on test day.

A half hour of vigorous activity—enough to raise a sweat—every day should be your aim. If you are really pressed for time, every other day is okay. Choose an activity you like and get out there and do it. Jogging with a friend always makes the time go faster, or take a radio.

But don't overdo it. You don't want to exhaust yourself. Moderation is the key.

Diet

First of all, cut out the junk. Go easy on caffeine and nicotine, and eliminate alcohol and any other drugs from your system at least two weeks before the exam. Promise yourself a treat the night after the exam, if need be.

What your body needs for peak performance is simply a balanced diet. Eat plenty of fruits and vegetables, along with protein and carbohydrates. Foods that are high in lecithin (an amino acid), such as fish and beans, are especially good "brain foods."

The night before the exam, you might carbo-load the way athletes do before a contest. Eat a big plate of spaghetti, rice and beans, or whatever your favorite carbohydrate is.

Rest

You probably know how much sleep you need every night to be at your best, even if you don't always get it. Make sure you do get that much sleep, though, for at least a week before the exam. Moderation is important here, too. Extra sleep will just make you groggy.

If you are not a morning person and your exam will be given in the morning, you should reset your internal clock so that your body doesn't think you are taking an exam at 3 A.M. You have to start this process well before the exam. The way it works is to get up half an hour earlier each morning, and then go to bed half an hour earlier that night. Don't try it the other way around; you will just toss and turn if you go to bed early without having gotten up early. The next morning, get up another half an hour earlier, and so on. How long you will have to do this depends on how late you are used to getting up. Use the Physical Preparation Checklist on the next page to make sure you are in tip-top form.

Physical Preparation Checklist

For the week before the exam, write down what physical exercise you engaged in and for how long, and what you ate for each meal. Remember, you are trying for at least half an hour of exercise every other day (preferably every day) and a balanced diet that's light on junk food.

Exam minus 7 days

Exercise: _____ for ____ minutes

Breakfast: _____

Lunch: _____

Dinner: _____

Snacks: _____

Exam minus 6 days

Exercise: _____ for ____ minutes

Breakfast: _____

Lunch: _____

Dinner: _____

Snacks: _____

Exam minus 5 days

Exercise: _____ for ____ minutes

Breakfast: _____

Lunch: _____

Dinner: _____

Snacks: _____

Exam minus 4 days

Exercise: _____ for ____ minutes

Breakfast: _____

Lunch: _____

Dinner: _____

Snacks: _____

Exam minus 3 days

Exercise: _____ for ____ minutes

Breakfast: _____

Lunch: _____

Dinner: _____

Snacks: _____

Exam minus 2 days

Exercise: _____ for ____ minutes

Breakfast: _____

Lunch: _____

Dinner: _____

Snacks: _____

Exam minus 1 day

Exercise: _____ for ____ minutes

Breakfast: _____

Lunch: _____

Dinner: _____

Snacks: _____

▶ Step 8: Get Your Act Together

Time to complete: 10 minutes to read; time to complete will vary.
Activity: Complete the Final Preparations worksheet.

You are in control of your mind and body; you are in charge of test anxiety, your preparation, and your test-taking strategies. Now it's time to take charge of external factors, like the testing site and the materials you need to take the exam.

Find Out Where the Exam Is and Make a Trial Run

Do you know how to get to the testing site? Do you know how long it will take to get there? If not, make a trial run, preferably on the same day of the week at the same time of day. Make note, on the Final Preparations worksheet on the next page, of the amount of time it will take you to get to the exam site. Plan on arriving 30–45 minutes early so you can get the lay of the land, use the bathroom, and calm down. Then figure out how early you will have to get up that morning, and make sure you get up that early every day for a week before the exam.

Gather Your Materials

The night before the exam, lay out the clothes you will wear and the materials you have to bring with you to the exam. Plan on dressing in layers; you won't have any control over the temperature of the examination room. Have a sweater or jacket you can take off if it's warm. Use the checklist on the Final Preparations worksheet to help you pull together what you will need.

Don't Skip Breakfast

Even if you don't usually eat breakfast, do so on exam morning. A cup of coffee doesn't count. Don't eat doughnuts or other sweet foods, either. A sugar high will leave you with a sugar low in the middle of the exam. A mix of protein and carbohydrates is best: Cereal with milk and just a little sugar, or eggs with toast, will do your body a world of good.

Final Preparations

Getting to the Exam Site

Location of exam: _____

Date: _____

Departure time: _____

Do I know how to get to the exam site? Yes _____ No _____
If no, make a trial run.

Time it will take to get to exam site: _____

Things to Lay Out the Night Before

Clothes I will wear	_____
Sweater/jacket	_____
Watch	_____
Photo ID	_____
No. 2 pencils	_____
Calculator	_____
_____	_____
_____	_____

▶ Step 9: Do It!

Time to complete: 10 minutes, plus test-taking time
Activity: Ace the Praxis I!

Fast-forward to exam day. You are ready. You made a study plan and followed through. You practiced your test-taking strategies while working through this book. You are in control of your physical, mental, and emotional state. You know when and where to show up and what to bring with you. In other words, you are better prepared than most of the other people taking the exam. You are psyched.

Just one more thing. When you are done with the exam, you will have earned a reward. Plan a celebration. Call up your friends and plan a party, or have a nice dinner for two—whatever your heart desires. Give yourself something to look forward to.

And then do it. Go into the exam, full of confidence, armed with test-taking strategies you have practiced until they're second nature. You are in control of yourself, your environment, and your performance on the exam. You are ready to succeed. So do it. Go in there and ace the exam. And look forward to your future career as a teacher!

3 ▶ Praxis I Practice Exam 1

CHAPTER SUMMARY

This is the first of the three practice exams in this book based on the three elements of the Praxis I, the Pre-Professional Skills Tests (PPSTs) of Reading, Mathematics, and Writing. Use this practice exam to see how you would do if you were to take the Praxis I today.

THIS PRACTICE EXAM CONTAINS three tests of the same type as the real exam you will be taking—that is, Reading (multiple-choice questions), Mathematics (multiple-choice questions), and Writing (multiple-choice questions and an essay).

As you take this first practice exam, do not worry too much about timing. Just take the three tests in as relaxed a manner as you can to find out which areas you are skilled in and which ones will need extra work.

The answer sheet you should use for the multiple-choice questions is on the following page. (You will write your essay on a separate piece of paper.) After you finish taking your test, you should review the answer explanations found at the end of this test. The answer explanations are followed by information on how to score your exam.

► Answer Sheet

SKILLS TEST IN READING	SKILLS TEST IN MATHEMATICS	SKILLS TEST IN WRITING, SECTION 1

SKILLS TEST IN READING

1. (a) (b) (c) (d) (e)
2. (a) (b) (c) (d) (e)
3. (a) (b) (c) (d) (e)
4. (a) (b) (c) (d) (e)
5. (a) (b) (c) (d) (e)
6. (a) (b) (c) (d) (e)
7. (a) (b) (c) (d) (e)
8. (a) (b) (c) (d) (e)
9. (a) (b) (c) (d) (e)
10. (a) (b) (c) (d) (e)
11. (a) (b) (c) (d) (e)
12. (a) (b) (c) (d) (e)
13. (a) (b) (c) (d) (e)
14. (a) (b) (c) (d) (e)
15. (a) (b) (c) (d) (e)
16. (a) (b) (c) (d) (e)
17. (a) (b) (c) (d) (e)
18. (a) (b) (c) (d) (e)
19. (a) (b) (c) (d) (e)
20. (a) (b) (c) (d) (e)
21. (a) (b) (c) (d) (e)
22. (a) (b) (c) (d) (e)
23. (a) (b) (c) (d) (e)
24. (a) (b) (c) (d) (e)
25. (a) (b) (c) (d) (e)
26. (a) (b) (c) (d) (e)
27. (a) (b) (c) (d) (e)
28. (a) (b) (c) (d) (e)
29. (a) (b) (c) (d) (e)
30. (a) (b) (c) (d) (e)
31. (a) (b) (c) (d) (e)
32. (a) (b) (c) (d) (e)
33. (a) (b) (c) (d) (e)
34. (a) (b) (c) (d) (e)
35. (a) (b) (c) (d) (e)
36. (a) (b) (c) (d) (e)
37. (a) (b) (c) (d) (e)
38. (a) (b) (c) (d) (e)
39. (a) (b) (c) (d) (e)
40. (a) (b) (c) (d) (e)

SKILLS TEST IN MATHEMATICS

1. (a) (b) (c) (d) (e)
2. (a) (b) (c) (d) (e)
3. (a) (b) (c) (d) (e)
4. (a) (b) (c) (d) (e)
5. (a) (b) (c) (d) (e)
6. (a) (b) (c) (d) (e)
7. (a) (b) (c) (d) (e)
8. (a) (b) (c) (d) (e)
9. (a) (b) (c) (d) (e)
10. (a) (b) (c) (d) (e)
11. (a) (b) (c) (d) (e)
12. (a) (b) (c) (d) (e)
13. (a) (b) (c) (d) (e)
14. (a) (b) (c) (d) (e)
15. (a) (b) (c) (d) (e)
16. (a) (b) (c) (d) (e)
17. (a) (b) (c) (d) (e)
18. (a) (b) (c) (d) (e)
19. (a) (b) (c) (d) (e)
20. (a) (b) (c) (d) (e)
21. (a) (b) (c) (d) (e)
22. (a) (b) (c) (d) (e)
23. (a) (b) (c) (d) (e)
24. (a) (b) (c) (d) (e)
25. (a) (b) (c) (d) (e)
26. (a) (b) (c) (d) (e)
27. (a) (b) (c) (d) (e)
28. (a) (b) (c) (d) (e)
29. (a) (b) (c) (d) (e)
30. (a) (b) (c) (d) (e)
31. (a) (b) (c) (d) (e)
32. (a) (b) (c) (d) (e)
33. (a) (b) (c) (d) (e)
34. (a) (b) (c) (d) (e)
35. (a) (b) (c) (d) (e)
36. (a) (b) (c) (d) (e)
37. (a) (b) (c) (d) (e)
38. (a) (b) (c) (d) (e)
39. (a) (b) (c) (d) (e)
40. (a) (b) (c) (d) (e)

SKILLS TEST IN WRITING, SECTION 1

1. (a) (b) (c) (d) (e)
2. (a) (b) (c) (d) (e)
3. (a) (b) (c) (d) (e)
4. (a) (b) (c) (d) (e)
5. (a) (b) (c) (d) (e)
6. (a) (b) (c) (d) (e)
7. (a) (b) (c) (d) (e)
8. (a) (b) (c) (d) (e)
9. (a) (b) (c) (d) (e)
10. (a) (b) (c) (d) (e)
11. (a) (b) (c) (d) (e)
12. (a) (b) (c) (d) (e)
13. (a) (b) (c) (d) (e)
14. (a) (b) (c) (d) (e)
15. (a) (b) (c) (d) (e)
16. (a) (b) (c) (d) (e)
17. (a) (b) (c) (d) (e)
18. (a) (b) (c) (d) (e)
19. (a) (b) (c) (d) (e)
20. (a) (b) (c) (d) (e)
21. (a) (b) (c) (d) (e)
22. (a) (b) (c) (d) (e)
23. (a) (b) (c) (d) (e)
24. (a) (b) (c) (d) (e)
25. (a) (b) (c) (d) (e)
26. (a) (b) (c) (d) (e)
27. (a) (b) (c) (d) (e)
28. (a) (b) (c) (d) (e)
29. (a) (b) (c) (d) (e)
30. (a) (b) (c) (d) (e)
31. (a) (b) (c) (d) (e)
32. (a) (b) (c) (d) (e)
33. (a) (b) (c) (d) (e)
34. (a) (b) (c) (d) (e)
35. (a) (b) (c) (d) (e)
36. (a) (b) (c) (d) (e)
37. (a) (b) (c) (d) (e)
38. (a) (b) (c) (d) (e)

▶ Skills Test in Reading

Directions: Read the following passages and answer the questions that follow.

Use the following passage to answer questions 1 and 2.

The English-language premiere of Samuel Beckett's play *Waiting for Godot* took place in London in August 1955. *Godot* is an avant-garde play with only five characters (not including Mr. Godot, who never arrives) and a minimal setting: one rock and one bare tree. The play has two acts; the second act repeats what little action occurs in the first with few changes: the tree, for instance, acquires one leaf. In a statement that was to become famous, the critic Vivian Mercer described *Godot* as "a play in which nothing happens twice." Opening night, critics and playgoers greeted the play with bafflement and derision. The line, "Nothing happens, nobody comes, nobody goes. It's awful," was met by a loud rejoinder of "Hear! Hear!" from an audience member. _____. However, Harold Hobson's review in the *Sunday Times* managed to recognize the play for what history has proven it to be, a revolutionary moment in theater.

1. Which sentence, if inserted in the blank space, would make the best sense in the context of the passage?
   a. The director, Peter Hall, had to beg the theater management not to close the play immediately but to wait for the Sunday reviews.
   b. Despite the audience reaction, the cast and director believed in the play.
   c. It looked as if *Waiting for Godot* was beginning a long run as the most controversial play of London's 1955 season.
   d. *Waiting for Godot* was in danger of closing the first week of its run and of becoming nothing more than a footnote in the annals of the English stage.
   e. The audience and critics all completely misunderstood Beckett's play.

2. Which of the following best describes the attitude of the author of the passage toward the play *Waiting for Godot*?
   a. It was a curiosity in theater history.
   b. It is the most important play of the twentieth century.
   c. It had no effect on theater.
   d. It is too repetitious.
   e. It represents a turning point in stage history.

Use the following passage to answer question 3.

In space flight there are the obvious hazards of meteors, debris, and radiation; however, astronauts must also deal with two vexing physiological foes—muscle atrophy and bone loss. Space shuttle astronauts, because they spend only about a week in space, undergo minimal wasting of bone and muscle. But when longer stays in microgravity or zero gravity are contemplated, as in the proposed space station or a two-year round-trip voyage to Mars, these problems are of particular concern because they could become acute.

3. The most appropriate audience for the passage would be students in a(n)
   a. physiology class.
   b. engineering class.
   c. physics class.
   d. astronomy class.
   e. history of science class.

Use the following passage to answer question 4.

Jessie Street is sometimes called the Australian Eleanor Roosevelt. Like Roosevelt, Street lived a life of privilege, while at the same time devoting her efforts to working for the rights of the disenfranchised, including workers, women, refugees, and Aborigines. In addition, she gained international fame when she was the only woman on the Australian delegation to the conference that founded the United Nations—just as Eleanor Roosevelt was for the United States.

4. Which of the following inferences may be drawn from the information presented in the passage?
   a. Eleanor Roosevelt and Jessie Street worked together to include women in the United Nations Charter.
   b. Usually, people who live lives of privilege do not spend much time participating in political activities.
   c. Discrimination in Australia is much worse than it ever was in the United States.
   d. At the time of the formation of the United Nations, few women were involved in international affairs.
   e. The United Nations has been ineffective in helping the disenfranchised all over the world.

Use the following passage to answer questions 5–7.

Mental and physical health professionals may consider referring clients and patients to a music therapist for a number of reasons. It seems a particularly good choice for the social worker who is coordinating a client's case. Music therapists use music to establish a relationship with the patient and to improve the patient's health, using highly structured musical interactions. Patients and therapists may sing, play instruments, compose music, dance, or simply listen to music.

The course of training for music therapists is comprehensive. In addition to their formal musical and therapy training, music therapists are taught to discern what kinds of interventions will be most beneficial for each individual patient. Because each patient is different and has different goals, the music therapist must be able to understand the patient's situation and choose the music and activities that will do the most toward helping the patient achieve his or her goals. The referring social worker can help this process by clearly articulating each client's history.

Although patients may develop their musical skills, that is not the main goal of music therapy. Any client who needs particular work on communication or on academic, emotional, and social skills, and who is not responding to traditional therapy, is an excellent candidate for music therapy.

5. Which of the following would be the most appropriate title for this passage?
   a. The Use of Music in the Treatment of Autism
   b. How to Use Music to Combat Depression
   c. Music Therapy: A Role in Social Work?
   d. Training for a Career in Music Therapy
   e. The Social Worker as Music Therapist

6. Which of the following inferences can be drawn from the passage?
   a. Music therapy can succeed where traditional therapies have failed.
   b. Music therapy is a relatively new field.
   c. Music therapy is particularly beneficial for young children.
   d. Music therapy probably will not work well for psychotic people.
   e. Music therapy is appropriate in only a limited number of circumstances.

7. Which of the following best organizes the main topics addressed in this passage?
   a. I.   the role of music therapy in social work
       II. locating a music therapist
       III. how to complete a music therapist referral
   b. I.   using music in therapy
       II. a typical music therapy intervention
       III. when to prescribe music therapy for sociopaths
   c. I.   music therapy and social work
       II. training for music therapists
       III. skills addressed by music therapy
   d. I.   how to choose a music therapist
       II. when to refer to a music therapist
       III. who benefits the most from music therapy
   e. I.   music therapy as a cost-effective treatment
       II. curriculum of a music therapy program
       III. music therapy and physical illness

Use the following passage to answer question 8.

According to a recent poll, the number of students in the high school environmental club has increased by 40% over the past three years. This increase is the reason why more students have begun recycling their paper and cans during this period.

8. Which of the following, if true, most significantly weakens the above argument?
   a. The school installed recycling bins in all classrooms five years ago.
   b. Most students join the environmental club in order to add one more activity to their college applications.
   c. Not all students participated in the poll.
   d. Two years ago, the school began giving detention to any student caught throwing recyclable materials in the regular trash.
   e. The environmental club has begun hanging up more posters about recycling.

Use the following passage to answer question 9.

The seemingly simple question of "what defines a sport?" has been the fodder for argument and conversation for years, among professional and armchair athletes alike. There seems to be no doubt that vigorous and highly competitive activities such as baseball, football, and soccer are truly sports, but when the subject of other activities such as darts, chess, and shuffleboard is broached we find ourselves at the heart of a controversy. Some people claim that a true sport first and foremost requires some form of physical exertion. Therefore, if a player does not break a sweat, what he or she plays is not a sport. Beyond that, more important criteria would be the need for decent hand-eye coordination, and the ever-present possibility of sustaining injury.

9. According to the criteria given in the passage, all of the following would be considered a true sport EXCEPT
   a. cheerleading.
   b. skiing.
   c. race car driving.
   d. horse shoes.
   e. gymnastics.

Use the following passage to answer questions 10–12.

Businesses today routinely keep track of large amounts of both financial and nonfinancial information. Sales departments keep track of current and potential customers; marketing departments keep track of product details and regional demographics; accounting departments keep track of financial data and issue reports. To be useful, all this data must be organized into a meaningful and useful system. Such a system is called a *management information system*, abbreviated MIS. The financial hub of the MIS is accounting.

Accounting is the information system that records, analyzes, and reports economic transactions, enabling decisionmakers to make informed choices when allocating scarce economic resources. It is a tool that enables the user, whether a business entity or an individual, to make wiser, more informed economic choices. It is an aid to planning, controlling, and evaluating a broad range of activities. A financial accounting system is intended for use by both the management of an organization and those outside the organization. Because it is important that financial accounting reports be interpreted correctly, financial accounting is subject to a set of stringent guidelines called generally accepted accounting principles (GAAP).

10. This passage is most likely taken from
   a. a newspaper column.
   b. an essay about modern business.
   c. a legal brief.
   d. a business textbook.
   e. a business machine catalog.

11. According to the information in the passage, which of the following is least likely to be a function of accounting?
   a. helping businesspeople make sound judgments
   b. producing reports of many different kinds of transactions
   c. assisting with the marketing of products
   d. assisting companies in important planning activities
   e. providing information to potential investors

12. According to the information in the first paragraph of the passage, all of the following would be included in a company's MIS EXCEPT
   a. potential customers.
   b. financial data.
   c. regional demographics.
   d. employee birthdates.
   e. product details.

Use the following passage to answer question 13.

The salesperson of the month at Smith's Used Cars sold 26 cars in February. Diana sold 22 cars in February.

13. Based only on the information above, which of the following must be true?
   a. Diana is not salesperson of the month at Smith's Used Cars.
   b. The salesperson of the month is the person who sold the most cars that month.
   c. Diana does not work at Smith's Used Cars.
   d. The salesperson of the month made more money in February than Diana did.
   e. The salesperson of the month is better at selling cars than Diana is.

Use the following passage to answer question 14.

Many studies make it clear that sleep deprivation is dangerous. Sleep-deprived people who are tested by using a driving simulator or by performing a hand-eye coordination task perform as badly as or worse than those who are intoxicated. Sleep deprivation also magnifies alcohol's effects on the body, so a fatigued person who drinks will become much more impaired than someone who is well rested. Since drowsiness is the brain's last step before falling asleep, driving while drowsy can—and often does—lead to disaster. Caffeine and other stimulants cannot overcome the effects of severe sleep deprivation.

14. In the passage, the term *impaired* most nearly means
   a. sentient.
   b. apprehensive.
   c. disturbed.
   d. blemished.
   e. hampered.

Use the following passage to answer question 15.

Because they have the ability to evoke an emotional response in readers, political cartoons can serve as a vehicle for swaying public opinion and can contribute to reform. Thomas Nast (1840–1902), the preeminent political cartoonist of the second half of the nineteenth century, demonstrated the power of his medium when he used his art to end the corrupt Boss Tweed Ring in New York City. His images, first drawn for *Harper's Weekly*, are still in currency today: Nast created the tiger as the symbol of Tammany Hall, the elephant for the Republican Party, and the donkey for the Democratic Party. Created under tight deadlines for ephemeral, commercial formats like newspapers and magazines, cartoons still manage to have lasting influence. Although they tackle the principal issues and leaders of their day, they often provide a vivid historical picture for generations to come.

15. The author cites Thomas Nast's depiction of an elephant for the Republican Party as an example of
   a. an image that is no longer recognized by the public.
   b. the saying, "the pen is mightier than the sword."
   c. art contributing to political reform.
   d. a graphic image that became an enduring symbol.
   e. the ephemeral nature of political cartooning.

Use the following passage to answer questions 16 and 17.

Typically people think of genius, whether it manifests in Mozart's composing symphonies at age five or Einstein's discovery of relativity, as having a quality not just of the supernatural, but also of the eccentric. People see genius as a "good" abnormality; moreover, they think of genius as a completely unpredictable abnormality. Until recently, psychologists regarded the quirks of genius as too erratic to describe intelligibly; however, Anna Findley's ground-breaking study uncovers predictable patterns in the biographies of geniuses. These patterns do not dispel the common belief that there is a kind of supernatural intervention in the lives of unusually talented men and women, however, even though they occur with regularity. For example, Findley shows that all geniuses experience three intensely productive periods in their lives, one of which always occurs shortly before their deaths; this is true whether the genius lives to 19 or 90.

16. Which of the following would be the best title for passage?
    a. Understanding Mozarts and Einsteins
    b. Predicting the Life of a Genius
    c. The Uncanny Patterns in the Lives of Geniuses
    d. Pattern and Disorder in the Lives of Geniuses
    e. Supernatural Intervention in the Life of the Genius

17. Given the information in the passage, which of the following statements is true?
    a. Anna Findley is a biographer.
    b. All geniuses are eccentric and unpredictable.
    c. A genius has three prolific periods in his or her life.
    d. Mozart discovered relativity.
    e. Geniuses experience three fallow periods in their lives.

Use the following passage to answer question 18.

A study conducted by the Centers for Disease Control (CDC) found that high school students who take part in team sports or are physically active outside of school are less likely to engage in risky behaviors, like using drugs or smoking. Physical activity does not need to be strenuous to be beneficial. The CDC recommends moderate, daily physical activity for people of all ages, such as brisk walking for 30 minutes or 15 to 20 minutes of more intense exercise. A survey conducted by the National Association for Sport and Physical Education questioned teens about their attitudes toward exercise and about what it would take to get them moving. Teens chose friends (56%) as their most likely motivators for becoming more active, followed by parents (18%) and professional athletes (11%).

18. Which of the following techniques is used in the last sentence of the passage?
   a. explanation of terms
   b. comparison of different arguments
   c. contrast of opposing views
   d. generalized statement
   e. illustration by example

Use the following passage to answer question 19.

Burgers, fries, pizza, raw fish. Raw fish? Fast food in America is changing. Sushi, the thousand-year-old Japanese delicacy, was once thought of in this country as unpalatable and too exotic. But tastes have changed, for a number of reasons. Beginning in the 1970s, Americans became increasingly more aware of diet and health issues, and began rejecting their traditional red-meat diets in favor of healthier, lower-fat choices such as fish, poultry, whole grains, rice, and vegetables. The way food was prepared began to change, too; rather than frying food, people started opting for broiled, steamed, and raw versions. Sushi, a combination of cold boiled rice and raw fish, fit the bill. In addition, that same decade saw Japan become an important global economic force, and companies began flocking to the country to do business. All things Japanese, including décor, clothing, and cuisine, became popular.

19. In the passage, *unpalatable* most nearly means
   a. not visually appealing.
   b. not good tasting.
   c. bad smelling.
   d. too expensive.
   e. rough to the touch.

Use the following passage to answer question 20.

The information on a standard compact disc (CD) is contained in a single spiral track of pits, starting at the inside of the disk and circling its way to the outside. This information is read by shining light from a 780 nm wavelength semiconductor laser. Information is read as the laser moves over the bumps (where no light will be reflected) and the areas that have no bumps, also known as *land* (where the laser light will be reflected off the aluminum). The changes in reflectivity are interpreted by a part of the compact disc player known as the *detector*. It is the job of the detector to convert the information collected by the laser into the music that was originally recorded onto the disk.

20. What would happen if the detector on a CD player malfunctioned?

    a. The spiral track would not be read properly.

    b. The pits and land would look like one unit.

    c. The changes in reflectivity would be absorbed back into the laser.

    d. The music would play backward.

    e. The information read by the laser would not be converted into music.

Use the following passage to answer questions 21–24.

The Caribbean island of Saint Martin is a favorite vacation spot, one that is popular with tourists from various countries. The French and Dutch settled on the island in the 1600s. Today, the island is divided between the two. The French capital is Marigot; the Dutch capital is Philipsburg.

    Tourists on vacation soon discover that Saint Martin has an intriguing history. Twelve hundred years ago, the Arawak Indians inhabited all the islands of the West Indies, and were a peaceful people living under the guidance of their chiefs. In the 1300s, three hundred years after the Arawaks first arrived on Saint Martin, they were defeated and forced to abandon the island by a more hostile tribe of Indians that originated in South America. This new tribe was called the Carib. The Caribbean Sea was named after them. Unlike the Arawaks, they had no permanent chiefs or leaders, except in times of strife. And they were extremely warlike. Worse, they were cannibalistic, eating the enemy warriors they captured. In fact, the very word *cannibal* comes from the Spanish name for the Carib Indians. The Spanish arrived in the fifteenth century and, unfortunately, they carried diseases to which the Indians had no immunity. Many Indians succumbed to common European illnesses. Others died from the hard labor forced upon them.

21. According to the passage, all of the following are true about the Carib Indians EXCEPT

    a. the sea was named after them.

    b. they were peaceful fishermen, hunters, and farmers.

    c. they ate human flesh.

    d. they settled after defeating the Arawak Indians.

    e. during times of war, they had temporary leaders.

22. According to the passage, the Carib Indians were finally defeated by

    a. sickness and forced labor.

    b. the more aggressive Arawak tribe.

    c. the Dutch West India Company.

    d. the French explorers.

    e. a cannibalistic tribe.

23. One can infer from the passage that the word *strife* means
    a. cannibalism.
    b. war.
    c. labor.
    d. chief.
    e. Carib.

24. According to the article, present-day Saint Martin
    a. belongs to the Spanish.
    b. is independent.
    c. belongs to the Carib.
    d. is part of the U.S. Virgin Islands.
    e. is shared by the French and the Dutch.

Use the following passage to answer question 25.

Although protected by the Australian government, the Great Barrier Reef faces environmental threats. Crown-of-thorns starfish feed on coral and can destroy large portions of reef. Pollution and rising water temperatures also threaten the delicate coral. But the most preventable of the hazards to the reef are tourists. Tourists have contributed to the destruction of the reef ecosystem by breaking off and removing pieces of coral to bring home as souvenirs. The government hopes that by informing tourists of the dangers of this seemingly harmless activity they will quash this creeping menace to the fragile reef.

25. The primary purpose of this passage is to
    a. inform the reader that coral reefs are a threatened, yet broadly functioning ecosystem.
    b. alert the reader to a premier vacation destination in the tropics.
    c. explain in detail how the Great Barrier Reef is constructed.
    d. recommend that tourists stop stealing coral off the Great Barrier Reef.
    e. dispel the argument that coral is a plant, not an animal.

Use the following passage to answer questions 26 and 27.

Although it is called Central Park, New York City's great green space has no "center"—no formal walkway down the middle of the park, no central monument or body of water, no single orienting feature. The paths wind, the landscape constantly shifts and changes, the sections spill into one another in a seemingly random manner. But this "decentering" was precisely the intent of the park's innovative design. Made to look as natural as possible, Frederick Law Olmsted's 1858 plan for Central Park had as its main goal the creation of a democratic playground—a place with many centers to reflect the multiplicity of its uses and users. Olmsted designed the park to allow interaction among the various members of society, without giving preference to one group or class. Thus Olmsted's ideal of a "commonplace civilization" could be realized.

26. In the passage, the author describes specific park features in order to
   a. present both sides of the argument.
   b. suggest the organization of the rest of the passage.
   c. provide evidence that the park has no center.
   d. demonstrate how large the park is.
   e. show how well the author knows the park.

27. The main idea of this passage is that
   a. New York City is a democratic city.
   b. Olmsted was a brilliant designer.
   c. more parks should be designed without centers.
   d. Central Park is used by many people for many different purposes.
   e. Central Park is democratic by design.

Use the following passage to answer questions 28 and 29.

Could good dental hygiene be man's earliest custom? The findings of paleontologist Leslea Hlusko suggest that 1.8 million years ago early hominids used grass stalks to clean their teeth. Many ancient hominid teeth unearthed in archaeological digs have curved grooves near the gumline. Hlusko posited that these grooves were evidence of teeth cleaning by early man. A stalk of grass is also about the same width as the marks found on the ancient teeth. To prove her theory Dr. Hlusko took a baboon tooth and patiently rubbed a grass stalk against it for eight hours. As she suspected, the result was grooves similar to those found on the ancient hominid teeth. She repeated the experiment with a human tooth and found the same result.

It seems that our early human ancestors may have used grass, which was easily found and ready to use, to floss between their teeth. As Hlusko suggests in the journal *Current Anthropology*, "Toothpicking with grass stalks probably represents the most persistent habit documented in human evolution."

28. In the passage, the word *posited* most nearly means
   a. insisted.
   b. demanded.
   c. questioned.
   d. suggested.
   e. argued.

29. The passage suggests the theory that early man used grass stalks as toothpicks is
   a. a possibility.
   b. very probable.
   c. absolutely certain.
   d. fanciful.
   e. uncorroborated.

Use the following passage to answer questions 30 and 31.

A recent *New York Times* "House and Home" article featured the story of a man who lives in a glass house. Every wall in his home is transparent; he has no walls to hide behind, not even in the bathroom. Of course, he lives in an isolated area, so he doesn't exactly have neighbors peering in and watching his every move. But he has chosen to live without any physical privacy in a home that allows every action to be seen. He has created a panopticon—a place in which everything is in full view of others.

The term *panopticon* was coined by Jeremy Bentham in the late eighteenth century when he was describing an idea for how prisons should be designed. The prisoners' cells would be placed in a circle with a guard tower in the middle. All walls facing the center of the circle would be glass. In that way, every prisoner's cell would be in full view of the guards. The prisoners could do nothing unobserved, but the prisoners would not be able to see the guard tower. They would know they were being watched—or rather, they would know it was possible they were being watched—but because they could not see the observer, they would never know when the guard was actually monitoring their actions.

30. According to the passage, a panopticon is
   a. a prison cell.
   b. a place in which everything can be seen by others.
   c. a tower that provides a panoramic view.
   d. a house that is transparent.
   e. a place in which surveillance cameras and other monitoring equipment are in use.

31. The description of how the panopticon would work in a prison implies that the panopticon

    a. can be an effective tool for social control.

    b. should be used regularly in public places.

    c. is not applicable outside of the prison dynamic.

    d. is an effective tool for sharing information.

    e. will redefine privacy for the twenty-first century.

Use the following passage to answer questions 32–34.

The postwar era marked a period of unprecedented energy against the second-class citizenship accorded to African Americans in many parts of the nation. Resistance to racial segregation and discrimination with strategies such as civil disobedience, nonviolent resistance, marches, protests, boycotts, freedom rides, and rallies received national attention as newspaper, radio, and television reporters and cameramen documented the struggle to end racial inequality.

When Rosa Parks refused to give up her seat to a white person in Montgomery, Alabama, and was arrested in December 1955, she set off a chain of events that generated a momentum the Civil Rights movement had never before experienced. Local civil rights leaders were hoping for such an opportunity to test the city's segregation laws. Deciding to boycott the buses, the African-American community soon formed a new organization to supervise the boycott, the Montgomery Improvement Association (MIA). The young pastor of the Dexter Avenue Baptist Church, Reverend Martin Luther King, Jr., was chosen as the first MIA leader. The boycott, more successful than anyone hoped, led to a 1956 Supreme Court decision banning segregated buses.

In 1960, four African-American freshmen from North Carolina Agricultural and Technical College in Greensboro strolled into the F. W. Woolworth store and quietly sat down at the lunch counter. They were not served, but they stayed until closing time. The next morning they came with 25 more students. Two weeks later similar demonstrations had spread to several other cities, and within a year similar peaceful demonstrations took place in over a hundred cities in the North and South. At Shaw University in Raleigh, North Carolina, the students formed their own organization, the Student Nonviolent Coordinating Committee (SNCC, pronounced "Snick"). The students' bravery in the face of verbal and physical abuse led to integration in many stores even before the passage of the Civil Rights Act of 1964.

32. The passage is primarily concerned with

    a. enumerating the injustices that African Americans faced.

    b. describing the strategies used in the struggle for civil rights.

    c. showing how effective sit-down strikes can be in creating change.

    d. describing the nature of discrimination and second-class citizenship.

    e. recounting the legal successes of the Civil Rights movement.

33. In the second paragraph, the word *test* most nearly means
   a. analyze.
   b. determine.
   c. prove.
   d. quiz.
   e. challenge.

34. The passage suggests that the college students in Greensboro, North Carolina,
   a. were regulars at the Woolworth lunch counter.
   b. wanted to provoke a violent reaction.
   c. were part of an ongoing national movement of lunch-counter demonstrations.
   d. inspired other students to protest peacefully against segregation.
   e. did not plan to create a stir.

Use the following passage to answer question 35.

The Environmental Protection Agency (EPA) has published regulations for schools to follow in order to protect against asbestos contamination and provide assistance to meet the requirements of the Asbestos Hazard Emergency Response Act (AHERA). These include performing an original inspection and periodic reinspections every three years for asbestos-containing material; developing, maintaining, and updating an asbestos management plan at the school; providing yearly notification to parent, teacher, and employee organizations regarding the availability of the school's asbestos management plan and any asbestos abatement actions taken or planned in the school; designating a contact person to ensure the responsibilities of the local education agency are properly implemented; performing periodic surveillance of known or suspected asbestos-containing building material; and providing custodial staff with asbestos awareness training.

35. The main purpose of this passage is to
   a. teach asbestos awareness in schools.
   b. explain the specifics of the AHERA.
   c. highlight the dangers of asbestos to your health.
   d. provide a list of materials that may include asbestos.
   e. frighten parents.

Use the following passage to answer question 36.

The ability to defer gratification is an essential skill for negotiating the adult world. In a study of four-year-olds, each child was offered a marshmallow. The child could choose to eat the marshmallow right away or wait 15 minutes to eat the marshmallow and receive another marshmallow as a reward for waiting. Researchers followed the children and found that by high school those children who ate their marshmallow right away were more likely to be lonely, more prone to stress, and more easily frustrated. Conversely, the children who demonstrated self-control were outgoing, confident, and dependable.

36. Based on the information in the passage, one can infer that children who are unable to defer gratification are most unlikely to succeed because
   a. they are unpopular.
   b. they lack empathy.
   c. their parents neglected them.
   d. they are unable to follow directions.
   e. they lack self-discipline.

Use the following passage to answer question 37.

The pioneering example set by Althea Gibson paved the way for future generations of African-American tennis players, and proved that beyond her tennis glory she was a true champion of the human spirit. In 1950, she was the first African American to play in the national indoor tournament, where she finished second. That year, she was refused an invitation to the U.S. Nationals, despite her talent. An editorial by tennis champion Alice Marble caused a national uproar that quickly led tournament officials to finally extend Althea an invitation to play in the Nationals. The following year she was the first African American to compete at Wimbledon. Althea once said that her extraordinary success was the product of being "game enough to take a lot of punishment along the way."

37. The author uses Althea's quote about *being game enough* to illustrate that
   a. Althea's career was plagued with injuries.
   b. the sport of tennis is more grueling than people realize.
   c. Althea believed the discrimination she faced served only to make her a stronger competitor.
   d. Althea was often fined for yelling at the referee.
   e. Althea believed talent was more important than mental toughness.

Use the following passage to answer questions 38 and 39.

The doctrine of judicial review gives the court the authority to declare executive actions and laws invalid if they conflict with the U.S. Constitution. The court's ruling on the constitutionality of a law is nearly final—it can be overcome only by a constitutional amendment or by a new ruling of the court. Through the power of judicial review, the court shapes the development of law, assures individual rights, and maintains the Constitution as a living document by applying its broad provisions to complex new situations.

Despite the court's role in interpreting the Constitution, the document itself does not grant this authority to the court. However, it is clear that several of the founding fathers expected the Court to act in this way. Alexander Hamilton and James Madison argued for the importance of judicial review in the *Federalist Papers*, a series of 85 political essays that urged the adoption of the Constitution. Hamilton argued that judicial review protected the will of the people by making the Constitution supreme over the legislature, which might only reflect the temporary will of the people. Madison wrote that if a public political process determined the constitutionality of laws, the Constitution would become fodder for political interests and partisanship. However, the practice of judicial review was, and continues to be, a controversial power because it gives justices—who are appointed rather than elected by the people—the authority to void legislation made by Congress and state lawmakers.

38. The passage suggests that the practice of judicial review allows the court to
    a. wield enormous power.
    b. determine foreign policy.
    c. make laws that reflect the principles of the Constitution.
    d. rewrite laws that are unconstitutional.
    e. make amendments to the Constitution.

39. The last sentence in the passage provides
    a. a specific example supporting the argument made earlier.
    b. a summary of the points made earlier.
    c. an explanation of the positions made earlier.
    d. a prediction based on the argument made earlier.
    e. a counterargument to the views referred to earlier.

Use the following passage to answer question 40.

If you have ever made a list of pros and cons to help you make a decision, you have used the utilitarian method of moral reasoning. One of the main ethical theories, utilitarianism posits that the key to deciding what makes an act morally right or wrong is its consequences. Whether our intentions are good or bad is irrelevant; what matters is whether the *result* of our actions is good or bad. To utilitarians, happiness is the ultimate goal of human beings and the highest moral good. Thus, if there is great unhappiness because of an act, then that action can be said to be morally wrong. If, on the other hand, there is great happiness because of an action, then that act can be said to be morally right.

40. In the passage, the author refers to a list of pros and cons in order to
   a. show that there are both positive and negative aspects of utilitarianism.
   b. suggest that making a list of pros and cons is not an effective way to make a decision.
   c. emphasize that utilitarians consider both the good and the bad before making a decision.
   d. indicate that readers will learn how to make decisions using pro/con lists.
   e. show readers that they are probably already familiar with the principles of utilitarian reasoning.

► Skills Test in Mathematics

Directions: Choose the best answer to each of the following questions.

Use the following figure to answer question 1.

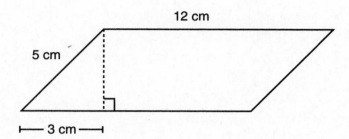

1. Find the area of the parallelogram.
   a. 48 cm²
   b. 60 cm²
   c. 72 cm²
   d. 90 cm²
   e. 240 cm²

2. Four squares are joined together to form one large square. If the perimeter of one of the original squares was 8x units, what is the perimeter of the new, large square?
   a. 16x units
   b. 20x units
   c. 24x units
   d. 32x units
   e. 64x units

3. All students at Central High School take math.
   Some students at Central High School take art.
   Charles takes math.

   If these statements are true, which of the following statements must also be true?
   a. Charles attends Central High School.
   b. All students at Central High School take art.
   c. Some students at Central High School take both math and art.
   d. Charles does not take art.
   e. Some students at Central High School do not take math.

4. Which of the following is equivalent to 150% of 0.0032?
   a. 0.48
   b. 0.048
   c. 0.0048
   d. 0.00048
   e. 0.000048

5. Which is greatest?
   a. $\frac{7}{12}$
   b. $\frac{5}{7}$
   c. 0.079
   d. 0.63
   e. 0.0108

Use the following graph to answer question 6.

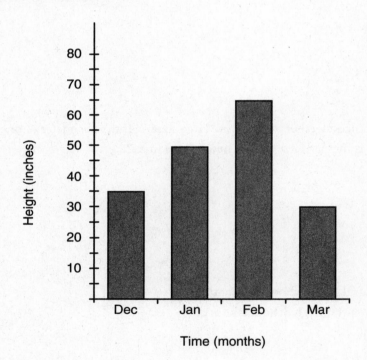

6. Which of the following represents the best choice for the title of the graph?
   a. Average Rainfall per Month for Winter Months in Northern United States
   b. Average Number of Hours of Sunlight for Winter Months in Northern United States
   c. Daily Snowfall Rates for Winter Months in Northern United States
   d. Average Snowfall per Month for Winter Months in Northern United States
   e. Average Heating Oil Costs for Winter Months in Northern United States

7. In Sunnyside, a special lottery is held for the elementary student who will attend the county's invention contest. There are 100 fifth graders, 150 fourth graders, and 200 third graders who qualify for the lottery. Each fifth grader's name is placed in the lottery three times; each fourth grader's name, twice; and each third grader's name, once. What is the probability that a fifth grader's name will be chosen?

    a. $\frac{1}{8}$

    b. $\frac{2}{9}$

    c. $\frac{2}{7}$

    d. $\frac{3}{8}$

    e. $\frac{1}{2}$

8. If three more than one-fourth of a number is three less than the number, what is the value of the number?

    a. $\frac{3}{4}$

    b. 4

    c. 6

    d. 8

    e. 12

9. A major city recently received a snowstorm that left a total of eight inches of snow. If it snowed at a constant rate of three inches every two hours, how much snow had fallen in the first five hours of the storm?

    a. 3 inches

    b. 3.3 inches

    c. 5 inches

    d. 7.5 inches

    e. 8 inches

Use the following graph to answer question 10.

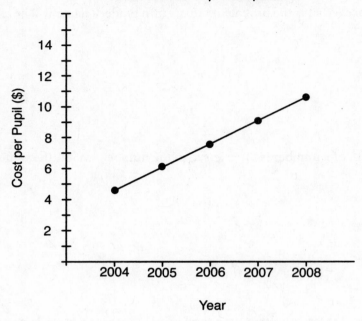

Cost of Field Trip Transportation

10. Based on the graph, if the current trend continues, what will be the approximate cost per pupil for field trip transportation in 2010?
   a. $10.50
   b. $11.50
   c. $12.00
   d. $13.00
   e. $13.50

11. During the semester break, Marcus can wax the floors of five classrooms in an hour. Josie can wax four of the same classrooms in an hour. If Marcus works for three hours and Josie works for two hours, what percentage of the 50 classrooms will be waxed?
   a. 23%
   b. 44%
   c. 46%
   d. 52%
   e. 56%

Use the following graph to answer questions 12–14.

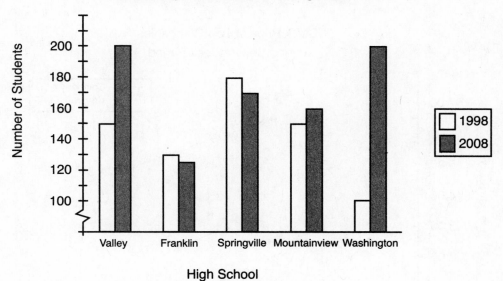

Graduating Class Size of Five High Schools

12. According to the graph, which of the schools doubled the size of its graduating class size from 1998 to 2008?
   a. Valley High
   b. Franklin High
   c. Springville High
   d. Mountainview High
   e. Washington High

13. Approximately how many more students graduated from Springville High than Valley High in 1998?
   a. 15
   b. 30
   c. 45
   d. 60
   e. 140

14. According to the graph, which of the schools had an average increase of about six graduating students per year between 1998 and 2008?
   a. Valley High
   b. Franklin High
   c. Springville High
   d. Mountainview High
   e. Washington High

Use the following graph to answer questions 15–17.

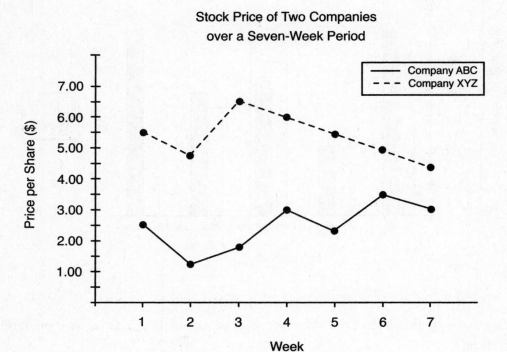

**Stock Price of Two Companies
over a Seven-Week Period**

15. According to the graph, if the trend of the past five weeks is expected to continue, at what point in the future should the price per share be the same for both companies?
   a. week 12
   b. week 11
   c. week 10
   d. week 9
   e. week 8

16. What is the approximate average price per share of stock in Company ABC over the weeks shown in the graph?
   a. $2.25
   b. $2.57
   c. $2.75
   d. $2.86
   e. $4.75

17. Based on the graph, in which week is the stock price for Company ABC exactly half the price per share for Company XYZ?
a. week 1
b. week 2
c. week 3
d. week 4
e. week 5

18. Which of the following has a 9 in the thousandths place?
a. 3.00950
b. 3.09050
c. 3.90050
d. 3.00590
e. 3.00509

19. Petra earns $10.40 per hour for the first eight hours that she works each day, and she earns time and a half for each hour after that. If she works an average of 9.5 hours per day, how much does she earn in a five-day workweek?
a. $83.20
b. $106.60
c. $416.00
d. $533.00
e. $790.40

Use the following figure to answer question 20.

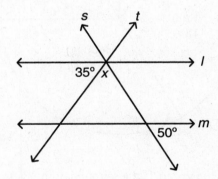

20. In the figure, line l is parallel to line m. What is the measure of the angle labeled x?
a. 15 degrees
b. 35 degrees
c. 50 degrees
d. 85 degrees
e. 95 degrees

21. Each teacher at Main Street School teaches at least three classes and no more than five classes per day. Each of the classes is 40 minutes in length. Which of the following statements must be true?

    a. The average class time for the teachers at the school is 160 minutes per day.

    b. The teachers have an average of four classes per day.

    c. Each teacher has between 120 and 200 minutes of class time per day, inclusive.

    d. choices **a** and **c** only

    e. choices **a**, **b**, and **c**

22. A rectangular patio has one side that measures 15 feet and another side one-third as long. What is the area of the patio?

    a. 37.5 square feet

    b. 40 square feet

    c. 55 square feet

    d. 75 square feet

    e. 85 square feet

Use the following graph to answer question 23.

Time Spent on Various Activities during the School Day

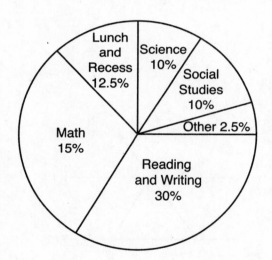

23. According to the information in the graph, if the school day consists of a total of 400 minutes, how many more minutes are spent during reading and writing than during social studies and science together?

    a. 20 minutes

    b. 40 minutes

    c. 60 minutes

    d. 80 minutes

    e. 120 minutes

24. According to recent statistics of a certain region of the United States, 5,000,000 students who took an aptitude test scored less than a perfect score and 8,000 earned a perfect score. What is the ratio of students who earned a perfect score to the students who did not receive a perfect score?

a. 1:624

b. 1:625

c. 1:626

d. 625:1

e. 626:1

25. The perimeter of a rectangular classroom is 148 feet. Its two longest sides add up to 86 feet. What is the length of each of the two shortest sides of the classroom?

a. 31 feet

b. 42 feet

c. 62 feet

d. 72 feet

e. 74 feet

26. If a, b, and c represent distinct real numbers, which of the following equations must be true?

a. $a \times b = b \times c$

b. $a + (b \times c) = ab \times ac$

c. $a(b + c) = ab + ac$

d. $ab + bc = b(a \times c)$

e. $a \times b + c = (a + b) \times (b + c)$

27. The East High School football team scored 20, 14, and 17 points in their last three games, respectively. What is the average number of points per game scored in their last three games?

a. 20 points

b. 19 points

c. 17 points

d. 14 points

e. 12 points

28. Given the following statements, which statement must be true?

All prime numbers are real numbers.

Some number q is a real number.

a. The number q is a prime number.

b. All real numbers are prime numbers.

c. No prime numbers are real numbers.

d. Some real numbers are prime numbers.

e. None of the above statements are necessarily true.

29. After three days, a group of hikers on a biology field trip discovers that they have used $\frac{2}{5}$ of their food supplies. They need enough food to make a round trip. At this rate, how many more days can they go forward before they have to turn around?

   a. 0.75 days

   b. 1.5 days

   c. 3.75 days

   d. 4.5 days

   e. 7.5 days

30. Which of the following has the greatest value?

   a. $\frac{2}{7}$

   b. $\frac{4}{11}$

   c. $\frac{1}{3}$

   d. $\frac{3}{8}$

   e. $\frac{3}{10}$

31. An administrative assistant can file 26 forms per hour. If 5,600 forms must be filed in an eight-hour day, how many assistants must you hire for that day?

   a. 24 assistants

   b. 25 assistants

   c. 26 assistants

   d. 27 assistants

   e. 28 assistants

32. Heading toward each other, one train travels due east at 35 miles per hour and a different train travels due west at 15 miles per hour. If the two trains start out 2,100 miles apart, how long will it take them to meet?

   a. 30 hours

   b. 42 hours

   c. 60 hours

   d. 105 hours

   e. 140 hours

33. During the spring bowling season, a bowler achieves the following scores: 116, 100, 104, 104, 114, 109, and 109. The bowler's three best scores are averaged for her final score on the season. What is her final score?

   a. 105

   b. 107

   c. 109

   d. 111

   e. 113

Use the following graph to answer question 34.

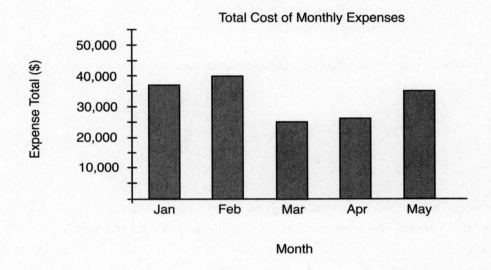

34. What were the total expenses for January, February, and April?

   a. $78,000

   b. $98,000

   c. $105,000

   d. $115,000

   e. $132,000

Use the following information to answer question 35.

x	y
2	5
4	11
6	17
8	23
10	29

35. Based on the table, which of the following expresses the relationship between x and y?
   a. $y = 2x + 3$
   b. $y = 2x - 1$
   c. $y = 3x + 2$
   d. $y = x + 3$
   e. $y = 3x - 1$

36. So far this week, Tory has worked a total of $26\frac{1}{4}$ hours at her job as a library clerk. If she is scheduled to work a total of $37\frac{1}{2}$ hours, how many more hours does she have to work this week?
   a. $10\frac{1}{4}$ hours
   b. $11\frac{1}{4}$ hours
   c. $11\frac{3}{4}$ hours
   d. $13\frac{1}{2}$ hours
   e. $13\frac{3}{4}$ hours

Use the following information to answer question 37.

Survey Regarding Reading Habits

Books per Month	Percentage
0	13
1–3	27
4–6	32
>6	28

37. Which of the following graphs most accurately represents the information in the table?

a.

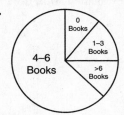

b.

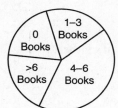

c.

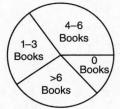

d.

e.

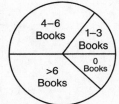

38. Some soccer players like to play in the rain.

All soccer players take science.

Sheila likes to play in the rain.

Based on this information, which of the following statements is true?

a. All soccer players like to play in the rain.

b. Only soccer players take science.

c. Sheila plays soccer.

d. Sheila takes science.

e. Some science students play soccer.

39. Tables in a cafeteria are arranged in four rows that are spaced 4 feet apart. Each table is 3 feet wide. If there is a distance of 4 feet from the wall to the rows of tables along the edges of the room, how wide is the cafeteria?

a. 20 feet

b. 28 feet

c. 32 feet

d. 36 feet

e. 40 feet

40. Kevin was half the age of his father 20 years ago. Kevin is 40. How old is Kevin's father?

a. 50

b. 60

c. 70

d. 80

e. 100

► Skills Test in Writing—Section 1, Part A

Directions: Choose the letter for the underlined portion that contains a grammatical error. If there is no error in the sentence, choose **e**.

1. After the <u>director and assistant</u> director both <u>resigned, we</u> could only guess <u>who would be</u> hired to take
           a   **b**   **c**

   <u>their</u> positions. <u>No error</u>
    d   **e**

2. The original shuttle bus <u>was</u> a horse-drawn wooden <u>carriage with</u> spoke wheels, it carried up to 15
                       a   **b**   **c**

   ferryboat passengers <u>to and from</u> the seaport. <u>No error</u>
                  d   **e**

3. <u>Frightened,</u> the parakeet chirped <u>loud</u> as the <u>neighbor's</u> curious cat <u>bounded up</u> to the birdcage.
    a   **b**   **c**   **d**

   <u>No error</u>
    e

4. *Kwanzaa,* a <u>S</u>wahili word meaning <u>a harvest's first fruits,</u> is a nonreligious holiday <u>that honors</u>
           a   **b**   **c**

   African-American <u>heritage and</u> culture. <u>No error</u>
            d   **e**

5. Last <u>Thursday,</u> as the <u>president of the university</u> addressed the <u>student body, she</u> made an <u>illusion to</u> the
        a   **b**   **c**   **d**

   construction of a new stadium for the football team. <u>No error</u>
                                  e

6. I thought <u>Johan's</u> dish of gumbo was <u>more spicier</u> than <u>Harold's,</u> but the <u>judges</u> disagreed. <u>No error</u>
             a   **b**   **c**   **d**   **e**

7. <u>Even as</u> the music industry pushes <u>further into</u> the realm of the digital world, <u>there is</u> still a large group
    a   **b**   **c**

   of people who collect vinyl records and old-style <u>amplifiers and</u> speakers. <u>No error</u>
                                    d   **e**

8. <u>If you hate</u> boring vacation <u>places, travel</u> off the beaten path to such faraway locations <u>such like</u>
     a   b   c

Madagascar, New Guinea, <u>or</u> the Himalayas. <u>No error</u>
                           d   e

9. <u>How</u> will the president's new <u>policies and</u> taxes <u>effect</u> the country's <u>morale?</u> <u>No error</u>
    a   b   c   d   e

10. <u>Each of</u> the players <u>have had</u> a <u>half-hour</u> warm-up <u>with</u> his or her personal trainer. <u>No error</u>
     a   b   c   d   e

11. <u>To find</u> the perimeter of a <u>polygon, add</u> the <u>lengths</u> of <u>it's</u> sides. <u>No error</u>
     a   b   c   d   e

12. Of the three boys <u>who</u> have <u>recently joined</u> the school's hockey <u>team</u>, Martin is the <u>taller</u>. <u>No error</u>
                   a   b   c   d   e

13. Cheryl <u>can't hardly</u> wait for election <u>day; she's</u> very curious to see who <u>will</u> be the next president.
            a   b c   d

<u>No error</u>
  e

14. Although <u>it usually has</u> a metal <u>frame and</u> exterior, some cars also <u>have</u> frames constructed <u>completely</u>
                  a   b   c   d

out of plastics. <u>No error</u>
             e

15. Despite the <u>boa's</u> daunting <u>ten-foot</u> length, the snake <u>will continue</u> to <u>grow;</u> it still has not reached
                a   b   c   d

maturity. <u>No error</u>
        e

16. The Department of State <u>has</u> foreign-policy <u>responsibilities</u> that include the promotion of peace,
                              a   b

<u>must protect</u> U.S. citizens abroad, <u>and</u> the assistance of U.S. businesses in the foreign marketplace.
    c   d

<u>No error</u>
  e

17. My <u>history</u> class, which is taught by <u>Professor Mendes</u>, is held on <u>Tuesdays and Fridays</u> from 9:00 A.M. to
         a   **b**   **c**
11:30 A.M. in <u>Grange Hall</u>. <u>No error</u>
              d   **e**

18. <u>Today's</u> ski jackets are made with synthetic fabrics <u>that are</u> very light <u>but yet</u> provide exceptional
     a   **b**   **c**
<u>warmth and</u> comfort. <u>No error</u>
   d   **e**

19. Here <u>are</u> one of the three <u>scarves</u> you <u>left</u> at my house <u>yesterday</u> morning. <u>No error</u>
      a   **b**   **c**   **d**   **e**

20. The florist <u>refused to</u> sell his last <u>orchid</u> because the <u>flowers</u> petals were <u>deformed and</u> discolored.
            a   **b**   **c**   **d**
<u>No error</u>
  e

21. Because they <u>close</u> resemble each other, many people think that Sara and Heather <u>are</u> identical <u>instead of</u>
          a   **b**   **c**   **d**
fraternal twins. <u>No error</u>
          e

▶ Skills Test in Writing—Section 1, Part B

Directions: Choose the best replacement for the underlined portion of the sentence. If no revision is necessary, choose **a**, which always repeats the original phrasing.

22. Any <u>passenger who is getting off at the next stop</u> should move to the front.
    a. passenger who is getting off at the next stop
    b. passenger, who is getting off at the next stop
    c. passenger who is getting off at the next stop,
    d. passenger, who is getting off at the next stop,
    e. passenger, whom is getting off at the next stop,

23. The Tour de France is a grueling trek through <u>France; and covering</u> almost 3,400 kilometers over the course of three weeks.
    a. France; and covering
    b. France, and covering
    c. France; it covers
    d. France it covers
    e. France; it covered

24. Shortly after landing upon the Red Planet, the Mars rover took a picture of <u>some own tire tracks.</u>
    a. some own tire tracks.
    b. it's own tire tracks.
    c. their own tire tracks.
    d. its own tire tracks.
    e. the tire tracks.

25. When the mayor took office, his plan was to bolster the economy, clean up the subways<u>, and reducing the crime rate.</u>
    a. , and reducing the crime rate.
    b. ; and reducing the crime rate.
    c. , and reduce the crime rate.
    d. , and reduction of the crime rate.
    e. ; and to reduce the rates of unlawful illegal criminal activities.

26. Our coach emphasizes teamwork <u>over individual accomplishment in his game plans.</u>

    a. over individual accomplishment in his game plans.

    b. onto individual accomplishment in his game plans.

    c. less better over individual accomplishment in his game plans.

    d. in his game plans over individual accomplishment instead.

    e. in his game plans with individual accomplishment instead.

27. <u>This was the third of the three assignments the professor gave during this the month of October.</u>

    a. This was the third of the three assignments the professor gave during this the month of October.

    b. Of the three assignments the professor gave during October, this was the third one.

    c. Thus far during the month of October, the professor gave three assignments and this was the third.

    d. This third assignment of the professor's given during the month of October was one of three assignments.

    e. This was the third assignment the professor gave during the month of October.

28. The horror film had <u>a frighteningly and unexpected ending.</u>

    a. a frighteningly and unexpected ending.

    b. a frighteningly and unexpectedly ending.

    c. an ending that was frightening and unexpectedly.

    d. a frightening and unexpected ending.

    e. an ending that was frightening and it was also an unexpected one.

29. An American writer of the twentieth century, <u>Jack Kerouac's collection of poems, *Mexico City Blues*,</u> celebrates freedom and individualism.

    a. Jack Kerouac's collection of poems, *Mexico City Blues*,

    b. *Mexico City Blues*, a collection of poems by Jack Kerouac,

    c. a collection of poems, *Mexico City Blues*, by Jack Kerouac,

    d. Jack Kerouac published poems, collected as *Mexico City Blues*, that

    e. Jack Kerouac published a collection of poems, *Mexico City Blues*, which

30. We loved our trip to the top of the <u>Empire State Building where you could see</u> the Statue of Liberty, all of New York's bridges, and the tiny people on the streets below.

    a. Empire State Building where you could see

    b. Empire State Building; you could see

    c. Empire State Building; where we saw

    d. Empire State Building; we saw

    e. Empire State Building in that you saw

31. <u>Conflicting to what stories you may have heard,</u> there was no curse written upon the entrance of King Tut's tomb.
   a. Conflicting in what you may have heard,
   b. Contrary in what you may have heard,
   c. Contrary to what you may have heard,
   d. To contrary what you have heard,
   e. Many stories of conflict you may have heard,

32. The senator did not <u>agree for the president's proposed tax hike.</u>
   a. agree for the president's proposed tax hike.
   b. agree the tax hike the president proposed with.
   c. agree with the president's proposed tax hike.
   d. agree with the tax hike that the president will propose.
   e. agree for the tax hike that the president will propose.

33. The student council has accused the members of the eighth-grade dance committee <u>with being careless with the spending of</u> the dance budget.
   a. with being careless with the spending of
   b. as to carelessness in the spending of
   c. of carelessness in the spending of
   d. of careless spending to
   e. with spending carelessly of

34. <u>Although England is surrounded by water,</u> it has always been important for the British to have a very powerful navy.
   a. Although England is surrounded by water,
   b. Although England was surrounded by water,
   c. England is surrounded by water,
   d. Because England is surrounded by water,
   e. Because England is surrounded by water;

35. The <u>principle objective of the documentary is to show you how global warming will effect</u> climates around the world.
   a. principle objective of the documentary is to show you how global warming will effect
   b. principle objective of the documentary is to show you how global warming will affect
   c. principal objective of the documentary is to show you how global warming will affect
   d. principal objective of the documentary is to show you how global warming will effect
   e. principle objective of the documentary is to show you how global warming will have effected

36. Built in Boston, the *U.S.S. Constitution* was given the nickname "Old Ironsides" because her thick oak planks had deflected many deadly cannonballs in battle.

    a. Built in Boston, the *U.S.S. Constitution* was given the nickname "Old Ironsides" because her thick oak planks had deflected

    b. Built in Boston, the *U.S.S. Constitution* was given the nickname "Old Ironsides" because her thick oak planks deflect

    c. The *U.S.S. Constitution*, being built in Boston, is nicknamed "Old Ironsides" because her thick oak planks had deflected

    d. Built in Boston, the *U.S.S. Constitution* will be given the nickname "Old Ironsides" because her thick oak planks had deflected

    e. The *U.S.S. Constitution*, to be built in Boston, was given the nickname "Old Ironsides" because her thick oak planks had deflected

37. Joe DiMaggio, the son of Italian immigrants, he was one of the most talented athletes of his generation and was later inducted into the baseball Hall of Fame.

    a. Joe DiMaggio, the son of Italian immigrants, he

    b. Joe DiMaggio, being the son of Italian immigrants,

    c. As he was the son of Italian immigrants, Joe DiMaggio

    d. The son of Italian immigrants, Joe DiMaggio

    e. Joe DiMaggio, the son of Italian immigrants, and he

38. The Gulf Stream is a warm current on the Atlantic's surface, it originates in the Gulf of Mexico and flows northeast.

    a. Atlantic's surface, it originates

    b. Atlantics' surface; it originates

    c. Atlantic's surface. Originating

    d. Atlantics' surface, and originating

    e. Atlantic's surface; it originates

▶ Skills Test in Writing—Section 2, Essay Writing

Carefully read the essay topic that follows. Plan and write an essay that addresses all points in the topic. Make sure that your essay is well organized and that you support your central argument with concrete examples. Allow 30 minutes for your essay.

School boards often discuss books that should not be included in a reading curriculum. Some think that some books should not only be part of the curriculum, but be required reading for students. Is there a book that you feel should be required reading for everyone? Choose a book you think should be required reading and write an essay persuading your audience why they should read this book. Be sure to support your position with logical arguments and specific examples.

▶ Answers

Skills Test in Reading

1. d. It is logical that a play would close after such a bad first-night reception, and the sentence in choice **d** also uses a metaphor about stage history that is extended in the next sentence. Choices **a**, **b**, and **c** do not fit the sense or syntax of the paragraph, because the *however* in the next sentence contradicts them. Choice **e** claims that all critics misunderstood the play, whereas the last sentence states that the critic Harold Hobson did see the importance of the play.

2. e. Although the writer seems amused by the negative criticisms of the play, he or she does give the opinion that it was revolutionary (a word that literally means a turning point). Choice **a** underplays and choice **b** overestimates the importance of the work to the author of the passage. Choice **c** is contradicted by the last sentence of the passage, and choice **d** mistakes Vivian Mercer's opinion for the author's.

3. a. Although students in the other classes might find the passage's subject matter somewhat appropriate, the passage talks mainly about physiological changes to astronauts in space.

4. d. Because the author mentions two women who attended an international conference as an accomplishment for which at least one of them gained international fame, the reader can surmise that it was a rare occurrence and choice **d** is the best answer. Choices **b**, **c**, and **e** are far beyond the scope of the passage; choice **a** might be true but would require information not contained in the passage.

5. c. This passage provides information to social workers about music therapy, as the title in choice **c** indicates. Choice **e** is incorrect because the first sentence speaks of mental and physical health professionals referring their clients and patients to music therapists; the second sentence indicates that *it* (meaning a referral) seems a particularly good choice for the social worker. Choice **d** is possible, but does not summarize the passage as well as choice **c**. Choices **a** and **b** refer to topics not covered in the passage.

6. a. Based particularly on the last sentence of the passage, **a** is the best choice. The other choices are beyond the scope of the passage.

7. c. Choice **c** provides the best outline of the passage. The other choices all contain points that are not covered by the passage.

8. d. If students have a strong motivation to recycle other than membership in the environmental club (i.e., fear of punishment), then this weakens the author's assertion that recycling has gone up because of increased membership in the club. Choice **a** is incorrect because it refers to a change made prior to the increase in the number of students recycling. Choice **b** is wrong because the students' motivation for joining the club is unrelated to whether they recycle. Choice **c** is incorrect because not all students need to participate in order for the poll to be valid. Finally, choice **e** is incorrect because it would strengthen the author's argument, not weaken it.

9. d. Cheerleading (choice **a**), skiing (choice **b**), race car driving (choice **c**), and gymnastics (choice **e**) are all strenuous activities that require good hand-eye coordination and run the risk of injury. Playing horse shoes (choice **d**) only requires good hand-eye coordination.

10. d. The passage contains objective language and straightforward information about accounting such as one might find in a textbook.

11. c. The second sentence of the passage speaks of a marketing department, separate from the accounting department.

12. d. All of the other choices are listed in the passage.

13. a. While all of the other choices may be true, the fact that Diana sold 22 cars in February and the salesperson of the month sold 26 means that they are not the same person. None of the other choices can be proved based on the information given.

14. e. The passage claims that lack of sleep *magnifies alcohol's effects on the body*, implying that it hampers a person's ability to function.

15. d. The author cites Thomas Nast's symbols for Tammany Hall and the Democratic and Republican Parties as examples of images that have entered the public consciousness and are *still in currency today*.

16. c. This title expresses the main point of the passage that, while there are predictable patterns in the life of a genius, the pattern increases the sense of something supernatural touching his or her life. Choices **a** and **b** are too general. Choice **d** is inaccurate because the passage does not talk about disorder in the life of a genius. Choice **e** covers only one of the two main ideas in the passage.

17. c. All the other statements are inaccurate.

18. e. The last sentence illustrates factors that motivate teenagers to exercise by using the results of a national survey to provide specific examples.

19. b. *Unpalatable* may be defined as not agreeable to taste (from the Latin *palatum*, which refers to the roof of the mouth). You know the word *palate* as the roof of the mouth, so unpalatable most likely has to do with the sense of taste. Another clue comes in the line that states that *tastes have changed*, indicating that *sushi*, which is now popular, was once considered unpleasant to eat.

20. e. The last sentence states that the detector's function is *to convert the information collected by the laser into . . . music.*

21. b. The Carib were not in any way described as peaceful, but rather as hostile people. Therefore, this answer is the exception. All other choices are descriptive of the Caribs and are explicit in the passage.

22. a. The last two lines of the passage directly state what defeated the Caribs. Choice **b** is incorrect because the Arawaks were defeated by the Carib, and neither the Dutch nor the French nor another cannibalistic tribe was mentioned in the role of conquerors.

23. b. *Strife* means war. Choice **a** is mentioned as a characteristic of the Carib toward their enemies in times of strife; it is not the meaning of strife. Choices **c** and **e** are not mentioned in conjunction with being warlike or with strife. Choice **d** makes no sense, because the times of strife were when the tribe allowed a chief to be chosen.

24. e. Present-day Saint Martin belongs to the French and the Dutch. Choices **b** and **d** have no support in the passage. Choices **a** and **c** are incorrect. The Spanish are mentioned in the passage only in conjunction with the Carib Indians.

25. a. This statement encapsulates the entire passage, not just a part of it. Choices **c** and **e** are too specific to be correct. Choices **b** and **d** are not supported by the passage.

26. c. The description of the winding paths, shifting landscape, and sections that *spill into one another* support the assertion that the park lacks a center.

27. e. The passage states that Olmsted wanted to create a *democratic playground*, so he designed the park to have many centers that would *allow interaction among the various members of society*.

28. d. To *posit* means to *suggest*. In this context, Hlusko suggests that grass stalks may have caused the grooves on early hominid teeth.

29. b. In the passage, the author states, *It seems that our early human ancestors may have used grass, which was easily found and ready to use, to floss between their teeth*. The use of *may* indicates that the author is not absolutely certain, but as the author does not suggest anything to contradict Dr. Hlusko's findings we can conclude that the author finds her theory very probable.

30. b. The passage defines panopticon: a place in which everything is in full view of others. The second paragraph repeats this definition: Every prisoner's cell would be in full view of the guards.

31. a. In the second paragraph, the author states that people behave differently when they know they are being watched—and that when we are being watched, or even think we are being watched, we will act the way we think we should act when we are being observed by others. Thus, the panopticon would be a useful tool for social control. If prisoners know they may be being watched by guards, it is logical to conclude that they are less likely to commit any wrongdoings; thus, the panopticon helps maintain order.

32. b. The passage illustrates several protest strategies used in the Civil Rights movement. Choices **c** and **e** are true statements but are too specific to be the primary focus of the passage. Choices **a** and **d** are not described in detail in the passage.

33. e. One meaning of *to test* is to apply a test as a means of analysis or diagnosis. In this context, *test* refers to putting something to a test or challenging something.

34. d. The protest at the Greensboro Woolworth lunch counter inspired others. The passage states *two weeks later similar demonstrations had spread to several other cities, and within a year similar peaceful demonstrations took place in over a hundred cities in the North and South*.

35. a. While the passage does include the other choices except choice **e**, the overall purpose of the passage is to teach asbestos awareness in schools.

36. e. This passage links the ability to defer gratification with self-control. Hence, children who are unable to defer gratification are unlikely to succeed because they lack self-discipline, or self-control.

37. c. Althea Gibson was an extraordinarily gifted athlete, yet because of the color of her skin and the time in which she lived, her path to success from the very beginning was obstructed by segregation and discrimination. Althea's ability to put these distractions aside and excel was a triumph of mental toughness, and the author uses the quote to illustrate that fact.

38. a. The fact that judicial review can override decisions made by the legislative and executive branches implies that it gives the court great authority.

39. e. The last sentence offers a view in opposition to the points made earlier in the passage supporting the Supreme Court's power to interpret the Constitution.

40. e. The opening sentence tells readers that making a list of pros and cons is a technique of utilitarian reasoning. Thus, readers who have used this technique will realize they are already familiar with the basic principles of utilitarianism.

Skills Test in Mathematics

1. **a.** In order to find the area of the parallelogram, first find the height. The vertical, dashed line drawn is the height and also forms a right triangle on the left side. Because two sides of this triangle are given, use the Pythagorean theorem to find the missing side; $a^2 + b^2 = c^2$. In this case, $a = 3$, $c = 5$, and $b =$ the height. Substitute; $3^2 + b^2 = 5^2$. Evaluate exponents; $9 + b^2 = 25$. Subtract 9 on both sides of the equation; $9 - 9 + b^2 = 25 - 9$; $b^2 = 16$. Therefore, $b = 4$. (The triangle is a 3–4–5 right triangle.) To find the area of the parallelogram, multiply the base of the figure by the height; $12 \times 4 = 48$ cm^2.

2. **a.** The perimeter of each small square is $8x$ units; therefore, the length of a side of each small square is $\frac{8x}{4} = 2x$ units. Because the new, large square is comprised of two sides from each of the four squares (the remaining four sides are now within the large square), the perimeter of the new, large square is equal to: $4(2x + 2x) = 4(4x) = 16x$ units.

3. **c.** Because *all* students at Central High School take math and *some* students take art, then some of the students will take both math and art. Choice **a** is incorrect because there is no information that shows that Charles attends Central High School. Choice **b** is incorrect because the second given statement says that *some* students take art and it cannot be assumed that this includes all students. Choice **d** is incorrect because there is no information given to prove that Charles does not also take art. Choice **e** is incorrect because the first given statement says that all students at Central High School do take math.

4. **c.** To find 150% of a number, multiply by 1.5; 0.0032 multiplied by 1.5 is equal to 0.0048.

5. **b.** The fractions are changed to decimals by dividing: $\frac{7}{12} = 7 \div 12 = 0.58$ and $\frac{5}{7} = 5 \div 7 = 0.71$. Change all numbers to decimal numbers with the same number of digits after the decimal point: 0.5800, 0.7100, 0.6300, 0.0790, 0.0108. The decimal 0.71 is the greatest, which was $\frac{5}{7}$.

6. **d.** In the bar graph, the horizontal axis is labeled with four different months and the vertical axis is labeled with height in inches. The title of this graph is then related to a quantity measured in inches and would occur during the winter months. The title in choice **d** represents a quantity (snowfall) that would be measured in inches during the winter. The amounts in the graph are not reasonable for rainfall amounts in choice **a**.

7. **d.** To determine the probability that a fifth grader's name will be chosen, you must determine the total number of fifth graders' names that are in the lottery and divide this number by the total number of names in the lottery. Because each fifth grader's name is placed in the lottery three times, there are $3 \times 100 = 300$ fifth-grade names. Likewise, there are $2 \times 150 = 300$ fourth-grade names and $1 \times 200 = 200$ third-grade names in the lottery. The probability that a fifth grader's name will be chosen is $\frac{300}{300 + 300 + 200} = \frac{300}{800} = \frac{3}{8}$.

8. d. This question translates into the equation $\frac{1}{4}x + 3 = x - 3$. First, subtract $\frac{1}{4}x$ from both sides of the equation: $3 = x - \frac{1}{4}x - 3$. Multiply both sides by 4: $12 = 4x - x - 12$. Combine like terms: $12 = 3x - 12$. Add 12 to both sides: $24 = 3x$. Divide both sides by 3: $8 = x$.

9. d. First, find the rate of snowfall per hour. Because it snowed at a constant rate of three inches every two hours, divide $\frac{3\text{ inches}}{2\text{ hours}}$ to get a rate of 1.5 inches per hour. The question asks for the amount of snow that fell in the first five hours, so multiply 1.5×5 hours $= 7.5$ inches to get the amount.

10. e. The cost of a field trip increases by approximately $1.50 each year. Because the cost per pupil in 2008 is $10.50 per pupil, the cost in 2009 will be approximately $10.50 + 1.50 = $12.00 and the cost in 2010 will be $12.00 + 1.50 = $13.50.

11. c. First, find the total number of floors they can wax in the specified time. This is arrived at by multiplying the rate for each person by the amount of time spent by each. Marcus waxes five floors an hour for three hours, or 15 floors; Josie waxes four floors an hour for two hours, or eight floors. Together they wax 23 floors. Because there are 50 classrooms total, the percentage waxed is $\frac{23}{50} = 0.46$, which is equal to 46%.

12. e. Be aware of the break in the scale on the vertical axis. This scale starts at zero, jumps to 100, and then increases by 10 at each mark. Washington High School has a graduating class size of approximately 100 students in 1998 and 200 students in 2008, thus doubling the size of its graduating class during that time.

13. b. Approximately 180 students from Springville High School and about 150 students from Valley High School graduated in 1998. Find the difference between them by subtracting $180 - 150 = 30$.

14. a. An average increase of six students per year over a period of ten years is an increase of about 60 students. Valley High School had about 140 students in the graduating class in 1998 and about 200 in 2008; $200 - 140 = 60$ students over the course of 10 years.

15. e. Over the five-week period between week 3 and week 7, Company ABC followed a pattern where the stock increased by $1 for week 4, decreased by $0.50 for week 5, increased by $1 for week 6, and decreased by $0.50 for week 7. If this trend continues, the price expected for week 8 would be $1 more than week 7, or $4.00 per share. Company XYZ decreased in price by $0.50 each week. Because the price for week 7 was $4.50, the expected price for week 8 would also be $4.00. The price per share for both companies would be the same for week 8.

16. b. To find the average price per share over the seven-week period, add the price per share for each week and divide the total by 7. By reading the graph, the price per share for each week is: week 1 = $2.50, week 2 = $1.50, week 3 = $2.00, week 4 = $3.00, week 5 = $2.50, week 6 = $3.50, and week 7 = $3.00. Adding the price for each week results in a total of $18; $18 divided by 7 weeks equals approximately $2.57.

17. **d.** During week 4, the price per share for Company XYZ was $6.00 and the price per share of Company ABC was $3.00. Since 3 is half of 6, this is the week where the stock price is exactly half.

18. **a.** The thousandths place is three places to the right of the decimal point. Choice **a** has a 9 in the thousandths place. In choice **b**, the 9 is in the hundredths place; in **c** it is in the tenths place; in **d** it is in the ten-thousandths place; in choice **e** it is the hundred-thousandths place.

19. **d.** First calculate her earnings for one day; $10.40 times 8 hours per day is equal to $83.20. For any amount of time she worked over 8 hours she earns time and a half, or 1.5 times her regular pay. This is equal to $10.40 $\times$ 1.5 = $15.60 per hour overtime. Because she worked $1\frac{1}{2}$ hours overtime on average, this is equal to $15.60 $\times$ 1.5 = $23.40 extra pay per day. Therefore, her total pay per day is equal to $83.20 + $23.40 = $106.60. Multiply this amount by 5 days per week to get her weekly pay: $106.60 $\times$ 5 = $533.00.

20. **e.** Because lines l and m are parallel, there are a number of angle relationships that allow you to solve for x. As shown in the following figure, the angle labeled 35° and its corresponding angle are congruent. In addition, the angle vertical to, or across from, the angle labeled 50° is also 50°.

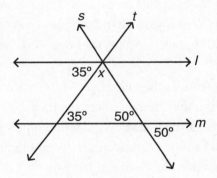

The two newly labeled angles and the angle labeled x are three angles of a triangle, so subtract the sum of the two known angles from 180 to solve for x; $180 - (50 + 35) = 180 - 85 = 95°$.

21. **c.** The words *at least* and *at most* in the first sentence indicate that a teacher at this school has between three and five classes, inclusively, but no more and no less. Because the actual number of teachers at the school is not known, the average number of classes and the average time spent teaching cannot be determined. Therefore, it can only be concluded that each teacher has from three to five classes at 40 minutes each, for a total between 120 and 200 minutes per day, inclusive.

22. **d.** The area of the patio is found by multiplying the length times width. Because the length is 15 feet and the width is $\frac{1}{3}$ as long as the length, the width is $\frac{1}{3} \times 15 = 5$ feet. Multiplying the length by the width yields the area: 15 feet $\times$ 5 feet = 75 square feet.

23. b. Use the percent of each section to find the total number of minutes spent in the specific areas. Because 30% of the day is spent on reading, multiply $0.30 \times 400 = 120$ minutes. Because 10% of the day is spent on social studies and another 10% on science, multiply $0.10 \times 400 = 40$ minutes for each. Therefore, the total time for reading (120 minutes) minus the total time for social studies and science together (80) is equal to 40 minutes.

24. b. The ratio is *number of perfect scores:number of nonperfect scores*. This unreduced ratio is 8,000:5,000,000 or 8:5,000. Because 5,000 divided by 8 equals 625, this ratio then becomes 1:625.

25. a. The first step in solving the problem is to subtract the length of the two known sides from the perimeter; $148 - 86 = 62$. This amount is the sum of the two shorter sides. Divide 62 by 2 to get 31 feet, the measure of each of the shorter sides.

26. c. Choice **c** represents the distributive property of multiplication over addition. This property can be checked by substituting numbers for *a*, *b*, and *c*. For example, if $a = 3$, $b = 4$, and $c = 5$ the equation would become $3(4 + 5) = 3 \times 4 + 3 \times 5$. The equation then simplifies to $3(9) = 12 + 15$, which then becomes $27 = 27$. Because both sides are equal, the equation is true. Each of the other choices would not be true if different numbers were substituted in for *a*, *b*, and *c*.

27. c. To find the average points scored per game, you add the total points for each game and divide by the number of games. $\frac{20 + 17 + 14}{3} = \frac{51}{3} = 17$ average points per game.

28. d. Because it is given that all prime numbers are real numbers, then it can be inferred that at least *some* real numbers are also prime numbers. However, it cannot be assumed that *all* real numbers are also prime numbers for answer choice **b**. We know only that *q* is a real number, so it is not for certain that it is also a prime number for answer choice **a**. Answer choice **c** contradicts the first statement that was given.

29. a. First, find out how long the entire hike can be, based on the rate at which the hikers are using their supplies. $\frac{\frac{2}{5}}{3} = \frac{1}{x}$, where 1 is the total amount of supplies and *x* is the number of days for the whole hike. Cross multiplying, you get $\frac{2}{5}x = 3$. Multiply each side of the equation by $\frac{5}{2}$ to get $x = \frac{5}{2} \times 3 = \frac{15}{2}$ $= 7\frac{1}{2}$ days for the length of the entire hike, which includes the trip back. Because half of $7\frac{1}{2}$ is $3\frac{3}{4}$ or 3.75, the hikers could go forward for 3.75 days altogether before they would have to turn around. They have already hiked for three days, so $3.75 - 3 = 0.75$ (days) is the amount of time they can now go forward before they have to turn around.

30. d. Another way to complete the problem, or simply check your answer, is to change each of the fractions to decimal form to the nearest hundredth to compare; $\frac{2}{7} \approx 0.29$, $\frac{4}{11} \approx 0.36$, $\frac{1}{3} \approx 0.33$, $\frac{3}{8} \approx 0.38$, $\frac{3}{10} \approx 0.30$. Choice **d** is greater than the others.

31. d. Multiply: 26 forms times 8 hours is 208 forms per day per assistant. Divide the total forms that need to be filed by the amount of forms one assistant can file per day; 5,600 divided by 208 is approximately 26.9. You can't hire 0.9 of an assistant, so you have to hire 27 assistants for the day.

32. b. Because they are traveling toward each other, the trains' combined rate of travel is 35 miles per hour plus 15 miles per hour. This is equal to 50 miles per hour. Because distance = rate $\times$ time, time = $\frac{\text{distance}}{\text{rate}}$. Divide the rate of travel into the total distance that they need to go; 2,100 miles divided by 50 miles per hour equals 42 hours.

33. e. The bowler's three best scores are the highest three scores. These are 116, 114, and 109. To find the average, divide the sum of these three scores by 3; $\frac{116 + 114 + 109}{3} = \frac{339}{3} = 113$.

34. c. January's expenses are approximately $38,000; February is approximately $41,000, and April is approximately $26,000. These added together give a total of $105,000.

35. e. One of the best ways to solve a question such as this one is to substitute the values for x into the equations and see which one has the matching y-values from the table. If 2 is substituted for x, only choices **d** and **e** result in a y-value of 5; $y = 2 + 3$; $y = 5$. $y = 3(2) - 1$; $y = 6 - 1$; $y = 5$. Now try each of these equations with other values from the table. If 4 is substituted for x, answer choice **d** gives a result of 7 and answer choice **e** gives a result of 11. Because 11 is the y-value in the table, the solution is choice **e**.

36. b. Subtract the number of hours she has worked so far this week from the total number of hours she needs to work. The expression becomes: $37\frac{1}{2} - 26\frac{1}{4} = 37\frac{2}{4} - 26\frac{1}{4} = 11\frac{1}{4}$.

37. c. Three out of the four sections are each close to 30%, so look for the answer choice with three of the four sections about the same size and that together make up about 90% of the circle. Only choice **c** has three sections about the same size that take up most of the circle and the fourth section about half the size of one of the others.

38. e. Because all soccer players take science, then at least some of the science students are also soccer players. Only some soccer players like to play in the rain, so it cannot be concluded that *all* soccer players like to play in the rain. In addition, we cannot conclude from this information that *only* soccer players take science. The fact that Sheila likes to play in the rain does not give you any information as to whether she is a soccer player or whether she takes science. Thus, there is not enough information to draw a conclusion about answer choices **b**, **c**, or **d**.

39. c. The width of the room can be determined by two factors: (1) the width of each table and the number of tables across the width of the room, and (2) the width of the spaces between the tables and the walls, and the number of these spaces. Because there are four tables that are each 3 feet in width, there is $4 \times 3 = 12$ feet to include for the width of the tables. In addition, there are five spaces either between tables or between a table and the wall that measure 4 feet in width; $5 \times 4 = 20$ feet. Combine these two together: $12 + 20 = 32$ feet.

40. b. Kevin is 40, so 20 years ago he was $40 - 20 = 20$ years old. At that time in the past, Kevin's father was twice his age, so his father was 40, 20 years ago. Therefore, Kevin's father is $40 + 20 = 60$ years old now.

Skills Test in Writing—Section 1, Part A

1. e. Because there are no grammatical, idiomatic, logical, or structural errors in this sentence, choice **e** is the best answer.

2. c. The comma is incorrect punctuation. Because this sentence contains two independent clauses, a semicolon (;) should be used instead.

3. b. The word *loud* is an adjective and should modify a noun. In this sentence the adverb *loudly* should be used, because it would correctly modify the verb *chirped*.

4. e. Because there are no grammatical, idiomatic, logical, or structural errors in this sentence, choice **e** is the best answer.

5. d. This is an error in word choice. The use of the word *illusion* makes this sentence illogical. An illusion is something that is not what it seems. The correct word choice would be *allusion*, which means a reference or hint.

6. b. Using *more* or *most* before an adjective or adverb is an example of a double comparison. In this sentence, just using the word *spicier* is enough to establish the proper comparison between the two dishes of gumbo.

7. e. Because there are no grammatical, idiomatic, logical, or structural errors in this sentence, choice **e** is the best answer.

8. c. In this comparison the word *as* should be used instead of *like*. The use of *as* completes the idiom *such as*.

9. c. This is a word-choice error. In this sentence the verb *affect*, meaning to influence, should be used. *Effect* is most often used as a noun, but when it is used as a verb, it means to bring about. In this sentence, the use of *effect* as a verb makes this sentence illogical.

10. b. The error is grammatical; there is no subject-verb agreement in this sentence. The subject *each* is singular and requires a singular verb form. In this sentence, the correct form is *has had*.

11. d. This is a grammatical error. The contraction *it's* (meaning *it is*) should be replaced by the possessive pronoun *its*.

12. d. This sentence makes a comparison among Martin and two other boys (three people); therefore, the superlative *tallest* should be used. *Taller* is incorrect because it is the comparative form and should be used only when there is a comparison between two people.

13. a. The phrase *can't hardly* is an example of a double negative. In this sentence, the proper form would be to use *can hardly wait* or simply, *cannot wait*.

14. a. This is an error of agreement. The singular pronoun *it* does not agree with the plural noun *cars*. In this sentence *it . . . has* should be replaced by the plural *they . . . have*.

15. e. Because there are no grammatical, idiomatic, logical, or structural errors in this sentence, choice **e** is the best answer.

16. c. This is an error in sentence construction. For proper parallel construction in the sentence, *must protect* should be changed to *the protection of*.

17. e. Because there are no grammatical, idiomatic, logical, or structural errors in this sentence, choice **e** is the best answer.

18. c. Because the words *but* and *yet* mean the same thing, this sentence contains a redundancy. Either one of these words should be deleted.

19. a. This is an error in agreement. The singular noun *one* requires the singular verb *is*. When the subject (in this case *one*) follows the verb, as in a sentence beginning with *here* or *there*, be careful to determine the subject. In this sentence, the subject is not the plural noun *scarves*.

20. c. This is an error in the possessive case. The possessive indicates ownership (a flower's petals). With singular nouns, the possessive case is formed by adding an *'s*.

21. a. This is a grammatical error. Because the word modifies the verb *resemble*, the adverb *closely* should be used instead of the adjective *close*.

Skills Test in Writing—Section 1, Part B

22. a. The clause *who is getting off at the next stop* is a restrictive (essential) clause and should not be set off by commas. Choices **b**, **c**, **d**, and **e** are all punctuated incorrectly. In addition, choice **e** uses the pronoun *whom*, which is the wrong case.

23. c. This is the only choice in which the sentence construction is clear and error-free. Choices **a** and **b** create faulty subordination. In addition, choice **b** also uses incorrect punctuation between the two clauses. Choice **d** fails to include any punctuation between the two clauses. In choice **e**, *covered* represents an incorrect shift in verb tense.

24. d. This is the only choice that contains the pronoun (*its*) that grammatically agrees with the noun *Mars rover*. Choices **a** and **c** contain incorrect pronouns. Choice **b** mistakenly uses the contraction *it's* (*it is*), and choice **e** incorrectly implies that the rover did not create the tire tracks.

25. c. The item in the underlined portion of the sentence should be parallel with the rest of the sentence and possess the appropriate punctuation. Only choice **c** has the appropriate parallel construction and punctuation. Choices **a**, **b**, and **d** break the parallel flow of the sentence with the use of the words *reducing* or *reduction*. Choice **e** incorrectly uses a semicolon and is also unnecessarily wordy and redundant.

26. a. This sentence requires that the comparison between *teamwork* and *individual accomplishment* be logical and clear. Choice **b** is incorrect because the use of the preposition *onto* is confusing and does not observe standard usage conventions. The phrase *less better* in choice **c** makes no sense. Choices **d** and **e** result in an unclear comparison.

27. e. This is the only choice that does not contain excessive wordiness or a redundancy. In choice **a**, the phrase *the third of three* is a redundancy. Choice **b** also repeats by using both *three* and *third*. Choices **c** and **d**, although constructed differently, make the same error.

28. d. Adjectives modify nouns and adverbs modify verbs. In choice **d**, the adjectives *frightening* and *unexpected* correctly modify the noun *ending*. In choices **a** and **b** *frighteningly* is an adverb incorrectly modifying a noun. In choice **c**, the adverb *unexpectedly* incorrectly modifies a noun. Choice **e** is incorrect because it is excessively wordy.

29. e. The opening phrase, *An American writer of the twentieth century*, should modify a noun that identifies the *writer*. Only choices **d** and **e** do this. In choices **a**, **b**, and **c**, either *collection* or *Mexico City Blues* is illogically credited with being the writer. Choice **d** is incorrect because the subject of the resulting dependent clause, *poems*, would not agree with its verb, *celebrates*.

30. d. Choice **d** is correctly punctuated with a semicolon between two independent clauses, and there is no shift in person (e.g., everything is in the first person). Choices **a**, **b**, and **e** are incorrect because the sentence shifts from the first person (*we*) to the second person (*you*). Choice **c** uses a semicolon when no punctuation is necessary.

31. c. This is the only choice that is clear, logical, and idiomatic. In this sentence *contrary to*, which means a viewpoint that is opposite to or in conflict with another viewpoint, is used correctly in this context. Choices **a** and **b** are incorrect because the preposition *in* is inappropriately used with *conflicting* (choice **a**) and *contrary* (choice **b**). Similarly, choice **d** does not use standard-usage phrasing. Choice **e** simply does not make sense in context.

32. c. This is the only choice that is clear and idiomatic. In choice **a**, the preposition *for* is incorrectly paired with *agree*. In choice **b**, the sentence is awkward and does not make sense. Choice **d** is idiomatically correct, but like choice **e**, it uses awkward phrasing.

33. c. This choice is the only one that uses the idioms of standard English correctly. Choice **a** is wordy and awkward. Choices **b** and **e** also use awkward phrasing. Choice **d** is unclear and ambiguous; the use of the preposition *to* distorts the meaning of the sentence.

34. d. This is the only choice that employs the correct conjunction *because* and uses the proper punctuation between the two clauses. The use of the conjunction *although* in choices **a** and **b** sets up faulty coordination between the two clauses. In addition, the use of *was* in choice **b** is a verb tense error that creates a nonparallel sentence. Choice **c** lacks a proper conjunction, and is therefore incorrect. Choice **e** is properly coordinated, but the incorrect use of a semicolon instead of a comma creates a punctuation error.

35. c. The word *principle*, meaning rule, can only be used as a noun. *Principal*, meaning chief, can be used as a noun or as an adjective. In this sentence, it is clearly an adjective, which rules out choices **a**, **b**, and **e**. Choice **d** incorrectly uses the word *effect*. The verb *affect* means to produce an *effect* (noun) on something.

36. a. When constructing sentences, unnecessary shifts in verb tenses should be avoided. Choice **a** is best because all three verbs in the sentence indicate that the action occurred in the past (*built*, *was given*, and *had deflected*). In choice **b**, there is a shift to the present (*deflect*). Choice **c** begins in the present (*being built*, *is nicknamed*), and then shifts to the past (*had deflected*). Choice **d** starts in the past tense (*built*), shifts to the future (*will be given*), and then reverts back to the past (*had deflected*). Finally, choice **e** shifts from the future (*to be built*) to past tense (*was given*, *had deflected*).

37. d. This is the only choice that is both grammatically and logically correct. Choice **a** has a shift in construction; there are two subjects that mean the same thing (*Joe DiMaggio* and *he*). Choice **b** has a modifier problem; the sentence implies that Joe DiMaggio was a talented athlete because he was the son of immigrants. Choice **c**, though constructed differently, results in the same faulty logic. Choice **e** creates faulty subordination.

38. e. There are two potential problems in this sentence. One is the possessive form of the word *Atlantic*, and the other is the punctuation between the two clauses. Choice **e** uses the correct possessive form (there is only one Atlantic), and the correct punctuation (a semicolon should be used between two independent clauses). Choice **a** is incorrect because it creates a comma splice. Choice **b** uses the incorrect possessive form. Choice **c** creates a sentence fragment. Choice **d** creates faulty subordination.

Skills Test in Writing—Section 2, Essay Writing

Following are sample criteria for scoring a PPST essay.

A score "6" writer will

- create an exceptional composition that appropriately addresses the audience and given task
- organize ideas effectively, include very strong supporting details, and use smooth transitions
- present a definitive, focused thesis and clearly support it throughout the composition
- include vivid details, clear examples, and strong supporting text to enhance the themes of the composition
- exhibit an exceptional level of skill in the usage of the English language and the capacity to employ an assortment of sentence structures
- build essentially error-free sentences that accurately convey intended meaning

A score "5" writer will

- create a commendable composition that appropriately addresses the audience and given task
- organize ideas, include supporting details, and use smooth transitions
- present a thesis and support it throughout the composition
- include details, examples, and supporting text to enhance the themes of the composition
- generally exhibit a high level of skill in the usage of the English language and the capacity to employ an assortment of sentence structures
- build mostly error-free sentences that accurately convey intended meaning

A score "4" writer will

- create a composition that satisfactorily addresses the audience and given task
- display satisfactory organization of ideas, include adequate supporting details, and generally use smooth transitions
- present a thesis and mostly support it throughout the composition
- include some details, examples, and supporting text that typically enhance most themes of the composition
- exhibit a competent level of skill in the usage of the English language and the general capacity to employ an assortment of sentence structures
- build sentences with several minor errors that generally do not confuse the intended meaning

A score "3" writer will

- create an adequate composition that basically addresses the audience and given task
- display some organization of ideas, include some supporting details, and use mostly logical transitions
- present a somewhat underdeveloped thesis but attempt to support it throughout the composition
- display limited organization of ideas, have some inconsistent supporting details, and use few transitions
- exhibit an adequate level of skill in the usage of the English language and a basic capacity to employ an assortment of sentence structures
- build sentences with some minor and major errors that may obscure the intended meaning

A score "2" writer will

- create a composition that restrictedly addresses the audience and given task
- display little organization of ideas, have inconsistent supporting details, and use very few transitions
- present an unclear or confusing thesis with little support throughout the composition
- include very few details, examples, and supporting text
- exhibit a less than adequate level of skill in the usage of the English language and a limited capacity to employ a basic assortment of sentence structures
- build sentences with a few major errors that may confuse the intended meaning

A score "1" writer will

- create a composition that has a limited sense of the audience and given task
- display illogical organization of ideas, include confusing or no supporting details, and lack the ability to effectively use transitions
- present a minimal or unclear thesis
- include confusing or irrelevant details and examples, and little or no supporting text
- exhibit a limited level of skill in the usage of the English language and little or no capacity to employ basic sentence structure
- build sentences with many major errors that obscure or confuse the intended meaning

Sample 6 Essay

Most people know who Frankenstein is—or at least they think they do. Because of the way Mary Shelley's brilliant 1818 novel was adapted to film, most Americans think that Frankenstein is a towering, scar-faced monster who brings terror wherever he goes. In Shelley's novel, however, the real monster is Victor Frankenstein, the scientist who is the monster's creator. In her story of how Victor Frankenstein creates the monster and what he does after the monster comes to life, Shelley conveys several timeless messages about the dangers of science, the dangers of isolation, and the importance of being a good parent. It is a novel that everyone should read.

In the story, Frankenstein, eager for glory, wants to discover the "elixir of life" so that he can have the power to bring the dead back to life. He wants to create a new race of superhuman beings and wants them to worship him like a god. He wants to unlock the secrets of nature and use that power for his own selfish goals. Shelley's novel warns us that we must be careful what we do with science—how we apply the knowledge we discover. For when Frankenstein does discover the "elixir of life," and when he does create a superhuman being, he creates a creature that is beyond his control. The creature is more powerful and more intelligent than Victor Frankenstein, and the creature engineers Frankenstein's demise.

Shelley's novel also warns us about the dangers of isolation. Frankenstein's creation is so revolting and dangerous in part because Frankenstein works completely alone. He becomes so absorbed with his project that he completely blocks out family and friends. He stops communicating with others and works secretly; he does not consult with anyone about his project, both because he knows that what he is doing is wrong, and because he wants all the glory. But because he does not work with others, and because he loses touch with his community of family and friends, he also loses touch with his responsibility to other human beings. When the creature comes to life, Frankenstein runs away, abandoning his creation even though he knows the creature might harm others.

This abandonment brings us to the novel's third timeless message: the importance of being a good parent. Frankenstein creates a living being and then abandons him because he is an "ugly wretch." He totally ignores his responsibility to the creature, who is born as innocent as a child, even though he is the size of a giant. The creature is abhorred by everyone he meets, and because no one has ever shown him love, he learns to hate. And the person he comes to hate most is the father who abandoned him. Shelley's message is clear: you are responsible for what you create, and if you are a parent, you must love your child, whatever his or her appearance.

In our age of cloning and genetic engineering, of scattered communities and neighbors who don't know each other's names, of abandoned children and neglectful parents, Shelley's book may have more importance than ever. But it is not just the message that makes this book great. It is also a great read, powerful and suspense-filled. Will Frankenstein capture the creature? Will he create a "bride" for the monster? Will Walton, the ship captain who records Frankenstein's story, learn from Frankenstein's tale? Shelley's *Frankenstein* should be required reading for everyone.

Sample 4 Essay

Frankenstein isn't who most people think he is—a monster. The real Frankenstein is the scientist who brings the monster to life. The confusion comes from the fact that many rely on the movie version of the story, rather than the original book by Mary Shelley. *Frankenstein* should be required reading for a number of reasons. It teaches some important lessons, which are maybe even more important to day than they were in Shelly's time (the 1800s.)

One lesson is about how to use science. Dr. Frankenstein in the story discovers how to bring a dead person back to life. But everything goes wrong after the creature wakes up. What was supposed to be a great thing that would bring Frankenstein glory and make him a master creator instead brought him and many other people all kinds of terrible horror. I think Mary is telling us to be very careful how we use science.

She also is telling us in this story to stay close to others. Frankenstein makes the creature by himself. While working on the monster; he doesn't talk to anyone, and no one in the university knows what he's up to. He's so obsessed that he doesn't consider what will happen once this giant creature comes to life. He doesn't think about being responsible to and for the creature.

Another lesson is that we need to be good parents. Frankenstein is like the creature's father and mother. He created him, and he needs to take care of him. But he doesn't, he just runs away. That's when the horror begins. The creature is hated by everyone and his life is really sad.

There are many other important lessons to be learned from Frankenstein, including the need to learn from other's mistakes. Walton, a ship captain, learns the story from Frankenstien, and then writes about it in letters to his sister. The reader is left wondering if Walton will understand the messages of Frankenstein's story and live his life differently as a result.

Another message is the need to tell the truth, and the consequences of not doing so. Victor Frankenstein knows that the monster strangled his brother, but he does not want to tell anyone. Even when an innocent girl is accused of the crime, he keeps his silence. The girl is found guilty and executed as a result of his unwillingness to tell the truth. Shelley's *Frankenstein* is filled with important lessons, and I think it should be required reading for everyone.

Sample 1 Essay

Every school has a required reading list. They are filled with "the classics." Classics are books thought to be important by teachers. Some books leave the list, and others are added. But for the last century, many books have stayed the same. Some of them probably shouldn't be considered classics, but they remain on the list. Others are great books that are enjoyed by millions of people. One of these books is Mary Shelly's *Frankenstien.*

It is the story of a monster. Many people think the monster's name is Frankenstien, but this is really the name of the doctor who creates him. This is due to the 1931 movie version of the novel, which starred Boris Karloff. The movie was directed by James Whale. It was based on a play of the Shelly book. When people hear the name Frankenstien, they think of Boris Karloff.

In the book, Victor Frankenstien makes the monster out of dead body parts. Then he makes the monster come to life. But then he abandons the childlike monster and trouble starts. Everyone hates the monster, and he starts to hate, too. There is also a story about a sailor named Walton. He writes letters to someone in his family. They are about the story of Frankenstien. Frankenstine deserves to be on the list of classics.

▶ Praxis I Scoring

Your scores on the multiple-choice parts of the exam are based on the number of questions you answered correctly; there is no "guessing penalty" for incorrect answers and no penalty for unanswered questions. The Educational Testing Service does not set passing scores for these tests, leaving this up to the institutions, state agencies, and associations that use the tests. Therefore, the interpretation of your score depends on the reason you are taking the test. For example, there will be a difference in the interpretation of your score if you are applying for a teacher-training program than if you are a candidate for educational credentials or for teacher selection. Whatever the case, though, it is necessary for you to do well on all three segments of the Praxis I—Reading, Mathematics, and Writing—so you must figure your score on each test separately.

The Reading test, the Mathematics test, and the multiple-choice sections of the Writing test are scored the same way: First find the number of questions you got right on each test. As noted earlier, questions you skipped or got wrong don't count; just add up how many questions you got right. Then divide the number of questions you got right by the number of questions in the section to arrive at a percentage. You can check your score against the passing scores in the state or organization that requires you to take the exam.

In addition to passing the multiple-choice questions, you must receive a passing score on the essay portion of the PPST Writing test. On this portion, the essay is read and scored by at least two writing experts, using a scale of 1 to 6, where 6 is the highest. The scores of the two experts are then combined. The scoring criteria are outlined in detail in the answer explanations. The best way to see how you did on the essay portion of the exam is to give your essay and the scoring criteria to a teacher or other reader whom you trust to see what scores he or she would assign.

What's much more important than your scores, for now, is how you did on each of the basic skills tested by the exam. You need to diagnose your strengths and weaknesses so that you can concentrate your efforts as you prepare for the exam.

Use your percentage scores in conjunction with the LearningExpress Test Preparation guide in Chapter 2 of this book to help you devise a study plan. Then, turn to the review chapters that cover each of the basic skills tested on the Praxis I. You should plan to spend more time on the lessons that correspond to the questions you found hardest and less time on the lessons that correspond to areas in which you did well.

4 ▶ Reading Test Review

CHAPTER SUMMARY

Reading comprehension is an important skill to have in life and on tests. This chapter covers the most essential reading and reading comprehension strategies for success. You will learn to become an active reader, to understand the difference between main idea and supporting ideas, and to recognize information that is implied, but not stated in a passage.

DEVELOPING STRONG READING comprehension skills is crucial for success as a prospective teacher. The PPST Reading test measures your ability to understand written passages and demonstrate insight and discrimination about what you read. The test contains passages of varying lengths: long passages of about 200 words, shorter passages of approximately 100 words, and short statements of a few sentences. One or more multiple-choice questions follow each passage or statement. You will be asked to answer 40 questions in 60 minutes (46 questions in 75 minutes on the computer version of the test).

The topics presented in the passages reflect a range of subjects, from art, science, politics, and history to real-life situations. Although you do not need any specialized knowledge or a background in the subject to answer the questions, you do need to show that you can extract information from the passage. Some questions will focus on the explicit information offered in a passage: its main purpose, supporting details, and organization. Other questions will ask you to interpret and evaluate the assumptions that are implicit in the passage: the text's underlying message, arguments, and logic.

Although the content of the computer-based Praxis Reading test is similar to that of the paper-based test, the format of the two exams varies slightly. The way you view reading passages and related questions on the computer-based test is different from the paper test. You will view a split screen on your computer, with the reading passage displayed on the left-hand side and a question on the right-hand side; you will view one question at a time. By using a special marking tool, you can check off a difficult question so that you can go back to it later and review or change it. A review screen will tell you if a question is marked for review. Other differences between the two formats are outlined here:

	COMPUTER-BASED TEST	PAPER-BASED TEST
Total time	75 minutes	60 minutes

Number of questions	46 multiple-choice questions:
	21 literal comprehension
	    questions
	25 critical and inferential
	    comprehension questions
		40 multiple-choice questions:
		18 literal comprehension
		    questions
		22 critical and inferential
		    comprehension questions

▶ Types of Questions

Some of the questions on the PPST Reading test focus on *what* information is presented in a passage, while others deal with *how* information is presented. The questions fall into two basic categories: literal comprehension and critical and inferential comprehension. About 45% of the test questions deal with literal comprehension, whereas 55% focus on critical and inferential comprehension.

▶ Literal Comprehension

Literal comprehension questions measure your ability to understand the literal content of a passage. You might be asked to identify the main purpose of a passage, locate a fact or detail, describe how the passage is organized, or define how a word is used in a passage. There are four types of literal comprehension questions:

1. **Main Idea.** For this question type, you need to be able to identify the main idea of the passage or a specific paragraph in the passage.

   Examples
   - The passage is primarily concerned with . . . ?
   - What is the author's main purpose in this passage?
   - Which of the following would be the best title for this passage?

2. **Supporting Idea.** This question type asks you to summarize a supporting idea in the passage. You will need to be able to locate specific information in the passage, such as a fact, figure, or name.

   Examples
   - According to the passage, how many people in the United States have Type II diabetes?
   - The passage states that a lunar eclipse occurs when . . . ?
   - Which of the following is NOT mentioned as one of the reasons for the Cuban Missile Crisis?

3. **Organization.** In this type of question, you will be asked to recognize how a reading passage is organized. Organization questions may ask you to identify how a passage uses transitions and key phrases or how ideas within a passage relate to each other.

   Examples
   - Which of the following best describes the organization of the passage?
   - This passage is most likely taken from a . . . (newspaper column, textbook, etc.)?
   - The phrase *the contrast in meaning and tone* refers to the contrast between . . . ?
   - Why is the word *indescribably* used in sentence 4?

4. **Vocabulary.** This question type asks you to determine the meaning of a word as it is used in the passage.

   Examples
   - Which of the following words, if substituted for the word *indelible* in the passage, would introduce the least change in the meaning of the sentence?
   - The word *protest* in the passage could best be replaced by . . . ?
   - Which of the following is the best meaning of the word *experience* as it is used in the passage?

▶ Critical and Inferential Comprehension

Whereas literal comprehension questions are straightforward, critical and inferential comprehension questions ask you to read between the lines of a text. These questions are about what is *implied* in the passage or statement. They ask you to identify the author's assumptions and attitudes and evaluate the weaknesses and strengths of the author's argument or logic. Critical and inferential comprehension questions include three types:

1. **Evaluation.** This question type asks you to evaluate the strengths and weaknesses of the argument presented in a passage. Evaluation questions will ask you to judge whether something is fact or opinion, or whether the evidence presented supports the message of the passage.

Examples

- In order to evaluate the validity of the author's claim regarding Jackson Pollock, it would be most helpful to know which of the following?
- Which of the following is NOT mentioned in the passage as a weakness in the new law?
- Which of the following numbered sentences of the passage expresses a fact rather than an opinion?

2. **Inference.** This type of question asks you to make an inference (draw a logical conclusion) based on the content of the passage. Inference questions will ask you to determine an author's underlying assumptions or attitude toward the subject of the passage.

Examples

- Which of the following is an unstated assumption made by the author of the passage?
- It can be inferred from the passage that the art of Picasso and Matisse differ in all of the following ways EXCEPT . . .
- This passage suggests that Greek tragedies are still so powerful because . . .
- The author would be least likely to agree with which of the following statements?

3. **Generalization.** This question type requires you to apply the ideas of a passage to new situations, recognize similar situations, and draw conclusions about the content of the passage.

Examples

- Which of the following conclusions can you make based on the passage?
- Given the information in the passage, what appeared to be an important post–World War II trend in the United States?

Now that you are have a better idea of what to expect on the PPST Reading test, you can begin to review some reading comprehension skills and test-taking strategies. By honing these skills, you will be better equipped to understand reading passages and to do your best on the exam.

▶ Reading Skill Builders

Reading may seem like a passive activity—after all, you are sitting, looking at words on a page. However, to improve your reading comprehension you need to read *actively*, meaning that you need to interact with the text. Incorporate these active-reading techniques into your study plan for the PPST Reading test. Each time you read a magazine, newspaper, or book, sharpen your reading comprehension skills using these strategies:

- **Skim ahead.** Scan the text *before* you read. Look at how the text is organized: How is it broken into sections? In what order are the topics presented? Note key words and ideas that are highlighted in boldface type or in bulleted lists.

- **Jump back.** Review the text after you read. By looking at summaries, headings, and highlighted information, you increase your ability to remember information and make connections between ideas.

- **Look up new words.** Keep a dictionary on hand as you read. Look up unfamiliar words and list them with their definitions in a notebook or make flash cards. To help you remember new words, connect them to something in your life or reading. Make a point to use new words in your writing and conversation. By increasing your vocabulary, you build your reading comprehension.

- **Highlight key ideas.** As you read, highlight or underline key terms, main ideas, or concepts that are new to you. Be selective—if you highlight too much of the text, nothing will stand out for you on the page. (If you don't own the book, use a notebook to jot down information.)

- **Take notes.** Note taking can help you remember material, even if you never look at your notes again. That's because it's a muscle activity, and using your muscles can actually aid your memory. Record your questions, observations, and opinions as you read. Write down the main idea of the passage, the author's point of view, and whether you agree with the author.

- **Make connections.** When you connect two ideas, you improve your chances of remembering the material. For example, if you are reading about a current presidential race, you may note how it is similar to or different from past elections. How have circumstances changed? You may also connect the topic to your own experience: How did you feel about the past election versus the current race?

▶ Locate the Main Idea

When standardized reading tests ask you to find the main idea of a passage, they are asking you to determine an overall feeling or thought that a writer wants to convey about her subject. To find the main idea, think about a **general statement** that brings together all of the ideas in a paragraph or passage. Look out for statements that are too specific—a main idea must be broad enough to contain all of the concepts presented in a passage. Test takers often confuse the main idea of a passage with its main topic. The topic is the *subject*—what the passage is about. The main idea is what the author wants to express *about* the subject.

Main Topic versus Main Idea

Topic/subject: what the passage is about
Main idea: what the author wants to say about a subject

Textbook writing and the passages on the PPST Reading test often follow a basic pattern of **general idea →** **specific idea**. In other words, a writer states her main idea (makes a general claim about her subject) and then provides evidence for it through specific details and facts. Do you always find main ideas in the first sentence of the passage? The answer is no; although a first sentence may contain the main idea, an author may decide to build up to her main point. In that case, you may find the main idea in the last sentence of an introductory paragraph, or even in the last paragraph of the passage.

Read the following paragraph and answer the practice question that follows.

Experts say that if you feel drowsy during the day, even during boring activities, you haven't had enough sleep. If you routinely fall asleep within five minutes of lying down, you probably have severe sleep deprivation, possibly even a sleep disorder. *Microsleep*, or very a brief episode of sleep in an otherwise awake person, is another mark of sleep deprivation. In many cases, people are not aware that they are experiencing microsleeps. The widespread practice of "burning the candle at both ends" in western industrialized societies has created so much sleep deprivation that what is really abnormal sleepiness is now almost the norm.

Source: National Institute of Neurological Disorders and Stroke, National Institutes of Health, www.ninds.nih.gov

What is the main point of this passage?
a. If you fall asleep within five minutes every time you lie down, you are sleep deprived.
b. If you experience enough microsleeps, you can attain the sleep you need to function.
c. Sleep deprivation is a pervasive problem in the United States and other western nations.
d. If trends in sleep deprivation continue, our society will experience grave consequences.
e. Sleep deprivation is responsible for approximately 100,000 car accidents each year.

Choice **a** is a true statement, but too specific to be a main idea. Choice **b** is a false statement. Choice **d** is a speculative statement that is not implied in the passage, and choice **e** is a detail or fact that is not supported by the information in the paragraph. Only choice **c** represents a general or umbrella statement that covers all of the information in the paragraph. Notice that in the sample passage, the author does not present the main idea in the first sentence, but rather builds up to the main point, which is expressed in the last sentence of the paragraph.

▶ Find Essential Facts

Some of the literal comprehension questions on the PPST Reading test will ask you identify a paraphrase or rewording of supporting details. How can you distinguish a main idea from a supporting idea? Unlike main ideas, supporting ideas present facts or **specific information**. They often answer the questions *what? when? why?* or *how?*

How can you locate a supporting detail in a passage that is 200 words long? One thing you don't have to do is memorize the passage. This test does not require that you have perfect recall. Instead, it measures your ability to read carefully and know where to look for specific information. Here are some tips for finding supporting details.

- **Look for language clues.** Writers often use transitional words or phrases to signal that they are introducing a fact or supporting idea. As you read, keep your eye out for these common phrases:

for example	for instance	in particular
in addition	furthermore	some
other	specifically	such as

- **Focus on key words from the question.** Questions often contain two or three important words that signal what information to look for in the passage. For example, a question following a passage about the American car industry reads, "The passage states that hybrid automobiles work best if. . . ." The key words are *hybrid automobiles* and *best*. They tell you to look for a sentence that contains the phrase *hybrid automobiles* and describes an optimal situation. Instead of rereading the passage, *skim* through the paragraphs looking for the key word. Keep in mind that the passage may use a slightly different wording than the key word. As you scan, look for words that address the same idea.

- **Pay attention to the structure of the passage.** Take note of how the passage is organized as you read. Does the author begin with or build to his main point? Is information presented chronologically? Where does the author offer evidence to back up his main point? Understanding how a passage is structured can help you locate the information you need. Read on for more about common organizational models.

Read the following paragraph, focusing on its main idea and the details that support the main idea. Then, answer the practice questions that follow.

(1) The history of microbiology begins with a Dutch haberdasher named Antoni van Leeuwenhoek, a man of no formal scientific education. (2) In the late 1600s, Leeuwenhoek, inspired by the magnifying lenses used by drapers to examine cloth, assembled some of the first microscopes. (3) He developed a technique for grinding and polishing tiny, convex lenses, some of which could magnify an object up to 270 times. (4) After scraping some plaque from between his teeth and examining it under a lens, Leeuwenhoek found tiny squirming creatures, which he called "animalcules." (5) His observations, which he reported to the Royal Society of London, are among the first descriptions of living bacteria.

1. What inspired Leeuwenhoek's invention of the microscope?

    a. his training in science

    b. the great microbiologists of his era

    c. the lenses used by the practitioners of his profession

    d. the desire to observe bacteria

    e. the common practice of teeth scraping

2. In which sentence does the author give Leeuwenhoek's description of living bacteria?

    a. sentence 1

    b. sentence 2

    c. sentence 3

    d. sentence 4

    e. sentence 5

Answers

1. **c.** The first paragraph provides the supporting detail to answer this question. Leeuwenhoek, a haberdasher, was *inspired by the magnifying lenses used by drapers to examine cloth.* One of the key words from the question—*inspired*—leads you to the location of the detail in the passage. Choice **a** is refuted by a detail presented in the line: *a man of no formal scientific education.* Choice **b** is untrue, because the first sentence of the passage states that *the history of microbiology begins with* Leeuwenhoek. Choice **d** is also incorrect, because Leeuwenhoek did not know *what* he would discover under his microscope, and choice **e** is a silly choice used as a distracter.

2. **d.** You can find Leeuwenhoek's description of bacteria in sentence 4: *tiny squirming creatures, which he called "animalcules."* You may have been tricked into selecting choice **e**, because of its repetition of the phrase *descriptions of living bacteria*, from sentence 5. Be sure to always refer back to the passage when answering a question—do not rely on your memory. Choice **e** is incorrect, because it does not refer to Leeuwenhoek's own description, but rather the significance of his observation. This question highlights the importance of taking note of where crucial details are located in a passage. Again, do not try to memorize or learn facts or details, but have an idea about where to find them.

▶ All about Organization

Organization questions on the PPST Reading test ask you to identify how a passage is structured. You need to be able to recognize organizational patterns, common transitional phrases, and how ideas relate within a passage. Understanding the structure of a passage can also help you locate concepts and information, such as the main idea or supporting details.

To organize their ideas effectively, writers rely on one of several basic organizational patterns. The four most common strategies are:

1. chronological order
2. order of importance
3. comparison and contrast
4. cause and effect

Chronological order arranges events by the order in which they happened, from beginning to end. Textbooks, instructions and procedures, essays about personal experiences, and magazine feature articles may use this organizing principle. Passages organized by chronology offer language cues—in the form of transitional words or phrases—to signal the passage of time and link one idea or event to the next. Here are some of the most common chronological transitions:

first, second, third, etc.	before	after	next	now
then	when	as soon as	immediately	suddenly
soon	during	while	meanwhile	later
in the meantime	at last	eventually	finally	afterward

Order of importance organizes ideas by rank instead of by time. Instead of describing what happened next, this pattern presents what is most, or least, important. The structure can work two ways: Writers can organize their ideas either by increasing importance (least important idea → most important idea) or by decreasing importance (most important idea → least important idea).

Newspaper articles follow the principle of decreasing importance; they cover the most important information in the first sentence or paragraph (the *who, what, when, where,* and *why* about an event). As a result, readers can get the facts of an event without reading the entire article. Writing that is trying to persuade its readers or make an argument often uses the pattern of increasing importance. By using this structure, a writer creates a snowball effect, building and building upon her idea. "Saving the best for last" can create suspense for the reader and leave a lasting impression of the writer's main point.

Just as a chronological arrangement uses transitions, so does the order of importance principle. Keep your eye out for the following common transitional words and phrases:

first and foremost	most important	more important	moreover
above all	first, second, third	last but not least	finally

Comparison and contrast arranges two things or ideas side by side to show the ways in which they are similar or different. This organizational model allows a writer to analyze two things and ideas and determine how they measure up to one another. For example, this description of the artists Pablo Picasso and Henri Matisse uses comparison and contrast:

> The grand old lions of modernist innovation, Picasso and Matisse, originated many of the most significant developments of twentieth-century art (comparison). However, although they worked in the same tradition, they each had a different relationship to painting (contrast). For example, Picasso explored signs and symbols in his paintings, whereas Matisse insisted that the things represented in his paintings were merely things: The oranges on the table of a still life were simply oranges on the table (contrast).

Writers use two basic methods to compare and contrast ideas. In the **point-by-point** method, each aspect of idea A is followed by a comparable aspect of idea B, so that a paragraph resembles this pattern: ABABABAB. In the **block** method, a writer presents several aspects of idea A, followed by several aspects of idea B. The pattern of the block method looks like this: AAAABBBB.

Again, transitions can signal whether a writer is using the organizing principle of comparison and contrast. Watch for these common transitions:

Transitions Showing Similarity

similarly	in the same way	likewise
like	in a like manner	just as
and	also	both

Transitions Showing Difference

but	on the other hand	yet
however	on the contrary	in contrast
conversely	whereas	unlike

Cause and effect arranges ideas to explain why an event took place (cause) and what happened as a result (effect). Sometimes one cause has several effects, or an effect may have several causes. For example, a historian writing about World War I might investigate several causes of the war (assassination of the heir to the Austro-Hungarian throne, European conflicts over territory and economic power), and describe the various effects of the war (ten million soldiers killed, weakened European powers, enormous financial debt).

Key words offer clues that a writer is describing cause and effect. Pay attention to these words as you read:

Words Indicating Cause

because	created by
since	caused by

Words Indicating Effect

therefore	so
hence	consequently
as a result	

A writer might also describe a **contributing** cause, which is a factor that *helps* to make something happen but can't make that thing happen by itself. On the opposite end of the spectrum is a **sufficient** cause, which is an event that, by itself, is strong enough to make the event happen. Often an author will offer her opinion about the cause or effect of an event. In that case, readers must judge the validity of the author's analysis. Are the author's ideas logical? Does she support the conclusions that she comes to?

Read the following excerpt and answer the practice question.

When Rosa Parks refused to give up her seat to a white person in Montgomery, Alabama, and was arrested in December 1955, she set off a train of events that generated a momentum the Civil Rights movement had never before experienced. Local civil rights leaders were hoping for such an opportunity to test the city's segregation laws. Deciding to boycott the buses, the African-American community soon formed a new organization to supervise the boycott, the Montgomery Improvement Association (MIA). The young pastor of the Dexter Avenue Baptist Church, Reverend Martin Luther King, Jr., was chosen as the first MIA leader. The boycott, more successful than anyone hoped, led to a 1956 Supreme Court decision banning segregated buses.

Source: Excerpt from the Library of Congress, "The African American Odyssey: A Quest for Full Citizenship."

The author implies that the action and arrest of Rosa Parks directly resulted in
   a. the 1956 Supreme Court decision banning segregated buses.
   b. Martin Luther King, Jr.'s ascendancy as a civil rights leader.
   c. the formation of the Civil Rights movement in Montgomery, Alabama.
   d. the bus boycott in Montgomery, Alabama.
   e. the birth of a nationwide struggle for civil rights.

The correct answer is choice **d**. According to the passage, Rosa Parks's action directly inspired local civil rights leaders to institute the Montgomery bus boycott. Although Rosa Parks's action may have been a *contributing* factor to King's emergence as a civil rights leader (choice **b**) and the Supreme Court's later decision to ban segregated buses (choice **a**), it was not the *direct* cause of these events, according to the passage. Choice **c** is incorrect because the passage makes clear that a local Civil Rights movement already existed and was not the result of Rosa Parks's refusal to give up her bus seat. Likewise, choice **e** is incorrect. Rosa Parks may have furthered the national Civil Rights movement, but she was not its direct cause.

▶ Strategies for Vocabulary Questions

If you encounter an unfamiliar word when you are reading, you may likely grab a dictionary and look it up. During the PPST Reading test, you can't use a dictionary to check the meaning of new words. However, you can use a number of strategies to figure out what a word means.

Vocabulary questions measure your word power, but they also evaluate an essential reading comprehension skill, which is your ability to determine the meaning of a word from its **context**. The sentences that surround the word offer important clues about its meaning. For example, see if you can figure out the meaning of the word *incessant* from this context:

The incessant demands of the job are too much for me. The responsibilities are endless!

The word *incessant* most nearly means
   a. inaccessible.
   b. difficult.
   c. unceasing.
   d. compatible.
   e. manageable.

The best answer is **c**. The second sentence, *The responsibilities are endless*, restates the phrase in the first sentence, *incessant demands*. This restatement, or elaboration, suggests the meaning of *incessant*: continuing or following without interruption.

If the context of an unfamiliar word does not restate its meaning, try these two steps to figure out what the word means:

1. **Is the word positive or negative?** Using the context of the passage, determine whether the unfamiliar word is a positive or negative term. If a word is used in a positive context, you can eliminate the answer choices that are negative. In the preceding example, you can guess that the word *incessant* is used negatively. The phrase, *too much for me*, suggests that the demands of the job are overwhelming and negative. Thus, you can eliminate the answer choices **d** and **e** because they represent positive terms.
2. **Replace the vocabulary word** with the remaining answer choices, one at a time. Does the answer choice make sense when you read the sentence? If not, eliminate the answer choice. In the previous example, choice **a**, *inaccessible*, simply does not make sense in the sentence. Choice **b**, *difficult*, is too general to be a likely synonym. Only choice **c**, *unceasing*, makes sense in the context.

▶ Fact versus Opinion

Just because something is in print does not mean that it is fact. Most writing contains some *bias*—the personal judgment of a writer. Sometimes a writer's beliefs unknowingly affect how he or she writes about a topic. In other cases, a writer deliberately attempts to shape the reader's reaction and position. For example, a writer may present only one perspective about a subject or include only facts that support his or her point of view. Critical and inferential questions on the PPST Reading test—specifically evaluation questions—will ask you to judge the strengths or weaknesses of an author's argument. You will be required to distinguish between fact and opinion, and decide whether the supporting details or evidence effectively backs up the author's main point.

To separate fact from opinion, consider these differences:

- A **fact** is a statement that can be verified by a reliable source.
- An **opinion** is a statement about the beliefs or feelings of a person or group.

When determining whether a statement is factual, consider whether a source gives researched, accurate information. The following is an example of a factual statement—it can be supported by the recent national census:

The U.S. population is growing older—in fact, adults over age 85 are the fastest-growing segment of today's population.

Opinions, on the other hand, reflect judgments that may or may not be true. Opinions include speculation or predictions of the future that cannot be proven at the present time. The following statement represents an opinion—it offers a belief about the future. Others may disagree with the prediction:

Many believe that the population boom among elderly Americans will create a future healthcare crisis.

Language clues can alert you to a statement that reflects an opinion. Look for these common words that introduce opinions:

likely	should/could	say
possibly	think	charge
probably	believe	attest

Exhibit A—Evidence

Most writing presents *reasonable opinions*, based on fact: A writer asserts her opinion and supports it with facts or other evidence. A writer can use different types of evidence to build an argument—some forms of proof are more reliable than other types. When you read, look for the forms of evidence listed here and consider how accurate each might be:

observations   experiments
interviews   personal experience
surveys and questionnaires   expert opinions

► Reading between the Lines

Inference questions on the PPST Reading test will ask you to make an inference, or draw a logical conclusion, about what you read. Sometimes a writer does not explicitly state his main idea or offer a conclusion. The reader must infer the writer's meaning. To determine a writer's underlying assumptions or attitude, you need to look for clues in the context of the passage. One revealing clue to the writer's meaning is his word choice.

Word choice, also called **diction,** is the specific language the writer uses to describe people, places, and things. Word choice includes these forms:

- particular words or phrases a writer uses
- the way words are arranged in a sentence
- repetition of words or phrases
- inclusion of particular details

Consider how word choice affects the following sentences:

a. Lesson preparation benefits a teacher's performance in the classroom.
b. Lesson preparation improves a teacher's performance in the classroom.

The only difference between the two sentences is that sentence **a** uses *benefits*, and sentence **b** uses *improves*. Both sentences state that lesson preparation has a positive influence on a teacher's performance in the classroom. However, sentence **a** is stronger because of word choice: *to benefit* means to be useful or advantageous, whereas *to improve* means to enhance in value. The writer of sentence **b** believes that preparation is not only useful, it actually increases a teacher's effectiveness. The writer doesn't have to spell this out for you, because his word choice makes his position clear.

▶ Denotation and Connotation

Even words with similar dictionary definitions (**denotations**) can have different suggested meanings (**connotations**). Consider the different implied meanings of the following word pairs:

- slim/thin
- perilous/dangerous
- rich/wealthy

Although they are nearly synonyms, these word pairs suggest varying degrees and have subtle differences in their effect. The word *slim* suggests fitness and grace. *Thin* is more neutral, or possibly negative, implying someone may be too skinny to be healthy. *Perilous* suggests a greater threat of harm than the term *dangerous*: It has a more ominous connotation and implies a more life-threatening situation. The subtle difference between *rich* and *wealthy* is, again, one of degree: *rich* implies having more than enough to fulfill normal needs; *wealthy* suggests an established and elevated societal class.

▶ Euphemism and Dysphemism

Writers also reveal their attitude toward a subject through the use of euphemism or dysphemism. Here is a quick definition of the terms:

- **euphemism**—a neutral or positive expression used in place of a negative one
- **dysphemism**—a negative expression substituted for a neutral or positive one

A euphemism is the substitution of an agreeable description of something that might be unpleasant. In contrast, a dysphemism is an offensive, disagreeable, or disparaging expression that describes something neutral or agreeable.

For example, a student who fails a test might use a euphemistic statement when reporting the grade to her parents:

"I didn't do very well on the test."

The student might feel more comfortable using a dysphemism when talking to her classmates:

"I bombed on that test. I tanked!"

Another example might be the sentence "I've been fired." A euphemism for this statement is "I've been let go," whereas a dysphemism for the statement is "I've been axed."

▶ Style

Just as word choice can alert you to a writer's underlying message, so can other aspects of a writer's style. **Style** is the distinctive way in which a writer uses language to inform or promote an idea. In addition to word choice, a writer's style consists of three basic components:

1. sentence structure
2. degree of detail or description
3. degree of formality

When you read a magazine, newspaper, or book, consider how the writer uses sentences. Does the writer use short, simple sentences or long, complex sentences, packed with clauses and phrases? Writers use different **sentence structures** to create different effects: They may make short declarative statements in order to persuade readers or long descriptions to create a flow that pleases the reader's ear.

Degree of detail refers to how specific an author is in describing something. For example, a writer may use a general term (dog, beach, government) or specific terms (German shepherd, Crane's Beach, British Parliament). In evaluating the strength of a writer's argument, consider whether terms are too general to provide adequate evidence.

Degree of formality refers to how formal or casual the writer's language is. Technical jargon or terminology is an example of formal language. Colloquial phrases and slang are examples of casual language. Writers create distance and a sense of objectivity when they use formal language, whereas slang expresses familiarity. The degree of formality a writer uses should be appropriate to his purpose and message. For example, a business missive that uses slang is likely to put off its audience, whereas a novel aimed at teenage readers may use slang to appeal to its audience.

► Emotional Language

When writers want to persuade a reader of something, they may rely on emotional language. **Emotional language** targets a reader's emotions—fears, beliefs, values, prejudices—instead of appealing to a reader's reason or critical thinking. Just as advertising often uses emotional language to sell a product, writers use emotional appeals to sell an idea. Here are five techniques to look out for as you read:

1. **Bandwagon.** The basic message of a bandwagon appeal is that "everyone else is doing something, so you should, too." It appeals to the reader's desire to join the crowd or be on the winning team. Examples from advertising include: "Americans buy more of our brand than any other brand," or "the toothpaste picky parents choose."
2. **Common man.** In this approach, writers try to convince a reader that their message is just plain old common sense. Colloquial language or phrases and common jokes are examples of this technique.
3. **Generalities.** In this approach, writers use words or phrases that evoke deep emotions and carry strong associations for most people. By doing so, a writer can appeal to readers' emotions so that they will accept his message without evaluating it. Generalities are vague so that readers supply their own interpretations and do not ask further questions. Examples of generalities are *honor*, *peace*, *freedom*, or *home*.
4. **Labeling or name calling.** This method links a negative label, name, or phrase to a person, group, or belief. Name calling can be a direct attack that appeals to hates or fears, or it can be indirect, appealing to a sense of ridicule. Labels can evoke deep emotions, such as *Communist* or *terrorist*. Others can be negatively charged, depending on the situation: *yuppie, slacker, reactionary.*
5. **Testimonial.** In advertising, athletes promote a range of products, from cereal to wristwatches. Likewise, a writer may use a public figure, expert, or other respected person to endorse an idea or support the writer's argument. Because readers may respect or admire the person, they may be less critical and more willing to accept an idea.

Tone Makes Meaning

You can detect a writer's tone—his mood or attitude as conveyed through language—from a writer's choices about point of view, language use, and style. PPST questions will sometimes ask you to evaluate and summarize a writer's tone. When you read material in preparation for the exam, always think about the tone of each passage. Here are some common words that describe tone:

cheerful	apologetic	sarcastic
complimentary	critical	playful
hopeful	humorous	authoritative
gloomy	ironic	indifferent

▶ Point of View

One strategy that writers use to convey their meaning to readers is through **point of view**. Point of view is the person or perspective through which the writer channels her information and ideas. It determines *who* is speaking to the reader. Depending on the writer's intentions, she may present a **subjective** point of view (a perspective based on her own thoughts, feelings, and experiences), or an **objective** one (one that discounts the writer's personal feelings and attempts to offer an unbiased view). Understanding the point of view of a passage will help you answer questions that ask you to identify an author's assumptions or attitude. Here are three approaches to point of view:

First-person point of view expresses the writer's personal feelings and experiences directly to the reader using these pronouns: *I, me, mine; we, our, us.* The first person creates a sense of intimacy between the reader and writer because it expresses a *subjective* point of view.

This excerpt from Walt Whitman's *Leaves of Grass* provides an example of first-person perspective:

> As I ponder'd in silence,
> Returning upon my poems, considering, lingering long,
> A Phantom arose before me with distrustful aspect,
> Terrible in beauty, age, and power,
> The genius of poets of old lands,
> As to me directing like flame its eyes,
> With finger pointing to many immortal songs,
> And menacing voice, What singest thou? it said,
> Know'st thou not there is but one theme for ever-enduring bards?

Second-person point of view is another personal perspective in which the writer speaks directly to the reader, addressing the reader as *you.* Writers use the second person to give directions or to make the reader feel directly involved with the argument or action of their message. The following excerpt from Mark Twain's *The Adventures of Huckleberry Finn* uses the second person:

> The widow rung a bell for supper, and you had to come to time. When you got to the table you couldn't go right to eating, but you had to wait for the widow to tuck down her head and grumble a little over the victuals, though there warn't really anything the matter with them—that is, nothing only everything was cooked by itself.

Third-person point of view expresses an impersonal point of view by presenting the perspective of an outsider (a "third person") who is not directly involved with the action. Writers use the third person to establish distance from the reader and present a seemingly *objective* point of view. The third person uses these pronouns: *he, him, his; she, her, hers; it, its;* and *they, them, theirs.* Most PPST passages are written in the third person. The following is an example of the third-person perspective:

The Sami are an indigenous people living in the northern parts of Norway, Sweden, Finland, and Russia's Kola peninsula. Originally, the Sami religion was animistic; that is, for them, nature and natural objects had a conscious life, a spirit.

▶ Practice

Read the following passage and answer the practice question. Consider the writer's choice of words, style, and point of view and how it affects the message presented in the text.

Jane Austen died in 1817, leaving behind six novels that have since become English classics. Most Austen biographers accept the image of Jane Austen as a sheltered spinster who knew little of life beyond the drawing rooms of her Hampshire village. They accept the claim of Austen's brother, Henry: "My dear sister's life was not a life of events."

Biographer Claire Tomalin takes this view to task. She shows that Jane's short life was indeed tumultuous. Not only did Austen experience romantic love (briefly, with an Irishman), but her many visits to London and her relationships with her brothers (who served in the Napoleonic wars) widened her knowledge beyond her rural county, and even beyond England. Tomalin also argues that Austen's unmarried status benefited her ability to focus on her writing. I believe that Jane herself may have viewed it that way. Although her family destroyed most of her letters, one relative recalled that "some of her [Jane's] letters, triumphing over married women of her acquaintance, and rejoicing in her freedom, were most amusing."

1. In order to evaluate the validity of the author's claim that Austen's marital status helped her writing, it would be helpful to know which of the following?
   a. why the author mentions the biographer Claire Tomalin
   b. how single women were regarded in Austen's time period
   c. whether marriage would actually prevent a woman from writing during Austen's era
   d. how reliable is the source of the quotation at the end of the passage
   e. more details about Austen's tumultuous life

2. What best describes the tone of the passage?
   a. somber
   b. critical
   c. apathetic
   d. appreciative
   e. amusing

Answers

1. **d.** This evaluation question asks you to consider the evidence used to support the author's claim that Jane Austen viewed her unmarried status as a benefit to her writing. Because the author employs a quotation from one of Austen's relatives to back up her claim, it would be helpful to know more about the source. A greater degree of detail and description (which relative? can the relative be considered reliable?) would strengthen the author's argument.

2. **b.** To determine the tone of the passage, you need to look at the author's point of view, style, and word choice. Because the author's style and word choice are not formal, you can eliminate choice **a**, *somber*. Her style and word choice are not overly casual, either, so you can strike choice **e**, *playful*. The author uses the third-person point of view for most of the passage, signaling that the passage is attempting to be objective. Because the author uses the first-person point of view to make a claim, you can infer that the author is not *apathetic* (choice **c**) about her subject. Although the author may indeed be *appreciative* (choice **d**) about her subject, her word choice does not support this.

▶ Test-Taking Tips

Now that you have reviewed the components that will help you understand and analyze what you read, you are ready to consider some specific test-taking strategies. The following techniques will help you read the PPST passages quickly and effectively and answer the multiple-choice questions strategically so that you can boost your score.

Reading passages for a standardized test is different than reading at home. For one thing, you have a time limit. You have one hour to complete 40 questions (the computer-based test gives 75 minutes for 46 questions). This means that you have about 90 seconds to answer each question! And the time you spend reading each passage detracts from the time you have to answer questions. Here are some basic guidelines for keeping you moving through the test in a time-efficient way:

- **Spend no more than two minutes on a question.** Circle difficult questions and return to them if you have time.
- **Skim and answer short passages quickly.** Short passages have only one or two questions, so you should move through them with speed. Give yourself a bit more time for long passages that are followed by four or more questions.
- **Guess, if necessary.** The PPST Reading test does not penalize for wrong answers. Make sure to answer each question, even if you think you might return to it later.
- **Circle, underline, and make notes.** You can write in your test booklet, so be sure to mark up the passage as you read. Scribble down quick notes that will help you answer the questions.
- **Target the first part of the passage.** The first third of many reading passages is packed with essential information. Often you can answer main-idea questions based on the information at the start of a passage. Likewise, for longer passages of 200 words, you will often find what each paragraph is about from its first two sentences.

■ **Locate details, but don't learn them.** Detail-heavy portions of passages can be dense and difficult to read. Don't spend precious time rereading and absorbing details—just make sure you know where to find them in the passage. That way you can locate a detail if a question asks about it.

▶ Eliminating Wrong Answers

Test makers use "distracters" in test questions that can confuse you into choosing an incorrect answer. Familiarizing yourself with some of the common distraction techniques that test makers use will increase your chances of eliminating wrong answers and selecting the right answer.

■ **The choice that does too little.** This distracter type often follows main idea questions. The answer choice makes a true statement, but it is too narrow, too specific to be a main idea of the passage. It zeros in on select elements or supporting ideas of a passage instead of expressing a main idea.

■ **The choice that does too much.** This distracter also relates to main idea questions. Unlike the type just discussed, this answer choice goes too far, or beyond the scope of the passage. It may be a true statement, but cannot be supported by what the author expresses in the text.

■ **The close, but not close enough, choice.** This type of answer is very close to the correct answer, but is wrong in some detail.

■ **The off-topic choice.** Test takers often find this answer choice the easiest to spot and eliminate. It may have nothing at all to do with the passage itself.

■ **The irrelevant choice.** This option uses language found in the text—elements, ideas, phrases, words— but does not answer the question correctly. These distracters are tricky because test designers bait them with a good deal of information from the passage.

■ **The contradictory choice.** This answer may in fact be opposite or nearly opposite to the correct answer. If two of the answer choices seem contrary to each other, there is a good chance that one of these choices will be correct.

■ **The choice that is too broad.** This distracter relates to supporting detail questions. Although it may be a true statement, it is too general and does not address the specifics the question is looking for.

▶ Look Out for Absolutes

Reading comprehension questions that use words that represent absolutes should alert you to the likely presence of clever distracters among the answer choices. Two or more answers may be close contenders—they may reflect language from the passage and be true in general principle, but not true in *all* circumstances. Beware of these commonly used absolutes in reading questions:

best	most closely	always	all
primarily	most nearly	never	none

Types of Readers

How you approach a reading passage may show what kind of reader you are. Each of the approaches listed here has some merit. When you practice reading passages as part of your PPST study plan, experiment with some of these different styles to see what works best for you.

- The **concentrator** reads the passage thoroughly before looking at the questions. By concentrating on the passage, you can locate answers quickly if you don't already know the answer.
- The **skimmer** skims the passage before looking at the questions. Once you understand how the passage is arranged, you can go back and find the answers.
- The **cautious reader** reads the questions and answer choices first. Because you know what questions to expect, you can be on the lookout as you read the passage.
- The **game player** reads the questions first and answers them by guessing. By guessing the answers, you become familiar with the questions and can recognize the answers when you read the passage.
- The **educated guesser** reads the questions first, but not the answers. When you find the answer in the passage, you can quickly look among the answer choices for the right one.
- The **efficiency expert** reads the questions first, looking for key words that indicate where an answer is located. By doing this, you can skim the passage for answers instead of reading the whole passage.

▶ Five-Step Approach to Answering Reading Questions

If you feel daunted by the task of quickly reading and understanding dense passages, here is a quick approach that you can use. Feel free to adapt it to your style or change the order of the steps, but try to incorporate each of the five steps somewhere in your process.

Step 1—Preview
To get an idea of the content and organization of a passage, begin by skimming it. With practice, you will quickly discern topic sentences and key adjectives. Often, the first two sentences in a paragraph are topic sentences—they will tell you what a paragraph is about. If the passage is several paragraphs long, read the first and last sentence of each paragraph. You can't depend 100% on this technique, though; use your judgment to determine if a sentence is truly a topic sentence.

Step 2—Skim the Questions

Quickly take in the question or questions that follow a passage, marking important words and phrases. Don't bother reading the multiple-choice answers. You simply want to gather clues about what to look for when you read.

Step 3—Read Actively

Although you do not want to memorize or analyze the passage, you do need to read it. Keep your pencil handy to mark the passage as you read, looking for information that applies to the questions you skimmed. Circle or underline topic sentences, main ideas, or phrases that reveal the author's point of view. Check important names, dates, or difficult words. Mark transitions and phrases, such as *however*, *on the other hand*, *most importantly*, *but*, or *except* that help you to follow the author's direction or the organization of the passage.

As you read, ask yourself some of the following questions:

- What is the main theme or idea in the passage?
- What is the author's purpose or goal?
- How do ideas in the passage relate to the main idea?
- What is the tone or mood of the passage? Informative? Critical? Playful?
- How is the passage structured?

Step 4—Review the Passage

After actively reading the passage, take a few seconds to look over the main idea, the topic sentences, or other elements you have marked. Ask yourself what you have just read. Your goal is not to understand the passage thoroughly, but rather to get the gist of it. Quickly summarize it in your own words.

Don't get hung up on difficult phrasing or technical elements in the passage that you might not even need to know. Instead of focusing on absorbing specific details, just know the location of details in the passage. Remember, you can refer back to the passage several times while answering the questions. Focus on the general direction, main ideas, organization, purpose, and point of view of the passage, rather than learning details.

Step 5—Answer the Questions

Now it's time to answer the questions. Base your answers only on what is stated and implied in the passage. Some answer choices will try to trick you with information that is beyond the scope of the passage. Read *all* five multiple-choice answers before rushing to choose one. Eliminate and mark off as many choices as possible. If you eliminate three of the answer choices, reach your decision quickly between the remaining two. After you have timed yourself working with the practice tests in this book, you will have a good idea of your time limitations.

▶ Using the Five-Step Approach

This practice applies the five-step approach to a sample passage. You may want to review the five-step approach before you begin.

Sample Passage

Read the following passage to answer questions 1 and 2.

In his famous study of myth, *The Hero with a Thousand Faces*, Joseph Campbell writes about the archetypal hero who has ventured outside the boundaries of the village and, after many trials and adventures, has returned with the boon that will save or enlighten his fellows. Like Carl Jung, Campbell believes that the story of the hero is part of the collective unconscious of all humankind. He likens the returning hero to the sacred or tabooed personage described by James Frazier in *The Golden Bough*. Such an individual must, in many instances of myth, be insulated from the rest of society, "not merely for his own sake but for the sake of others; for since the virtue of holiness is, so to say, a powerful explosive which the smallest touch can detonate, it is necessary in the interest of the general safety to keep it within narrow bounds."

There is much similarity between the archetypal hero who has journeyed into the wilderness and the poet who has journeyed into the realm of imagination. Both places are dangerous and full of wonders, and both, at their deepest levels, are journeys that take place into the kingdom of the unconscious mind, a place that, in Campbell's words, "goes down into unsuspected Aladdin caves. There not only jewels but dangerous jinn abide. . . ."

1. Based on the passage, which of the following best describes the story that will likely be told by Campbell's returning hero and Frazier's sacred or tabooed personage?
   a. a radically mind-altering story
   b. a story that will terrify people to no good end
   c. a warning of catastrophe to come
   d. a story based on a dangerous lie
   e. a parable aimed at establishing a religious movement

2. Which of the following is the most accurate definition of the word *boon* as it is used in the passage?
   a. present
   b. blessing
   c. charm
   d. prize
   e. curse

You can answer these questions by following the five-step approach explained in the previous lesson.

Preview

Read the first sentence of each paragraph: "In his famous study of myth . . ." and "There is much similarity. . . ."
Because of the length of the sentences in each passage, you may or may not wish to read the ending sentences in
each paragraph. Underline the topic sentences.

Skim the Questions

Now, skim the questions and mark them.

- Based on the passage, which of the following best describes the story that will likely be told by Campbell's
  returning hero and Frazier's sacred or tabooed personage? An important word in this question is *story*.
  Also note the use of the absolute, *best*. This means that more than one answer choice may be true, but
  only one is the best answer. Circle or mark these terms. You may also notice that this is an inference question; it asks you to infer something based on the information of the passage.
- Which of the following is the most accurate definition of the word *boon* as it is used in the passage? This
  is a vocabulary question that measures your literal comprehension. The most important elements in this
  question are *definition* and *boon*. Mark these words. Again, note that the question asks for the *most accurate* definition—more than one answer choice may apply, but only one offers the best answer.

Read Actively

Now, read actively, marking the passage. The following marked passage is an example of which things you
might choose to circle or underline in the passage:

In his famous study of myth, *The Hero with a Thousand Faces*, Joseph Campbell writes about the
archetypal hero who has ventured outside the boundaries of the village and, after many **trials** and
adventures, has returned with the **boon** that will **save** or **enlighten** his fellows. Like Carl Jung,
Campbell believes that the story of the hero is part of the collective unconscious of all humankind.
He likens the returning **hero** to the **sacred or tabooed personage** described by James Frazier in *The
Golden Bough*. (**comparison here**) Such an individual must, in many instances of myth, be insulated
from the rest of society, "not merely for his own sake but for the sake of others; for since the virtue of
holiness is, so to say, a powerful explosive which the smallest touch can detonate, it is necessary in
the interest of the general safety to keep it within narrow bounds."

There is much similarity between the archetypal hero who has journeyed into the wilderness
and the poet who has journeyed into the realm of imagination. (**comparison here**) Both places are
dangerous and **full of wonders**, and both, at their deepest levels, are journeys that take place into the
kingdom of the **unconscious mind**, a place that, in Campbell's words, "goes down into unsuspected
Aladdin caves. There not only jewels but dangerous jinn abide. . . ."

Like many reading comprehension passages, the sample text features topic sentences that begin each paragraph. Then, the paragraphs become detail-heavy. Although you may have marked different terms in the sample

passage, you should underscore the word *boon* in the first sentence, because it applies to the second question. The information you need to infer the answer to the first question (the story that is likely told by Campbell's hero and Frazier's sacred or tabooed personage) is also contained in the first paragraph. The quotation at the end of the first paragraph is dense and somewhat difficult to read and understand. Don't bother rereading difficult parts of a passage—in this case, you can answer the questions without completely comprehending the quotation.

Your system of marking this passage may vary. You may underline topic sentences, circle words that cue important details, or put a star beside words that indicate the author's attitude or purpose. The important thing is to mark the passage in a way that will help you answer the questions.

Depending on the answers you are seeking, you may jot down notes or make observations as you read:

- Regarding the main idea, it seems that the author is proposing that the act of creating is similar to the journey undertaken by Campbell's mythic hero—both make a kind of passage and return with a vital message for others. (This would apply to a question that asks you to summarize the main idea.)
- The passage uses comparison to describe Campbell's study of myth: it compares Jung and Campbell, Campbell and Frazier, and the hero and the poet. (This would apply to a question about organization of the passage.)
- The author cites quotes by Campbell to support the main idea. (This would apply to an evaluation question in which you are asked to look at the strengths and weaknesses of the author's argument.)
- The tone of the passage is measured and analytical. (This would apply to a question about the author's attitude or point of view.)

Review the Passage

Take a few seconds to summarize in your own words what the passage is about. Look again at how you have marked the passage.

The passage is about Joseph Campbell's mythic hero and how his journey and return home relate to the experience of a poet.

Answer the Questions

Look again at question 1:

1. Based on the passage, which of the following best describes the story that will likely be told by Campbell's returning hero and Frazier's sacred or tabooed personage?
   a. a radically mind-altering story
   b. a story that will terrify people to no good end
   c. a warning of catastrophe to come
   d. a story based on a dangerous lie
   e. a parable aimed at establishing a religious movement

The passage states that the hero's tale will *save* and *enlighten* his fellows, but that it will also be *dangerous*. Choice **a** is the best answer. You can infer from the information of the passage that such a story would surely be radically mind-altering. Choice **b** is directly contradicted in the passage. If the hero's tale would terrify people to no good end, it could not possibly be enlightening. There is nothing in the passage to imply that the tale is a warning of catastrophe, a dangerous lie, or a parable (choices **c**, **d**, and **e**).

Now, look again at question 2:

2. Which of the following is the most accurate definition of the word *boon* as it is used in the passage?
   a. present
   b. blessing
   c. charm
   d. prize
   e. curse

Even if you don't know the dictionary definition of the word *boon*, you can determine its meaning from the context of the passage. You can determine that *boon* is a positive term because the passage states that the hero's boon *will save or enlighten his fellows.* Therefore, you can eliminate choice **e**, *curse*, which is negative. You can also guess from the context of the passage that a boon is likely to be intangible, and not a concrete *present*, *charm*, or *prize* (choices **a**, **c**, and **d**). Choice **b** offers the most accurate definition of boon, which is a timely benefit, favor, or blessing.

Now, take the skills you have learned or honed in this review and apply them to the next practice test.

5▶ Mathematics Test Review

CHAPTER SUMMARY

This review covers the math skills you need to know for the PPST Mathematics test. First you will learn about the test, including question types, and then you will learn about arithmetic, measurement, algebra, geometry, and data analysis.

THE PPST MATHEMATICS TEST measures those mathematical skills and concepts that an educated adult might need. Many of the problems require the integration of multiple skills to achieve a solution. This test covers several types of questions, and several types of math. Before you start reviewing math concepts, you should familiarize yourself with the test.

Numbers and Operations
- **Order:** These questions require an understanding of order among integers, fractions, and decimals.
- **Equivalence:** These questions require an understanding that numbers can be represented in more than just one way.
- **Numeration and place value:** These questions require an understanding of how numbers are named, place value, and order of value.
- **Number properties:** These questions require an understanding of the properties of whole numbers.

- **Operation properties:** These questions require an understanding of the properties (commutative, associative, and distributive) of the basic operations (addition, subtraction, multiplication, and division).
- **Computation:** These questions require an ability to perform computations, change the result of a computation to fit the context of a problem, and recognize what is needed to solve a problem.
- **Estimation:** These questions require an ability to estimate and to determine the validity of an estimate.
- **Ratio, proportion, and percent:** These questions require an ability to solve problems dealing with ratio, proportion, and percent.
- **Numerical reasoning:** These questions require the ability to interpret statements that use logical connectives or quantifiers, use reasoning to determine whether an argument is valid or invalid, and identify a generalization or an assumption.

Algebra

- **Equations and inequalities:** These questions require an ability to solve simple equations and inequalities and to guess the result of changing aspects of a problem.
- **Algorithmic thinking:** These questions require an ability to understand an algorithmic view. In other words, you must follow procedure, understand different ways to solve a problem, identify or evaluate a procedure, and recognize patterns.
- **Patterns:** These questions require an ability to understand patterns in data, including variation.
- **Algebraic representations:** These questions require an ability to understand the relationship between verbal or symbolic expressions and graphical displays.
- **Algebraic reasoning:** These questions require the ability to interpret statements that use logical connectives or quantifiers, use reasoning to determine whether an argument is valid or invalid, and identify a generalization or an assumption.

Geometry and Measurement

- **Geometric properties:** These questions require an ability to use geometric properties and relationships in real-life applications.
- **The *xy*-coordinate plane:** These questions require you to use coordinate geometry to represent geometric concepts.
- **Geometric reasoning:** These questions require the ability to interpret statements that use logical connectives or quantifiers, use reasoning to determine whether an argument is valid or invalid, and identify a generalization or an assumption.
- **Systems of measurement:** These questions require an ability to demonstrate basic understanding of the U.S. customary and metric systems of measurement. You should be able to convert from one unit to another and recognize correct units for making measurements.
- **Measurement:** These questions require an ability to recognize the measurements needed to solve a problem. You must also be able to solve for area, volume, and length, including using formulas, estimation, and rates, and comparisons.

Data Analysis and Probability

- **Data interpretation:** These questions require an ability to read and interpret displays of information, including bar graphs, line graphs, pie charts, pictographs, tables, scatterplots, schedules, simple flowcharts, and diagrams. You must also have the ability to recognize relationships and understand statistics.
- **Data representation:** These questions require an understanding of the correspondence between data sets and their graphical displays.
- **Trends and inferences:** These questions require an ability to recognize, compare, contrast, and predict based on given information and an ability to make conclusions or inferences from given data.
- **Measures of central tendency:** These questions involve mean, median, mode, and range.
- **Probability:** These questions require an ability to evaluate numbers used to express simple probability and to figure the probability of a possible outcome.

► Computer versus Paper

There are small differences between the Praxis I written and computer-based tests:

	PAPER-BASED PRE-PROFESSIONAL SKILLS TEST: MATH	COMPUTER-BASED PRE-PROFESSIONAL SKILLS TEST: MATH
Test code	0730	5730
Time allotment	60 minutes	75 minutes
Number of questions	40, with 5 answer choices each	46, with 5 answer choices each
Format	Multiple-choice questions (calculators prohibited)	Multiple-choice questions (calculators prohibited)

TOPIC	PAPER-BASED TEST	COMPUTER-BASED TEST
Numbers and Operations	13 questions (32.5%)	15 questions (32.5%)
Algebra	8 questions (20%)	9 questions (20%)
Geometry and Measurement	9 questions (22.5%)	10 questions (22.5%)
Data Analysis and Probability	10 questions (25%)	12 questions (25%)

Now that you know more about the test specifications, following are the math skills you will need to review to succeed.

▶ Arithmetic

This section covers the basics of mathematical operations and their sequence. It also reviews variables, integers, fractions, decimals, and square roots.

Numbers and Symbols

Numbers and the Number Line

- **Counting numbers** (or natural numbers): 1, 2, 3, . . .
- **Whole numbers** include the counting numbers and zero: 0, 1, 2, 3, 4, 5, 6, . . .
- **Integers** include the whole numbers and their opposites. Remember, the opposite of zero is zero: . . . −3, −2, −1, 0, 1, 2, 3, . . .
- **Rational numbers** are all numbers that can be written as fractions, where the numerator and denominator are both integers, but the denominator is not zero. For example, $\frac{2}{3}$ is a rational number, as is $\frac{-6}{5}$. The decimal form of these numbers is either a terminating (ending) decimal, such as the decimal form of $\frac{3}{4}$ which is 0.75; or a repeating decimal, such as the decimal form of $\frac{1}{3}$, which is 0.3333333 . . .
- **Irrational numbers** are numbers that cannot be expressed as terminating or repeating decimals (i.e., nonrepeating, nonterminating decimals such as π, $\sqrt{2}$, $\sqrt{12}$).

The number line is a graphical representation of the order of numbers. As you move to the right, the value increases. As you move to the left, the value decreases.

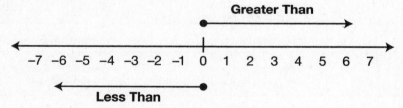

If we need a number line to reflect certain rational or irrational numbers, we can estimate where they should be.

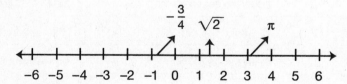

Comparison Symbols

The following table will illustrate some comparison symbols:

=	is equal to	5 = 5
≠	is not equal to	4 ≠ 3
>	is greater than	5 > 3
≥	is greater than or equal to	$x \geq 5$
		(x can be 5 or any number > 5)
<	is less than	4 < 6
≤	is less than or equal to	$x \leq 3$
		(x can be 3 or any number < 3)

Symbols of Addition

In addition, the numbers being added are called **addends**. The result is called a **sum**. The symbol for addition is called a **plus** sign. In the following example, 4 and 5 are addends and 9 is the sum:

$$4 + 5 = 9$$

Symbols of Subtraction

In subtraction, the number being subtracted is called the **subtrahend**. The number being subtracted *from* is called the **minuend**. The answer to a subtraction problem is called a **difference**. The symbol for subtraction is called a **minus** sign. In the following example, 15 is the minuend, 4 is the subtrahend, and 11 is the difference:

$$15 - 4 = 11$$

Symbols of Multiplication

When two or more numbers are being multiplied, they are called **factors**. The answer that results is called the **product**. In the following example, 5 and 6 are factors and 30 is their product:

$$5 \times 6 = 30$$

There are several ways to represent multiplication in this mathematical statement.

- A dot between factors indicates multiplication:
  $5 \cdot 6 = 30$
- Parentheses around any one or more factors indicate multiplication:
  $(5)6 = 30, 5(6) = 30$, and $(5)(6) = 30$.

- Multiplication is also indicated when a number is placed next to a variable: $5a = 30$. In this equation, 5 is being multiplied by a.

Symbols of Division

In division, the number being divided *by* is called the **divisor**. The number being divided *into* is called the **dividend**. The answer to a division problem is called the **quotient**.

There are a few different ways to represent division with symbols. In each of the following equivalent expressions, 3 is the divisor and 8 is the dividend:

$8 \div 3$, $8/3$, $\frac{8}{3}$, and $3\overline{)8}$

Prime and Composite Numbers

A positive integer that is greater than the number 1 is either prime or composite, but not both.

- A **prime** number is a number that has exactly two factors: 1 and itself.

    Examples
    2, 3, 5, 7, 11, 13, 17, 19, 23 . . .

- A **composite** number is a number that has more than two factors.

    Examples
    4, 6, 8, 9, 10, 12, 14, 15, 16 . . .

- The number 1 is neither prime nor composite since it has only one factor.

Operations

Addition

Addition is used when it is necessary to combine amounts. It is easiest to add when the addends are stacked in a column with the place values aligned. Work from right to left, starting with the ones column.

Example
Add $40 + 129 + 24$.

1. Align the addends in the ones column. Because it is necessary to work from right to left, begin to add starting with the ones column. The ones column totals 13, and 13 equals 1 ten and 3 ones, so write the 3 in the ones column of the answer, and regroup or "carry" the 1 ten to the next column as a 1 over the tens column so it gets added with the other tens:

$$
\begin{array}{r}
1 \\
40 \\
129 \\
+\ 24 \\
\hline
3
\end{array}
$$

2. Add the tens column, including the regrouped 1.

$$
\begin{array}{r}
1 \\
40 \\
129 \\
+\ 24 \\
\hline
93
\end{array}
$$

3. Then add the hundreds column. Because there is only one value, write the 1 in the answer.

$$
\begin{array}{r}
1 \\
40 \\
129 \\
+\ 24 \\
\hline
193
\end{array}
$$

Subtraction

Subtraction is used to find the difference between amounts. It is easiest to subtract when the minuend and subtrahend are in a column with the place values aligned. Again, just as in addition, work from right to left. It may be necessary to regroup.

Example

If Becky has 52 clients and Claire has 36, how many more clients does Becky have?

1. Find the difference between their client numbers by subtracting. Start with the ones column. Because 2 is less than the number being subtracted (6), regroup or "borrow" a ten from the tens column. Add the regrouped amount to the ones column. Now subtract 12 − 6 in the ones column.

$$
\begin{array}{r}
4\ 1 \\
\not{5}\not{2} \\
-\ 36 \\
\hline
6
\end{array}
$$

2. Regrouping 1 ten from the tens column left 4 tens. Subtract 4 – 3 and write the result in the tens column of the answer. Becky has 16 more clients than Claire. Check by addition: 16 + 36 = 52.

$$
\begin{array}{r}
^{4}\cancel{5}^{1}2 \\
-36 \\
\hline
6
\end{array}
$$

Multiplication

In multiplication, the same amount is combined multiple times. For example, instead of adding 30 three times, 30 + 30 + 30, it is easier to simply multiply 30 by 3. If a problem asks for the product of two or more numbers, the numbers should be multiplied to arrive at the answer.

Example

A school auditorium contains 54 rows, each containing 34 seats. How many seats are there in total?

1. In order to solve this problem, you could add 34 to itself 54 times, but we can solve this problem more easily with multiplication. Line up the place values vertically, writing the problem in columns. Multiply the number in the ones place of the top factor (4) by the number in the ones place of the bottom factor (4): $4 \times 4 = 16$. Because 16 = 1 ten and 6 ones, write the 6 in the ones place in the first partial product. Regroup or carry the ten by writing a 1 above the tens place of the top factor.

$$
\begin{array}{r}
^{1} \\
34 \\
\times54 \\
\hline
6
\end{array}
$$

2. Multiply the number in the tens place in the top factor (3) by the number in the ones place of the bottom factor (4): $4 \times 3 = 12$. Then add the regrouped amount: 12 + 1 = 13. Write the 3 in the tens column and the 1 in the hundreds column of the partial product.

$$
\begin{array}{r}
^{1} \\
34 \\
\times54 \\
\hline
136
\end{array}
$$

3. The last calculations to be done require multiplying by the tens place of the bottom factor. Multiply 5 (tens from bottom factor) by 4 (ones from top factor); $5 \times 4 = 20$, but because the 5 really represents a number of tens, the actual value of the answer is 200 ($50 \times 4 = 200$). Therefore, write the two zeros under the ones and tens columns of the second partial product and regroup or carry the 2 hundreds by writing a 2 above the tens place of the top factor.

$$
\begin{array}{r}
^{2} \\
34 \\
\times54 \\
\hline
136 \\
00
\end{array}
$$

4. Multiply 5 (tens from bottom factor) by 3 (tens from top factor); $5 \times 3 = 15$, but because the 5 and the 3 each represent a number of tens, the actual value of the answer is 1,500 ($50 \times 30 = 1,500$). Add the two additional hundreds carried over from the last multiplication: $15 + 2 = 17$ (hundreds). Write the 17 in front of the zeros in the second partial product.

$$
\begin{array}{r}
\overset{2}{}34 \\
\times\ \ 54 \\
\hline
136 \\
1{,}700 \\
\end{array}
$$

5. Add the partial products to find the total product:

$$
\begin{array}{r}
\overset{2}{}34 \\
\times\ \ 54 \\
\hline
136 \\
+\ \ 1{,}700 \\
\hline
1{,}836 \\
\end{array}
$$

Note: It is easier to perform multiplication if you write the factor with the greater number of digits in the top row. In this example, both factors have an equal number of digits, so it does not matter which is written on top.

Division

In division, the same amount is subtracted multiple times. For example, instead of subtracting 5 from 25 as many times as possible, $25 - 5 - 5 - 5 - 5 - 5$, it is easier to simply divide, asking how many 5s are in 25: $25 \div 5$.

Example

At a road show, three artists sold their beads for a total of $54. If they share the money equally, how much money should each artist receive?

1. Divide the total amount ($54) by the number of ways the money is to be split (3). Work from left to right. How many times does 3 divide 5? Write the answer, 1, directly above the 5 in the dividend, because both the 5 and the 1 represent a number of tens. Now multiply: since $1(\text{ten}) \times 3(\text{ones}) = 3(\text{tens})$, write the 3 under the 5, and subtract; $5(\text{tens}) - 3(\text{tens}) = 2(\text{tens})$.

$$
\begin{array}{r}
1 \\
3\overline{)54} \\
-3 \\
\hline
2 \\
\end{array}
$$

2. Continue dividing. Bring down the 4 from the ones place in the dividend. How many times does 3 divide 24? Write the answer, 8, directly above the 4 in the dividend. Because $3 \times 8 = 24$, write 24 below the other 24 and subtract $24 - 24 = 0$.

$$
\begin{array}{r}
18 \\
3\overline{)54} \\
-3\downarrow \\
\hline
24 \\
-24 \\
\hline
0
\end{array}
$$

Remainders

If you get a number other than zero after your last subtraction, this number is your remainder.

Example

9 divided by 4.

$$
\begin{array}{r}
2 \\
4\overline{)9} \\
-8 \\
\hline
1
\end{array}
$$

1 is the remainder.

The answer is 2 r1. This answer can also be written as $2\frac{1}{4}$, because there was one part left over out of the four parts needed to make a whole.

Working with Integers

Remember, an integer is a whole number or its opposite. Here are some rules for working with integers:

Adding

Adding numbers with the same sign results in a sum of the same sign:

(positive) + (positive) = positive   and   (negative) + (negative) = negative

When adding numbers of different signs, follow this two-step process:

1. Subtract the positive values of the numbers. Positive values are the values of the numbers without any signs.

2. Keep the sign of the number with the larger positive value.

Example

−2 + 3 =

1. Subtract the positive values of the numbers: 3 − 2 = 1.
2. The number 3 is the larger of the two positive values. Its sign in the original example was positive, so the sign of the answer is positive. The answer is positive 1.

Example

8 + −11 =

1. Subtract the positive values of the numbers: 11 − 8 = 3.
2. The number 11 is the larger of the two positive values. Its sign in the original example was negative, so the sign of the answer is negative. The answer is negative 3.

Subtracting

When subtracting integers, change the subtraction sign to addition and change the sign of the number being subtracted to its opposite. Then follow the rules for addition.

Examples

$(+10) − (+12) = (+10) + (−12) = −2$

$(−5) − (−7) = (−5) + (+7) = +2$

Multiplying and Dividing

A simple method for remembering the rules of multiplying and dividing is that if the signs are the same when multiplying or dividing two quantities, the answer will be positive. If the signs are different, the answer will be negative.

$(\text{positive}) \times (\text{positive}) = \text{positive}$

$(\text{positive}) \times (\text{negative}) = \text{negative}$

$(\text{negative}) \times (\text{negative}) = \text{positive}$

$\frac{(\text{positive})}{(\text{positive})} = \text{positive}$

$\frac{(\text{positive})}{(\text{negative})} = \text{negative}$

$\frac{(\text{negative})}{(\text{negative})} = \text{positive}$

Examples

$(10)(−12) = −120$

$−5 \times −7 = 35$

$\frac{12}{−3} = −4$

$\frac{15}{3} = 5$

Sequence of Mathematical Operations

There is an order in which a sequence of mathematical operations must be performed:

P: Parentheses/Grouping Symbols. Perform all operations within parentheses first. If there is more than one set of parentheses, begin to work with the innermost set and work toward the outside. If more than one operation is present within the parentheses, use the remaining rules of order to determine which operation to perform first.

E: Exponents. Evaluate exponents.

M/D: Multiply/Divide. Work from left to right in the expression.

A/S: Add/Subtract. Work from left to right in the expression.

This order is illustrated by the acronym PEMDAS, which can be remembered by using the first letter of each of the words in the phrase: **Please Excuse My Dear Aunt Sally.**

Example

$$\frac{(5+3)^2}{4} + 27$$

$$= \frac{(8)^2}{4} + 27$$

$$= \frac{64}{4} + 27$$

$$= 16 + 27$$

$$= 43$$

Properties of Arithmetic

There are several properties of mathematics:

- **Commutative Property:** This property states that the result of an arithmetic operation is not affected by reversing the order of the numbers. Multiplication and addition are operations that satisfy the commutative property.

Examples

$5 \times 2 = 2 \times 5$

$5a = a5$

$b + 3 = 3 + b$

However, neither subtraction nor division is commutative, because reversing the order of the numbers does not yield the same result.

Examples

$5 - 2 \neq 2 - 5$

$6 \div 3 \neq 3 \div 6$

- **Associative Property:** If parentheses can be moved to group different numbers in an arithmetic problem without changing the result, then the operation is associative. Addition and multiplication are associative.

  Examples

  $2 + (3 + 4) = (2 + 3) + 4$

  $2(ab) = (2a)b$

- **Distributive Property:** When a value is being multiplied by a sum or difference, multiply that value by each quantity within the parentheses. Then, take the sum or difference to yield an equivalent result.

  Examples

  $5(a + b) = 5a + 5b$

  $5(100 - 6) = (5 \times 100) - (5 \times 6)$

This second example can be proved by performing the calculations:

$$5(94) = 5(100 - 6)$$
$$= 500 - 30$$
$$470 = 470$$

Additive and Multiplicative Identities and Inverses

- The **additive identity** is the value that, when added to a number, does not change the number. For all of the sets of numbers defined previously (counting numbers, integers, rational numbers, etc.), the additive identity is 0.

  Examples

  $5 + 0 = 5$

  $-3 + 0 = -3$

Adding 0 does not change the values of 5 and −3, so 0 is the additive identity.

- The **additive inverse** of a number is the number that, when added to the number, gives you the additive identity.

  Example

  What is the additive inverse of −3?

This means, "What number can I add to –3 to give me the additive identity (0)?"

–3 + ___ = 0

–3 + 3 = 0

The answer is 3.

- The **multiplicative identity** is the value that, when multiplied by a number, does not change the number. For all of the sets of numbers defined previously (counting numbers, integers, rational numbers, etc.) the multiplicative identity is 1.

Examples

$5 \times 1 = 5$

$-3 \times 1 = -3$

Multiplying by 1 does not change the values of 5 and –3, so 1 is the multiplicative identity.

- The **multiplicative inverse** of a number is the number that, when multiplied by the number, gives you the multiplicative identity.

Example

What is the multiplicative inverse of 5?

This means, "What number can I multiply 5 by to give me the multiplicative identity (1)?"

$5 \times$ ___ $= 1$

$5 \times \frac{1}{5} = 1$

The answer is $\frac{1}{5}$.

There is an easy way to find the multiplicative inverse. It is the **reciprocal**, which is obtained by reversing the numerator and denominator of a fraction. In the preceding example, the answer is the reciprocal of 5; 5 can be written as $\frac{5}{1}$, so the reciprocal is $\frac{1}{5}$.

Here are some numbers and their reciprocals:

4	$\frac{1}{4}$
$\frac{2}{3}$	$\frac{3}{2}$
$-\frac{6}{5}$	$-\frac{5}{6}$
$\frac{1}{6}$	6

Note: Reciprocals do not change sign.

Note: The additive inverse of a number is the opposite of the number; the multiplicative inverse is the reciprocal.

Factors and Multiples

Factors

Factors are numbers that can be divided into a larger number without a remainder.

Example

$12 \div 3 = 4$

The number 3 is, therefore, a factor of the number 12. Other factors of 12 are 1, 2, 4, 6, and 12. The common factors of two numbers are the factors that both numbers have in common.

Examples

The factors of 24 = 1, 2, 3, 4, 6, 8, 12, and 24.
The factors of 18 = 1, 2, 3, 6, 9, and 18.

From the examples, you can see that the common factors of 24 and 18 are 1, 2, 3, and 6. From this list it can also be determined that the *greatest* common factor of 24 and 18 is 6. Determining the **greatest common factor** (GCF) is useful for simplifying fractions.

Example

Simplify $\frac{16}{20}$.

The factors of 16 are 1, 2, 4, 8, and 16. The factors of 20 are 1, 2, 4, 5, and 20. The common factors of 16 and 20 are 1, 2, and 4. The greatest of these, the GCF, is 4. Therefore, to simplify the fraction, both numerator and denominator should be divided by 4.

$$\frac{16 \div 4}{20 \div 4} = \frac{4}{5}$$

Multiples

Multiples are numbers that can be obtained by multiplying a number x by a positive integer.

Example

$5 \times 7 = 35$

The number 35 is, therefore, a multiple of the number 5 and of the number 7. Other multiples of 5 are 5, 10, 15, 20, and so on. Other multiples of 7 are 7, 14, 21, 28, and so on.

The common multiples of two numbers are the multiples that both numbers share.

Example
Some multiples of 4 are: 4, 8, 12, 16, 20, 24, 28, 32, 36 . . .
Some multiples of 6 are: 6, 12, 18, 24, 30, 36, 42, 48 . . .

Some common multiples are 12, 24, and 36. From the above it can also be determined that the *least* common multiple of the numbers 4 and 6 is 12, since this number is the smallest number that appeared in both lists. The **least common multiple**, or LCM, is used when performing addition and subtraction of fractions to find the least common denominator.

Example (using denominators 4 and 6 and LCM of 12)

$$\frac{1}{4} + \frac{5}{6} = \frac{1(3)}{4(3)} + \frac{5(2)}{6(2)}$$
$$= \frac{3}{12} + \frac{10}{12}$$
$$= \frac{13}{12}$$
$$= 1\frac{1}{12}$$

Decimals

The most important thing to remember about decimals is that the first place value to the right of the decimal point is the tenths place. The place values are as follows:

1	2	6	8	.	3	4	5	7
T H O U S A N D S	H U N D R E D S	T E N S	O N E S	D E C I M A L POINT	T E N T H S	H U N D R E D T H S	T H O U S A N D T H S	T E N T H O U S A N D T H S

In expanded form, this number can also be expressed as:

$1{,}268.3457 = (1 \times 1{,}000) + (2 \times 100) + (6 \times 10) + (8 \times 1) + (3 \times .1) + (4 \times .01) + (5 \times .001) + (7 \times .0001)$

Adding and Subtracting Decimals

Adding and subtracting decimals is very similar to adding and subtracting whole numbers. The most important thing to remember is to line up the decimal points. Zeros may be filled in as placeholders when all numbers do not have the same number of decimal places.

Examples

What is the sum of 0.45, 0.8, and 1.36?

$$
\begin{array}{r}
\overset{1\ 1}{} \\
0.45 \\
0.80 \\
+\ 1.36 \\
\hline
2.61 \\
\end{array}
$$

Take away 0.35 from 1.06.

$$
\begin{array}{r}
\overset{0\ 1}{\cancel{1}}.06 \\
-0.35 \\
\hline
0.71 \\
\end{array}
$$

Multiplication of Decimals

Multiplication of decimals is exactly the same as multiplication of integers, except one must make note of the total number of decimal places in the factors.

Example

What is the product of 0.14 and 4.3?

First, multiply as usual (do not line up the decimal points):

$$\begin{array}{r} 4.3 \\ \times .14 \\ \hline 172 \\ + 430 \\ \hline 602 \end{array}$$

Now, to figure out the answer, 4.3 has one decimal place and .14 has two decimal places. Add in order to determine the total number of decimal places the answer must have to the right of the decimal point. In this problem, there are a total of three (1 + 2) decimal places. When finished multiplying, start from the right side of the answer, and move to the left the number of decimal places previously calculated.

.602

In this example, 602 turns into .602, because there have to be three decimal places in the answer. If there are not enough digits in the answer, add zeros in front of the answer until there are enough.

Example

Multiply 0.03 × 0.2.

$$\begin{array}{r} .03 \\ \times .2 \\ \hline 6 \end{array}$$

There are three total decimal places in the problem; therefore, the answer must contain three decimal places. Starting to the right of 6, move left three places. The answer becomes 0.006.

Dividing Decimals

Dividing decimals is a little different from integers for the setup, and then the regular rules of division apply. It is easier to divide if the divisor does not have any decimals. In order to accomplish that, simply move the decimal place to the right as many places as necessary to make the divisor a whole number. If the decimal point is moved in the divisor, it must also be moved in the dividend in order to keep the answer the same as the original problem; 4 ÷ 2 has the same solution as its multiples 8 ÷ 4 and 28 ÷ 14. Moving a decimal point in a division problem is equivalent to multiplying a numerator and denominator of a fraction by the same quantity, which is the reason the answer will remain the same.

If there are not enough decimal places in the answer to accommodate the required move, simply add zeros until the desired placement is achieved. Add zeros after the decimal point to continue the division until the decimal terminates, or until a repeating pattern is recognized. The decimal point in the quotient belongs directly above the decimal point in the dividend.

Example

What is $.425\overline{)1.53}$?

First, to make .425 a whole number, move the decimal point three places to the right: 425.
Now move the decimal point three places to the right for 1.53: 1,530.
The problem is now a simple long division problem.

$$
\begin{array}{r}
3.6 \\
425.\overline{)1,530.0} \\
-1,275 \downarrow \\
\hline
2,550 \\
-2,550 \\
\hline
0
\end{array}
$$

Comparing Decimals

Comparing decimals is actually quite simple. Just line up the decimal points and then fill in zeros at the ends of the numbers until each one has an equal number of digits.

Example

Compare .5 and .005.

Line up decimal points.   .5
                            .005

Add zeros.   .500
                            .005

Now, ignore the decimal point and consider, which is bigger: 500 or 5?
500 is definitely bigger than 5, so .5 is larger than .005.

Rounding Decimals

It is often inconvenient to work with very long decimals. Often it is much more convenient to have an approximation for a decimal that contains fewer digits than the entire decimal. In this case, we **round** decimals to a certain number of decimal places. There are numerous options for rounding:

To the nearest integer: zero digits to the right of the decimal point
To the nearest tenth: one digit to the right of the decimal point (tenths unit)
To the nearest hundredth: two digits to the right of the decimal point (hundredths unit)

In order to round, we look at two digits of the decimal: the digit we are rounding to, and the digit to the immediate right. If the digit to the immediate right is less than 5, we leave the digit we are rounding to alone, and omit all the digits to the right of it. If the digit to the immediate right is 5 or greater, we increase the digit we are rounding by one, and omit all the digits to the right of it.

Example

Round $\frac{3}{7}$ to the nearest tenth and the nearest hundredth.

Dividing 3 by 7 gives us the repeating decimal .428571428571.... If we are rounding to the nearest tenth, we need to look at the digit in the tenths position (4) and the digit to the immediate right (2). Because 2 is less than 5, we leave the digit in the tenths position alone, and drop everything to the right of it. So, $\frac{3}{7}$ to the nearest tenth is .4.

To round to the nearest hundredth, we need to look at the digit in the hundredths position (2) and the digit to the immediate right (8). Because 8 is more than 5, we increase the digit in the hundredths position by 1, giving us 3, and drop everything to the right of it. So, $\frac{3}{7}$ to the nearest hundredth is .43.

Fractions

To work well with fractions, it is necessary to understand some basic concepts.

Simplifying Fractions

Rule:

$$\frac{ac}{bc} = \frac{a}{b}$$

- To simplify fractions, identify the greatest common factor (GCF) of the numerator and denominator and divide both the numerator and denominator by this number.

Example

Simplify $\frac{63}{72}$.

The GCF of 63 and 72 is 9, so divide 63 and 72 each by 9 to simplify the fraction:

$$\frac{63 \div 9 = 7}{72 \div 9 = 8}$$

$$\frac{63}{72} = \frac{7}{8}$$

Adding and Subtracting Fractions

Rules:

To add or subtract fractions with the same denominator:

$$\frac{a}{b} \pm \frac{c}{b} = \frac{a \pm c}{b}$$

To add or subtract fractions with different denominators:

$$\frac{a}{b} \pm \frac{c}{d} = \frac{ad \pm cb}{bd}$$

- To add or subtract fractions with like denominators, just add or subtract the numerators and keep the denominator.

Examples

$\frac{1}{7} + \frac{5}{7} = \frac{6}{7}$ and $\frac{5}{8} - \frac{2}{8} = \frac{3}{8}$

- To add or subtract fractions with unlike denominators, first find the least common denominator or LCD. The LCD is the smallest number divisible by each of the denominators.

For example, for the denominators 8 and 12, 24 would be the LCD because 24 is the smallest number that is divisible by both 8 and 12: $8 \times 3 = 24$, and $12 \times 2 = 24$.

Using the LCD, convert each fraction to its new form by multiplying both the numerator and denominator by the appropriate factor to get the LCD, and then follow the directions for adding/subtracting fractions with like denominators.

Example

$$\frac{1}{3} + \frac{2}{5} = \frac{1(5)}{3(5)} + \frac{2(3)}{5(3)}$$
$$= \frac{5}{15} + \frac{6}{15}$$
$$= \frac{11}{15}$$

Multiplication of Fractions

Rule:

$$\frac{a}{b} \times \frac{c}{d} = \frac{a \times c}{b \times d}$$

- Multiplying fractions is one of the easiest operations to perform. To multiply fractions, simply multiply the numerators and the denominators.

Example

$$\frac{4}{5} \times \frac{6}{7} = \frac{24}{35}$$

If any numerator and denominator have common factors, these may be simplified before multiplying. Divide the common multiples by a common factor. In the following example, 3 and 6 are both divided by 3 before multiplying.

Example

$$\frac{\overset{1}{\cancel{3}}}{5} \times \frac{1}{\underset{2}{\cancel{6}}} = \frac{1}{10}$$

Dividing Fractions

Rule:

$$\frac{a}{b} \div \frac{c}{d} = \frac{a}{b} \times \frac{d}{c} = \frac{a \times d}{b \times c}$$

- Dividing fractions is equivalent to multiplying the dividend by the reciprocal of the divisor. When dividing fractions, simply multiply the dividend by the divisor's reciprocal to get the answer.

Example

$$(\text{dividend}) \div (\text{divisor})$$
$$\frac{1}{4} \div \frac{1}{2}$$

Determine the reciprocal of the divisor:
$$\frac{1}{2} \to \frac{2}{1}$$

Multiply the dividend ($\frac{1}{4}$) by the reciprocal of the divisor ($\frac{2}{1}$) and simplify if necessary.

$$\frac{1}{4} \div \frac{1}{2} = \frac{1}{4} \times \frac{2}{1}$$
$$= \frac{2}{4}$$
$$= \frac{1}{2}$$

Comparing Fractions

Rules:

If $\frac{a}{b} = \frac{c}{d}$, then $ad = bc$

If $\frac{a}{b} < \frac{c}{d}$, then $ad < bc$

If $\frac{a}{b} > \frac{c}{d}$, then $ad > bc$

Sometimes it is necessary to compare the sizes of fractions. This is very simple when the fractions are familiar or when they have a common denominator.

Examples

$\frac{1}{2} < \frac{3}{4}$ and $\frac{11}{18} > \frac{5}{18}$

■ If the fractions are not familiar and/or do not have a common denominator, there is a simple trick to remember. Multiply the numerator of the first fraction by the denominator of the second fraction. Write this answer under the first fraction. Then multiply the numerator of the second fraction by the denominator of the first one. Write this answer under the second fraction. Compare the two numbers. The larger number represents the larger fraction.

Examples

Which is larger: $\frac{7}{11}$ or $\frac{4}{9}$?

Cross multiply.

$7 \times 9 = 63$ $4 \times 11 = 44$

$63 > 44$; therefore,

$$\frac{7}{11} > \frac{4}{9}$$

Compare $\frac{6}{18}$ and $\frac{2}{6}$.
Cross multiply.

$6 \times 6 = 36$ $2 \times 18 = 36$

$36 = 36$; therefore,

$$\frac{6}{18} = \frac{2}{6}$$

Converting Decimals to Fractions

■ To convert a nonrepeating decimal to a fraction, the digits of the decimal become the numerator of the fraction, and the denominator of the fraction is a power of 10 that contains that number of digits as zeros.

Example

Convert .125 to a fraction.

The decimal .125 means 125 *thousandths*, so it is 125 parts of 1,000. An easy way to do this is to make 125 the numerator, and since there are three digits in the number 125, the denominator is 1 with three zeros, or 1,000.

$$.125 = \frac{125}{1,000}$$

Then we just need to reduce the fraction.

$$\frac{125}{1,000} = \frac{125 \div 125}{1,000 \div 125} = \frac{1}{8}$$

■ When converting a repeating decimal to a fraction, the digits of the repeating pattern of the decimal become the numerator of the fraction, and the denominator of the fraction is the same number of 9s as digits.

Example

Convert $.\overline{3}$ to a fraction.

You may already recognize $.\overline{3}$ as $\frac{1}{3}$. The repeating pattern, in this case 3, becomes our numerator. There is one digit in the pattern, so 9 is our denominator.

$$.\overline{3} = \frac{3}{9} = \frac{3 \div 3}{9 \div 3} = \frac{1}{3}$$

Example

Convert $.\overline{36}$ to a fraction.

The repeating pattern, in this case 36, becomes our numerator. There are two digits in the pattern, so 99 is our denominator.

$$.\overline{36} = \frac{36}{99} = \frac{36 \div 9}{99 \div 9} = \frac{4}{11}$$

Converting Fractions to Decimals

■ To convert a fraction to a decimal, simply treat the fraction as a division problem.

Example

Convert $\frac{3}{4}$ to a decimal.

$$\begin{array}{r} .75 \\ 4\overline{)3.00} \end{array}$$

So, $\frac{3}{4}$ is equal to .75.

Converting Mixed Numbers to and from Improper Fractions

Rule:

$$a\frac{b}{c} = \frac{ac+b}{c}$$

- A mixed number is number greater than 1 that is expressed as a whole number joined to a proper fraction. Examples of mixed numbers are $5\frac{3}{8}$, $2\frac{1}{3}$, and $-4\frac{5}{6}$. To convert from a mixed number to an improper fraction (a fraction where the numerator is greater than the denominator), multiply the whole number and the denominator and add the numerator. This becomes the new numerator. The new denominator is the same as the original.

Note: If the mixed number is negative, temporarily ignore the negative sign while performing the conversion, and just make sure you replace the negative sign when you're done.

Example

Convert $5\frac{3}{8}$ to an improper fraction.

Using the conversion formula, $5\frac{3}{8} = \frac{5 \times 8 + 3}{8} = \frac{43}{8}$.

Example

Convert $-4\frac{5}{6}$ to an improper fraction.

Temporarily ignore the negative sign and perform the conversion: $4\frac{5}{6} = \frac{4 \times 6 + 5}{6} = \frac{29}{6}$. The final answer includes the negative sign: $-\frac{29}{6}$.

- To convert from an improper fraction to a mixed number, simply treat the fraction like a division problem, and express the answer as a fraction rather than a decimal.

Example

Convert $\frac{23}{7}$ to a mixed number.

Perform the division: $23 \div 7 = 3\frac{2}{7}$.

Percents

Percents are always "out of 100": 45% means 45 out of 100. Therefore, to write percents as decimals, move the decimal point two places to the left (to the hundredths place).

$$45\% = \frac{45}{100} = 0.45$$

$$3\% = \frac{3}{100} = 0.03$$

$$124\% = \frac{124}{100} = 1.24$$

$$0.9\% = \frac{.9}{100} = \frac{9}{1,000} = 0.009$$

Here are some conversions you should be familiar with:

FRACTION	DECIMAL	PERCENTAGE
$\frac{1}{2}$	.5	50%
$\frac{1}{4}$	.25	25%
$\frac{1}{3}$	.333 . . .	33.$\overline{3}$%
$\frac{2}{3}$	.666 . . .	66.$\overline{6}$%
$\frac{1}{10}$	.1	10%
$\frac{1}{8}$	.125	12.5%
$\frac{1}{6}$	.1666 . . .	16.$\overline{6}$%
$\frac{1}{5}$	.2	20%

Absolute Value

The absolute value of a number is the distance of that number from zero. Distances are always represented by positive numbers, so the absolute value of any number is positive. Absolute value is represented by placing small vertical lines around the value: $|x|$.

Examples

The absolute value of seven: $|7|$.

The distance from seven to zero is seven, so $|7| = 7$.

The absolute value of negative three: $|-3|$.

The distance from negative three to zero is three, so $|-3| = 3$.

Exponents

Positive Exponents

A positive exponent indicates the number of times a base is used as a factor to attain a product.

Example
Evaluate 2^5.

In this example, 2 is the base and 5 is the exponent. Therefore, 2 should be used as a factor 5 times to attain a product:

$$2^5 = 2 \times 2 \times 2 \times 2 \times 2 = 32$$

Zero Exponent

Any nonzero number raised to the zero power equals 1.

Examples
$5^0 = 1 \qquad 70^0 = 1 \qquad 29{,}874^0 = 1$

Negative Exponents

A base raised to a negative exponent is equivalent to the reciprocal of the base raised to the positive exponent (absolute value of the exponent).

Examples
$5^{-1} = \frac{1}{5}$
$7^{-2} = (\frac{1}{7})^2 = \frac{1}{49}$
$(\frac{2}{3})^{-2} = (\frac{3}{2})^2 = \frac{9}{4}$

Exponent Rules

- When multiplying identical bases, you add the exponents.

Examples
$2^2 \times 2^4 \times 2^6 = 2^{12}$
$a^2 \times a^3 \times a^5 = a^{10}$

- When dividing identical bases, you subtract the exponents.

Examples

$\dfrac{2^7}{2^3} = 2^4$ $\qquad\qquad$ $\dfrac{a^9}{a^4} = a^5$

- If a base raised to a power (in parentheses) is raised to another power, you multiply the exponents together.

Examples

$(3^2)^7 = 3^{14}$ $\qquad\qquad$ $(g^4)^3 = g^{12}$

Perfect Squares

The number 5^2 is read "5 to the second power," or, more commonly, "5 squared." Perfect squares are numbers that are second powers of other numbers. Perfect squares are always zero or positive, because when you multiply a positive or a negative by itself, the result is always positive. The perfect squares are $0^2, 1^2, 2^2, 3^2 \ldots$

Perfect squares: 0, 1, 4, 9, 16, 25, 36, 49, 64, 81, 100 . . .

Perfect Cubes

The number 5^3 is read "5 to the third power," or, more commonly, "5 cubed." (Powers higher than three have no special name.) Perfect cubes are numbers that are third powers of other numbers. Perfect cubes, unlike perfect squares, can be either positive or negative. This is because when a negative is multiplied by itself three times, the result is negative. The perfect cubes are $0^3, 1^3, 2^3, 3^3 \ldots$

Perfect cubes: 0, 1, 8, 27, 64, 125 . . .

- Note that 64 is both a perfect square and a perfect cube.

Square Roots

The square of a number is the product of the number and itself. For example, in the statement $3^2 = 3 \times 3 = 9$, the number 9 is the square of the number 3. If the process is reversed, the number 3 is the square root of the number 9. The symbol for square root is $\sqrt{}$ and is called a **radical**. The number inside of the radical is called the **radicand**.

Example

$5^2 = 25$; therefore, $\sqrt{25} = 5$

Because 25 is the square of 5, it is also true that 5 is the square root of 25.

The square root of a number might not be a whole number. For example, the square root of 7 is 2.645751311. . . . It is not possible to find a whole number that can be multiplied by itself to equal 7. Square roots of nonperfect squares are irrational.

Cube Roots

The cube of a number is the product of the number and itself for a total of three times. For example, in the statement $2^3 = 2 \times 2 \times 2 = 8$, the number 8 is the cube of the number 2. If the process is reversed, the number 2 is the cube root of the number 8. The symbol for cube root is the same as the square root symbol, except for a small 3: $\sqrt[3]{}$. It is read as "cube root." The number inside of the radical is still called the radicand, and the 3 is called the index. (In a square root, the index is not written, but it has an index of 2.)

Example

$5^3 = 125$; therefore, $\sqrt[3]{125} = 5$.

Like square roots, the cube root of a number might be not be a whole number. Cube roots of nonperfect cubes are irrational.

Probability

Probability is the numerical representation of the likelihood of an event occurring. Probability is always represented by a decimal or fraction between 0 and 1, 0 meaning that the event will never occur, and 1 meaning that the event will always occur. The higher the probability, the more likely the event is to occur.

A **simple event** is one action. Examples of simple events are: drawing one card from a deck, rolling one die, flipping one coin, or spinning a hand on a spinner once.

Simple Probability

The probability of an event occurring is defined as the number of desired outcomes divided by the total number of outcomes. The list of all outcomes is often called the **sample space**.

$$P(\text{event}) = \frac{\text{\# of desired outcomes}}{\text{total number of outcomes}}$$

Example

What is the probability of drawing a king from a standard deck of cards?

There are four kings in a standard deck of cards, so the number of desired outcomes is 4. There are 52 ways to pick a card from a standard deck of cards, so the total number of outcomes is 52. The probability of drawing a king from a standard deck of cards is $\frac{4}{52}$. So, $P(\text{king}) = \frac{4}{52}$.

Example

What is the probability of getting an odd number on the roll of one die?

There are three odd numbers on a standard die: 1, 3, and 5. So, the number of desired outcomes is 3. There are six sides on a standard die, so there are 6 possible outcomes. The probability of rolling an odd number on a standard die is $\frac{3}{6}$. So, P(odd) = $\frac{3}{6}$.

Note: It is not necessary to reduce fractions when working with probability.

Probability of an Event Not Occurring

The sum of the probability of an event occurring and the probability of the event *not* occurring = 1. Therefore, if we know the probability of the event occurring, we can determine the probability of the event *not* occurring by subtracting from 1.

Example

If the probability of rain tomorrow is 45%, what is the probability that it will *not* rain tomorrow?

45% = .45, and 1 − .45 = .55 or 55%. The probability that it will not rain is 55%.

Probability Involving the Word *Or*

Rule:

P(event A *or* event B) = P(event A) + P(event B) − P(overlap of event A and B)

When the word *or* appears in a simple probability problem, it signifies that you will be adding outcomes. For example, if we are interested in the probability of obtaining a king or a queen on a draw of a card, the number of desired outcomes is 8, because there are four kings and four queens in the deck. The probability of event A (drawing a king) is $\frac{4}{52}$, and the probability of drawing a queen is $\frac{4}{52}$. The overlap of event A and B would be any cards that are both a king and a queen at the same time, but there are no cards that are both a king and a queen at the same time. So the probability of obtaining a king or a queen is $\frac{4}{52} + \frac{4}{52} - \frac{0}{52} = \frac{8}{52}$.

Example

What is the probability of getting an even number or a multiple of 3 on the roll of a die?

The probability of getting an even number on the roll of a die is $\frac{3}{6}$, because there are three even numbers (2, 4, 6) on a die and a total of 6 possible outcomes. The probability of getting a multiple of 3 is $\frac{2}{6}$, because there are 2 multiples of three (3, 6) on a die. But because the outcome of rolling a 6 on the die is an overlap of both events, we must subtract $\frac{1}{6}$ from the result so we don't count it twice.

P(even *or* multiple of 3) = P(even) + P(multiple of 3) − P(overlap)
$$= \frac{3}{6} + \frac{2}{6} - \frac{1}{6} = \frac{4}{6}$$

Compound Probability

A **compound event** is performing two or more simple events in succession. Drawing two cards from a deck, rolling three dice, flipping five coins, having four babies are all examples of compound events.

This can be done "with replacement" (probabilities do not change for each event) or "without replacement" (probabilities change for each event).

The probability of event A followed by event B occurring is $P(A) \times P(B)$. This is called the **counting principle** for probability.

Note: In mathematics, the word *and* usually signifies addition. In probability, however, *and* signifies multiplication and *or* signifies addition.

Example

You have a jar filled with three red marbles, five green marbles, and two blue marbles. What is the probability of getting a red marble followed by a blue marble, with replacement?

"With replacement" in this case means that you will draw a marble, note its color, and then replace it back into the jar. This means that the probability of drawing a red marble does not change from one simple event to the next.

Note that there are a total of ten marbles in the jar, so the total number of outcomes is 10.

$P(\text{red}) = \frac{3}{10}$ and $P(\text{blue}) = \frac{2}{10}$ so $P(\text{red followed by blue})$ is $\frac{3}{10} \times \frac{2}{10} = \frac{6}{100}$.

If the problem was changed to say "without replacement," that would mean you are drawing a marble, noting its color, but not returning it to the jar. This means that for the second event, you no longer have a total number of 10 outcomes; you have only 9, because you have taken one red marble out of the jar. In this case,

$P(\text{red}) = \frac{3}{10}$ and $P(\text{blue}) = \frac{2}{9}$ so $P(\text{red followed by blue})$ is $\frac{3}{10} \times \frac{2}{9} = \frac{6}{90}$.

Statistics

Statistics is the field of mathematics that deals with describing sets of data. Often, we want to understand trends in data by looking at where the center of the data lies. There are a number of ways to find the center of a set of data.

Mean

When we talk about average, we usually are referring to the **arithmetic mean** (usually just called the **mean**). To find the mean of a set of numbers, add all of the numbers together and divide by the quantity of numbers in the set.

average = (sum of set) ÷ (quantity of set)

Example

Find the average of 9, 4, 7, 6, and 4.

$$\frac{9 + 4 + 7 + 6 + 4}{5} = \frac{30}{5} = 6$$

The mean, or average, of the set is 6.

(Divide by 5 because there are five numbers in the set.)

Median

Another center of data is the median. It is literally the center number if you arrange all the data in ascending or descending order. To find the median of a set of numbers, arrange the numbers in ascending or descending order and find the middle value.

- If the set contains an odd number of elements, then simply choose the middle value.

  Example

  Find the median of the number set: 1, 5, 4, 7, 2.

  First arrange the set in order—1, 2, 4, 5, 7—and then find the middle value. Because there are five values, the middle value is the third one: 4. The median is 4.

- If the set contains an even number of elements, simply average the two middle values.

  Example

  Find the median of the number set: 1, 6, 3, 7, 2, 8.

  First arrange the set in order—1, 2, 3, 6, 7, 8—and then find the middle values, 3 and 6. Find the average of the numbers 3 and 6: $\frac{3 + 6}{2} = \frac{9}{2} = 4.5$. The median is 4.5.

Mode

Sometimes when we want to know the average, we just want to know what occurs most often. The **mode** of a set of numbers is the number that appears the greatest number of times.

  Example

  For the number set 1, 2, 5, 9, 4, 2, 9, 6, 9, 7, the number 9 is the mode because it appears the most frequently.

▶ Measurement

This section reviews the basics of measurement systems used in the United States (sometimes called customary measurement) and other countries, methods of performing mathematical operations with units of measurement, and the process of converting between different units.

The use of measurement enables a connection to be made between mathematics and the real world. To measure any object, assign a number and a unit of measure. For instance, when a fish is caught, it is often weighed in ounces and its length measured in inches. The following lesson will help you become more familiar with the types, conversions, and units of measurement.

Types of Measurements

The types of measurements used most frequently in the United States are listed here:

Units of Length

12 inches (in.) = 1 foot (ft.)

3 feet = 36 inches = 1 yard (yd.)

5,280 feet = 1,760 yards = 1 mile (mi.)

Units of Volume

8 ounces* (oz.) = 1 cup (c.)

2 cups = 16 ounces = 1 pint (pt.)

2 pints = 4 cups = 32 ounces = 1 quart (qt.)

4 quarts = 8 pints = 16 cups = 128 ounces = 1 gallon (gal.)

Units of Weight

16 ounces* (oz.) = 1 pound (lb.)

2,000 pounds = 1 ton (T.)

Units of Time

60 seconds (sec.) = 1 minute (min.)

60 minutes = 1 hour (hr.)

24 hours = 1 day

7 days = 1 week

52 weeks = 1 year (yr.)

12 months = 1 year

365 days = 1 year

*Notice that ounces are used to measure the dimensions of both volume and weight.

Converting Units

When performing mathematical operations, it may be necessary to convert units of measure to simplify a problem. Units of measure are converted by using either multiplication or division.

- To convert from a larger unit into a smaller unit, *multiply* the given number of larger units by the number of smaller units in only one of the larger units:

(given number of the larger units) $\times$ (the number of smaller units per larger unit) = answer in smaller units

For example, to find the number of inches in five feet, multiply 5, the number of larger units, by 12, the number of inches in one foot:

5 feet = _?_ inches

5 feet $\times$ 12 (the number of inches in a single foot) = 60 inches: $5 \text{ ft.} \times \frac{12 \text{ in.}}{1 \text{ ft.}} = 60 \text{ in.}$

Therefore, there are 60 inches in five feet.

Example

Change 3.5 tons to pounds.

3.5 tons = _?_ pounds

$3.5 \text{ tons} \times \frac{2{,}000 \text{ pounds}}{1 \text{ ton}} = 7{,}000 \text{ pounds}$

Therefore, there are 7,000 pounds in 3.5 tons.

- To change a smaller unit to a larger unit, *divide* the given number of smaller units by the number of smaller units in only one of the larger units:

$$\frac{\text{given number of smaller units}}{\text{the number of smaller units per larger unit}} = \text{answer in larger units}$$

For example, to find the number of pints in 64 ounces, divide 64, the number of smaller units, by 16, the number of ounces in one pint.

64 ounces = _?_ pints

$\frac{64 \text{ ounces}}{16 \text{ ounces per pint}} = 4 \text{ pints}$

Therefore, 64 ounces equals four pints.

Example

Change 32 ounces to pounds.

32 ounces = _?_ pounds

$\frac{32 \text{ ounces}}{16 \text{ ounces per pound}} = 2 \text{ pounds}$

Therefore, 32 ounces equals two pounds.

Basic Operations with Measurement

You may need to add, subtract, multiply, and divide with measurement. The mathematical rules needed for each of these operations with measurement follow.

Addition with Measurements

To add measurements, follow these two steps:

1. Add like units.
2. Simplify the answer by converting smaller units into larger units when possible.

Example

Add 4 pounds 5 ounces to 20 ounces.

$$
\begin{array}{ll}
4 \text{ lb. } 5 \text{ oz.} & \text{Be sure to add ounces to ounces.} \\
\underline{+ \quad 20 \text{ oz.}} & \\
4 \text{ lb. } 25 \text{ oz.} &
\end{array}
$$

Because 25 ounces is more than 16 ounces (1 pound), simplify by dividing by 16:

$$
\begin{array}{r}
1 \text{ lb. r}9 \text{ oz.} \\
16 \text{ oz.}\overline{)25 \text{ oz.}} \\
\underline{-16 \text{ oz.}} \\
9 \text{ oz.}
\end{array}
$$

Then add the 1 pound to the 4 pounds:

4 pounds 25 ounces = 4 pounds + 1 pound 9 ounces = 5 pounds 9 ounces

Subtraction with Measurements

1. Subtract like units if possible.
2. If not, regroup units to allow for subtraction.
3. Write the answer in simplest form.

For example, 6 pounds 2 ounces subtracted from 9 pounds 10 ounces.

$$
\begin{array}{ll}
9 \text{ lb. } 10 \text{ oz.} & \text{Subtract ounces from ounces.} \\
\underline{- 6 \text{ lb. } 2 \text{ oz.}} & \text{Then subtract pounds from pounds.} \\
3 \text{ lb. } 8 \text{ oz.} &
\end{array}
$$

Sometimes, it is necessary to regroup units when subtracting.

Example

Subtract 3 yards 2 feet from 5 yards 1 foot.

Because 2 feet cannot be taken from 1 foot, regroup 1 yard from the 5 yards and convert the 1 yard to 3 feet. Add 3 feet to 1 foot. Then subtract feet from feet and yards from yards:

$$\begin{array}{r} \overset{4}{\cancel{5}} \text{ yd. } \overset{4}{\cancel{1}} \text{ ft.} \\ - \quad 3 \text{ yd. } 2 \text{ ft.} \\ \hline 1 \text{ yd. } 2 \text{ ft.} \end{array}$$

Therefore, 5 yards 1 foot − 3 yards 2 feet = 1 yard 2 feet.

Multiplication with Measurements

1. Multiply like units if units are involved.
2. Simplify the answer.

Example
Multiply 5 feet 7 inches by 3.

$$\begin{array}{r} 5 \text{ ft. } 7 \text{ in.} \\ \times \qquad 3 \\ \hline 15 \text{ ft. } 21 \text{ in.} \end{array}$$

Multiply 7 inches by 3, then multiply 5 feet by 3. Keep the units separate.

Because 12 inches = 1 foot, simplify 21 inches.

15 ft. 21 in. = 15 ft. + 1 ft. 9 in. = 16 ft. 9 in.

Example
Multiply 9 feet by 4 yards.

First, decide on a common unit: either change the 9 feet to yards, or change the 4 yards to feet. Both options are explained below:

Option 1:
To change yards to feet, multiply the number of feet in a yard (3) by the number of yards in this problem (4).

    3 feet in a yard • 4 yards = 12 feet

Then multiply: 9 feet × 12 feet = 108 square feet.

(Note: feet • feet = square feet = ft.^{2})

Option 2:
To change feet to yards, divide the number of feet given (9), by the number of feet in a yard (3).

    9 feet ÷ 3 feet in a yard = 3 yards

Then multiply 3 yards by 4 yards = 12 square yards.

(Note: yards • yards = square yards = yd.^{2})

Division with Measurements

1. Divide into the larger units first.
2. Convert the remainder to the smaller unit.
3. Add the converted remainder to the existing smaller unit, if any.
4. Divide into smaller units.
5. Write the answer in simplest form.

Example

Divide 5 quarts 4 ounces by 4.

1. Divide into the larger unit:

$$
\begin{array}{r}
1 \text{ qt. r1 qt.} \\
4\overline{)5 \text{ qt.}} \\
-4 \text{ qt.} \\
\hline
1 \text{ qt.}
\end{array}
$$

2. Convert the remainder:

   1 qt. = 32 oz.

3. Add remainder to original smaller unit:

   32 oz. + 4 oz. = 36 oz.

4. Divide into smaller units:

   36 oz. ÷ 4 = 9 oz.

5. Write the answer in simplest form:

   1 qt. 9 oz.

Metric Measurements

The metric system is an international system of measurement also called the **decimal system**. Converting units in the metric system is much easier than converting units in the customary system of measurement. However, making conversions between the two systems is much more difficult. The basic units of the metric system are the meter, gram, and liter. Here is a general idea of how the two systems compare:

METRIC SYSTEM	CUSTOMARY SYSTEM
1 meter	A meter is a little more than a yard; it is equal to about 39 inches.
1 gram	A gram is a very small unit of weight; there are about 30 grams in one ounce.
1 liter	A liter is a little more than a quart.

Prefixes are attached to the basic metric units to indicate the amount of each unit. For example, the prefix *deci* means one-tenth ($\frac{1}{10}$); therefore, one decigram is one-tenth of a gram, and one decimeter is one-tenth of a meter. The following six prefixes can be used with every metric unit:

KILO	HECTO	DEKA	DECI	CENTI	MILLI
(k)	(h)	(dk)	(d)	(c)	(m)
1,000	100	10	$\frac{1}{10}$	$\frac{1}{100}$	$\frac{1}{1,000}$

Examples

- 1 hectometer = 1 hm = 100 meters
- 1 millimeter = 1 mm = $\frac{1}{1,000}$ meter = .001 meter
- 1 dekagram = 1 dkg = 10 grams
- 1 centiliter = 1 cL* = $\frac{1}{100}$ liter = .01 liter
- 1 kilogram = 1 kg = 1,000 grams
- 1 deciliter = 1 dL* = $\frac{1}{10}$ liter = .1 liter

*Notice that liter is abbreviated with a capital letter—*L*.

The following chart illustrates some common relationships used in the metric system:

LENGTH	WEIGHT	VOLUME
1 km = 1,000 m	1 kg = 1,000 g	1 kL = 1,000 L
1 m = .001 km	1 g = .001 kg	1 L = .001 kL
1 m = 100 cm	1 g = 100 cg	1 L = 100 cL
1 cm = .01 m	1 cg = .01 g	1 cL = .01 L
1 m = 1,000 mm	1 g = 1,000 mg	1 L = 1,000 mL
1 mm = .001 m	1 mg = .001 g	1 mL = .001 L

Conversions within the Metric System

An easy way to do conversions with the metric system is to move the decimal point either to the right or to the left, because the conversion factor is always ten or a power of ten. Remember, when changing from a large unit to a smaller unit, multiply. When changing from a small unit to a larger unit, divide.

Making Easy Conversions within the Metric System

When multiplying by a power of ten, move the decimal point to the right, because the number becomes larger. When dividing by a power of ten, move the decimal point to the left, because the number becomes smaller.

To change from a larger unit to a smaller unit, move the decimal point to the right.

$\rightarrow$

kilo hecto deka UNIT deci centi milli

$\leftarrow$

An easy way to remember the metric prefixes is to remember the mnemonic: "King Henry Died Of Drinking Chocolate Milk." The first letter of each word represents a corresponding metric heading from Kilo down to Milli: "King"—Kilo, "Henry"—Hecto, "Died"—Deka, "Of"—Original Unit, "Drinking"—Deci, "Chocolate"—Centi, and "Milk"—Milli.

To change from a smaller unit to a larger unit, move the decimal point to the left.

Example

Change 520 grams to kilograms.

1. Be aware that changing meters to kilometers is going from small units to larger units and, thus, requires that the decimal point move to the left.
2. Beginning at the unit (for grams), note that the kilo heading is three places away. Therefore, the decimal point will move three places to the left.

k h dk unit d c m

3. Move the decimal point from the end of 520 to the left three places.
520
←
.520
Place the decimal point before the 5: .520
The answer is 520 grams = .520 kilograms.

Example

Ron's supply truck can hold a total of 20,000 kilograms. If he exceeds that limit, he must buy stabilizers for the truck that cost $12.80 each. Each stabilizer can hold 100 additional kilograms. If he wants to pack 22,300,000 grams of supplies, how much money will he have to spend on the stabilizers?

1. First, change 22,300,000 grams to kilograms.

kg hg dkg g dg cg mg

2. Move the decimal point three places to the left: 22,300,000 g = 22,300.000 kg = 22,300 kg.
3. Subtract to find the amount over the limit: 22,300 kg − 20,000 kg = 2,300 kg.
4. Because each stabilizer holds 100 kilograms and the supplies exceed the weight limit of the truck by 2,300 kilograms, Ron must purchase 23 stabilizers: 2,300 kg ÷ 100 kg per stabilizer = 23 stabilizers.
5. Each stabilizer costs $12.80, so multiply $12.80 by 23: $12.80 × 23 = $294.40.

▶ Algebra

This section will help in mastering algebraic equations by reviewing variables, cross multiplication, algebraic fractions, reciprocal rules, and exponents. Algebra is arithmetic using letters, called **variables**, in place of numbers. By using variables, the general relationships among numbers can be easier to see and understand.

Algebra Terminology

A **term** of a polynomial is an expression that is composed of variables and their exponents, and coefficients. A **variable** is a letter that represents an unknown number. Variables are frequently used in equations, in formulas, and in mathematical rules to help illustrate numerical relationships. When a number is placed next to a variable, indicating multiplication, the number is said to be the **coefficient** of the variable.

Examples

$8c$ 8 is the coefficient to the variable c.

$6ab$ 6 is the coefficient to both variables, a and b.

Three Kinds of Polynomials

- **Monomials** are single terms that are composed of variables and their exponents and a positive or negative coefficient. The following are examples of monomials: x, $5x$, $-6y^3$, $10x^2y$, 7, 0.
- **Binomials** are two nonlike monomial terms separated by + or − signs. The following are examples of binomials: $x + 2$, $3x^2 - 5x$, $-3xy^2 + 2xy$.
- **Trinomials** are three nonlike monomial terms separated by + or − signs. The following are examples of trinomials: $x^2 + 2x - 1$, $3x^2 - 5x + 4$, $-3xy^2 + 2xy - 6x$.
- Monomials, binomials, and trinomials are all examples of **polynomials**, but we usually reserve the word *polynomial* for expressions formed by more than three terms.
- The **degree** of a polynomial is the largest sum of the terms' exponents.

Examples

- The degree of the trinomial $x^2 + 2x - 1$ is 2, because the x^2 term has the highest exponent of 2.
- The degree of the binomial $x + 2$ is 1, because the x term has the highest exponent of 1.
- The degree of the binomial $-3x^4y^2 + 2xy$ is 6, because the x^4y^2 term has the highest exponent sum of 6.

Like Terms

If two or more terms have exactly the same variable(s), and these variables are raised to exactly the same exponents, they are said to be **like terms**. Like terms can be simplified when added and subtracted.

Examples

$7x + 3x = 10x$

$6y^2 - 4y^2 = 2y^2$

However, $3cd^2 + 5c^2d$ cannot be simplified. Since the exponent of 2 is on d in $3cd^2$ and on c in $5c^2d$, they are not like terms.

The process of adding and subtracting like terms is called **combining** like terms. It is important to combine like terms carefully, making sure that *the variables are exactly the same.*

Algebraic Expressions

An algebraic expression is a combination of monomials and operations. The difference between algebraic expressions and algebraic equations is that algebraic expressions are evaluated at different given values for variables, while algebraic equations are solved to determine the value of the variable that makes the equation a true statement.

There is very little difference between expressions and equations, because equations are nothing more than two expressions set equal to each other. Their usage is subtly different.

Example
A mobile phone company charges a $39.99 a month flat fee for the first 600 minutes of calls, with a charge of $.55 for each minute thereafter.

Write an algebraic expression for the cost of a month's mobile phone bill:
$39.99 + $.55$x$, where x represents the number of additional minutes used.

Write an equation for the cost (C) of a month's mobile phone bill:
$C = $39.99 + $.55$x$, where x represents the number of additional minutes used.

In the preceding example, you might use the expression $39.99 + $.55$x$ to determine the cost if you are given the value of x by substituting the value for x. You could also use the equation $C = $39.99 + $.55$x$ in the same way, but you can also use the equation to determine the value of x if you were given the cost.

Simplifying and Evaluating Algebraic Expressions

We can use the mobile phone company example above to illustrate how to simplify algebraic expressions. Algebraic expressions are evaluated by a two-step process: substituting the given value(s) into the expression, and then simplifying the expression by following the order of operations (PEMDAS).

Example
Using the cost expression $39.99 + $.55$x$, determine the total cost of a month's mobile phone bill if the owner made 700 minutes of calls.
Let x represent the number of minutes over 600 used, so in order to find out the difference, subtract $700 - 600$; $x = 100$ minutes over 600 used.

Substitution: Replace x with its value, using parentheses around the value.

$39.99 + $.55$x$

$39.99 + $.55(100)

Evaluation: PEMDAS tells us to evaluate parentheses and exponents first. There is no operation to perform in the parentheses, and there are no exponents, so the next step is to multiply, and then add.

$39.99 + $.55(100)

$39.99 + $55 = $94.99

The cost of the mobile phone bill for the month is $94.99.

You can evaluate algebraic expressions that contain any number of variables, as long as you are given all of the values for all of the variables.

Simple Rules for Working with Linear Equations

A linear equation is an equation whose variables' highest exponent is 1. It is also called a **first-degree equation**. An equation is solved by finding the value of an unknown variable.

1. The equal sign separates an equation into two sides.
2. Whenever an operation is performed on one side, the same operation must be performed on the other side.
3. The first goal is to get all of the variable terms on one side and all of the numbers (called **constants**) on the other side. This is accomplished by *undoing* the operations that are attaching numbers to the variable, thereby isolating the variable. The operations are always done in reverse PEMDAS order: start by adding/subtracting, then multiply/divide.
4. The final step often will be to divide each side by the coefficient, the number in front of the variable, leaving the variable alone and equal to a number.

Example

$$5m + 8 = 48$$
$$-8 = -8$$
$$\frac{5m}{5} = \frac{40}{5}$$
$$m = 8$$

Undo the addition of 8 by subtracting 8 from both sides of the equation. Then undo the multiplication by 5 by dividing by 5 on both sides of the equation. The variable, m, is now isolated on the left side of the equation, and its value is 8.

Checking Solutions to Equations

To check an equation, substitute the value of the variable into the original equation.

Example

To check the solution of the previous equation, substitute the number 8 for the variable m in $5m + 8 = 48$.

$$5(8) + 8 = 48$$
$$40 + 8 = 48$$
$$48 = 48$$

Because this statement is true, the answer $m = 8$ must be correct.

Isolating Variables Using Fractions

Working with equations that contain fractions is almost exactly the same as working with equations that do not contain variables, except for the final step. The final step when an equation has no fractions is to divide each side by the coefficient. When the coefficient of the variable is a fraction, you will instead multiply both sides by the reciprocal of the coefficient. Technically, you could still divide both sides by the coefficient, but that involves division of fractions, which can be trickier.

Example

$$\frac{2}{3}m + \frac{1}{2} = 12$$
$$-\frac{1}{2} = -\frac{1}{2}$$
$$\frac{2}{3}m = 11\frac{1}{2}$$
$$\frac{3}{2} \cdot \frac{2}{3}m = 11\frac{1}{2} \cdot \frac{3}{2}$$
$$\frac{3}{2} \cdot \frac{2}{3}m = \frac{23}{2} \cdot \frac{3}{2}$$
$$m = \frac{69}{4}$$

Undo the addition of $\frac{1}{2}$ by subtracting $\frac{1}{2}$ from both sides of the equation. Multiply both sides by the reciprocal of the coefficient. Convert the $11\frac{1}{2}$ to an improper fraction to facilitate multiplication. The variable m is now isolated on the left side of the equation, and its value is $\frac{69}{4}$.

Equations with More than One Variable

Equations can have more than one variable. Each variable represents a different value, although it is possible that the variables have the same value.

Remember that like terms have the same variable and exponent. All of the rules for working with variables apply in equations that contain more than one variable, but you must remember not to combine terms that are not alike.

Equations with more than one variable cannot be solved, because if there is more than one variable in an equation there is usually an infinite number of values for the variables that would make the equation true. Instead, we are often required to "solve for a variable," which instead means to isolate that variable on one side of the equation.

Example

Solve for y in the equation $2x + 3y = 5$.

There are an infinite number of values for x and y that that satisfy the equation. Instead, we are asked to isolate y on one side of the equation.

$$2x + 3y = 5$$
$$-2x = -2x$$
$$\frac{3y}{3} = \frac{-2x + 5}{3}$$
$$y = \frac{-2x + 5}{3}$$

Cross Multiplying

Because algebra uses percents and proportions, it is necessary to learn how to cross multiply. You can solve an equation that sets one fraction equal to another by **cross multiplication**. Cross multiplication involves setting the cross products of opposite pairs of terms equal to each other.

Example

$$\frac{x}{10} = \frac{70}{100}$$

$$100x = 700$$

$$\frac{100x}{100} = \frac{700}{100}$$

$$x = 7$$

Algebraic Fractions

Working with algebraic fractions is very similar to working with fractions in arithmetic. The difference is that algebraic fractions contain algebraic expressions in the numerator and/or denominator.

Example

A hotel currently has only one-fifth of its rooms available. If x represents the total number of rooms in the hotel, find an expression for the number of rooms that will be available if another tenth of the total rooms are reserved.

Because x represents the total number of rooms, $\frac{x}{5}$ (or $\frac{1}{5}x$) represents the number of available rooms. One-tenth of the total rooms in the hotel would be represented by the fraction $\frac{x}{10}$. To find the new number of available rooms, find the difference: $\frac{x}{5} - \frac{x}{10}$.
Write $\frac{x}{5} - \frac{x}{10}$ as a single fraction.

Just like in arithmetic, the first step is to find the LCD of 5 and 10, which is 10. Then change each fraction into an equivalent fraction that has 10 as a denominator.

$$\frac{x}{5} - \frac{x}{10} = \frac{x(2)}{5(2)} - \frac{x}{10}$$
$$= \frac{2x}{10} - \frac{x}{10}$$
$$= \frac{x}{10}$$

Therefore, $\frac{x}{10}$ rooms will be available after another tenth of the rooms are reserved.

Reciprocal Rules

There are special rules for the sum and difference of reciprocals. The reciprocal of 3 is $\frac{1}{3}$ and the reciprocal of x is $\frac{1}{x}$.

- If x and y are not 0, then $\frac{1}{x} + \frac{1}{y} = \frac{y}{xy} + \frac{x}{xy} = \frac{y+x}{xy}$.
- If x and y are not 0, then $\frac{1}{x} - \frac{1}{y} = \frac{y}{xy} - \frac{x}{xy} = \frac{y-x}{xy}$.

Translating Words into Numbers

The most important skill needed for word problems is being able to translate words into mathematical operations. The following will be helpful in achieving this goal by providing common examples of English phrases and their mathematical equivalents.

Phrases meaning addition: *increased by; sum of; more than; exceeds by.*

Examples

A number increased by five: $x + 5$.

The sum of two numbers: $x + y$.

Ten more than a number: $x + 10$.

Phrases meaning subtraction: *decreased by; difference of; less/fewer than; diminished by.*

Examples

Ten less than a number: $x - 10$.

The difference of two numbers: $x - y$.

Phrases meaning multiplication: *times; times the sum/difference; product; of.*

Examples

Three times a number: $3x$.

Twenty percent of 50: $20\% \times 50$.

Five times the sum of a number and three: $5(x + 3)$.

Phrases meaning "equals": *is*; *result is.*

Examples
Fifteen is 14 plus 1: $15 = 14 + 1$.
Ten more than two times a number is 15: $2x + 10 = 15$.

Assigning Variables in Word Problems
It may be necessary to create and assign variables in a word problem. To do this, first identify any knowns and unknowns. The known may not be a specific numerical value, but the problem should indicate something about its value. Then let x represent the unknown you know the least about.

Examples
Max has worked for three more years than Ricky.
Unknown: Ricky's work experience $= x$
Known: Max's experience is three more years $= x + 3$

Heidi made twice as many sales as Rebecca.
Unknown: number of sales Rebecca made $= x$
Known: number of sales Heidi made is twice Rebecca's amount $= 2x$

There are six less than four times the number of pens than pencils.
Unknown: the number of pencils $= x$
Known: the number of pens $= 4x - 6$

Todd has assembled five more than three times the number of cabinets that Andrew has.
Unknown: the number of cabinets Andrew has assembled $= x$
Known: the number of cabinets Todd has assembled is five more than three times the number Andrew has assembled $= 3x + 5$

Percentage Problems
To solve percentage problems, determine what information has been given in the problem and fill this information into the following template:

_____ is _____% of _____

Then translate this information into a one-step equation and solve. In translating, remember that *is* translates to = and *of* translates to ×. Use a variable to represent the unknown quantity.

Examples

Finding a percentage of a given number:

In a new housing development there will be 50 houses. 40% of the houses must be completed in the first stage. How many houses are in the first stage?

1. Translate.

_____ is 40% of 50.

x is .40 × 50.

2. Solve.

x = .40 × 50

x = 20

20 is 40% of 50. There are 20 houses in the first stage.

Finding a number when a percentage is given:

40% of the cars on the lot have been sold. If 24 were sold, how many total cars were there on the lot originally?

1. Translate.

24 is 40% of _____.

24 = .40 × x.

2. Solve.

$$\frac{24}{.40} = \frac{.40x}{.40}$$

60 = x

24 is 40% of 60. There were 60 total cars on the lot.

Finding what percentage one number is of another:

Matt has 75 employees. He is going to give 15 of them raises. What percent of the employees will receive raises?

1. Translate.

15 is _____% of 75.

15 = x × 75.

2. Solve.

$$\frac{15}{75} = \frac{75x}{75}$$

$.20 = x$

$20\% = x$

15 is 20% of 75. Therefore, 20% of the employees will receive raises.

Problems Involving Ratio

A **ratio** is a comparison of two quantities measured in the same units. It is symbolized by the use of a colon—$x{:}y$. Ratios can also be expressed as fractions ($\frac{x}{y}$) or using words (x to y).

Ratio problems are solved using the concept of multiples.

Example

A bag contains 60 screws and nails. The ratio of the number of screws to nails is 7:8. How many of each kind are there in the bag?

From the problem, it is known that 7 and 8 share a multiple and that the sum of their product is 60. Whenever you see the word *ratio* in a problem, place an "x" next to each of the numbers in the ratio, and those are your unknowns.

Let $7x =$ the number of screws.

Let $8x =$ the number of nails.

Write and solve the following equation:

$7x + 8x = 60$

$$\frac{15x}{15} = \frac{60}{15}$$

$x = 4$

Therefore, there are $(7)(4) = 28$ screws and $(8)(4) = 32$ nails.

Check: $28 + 32 = 60$ screws, $\frac{28}{32} = \frac{7}{8}$.

Problems Involving Variation

Variation is a term referring to a constant ratio in the change of a quantity.

- Two quantities are said to vary directly if their ratios are constant. Both variables change in an equal direction. In other words, two quantities vary directly if an increase in one causes an increase in the other. This is also true if a decrease in one causes a decrease in the other.

Example

If it takes 300 new employees a total of 58.5 hours to train, how many hours of training will it take for 800 employees?

Because each employee needs about the same amount of training, you know that they vary directly. Therefore, you can set the problem up the following way:

$$\frac{\text{employees}}{\text{hours}} \rightarrow \frac{300}{58.5} = \frac{800}{x}$$

Cross multiply to solve:

$$(800)(58.5) = 300x$$
$$\frac{46,800}{300} = \frac{300x}{300}$$
$$156 = x$$

Therefore, it would take 156 hours to train 800 employees.

- Two quantities are said to vary inversely if their products are constant. The variables change in opposite directions. This means that as one quantity increases, the other decreases, or as one decreases, the other increases.

Example
If two people plant a field in six days, how many days will it take six people to plant the same field? (Assume each person is working at the same rate.)

As the number of people planting increases, the days needed to plant decreases. Therefore, the relationship between the number of people and days varies inversely. Because the field remains constant, the two products can be set equal to each other.

2 people $\times$ 6 days = 6 people $\times$ x days

$$2 \times 6 = 6x$$
$$\frac{12}{6} = \frac{6x}{6}$$
$$2 = x$$

Thus, it would take six people two days to plant the same field.

Rate Problems
In general, there are three different types of rate problems likely to be encountered in the workplace: cost per unit, movement, and work output. **Rate** is defined as a comparison of two quantities with different units of measure.

$$\text{rate} = \frac{x \text{ units}}{y \text{ units}}$$

Examples
$$\frac{\text{dollars}}{\text{hour}}, \frac{\text{cost}}{\text{pound}}, \frac{\text{miles}}{\text{hour}}$$

Cost per Unit

Some problems will require the calculation of unit cost.

Example

If 100 square feet cost $1,000, how much does 1 square foot cost?

$$\frac{\text{total cost}}{\text{\# of square feet}} = \frac{\$1,000}{100 \text{ ft.}^2}$$
$$= \$10 \text{ per square foot}$$

Movement

In working with movement problems, it is important to use the following formula:

(rate)(time) = distance

Example

A courier traveling at 15 mph traveled from his base to a company in $\frac{1}{4}$ of an hour less than it took when the courier traveled at 12 mph. How far away was his drop-off?

First, write what is known and unknown.

Unknown: time for courier traveling 12 mph = x

Known: time for courier traveling 15 mph = $x - \frac{1}{4}$.

Then, use the formula (rate)(time) = distance to find expressions for the distance traveled at each rate:

12 mph for x hours = a distance of $12x$ miles

15 mph for $x - \frac{1}{4}$ mph = a distance of $15x - \frac{15}{4}$ miles.

The distance traveled is the same; therefore, make the two expressions equal to each other:

$$12x = 15x - 3.75$$
$$-15x = -15x$$
$$\frac{-3x}{-3} = \frac{-3.75}{-3}$$
$$x = 1.25$$

Be careful: 1.25 is not the distance; it is the time. Now you must plug the time into the formula (rate)(time) = distance. Either rate can be used.

$12x$ = distance

$12(1.25)$ = distance

15 miles = distance

Work Output

Work-output problems are word problems that deal with the rate of work. The following formula can be used on these problems:

(rate of work)(time worked) = job or part of job completed

Example

Danette can wash and wax two cars in six hours, and Judy can wash and wax the same two cars in four hours. If Danette and Judy work together, how long will it take to wash and wax one car?

Because Danette can wash and wax two cars in six hours, her rate of work is $\frac{2 \text{ cars}}{6 \text{ hours}}$, or one car every three hours. Judy's rate of work is $\frac{2 \text{ cars}}{4 \text{ hours}}$, or one car every two hours. In this problem, making a chart will help:

	Rate	Time	=	Part of job completed
Danette	$\frac{1}{3}$	x	=	$\frac{1}{3}x$
Judy	$\frac{1}{2}$	x	=	$\frac{1}{2}x$

Because they are both working on only one car, you can set the equation equal to one: Danette's part + Judy's part = 1 car:

$$\frac{1}{3}x + \frac{1}{2}x = 1$$

Solve by using 6 as the LCD for 3 and 2 and clear the fractions by multiplying by the LCD:

$$6(\tfrac{1}{3}x) + 6(\tfrac{1}{2}x) = 6(1)$$
$$2x + 3x = 6$$
$$\frac{5x}{5} = \frac{6}{5}$$
$$x = 1\tfrac{1}{5}$$

Thus, it will take Judy and Danette $1\frac{1}{5}$ hours to wash and wax one car.

Patterns and Functions

The ability to detect patterns in numbers is a very important mathematical skill. Patterns exist everywhere in nature, business, and finance.

When you are asked to find a pattern in a series of numbers, look to see if there is some common number you can add, subtract, multiply, or divide each number in the pattern by to give you the next number in the series.

For example, in the sequence 5, 8, 11, 14 . . . you can add 3 to each number in the sequence to get the next number in the sequence. The next number in the sequence is 17.

Example

What is the next number in the sequence $\frac{3}{4}$, 3, 12, 48?

Each number in the sequence can be multiplied by the number 4 to get the next number in the sequence: $\frac{3}{4} \times 4 = 3$, $3 \times 4 = 12$, $12 \times 4 = 48$, so the next number in the sequence is $48 \times 4 = 192$.

Sometimes it is not that simple. You may need to look for a combination of multiplying and adding, dividing and subtracting, or some combination of other operations.

Example

What is the next number in the sequence 0, 1, 2, 5, 26?

Keep trying various operations until you find one that works. In this case, the correct procedure is to square the term and add 1: $0^2 + 1 = 1$, $1^2 + 1 = 2$, $2^2 + 1 = 5$, $5^2 + 1 = 26$, so the next number in the sequence is $26^2 + 1 = 677$.

Properties of Functions

A **function** is a relationship between two variables x and y where for each value of x, there is one and only one value of y. Functions can be represented in four ways:

1. a table or chart
2. an equation
3. a word problem
4. a graph

For example, the following four representations are equivalent to the same function:

Word Problem
Javier has one more than two times the
number of books Susanna has.

Equation

$y = 2x + 1$

Graph

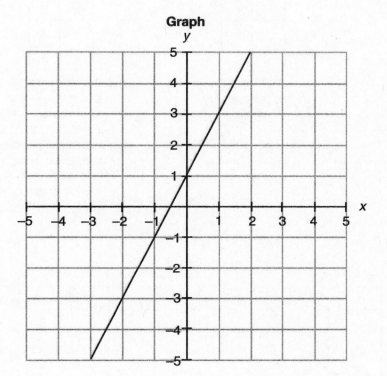

Table

x	y
−3	−5
−2	−3
−1	−1
0	1
1	3
2	5

Helpful hints for determining if a relationship is a function:

- If you can isolate y in terms of x using only one equation, it **is** a function.
- If the equation contains y^2, it will **not** be a function.
- If you can draw a vertical line anywhere on a graph such that it touches the graph in more than one place, it is **not** a function.
- If there is a value for x that has more than one y-value assigned to it, it is **not** a function.

x	y
5	2
3	−1
2	0
6	1
5	4

In this table, the x-value of 5 has **two** corresponding y-values, 2 and 4. Therefore, it is **not** a function.

x	y
−2	5
−1	6
0	7
1	8
2	9

In this table, every x-value {−2, −1, 0, 1, 2, 3} has **one** corresponding y-value. This **is** a function.

x	y
−2	3
−1	3
0	3
1	3
2	3

In this table, every x-value {−2, −1, 0, 1, 2, 3} has **one** corresponding y-value, even though that value is 3 in every case. This **is** a function.

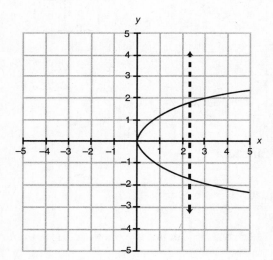

In this graph, there is at least one vertical line that can be drawn (the dotted line) that intersects the graph in more than one place. Therefore, this is **not** a function.

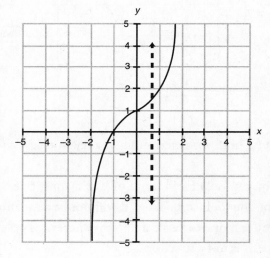

In this graph, there is no vertical line that can be drawn that intersects the graph in more than one place. This **is** a function.

Examples

$x = 5$ Contains no variable y, so you cannot isolate y. This is **not** a function.

$2x + 3y = 5$ Isolate y:

$$2x + 3y = \quad 5$$
$$\underline{-2x \qquad\quad -2x}$$
$$\frac{3y}{3} = \frac{-2x + 5}{3}$$
$$y = -\frac{2}{3x} + \frac{5}{3}$$

This is a **linear function**, of the form $y = mx + b$.

$x^2 + y^2 = 36$ Contains y^2, so it is **not** a function.

$|y| = 5$ There is no way to isolate y with a single equation; therefore, it is **not** a function.

Function Notation

Instead of using the variable y, often you will see the variable $f(x)$. This is shorthand for "function of x" to automatically indicate that an equation is a function. This can be confusing; $f(x)$ does not indicate two variables f and x multiplied together; it is a notation that means the single variable y.

Although it may seem that $f(x)$ is not an efficient shorthand (it has more characters than y), it is very eloquent way to indicate that you are being given expressions to evaluate. For example, if you are given the equation $f(x) = 5x - 2$, and you are being asked to determine the value of the equation at $x = 2$, you need to write "evaluate the equation $f(x) = 5x - 2$ when $x = 2$." This is very wordy. With function notation, you only need to write "determine $f(2)$." The x in $f(x)$ is replaced with a 2, indicating that the value of x is 2. This means that $f(2) = 5(2) - 2 = 10 - 2 = 8$.

All you need to do when given an equation $f(x)$ and told to evaluate $f(value)$ is to replace the *value* for every occurrence of x in the equation.

Example

Given the equation $f(x) = 2x^2 + 3x + 1$, determine $f(0)$ and $f(-1)$.

$f(0)$ means replace the value 0 for every occurrence of x in the equation and evaluate.
$$f(0) = 2(0)^2 + 3(0) + 1$$
$$= 0 + 0 + 1$$
$$= 1$$

$f(-1)$ means replace the value -1 for every occurrence of x in the equation and evaluate.
$$f(0) = 2(-1)^2 + 3(-1) + 1$$
$$= 2(1) + -3 + 1$$
$$= 2 - 3 + 1$$
$$= 0$$

Families of Functions

There are a number of different types, or families, of functions. Each function family has a certain equation and its graph takes on a certain appearance. You can tell what type of function an equation is by just looking at the equation or its graph.

These are the shapes that various functions have. They can appear thinner or wider, higher or lower, or upside down.

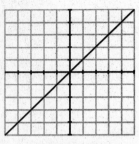

Linear Function
$f(x) = mx + b$
$y = mx + b$

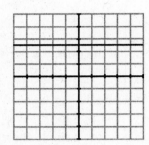

Constant Function
$f(x) = c$
$y = c$
The equation contains no variable x.

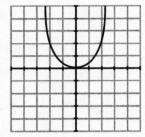

Quadratic Function
$f(x) = ax^2 + bx + c$
$y = ax^2 + bx + c$
This is the function name for a parabola.

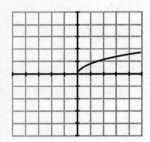

Square Root Function
The equation has to contain a square root symbol.

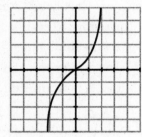

Cubic Function
$f(x) = ax^3 + bx^2 + cx + d$
$y = ax^3 + bx^2 + cx + d$

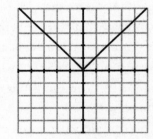

Absolute Value Function
The equation has to have an absolute value symbol in it.

Systems of Equations

A system of equations is a set of two or more equations with the same solution. Two methods for solving a system of equations are substitution and elimination.

Substitution

Substitution involves solving for one variable in terms of another and then substituting that expression into the second equation.

Example
$2p + q = 11$ and $p + 2q = 13$

- First, choose an equation and rewrite it, isolating one variable in terms of the other. It does not matter which variable you choose.

  $2p + q = 11$ becomes $q = 11 - 2p$.

- Second, substitute $11 - 2p$ for q in the other equation and solve:

  $p + 2(11 - 2p) = 13$

  $p + 22 - 4p = 13$

  $22 - 3p = 13$

  $22 = 13 + 3p$

  $9 = 3p$

  $p = 3$

- Now substitute this answer into either original equation for p to find q.

  $2p + q = 11$

  $2(3) + q = 11$

  $6 + q = 11$

  $q = 5$

- Thus, $p = 3$ and $q = 5$.

Elimination

The elimination method involves writing one equation over another and then adding or subtracting the like terms on the same sides of the equal sign so that one letter is eliminated.

Example
$x - 9 = 2y$ and $x - 3 = 5y$

- Rewrite each equation in the same form.

  $x - 9 = 2y$ becomes $x - 2y = 9$ and $x - 3 = 5y$ becomes $x - 5y = 3$.

- If you subtract the two equations, the "x" terms will be eliminated, leaving only one variable:

  Subtract:

  $x - 2y = 9$

  $-(x - 5y = 3)$

  $\dfrac{3y}{3} = \dfrac{6}{3}$

  $y = 2$ is the answer.

- Substitute 2 for y in one of the original equations and solve for x.

$x - 9 = 2y$
$x - 9 = 2(2)$
$x - 9 = 4$
$x - 9 + 9 = 4 + 9$
$x = 13$

- The answer to the system of equations is $y = 2$ and $x = 13$.

If the variables do not have the same or opposite coefficients as in the preceding example, adding or subtracting will not eliminate a variable. In this situation, it is first necessary to multiply one or both of the equations by some constant or constants so that the coefficients of one of the variables are the same or opposite. There are many different ways you can choose to do this.

Example
$3x + y = 13$
$x + 6y = -7$

We need to multiply one or both of the equations by some constant that will give equal or opposite coefficients of one of the variable. One way to do this is to multiply every term in the second equation by −3.

$3x + y = 13$
$-3(x + 6y = -7) \rightarrow -3x - 18y = 21$

Now if you add the two equations, the "x" terms will be eliminated, leaving only one variable. Continue as in the preceding example.

$3x + y = 13$
$-3x - 18y = 21$
$\frac{-17y}{-17} = \frac{34}{-17}$
$y = -2$ is the answer.

- Substitute −2 for y in one of the original equations and solve for x.

$3x + y = 13$
$3x + (-2) = 13$
$3x + (-2) + -2 = 13 + -2$
$3x = 11$
$x = \frac{11}{3}$

- The answer to the system of equations is $y = -2$ and $x = \frac{11}{3}$.

Inequalities

Linear inequalities are solved in much the same way as simple equations. The most important difference is that when an inequality is multiplied or divided by a negative number, the inequality symbol changes direction.

Example

$$10 > 5 \qquad \text{so} \qquad (10)(-3) < (5)(-3)$$
$$-30 < -15$$

Solving Linear Inequalities

To solve a linear inequality, isolate the letter and solve the same way as you would in a linear equation. Remember to reverse the direction of the inequality sign if you divide or multiply both sides of the equation by a negative number.

Example

If $7 - 2x > 21$, find x.

- Isolate the variable.

$$7 - 2x > 21$$
$$\underline{-7 \qquad\quad -7}$$
$$-2x > 14$$

- Because you are dividing by a negative number, the inequality symbol changes direction.

$$\frac{-2x}{-2} > \frac{14}{-2}$$
$$x < -7$$

- The answer consists of all real numbers less than -7.

Solving Compound Inequalities

To solve an inequality that has the form $c < ax + b < d$, isolate the letter by performing the same operation on each part of the equation.

Example

If $-10 < -5y - 5 < 15$, find y.

- Add five to each member of the inequality.

$$-10 + 5 < -5y - 5 + 5 < 15 + 5 - 5 < -5y < 20$$

- Divide each term by -5, changing the direction of both inequality symbols:

$$\frac{-5}{-5} < -\frac{5y}{-5} < \frac{20}{-5} = 1 > y > -4$$

The solution consists of all real numbers less than 1 and greater than -4.

► Geometry

This section will familiarize you with the properties of angles, lines, polygons, triangles, and circles, as well as the formulas for area, volume, and perimeter.

Geometry is the study of shapes and the relationships among them. Basic concepts in geometry will be detailed and applied in this section. The study of geometry always begins with a look at basic vocabulary and concepts. Therefore, a list of definitions and important formulas is provided.

Geometry Terms

area	the space inside a two-dimensional figure
circumference	the distance around a circle
chord	a line segment that goes through a circle, with its endpoints on the circle
congruent	equal, in reference to lengths, measures of angles, or size of figures
diameter	a chord that goes directly through the center of a circle—the longest line segment that can be drawn in a circle
hypotenuse	the longest side of a right triangle, always opposite the right angle
leg	either of the two sides of a right triangle that make the right angle
perimeter	the distance around a figure
π (pi)	the ratio of any circle's circumference to its diameter (pi is an irrational number, but most of the time it is okay to approximate π with 3.14)
radius	a line segment from the center of a circle to a point on the circle (half of the diameter)
surface area	the sum of the areas of all of a three-dimensional figure's faces
volume	the space inside a three-dimensional figure

Coordinate Geometry

Coordinate geometry is a form of geometrical operations in relation to a coordinate plane. A **coordinate plane** is a grid of square boxes divided into four quadrants by both a horizontal *x*-axis and a vertical *y*-axis. These two axes intersect at one coordinate point, (0,0), the **origin**. A **coordinate point**, also called an **ordered pair**, is a specific point on the coordinate plane with the first number representing the horizontal placement and the second number representing the vertical placement. Coordinate points are given in the form of (*x,y*).

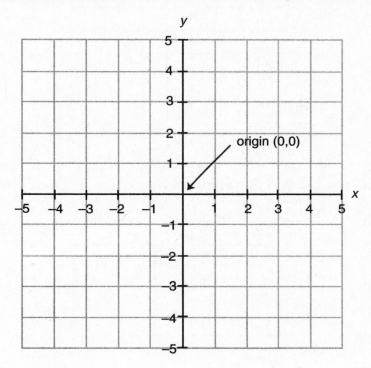

Graphing Ordered Pairs (Points)

- The *x*-coordinate is listed first in the ordered pair and tells you how many units to move to either the left or the right. If the *x*-coordinate is positive, move to the right. If the *x*-coordinate is negative, move to the left.
- The *y*-coordinate is listed second and tells you how many units to move up or down. If the *y*-coordinate is positive, move up. If the *y*-coordinate is negative, move down.

Example

Graph the following points: (2,3), (3,–2), (–2,3), and (–3,–2).

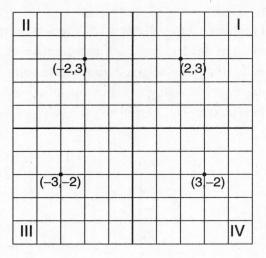

■ Notice that the graph is broken up into four quadrants with one point plotted in each one. Here is a chart to indicate which quadrants contain which ordered pairs based on their signs:

Points	Sign of Coordinates	Quadrant
(2,3)	(+,+)	I
(−2,3)	(−,+)	II
(−3,−2)	(−,−)	III
(3,−2)	(+,−)	IV

Lines, Line Segments, and Rays

A **line** is a straight geometric object that goes on forever in both directions. It is infinite in length, and is represented by a straight line with an arrow at both ends. Lines can be labeled with one letter (usually in italics) or with two capital letters near the arrows. **Line segments** are portions of lines. They have two endpoints and a definitive length. Line segments are named by their endpoints. **Rays** have an endpoint and continue straight in one direction. Rays are named by their endpoint and one point on the ray.

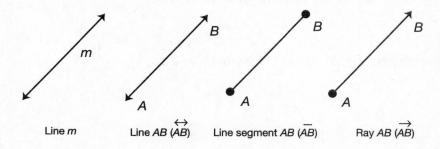

Line *m*   Line *AB* ($\overleftrightarrow{AB}$)   Line segment *AB* ($\overline{AB}$)   Ray *AB* ($\overrightarrow{AB}$)

Parallel and Perpendicular Lines

Parallel lines (or line segments) are a pair of lines that, if extended, would never intersect or meet. The symbol || is used to denote that two lines are parallel. **Perpendicular lines** (or line segments) are lines that intersect to form right angles, and are denoted with the symbol ⊥.

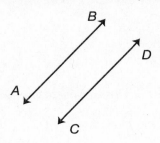

Parallel Lines *AB* and *CD*

$$\overleftrightarrow{AB} \parallel \overleftrightarrow{CD}$$

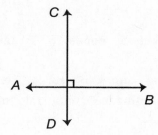

Parallel Lines *AB* and *CD*

$$\overleftrightarrow{AB} \perp \overleftrightarrow{CD}$$

Lengths of Horizontal and Vertical Segments

Two points with the same *y*-coordinate lie on the same horizontal line and two points with the same *x*-coordinate lie on the same vertical line. The distance between a horizontal or vertical segment can be found by taking the absolute value of the difference of the two points.

Example

Find the lengths of line segments $\overline{AB}$ and $\overline{BC}$.

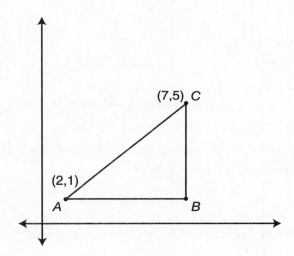

$$|2 - 7| = 5 = AB$$
$$|1 - 5| = 4 = BC$$

Distance of Coordinate Points

The distance between any two points is given by the formula $d = \sqrt{(x_2 - x_1)^2 + (y_2 - y_1)^2}$, where (x_1, y_1) represents the coordinates of one point and (x_2, y_2) is the other. The subscripts are used to differentiate between the two different coordinate pairs.

Example

Find the distance between points $A(-3,5)$ and $B(1,-4)$.

Let (x_1, y_1) represent point A and let (x_2, y_2) represent point B. This means that $x_1 = -3$, $y_1 = 5$, $x_2 = 1$, and $y_2 = -4$. Substituting these values into the formula gives us:

$$d = \sqrt{(x_2 - x_1)^2 + (y_2 - y_1)^2}$$
$$d = \sqrt{(-3 - 1)^2 + (5 - (-4))^2}$$
$$d = \sqrt{(-4)^2 + (9)^2}$$
$$d = \sqrt{16 + 81}$$
$$d = \sqrt{97}$$

Midpoint

The midpoint of a line segment is a point located at an equal distance from each endpoint. This point is in the exact center of the line segment, and is said to be **equidistant** from the segment's endpoints.

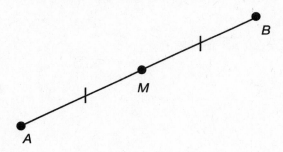

M is the midpoint of $\overline{AB}$

In coordinate geometry, the formula for finding the coordinates of the midpoint of a line segment whose endpoints are (x_1, y_1) and (x_2, y_2) is given by $M = (\frac{x_1 + x_2}{2}, \frac{y_1 + y_2}{2})$.

Example

Determine the midpoint of the line segment $\overline{AB}$ with $A(-3,5)$ and $B(1,-4)$.

Let (x_1, y_1) represent point A and let (x_2, y_2) represent point B. This means that $x_1 = -3$, $y_1 = 5$, $x_2 = 1$, and $y_2 = -4$. Substituting these values into the formula gives us:

$$M = (\frac{-3 + 1}{2}, \frac{5 + (-4)}{2})$$

$$M = (-\frac{2}{2}, \frac{1}{2})$$

$$M = (-1, \frac{1}{2})$$

Note: There is no such thing as the midpoint of a line, as lines are infinite in length.

Slope

The **slope** of a line (or line segment) is a numerical value given to show how steep a line is. A line or segment can have one of four types of slope:

1. A line with a **positive slope** increases from the bottom left to the upper right on a graph.
2. A line with a **negative slope** decreases from the upper left to the bottom right on a graph.
3. A horizontal line is said to have a **zero slope**.
4. A vertical line is said to have **no slope** (undefined).

Parallel lines have **equal slopes**.
Perpendicular lines have slopes that are negative reciprocals of each other.

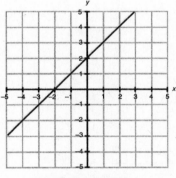

Positive slope

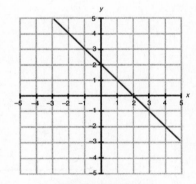

Negative slope

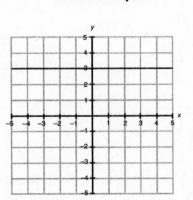

Zero slope

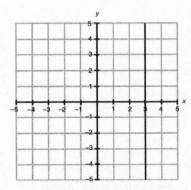

Undefined (no) slope

The slope of a line can be found if you know the coordinates of any two points that lie on the line. It does not matter which two points you use. It is found by writing the change in the y-coordinates of any two points on the line, over the change in the corresponding x-coordinates. (This is also known as the *rise* over the *run*.)

The formula for the slope of a line (or line segment) containing points (x_1, y_1) and (x_2, y_2): $m = \frac{y_2 - y_1}{x_2 - x_1}$.

Example

Determine the slope of the line joining points $A(-3,5)$ and $B(1,-4)$.

Let (x_1, y_1) represent point A and let (x_2, y_2) represent point B. This means that $x_1 = -3$, $y_1 = 5$, $x_2 = 1$, and $y_2 = -4$. Substituting these values into the formula gives us:

$m = \frac{y_2 - y_1}{x_2 - x_1}$

$m = \frac{-4 - 5}{1 - (-3)}$

$m = \frac{-9}{4}$

Example

Determine the slope of the line graphed below.

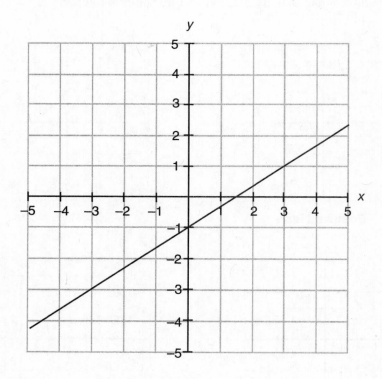

Two points that can be easily determined on the graph are $(3,1)$ and $(0,-1)$. Let $(3,1) = (x_1, y_1)$, and let $(0,-1) = (x_2, y_2)$. This means that $x_1 = 3$, $y_1 = 1$, $x_2 = 0$, and $y_2 = -1$. Substituting these values into the formula gives us:

$$m = \frac{-1-1}{0-3}$$
$$m = \frac{-2}{-3} = \frac{2}{3}$$

Note: If you know the slope and at least one point on a line, you can find the coordinate point of other points on the line. Simply move the required units determined by the slope. For example, from (8,9), given the slope $\frac{7}{5}$, move up seven units and to the right five units. Another point on the line, thus, is (13,16).

Determining the Equation of a Line

The equation of a line is given by $y = mx + b$ where:

- y and x are variables such that every coordinate pair (x,y) is on the line
- m is the slope of the line
- b is the **y-intercept**, the y-value at which the line intersects (or intercepts) the y-axis

In order to determine the equation of a line from a graph, determine the slope and y-intercept and substitute it in the appropriate place in the general form of the equation.

Example

Determine the equation of the line in the graph below.

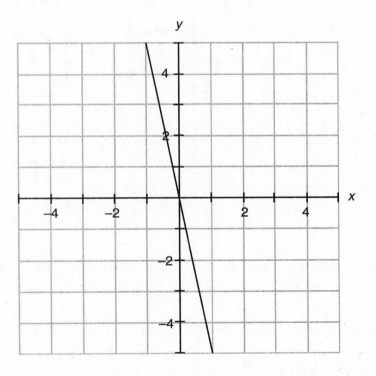

In order to determine the slope of the line, choose two points that can be easily determined on the graph. Two easy points are (–1,4) and (1,–4). Let (–1,4) = (x_1, y_1), and let (1,–4) = (x_2, y_2). This means that $x_1 = -1$, $y_1 = 4$, $x_2 = 1$, and $y_2 = -4$. Substituting these values into the formula gives us: $m = \frac{-4-4}{1-(-1)} = \frac{-8}{2} = -4$.

Looking at the graph, we can see that the line crosses the y-axis at the point (0,0). The y-coordinate of this point is 0. This is the y-intercept.

Substituting these values into the general formula gives us $y = -4x + 0$, or just $y = -4x$.

Example

Determine the equation of the line in the following graph.

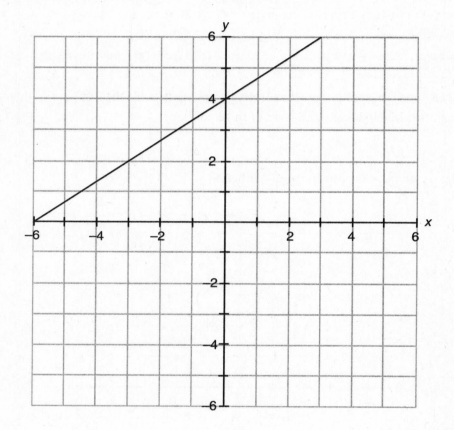

Two points that can be easily determined on the graph are (–3,2) and (3,6). Let (–3,2) = (x_1, y_1), and let (3,6) = (x_2, y_2). Substituting these values into the formula gives us:
$m = \frac{6-2}{3-(-3)} = \frac{4}{6} = \frac{2}{3}$.

We can see from the graph that the line crosses the y-axis at the point (0,4). This means the y-intercept is 4.

Substituting these values into the general formula gives us $y = \frac{2}{3}x + 4$.

Angles

Naming Angles

An angle is a figure composed of two rays or line segments joined at their endpoints. The point at which the rays or line segments meet is called the **vertex** of the angle. Angles are usually named by three capital letters, where the first and last letter are points on the end of the rays, and the middle letter is the vertex.

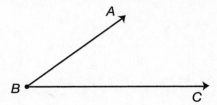

This angle can be named either ∠*ABC* or ∠*CBA*, but because the vertex of the angle is point *B*, letter *B* must be in the middle.

We can sometimes name an angle by its vertex, as long as there is no ambiguity in the diagram. For example, in the angle above, we may call the angle ∠*B*, because there is only one angle in the diagram that has *B* as its vertex.

But, in the following diagram, there are a number of angles that have point *B* as their vertex, so we must name each angle in the diagram with three letters.

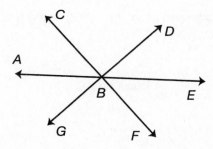

Angles may also be numbered (not measured) with numbers written between the sides of the angles, in the interior of the angle, near the vertex.

Classifying Angles

The unit of measure for angles is the degree.

Angles can be classified into the following categories: acute, right, obtuse, and straight.

■ An **acute angle** is an angle that measures between 0 and 90 degrees.

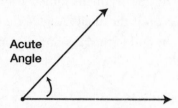

Acute
Angle

■ A **right angle** is an angle that measures exactly 90°. A right angle is symbolized by a square at the vertex.

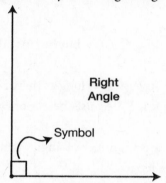

Right
Angle

Symbol

■ An **obtuse angle** is an angle that measures more than 90°, but less than 180°.

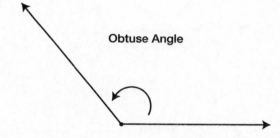

Obtuse Angle

■ A **straight angle** is an angle that measures 180°. Thus, both of its sides form a line.

Straight Angle

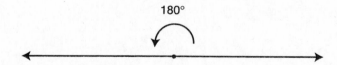

180°

Special Angle Pairs

- **Adjacent angles** are two angles that share a common vertex and a common side. There is no numerical relationship between the measures of the angles.

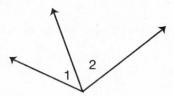

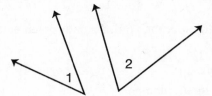

Adjacent angles ∠1 and ∠2   Nonadjacent angles ∠1 and ∠2

- A **linear pair** is a pair of adjacent angles whose measures add to 180°.
- **Supplementary angles** are any two angles whose sum is 180°. A linear pair is a special case of supplementary angles. A linear pair is always supplementary, but supplementary angles do not have to form a linear pair.

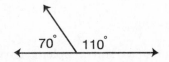

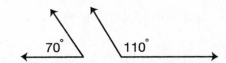

Linear pair (also supplementary)   Supplementary angles (but not a linear pair)

- **Complementary angles** are two angles whose sum measures 90 degrees. Complementary angles may or may not be adjacent.

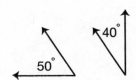

Adjacent complementary angles   Nonadjacent complementary angles

Example

Two complementary angles have measures $2x°$ and $3x + 20°$. What are the measures of the angles?

Because the angles are complementary, their sum is 90°. We can set up an equation to let us solve for x:

$2x + 3x + 20 = 90$

$5x + 20 = 90$

$5x = 70$

$x = 14$

Substituting $x = 14$ into the measures of the two angles, we get $2(14) = 28°$ and $3(14) + 20 = 62°$. We can check our answers by observing that $28 + 62 = 90$, so the angles are indeed complementary.

Example

One angle is 40 more than 6 times its supplement. What are the measures of the angles?

Let x = one angle.

Let $6x + 40$ = its supplement.

Because the angles are supplementary, their sum is 180°. We can set up an equation to let us solve for x:

$x + 6x + 40 = 180$

$7x + 40 = 180$

$7x = 140$

$x = 20$

Substituting $x = 20$ into the measures of the two angles, we see that one of the angles is 20° and its supplement is $6(20) + 40 = 160°$. We can check our answers by observing that $20 + 160 = 180$, proving that the angles are supplementary.

Note: A good way to remember the difference between supplementary and complementary angles is that the letter c comes before s in the alphabet; likewise 90 comes before 180 numerically.

Angles of Intersecting Lines

Important mathematical relationships between angles are formed when lines intersect. When two lines intersect, four smaller angles are formed.

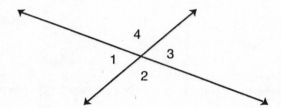

Any two adjacent angles formed when two lines intersect form a linear pair, therefore they are supplementary. In this diagram, $\angle 1$ and $\angle 2$, $\angle 2$ and $\angle 3$, $\angle 3$ and $\angle 4$, and $\angle 4$ and $\angle 1$ are all examples of linear pairs.

Also, the angles that are opposite each other are called **vertical angles**. Vertical angles are angles that share a vertex and whose sides are two pairs of opposite rays. Vertical angles are congruent. In this diagram, $\angle 1$ and $\angle 3$ are vertical angles, so $\angle 1 \cong \angle 3$; $\angle 2$ and $\angle 4$ are congruent vertical angles as well.

Note: Vertical angles is a name given to a special angle pair. Try not to confuse this with right angles or perpendicular angles, which often have vertical components.

Example

Determine the value of y in the following diagram:

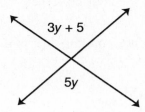

The angles marked $3y + 5$ and $5y$ are vertical angles, so they are congruent and their measures are equal. We can set up and solve the following equation for y:

$3y + 5 = 5y$

$\quad 5 = 2y$

$\quad 2.5 = y$

Replacing y with the value 2.5 gives us the $3(2.5) + 5 = 12.5$ and $5(2.5) = 12.5$. This proves that the two vertical angles are congruent, with each measuring 12.5°.

Parallel Lines and Transversals

Important mathematical relationships are formed when two parallel lines are intersected by a third, nonparallel line called a **transversal**.

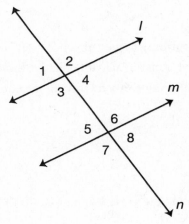

In the preceding diagram, parallel lines l and m are intersected by transversal n. Supplementary angle pairs and vertical angle pairs are formed in this diagram, too.

SUPPLEMENTARY ANGLE PAIRS		VERTICAL ANGLE PAIRS
$\angle 1$ and $\angle 2$	$\angle 2$ and $\angle 4$	$\angle 1$ and $\angle 4$
$\angle 4$ and $\angle 3$	$\angle 3$ and $\angle 1$	$\angle 2$ and $\angle 3$
$\angle 5$ and $\angle 6$	$\angle 6$ and $\angle 8$	$\angle 5$ and $\angle 8$
$\angle 8$ and $\angle 7$	$\angle 7$ and $\angle 5$	$\angle 6$ and $\angle 7$

Other congruent angle pairs are formed:

- Alternate interior angles are angles on the **interior** of the parallel lines, on **alternate** sides of the transversal: $\angle 3$ and $\angle 6$; $\angle 4$ and $\angle 5$.
- Corresponding angles are angles on **corresponding** sides of the parallel lines, on **corresponding** sides of the transversal: $\angle 1$ and $\angle 5$; $\angle 2$ and $\angle 6$; $\angle 3$ and $\angle 7$; $\angle 4$ and $\angle 8$.

Example

In the following diagram, line l is parallel to line m. Determine the value of x.

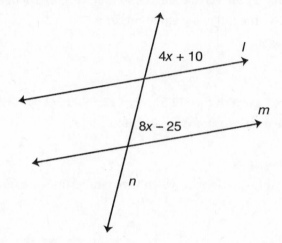

The two angles labeled are **corresponding** angle pairs, because they are located on top of the parallel lines and on the same side of the transversal (same relative location). This means that they are congruent, and we can determine the value of x by solving the equation:

$$4x + 10 = 8x - 25$$
$$10 = 4x - 25$$
$$35 = 4x$$
$$8.75 = x$$

We can check our answer by replacing the value 8.75 in for x in the expressions $4x + 10$ and $8x - 25$:
$$4(8.75) + 10 = 8(8.75) - 25$$
$$45 = 45$$

Note: If the diagram showed the two angles were a vertical angle pair or alternate interior angle pair, the problem would be solved in the same way.

Area, Circumference, and Volume Formulas

Here are the basic formulas for finding area, circumference, and volume. They are discussed in detail in the sections that follow.

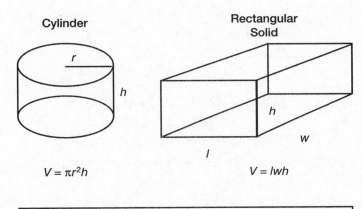

Circle

$C = 2\pi r$
$A = \pi r^2$

Rectangle

w

l

$A = lw$

Triangle

h

b

$A = \frac{1}{2}bh$

Cylinder

r

h

$V = \pi r^2 h$

Rectangular Solid

h

w

l

$V = lwh$

C	=	Circumference	w	=	Width
A	=	Area	h	=	Height
r	=	Radius	v	=	Volume
l	=	Length	b	=	Base

Triangles

The sum of the measures of the three angles in a triangle always equals 180°.

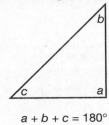

$a + b + c = 180°$

Exterior Angles

An **exterior angle** can be formed by extending a side from any of the three vertices of a triangle. Here are some rules for working with exterior angles:

- An exterior angle and an interior angle that share the same vertex are supplementary. In other words, exterior angles and interior angles form straight lines with each other.
- An exterior angle is equal to the sum of the nonadjacent interior angles.
- The sum of the exterior angles of a triangle equals 360°.

Example

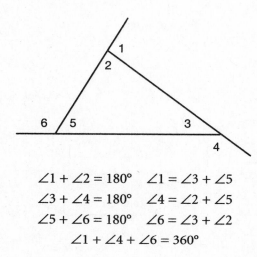

$$\angle 1 + \angle 2 = 180° \quad \angle 1 = \angle 3 + \angle 5$$
$$\angle 3 + \angle 4 = 180° \quad \angle 4 = \angle 2 + \angle 5$$
$$\angle 5 + \angle 6 = 180° \quad \angle 6 = \angle 3 + \angle 2$$
$$\angle 1 + \angle 4 + \angle 6 = 360°$$

Classifying Triangles

It is possible to classify triangles into three categories based on the number of congruent (indicated by the symbol ≅) sides. Sides are congruent when they have equal lengths.

SCALENE TRIANGLE	ISOSCELES TRIANGLE	EQUILATERAL TRIANGLE
no sides congruent	two congruent sides	all sides congruent

It is also possible to classify triangles into three categories based on the measure of the greatest angle:

ACUTE TRIANGLE	RIGHT TRIANGLE	OBTUSE TRIANGLE
greatest angle is acute	greatest angle is 90°	greatest angle is obtuse

Angle-Side Relationships

Knowing the angle-side relationships in isosceles, equilateral, and right triangles is helpful.

- In isosceles triangles, congruent angles are opposite congruent sides.

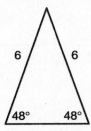

- In equilateral triangles, all sides are congruent and all angles are congruent. The measure of each angle in an equilateral triangle is always 60°.

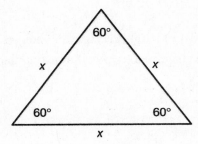

- In a right triangle, the side opposite the right angle is called the **hypotenuse** and the other sides are called **legs**. The box in the angle of the 90-degree angle symbolizes that the triangle is, in fact, a right triangle.

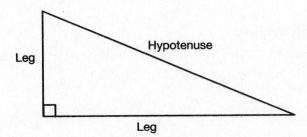

Pythagorean Theorem

The **Pythagorean theorem** is an important tool for working with right triangles. It states: $a^2 + b^2 = c^2$, where a and b represent the legs and c represents the hypotenuse.

This theorem makes it easy to find the length of any side as long as the measures of two sides are known. So, if leg $a = 1$ and leg $b = 2$ in the triangle below, it is possible to find the measure of the hypotenuse, c.

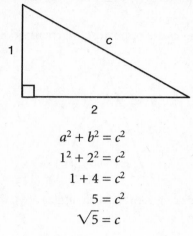

$$a^2 + b^2 = c^2$$
$$1^2 + 2^2 = c^2$$
$$1 + 4 = c^2$$
$$5 = c^2$$
$$\sqrt{5} = c$$

Pythagorean Triples

Sometimes, the measures of all three sides of a right triangle are integers. If three integers are the lengths of the sides of a right triangle; we call them **Pythagorean triples**. Some popular Pythagorean triples are:

3, 4, 5
5, 12, 13
8, 15, 17
9, 40, 41

The smaller two numbers in each triple represent the lengths of the legs, and the largest number represents the length of the hypotenuse.

Multiples of Pythagorean Triples

Whole-number multiples of each triple are also triples. For example, if we multiply each of the lengths of the triple 3, 4, 5 by 2, we get 6, 8, 10. This is also a triple.

Example

If given a right triangle with sides measuring 6, x, and a hypotenuse 10, what is the value of x?

3, 4, 5 is a Pythagorean triple, and a multiple of that is 6, 8, 10. Therefore, the missing side length is 8.

Comparing Triangles

Triangles are said to be congruent (indicated by the symbol $\cong$) when they have exactly the same size and shape. Two triangles are congruent if their corresponding parts (their angles and sides) are congruent. Sometimes, it is easy to tell if two triangles are congruent by looking at them. However, in geometry, we must be able to prove that the triangles are congruent.

There are a number of ways to prove that two triangles are congruent:

Side-Side-Side (SSS)   If the three sides of one triangle are congruent to the three corresponding sides of another triangle, the triangles are congruent.

Side-Angle-Side (SAS)   If two sides and the included angle of one triangle are congruent to the corresponding two sides and included angle of another triangle, the triangles are congruent.

Angle-Side-Angle (ASA)   If two angles and the included side of one triangle are congruent to the corresponding two angles and included side of another triangle, the triangles are congruent.

Used less often but also valid:

Angle-Angle-Side (AAS)   If two angles and the non-included side of one triangle are congruent to the corresponding two angles and non-included side of another triangle, the triangles are congruent.

Hypotenuse-Leg (Hy-Leg)   If the hypotenuse and a leg of one right triangle are congruent to the hypotenuse and leg of another right triangle, the triangles are congruent.

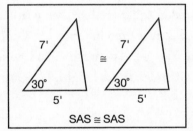

SAS ≅ SAS

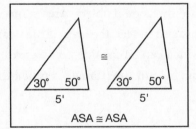

ASA ≅ ASA

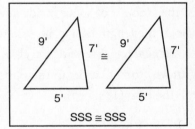

SSS ≅ SSS

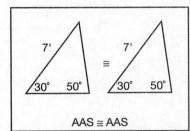

AAS ≅ AAS

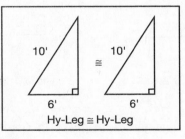

Hy-Leg ≅ Hy-Leg

Example

Determine if these two triangles are congruent.

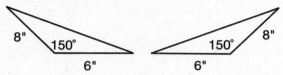

Although the triangles are not aligned the same, there are two congruent corresponding sides, and the angle between them (150°) is congruent. Therefore, the triangles are congruent by the SAS postulate.

Example

Determine if these two triangles are congruent.

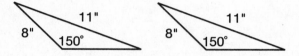

Although the triangles have two congruent corresponding sides and a corresponding congruent angle, the 150° angle is not included between them. This would be SSA, but SSA is not a way to prove that two triangles are congruent.

Area of a Triangle

Area is the amount of space inside a two-dimensional object. Area is measured in square units, often written as *unit*². So, if the length of a triangle is measured in feet, the area of the triangle is measured in *feet*².

A triangle has three sides, each of which can be considered a **base** of the triangle. A perpendicular line segment drawn from a vertex to the opposite base of the triangle is called the **altitude**, or the **height**. It measures how tall the triangle stands.

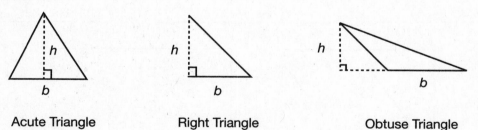

Acute Triangle   Right Triangle   Obtuse Triangle

It is important to note that the height of a triangle is not necessarily one of the sides of the triangle. The correct height for the following triangle is 8, not 10. The height will always be associated with a line segment (called an **altitude**) that comes from one vertex (angle) to the opposite side and forms a right angle (signified by the box). In other words, the height must always be perpendicular to (form a right angle with) the base. Note that in an obtuse triangle, the height can be outside the triangle, and in a right triangle the height is usually one of the sides.

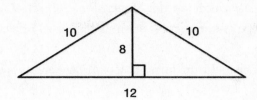

The formula for the area of a triangle is given by $A = \frac{1}{2}bh$, where b is the base of the triangle, and h is the height.

Example

Determine the area of the following triangle.

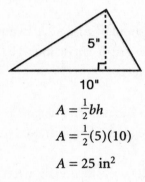

$A = \frac{1}{2}bh$

$A = \frac{1}{2}(5)(10)$

$A = 25 \text{ in}^2$

Volume Formulas

A **prism** is a three-dimensional object that has matching polygons as its top and bottom. The matching top and bottom are called the **bases** of the prism. The prism is named for the shape of the prism's base, so a **triangular prism** has congruent triangles as its bases.

Height of Prism

Base of Prism

Note: This can be confusing. The **base** of the prism is the shape of the polygon that forms it; the **base** of a triangle is one of its sides.

Volume is the amount of space inside a three-dimensional object. Volume is measured in cubic units, often written as $unit^3$. So, if the edge of a triangular prism is measured in feet, the volume of it is measured in $feet^3$.

The volume of ANY prism is given by the formula $V = A_b h$, where A_b is the area of the prism's base, and h is the height of the prism.

Example
Determine the volume of the following triangular prism:

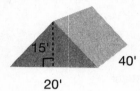

The area of the triangular base can be found by using the formula $A = \frac{1}{2}bh$, so the area of the base is $A = \frac{1}{2}(15)(20) = 150$. The volume of the prism can be found by using the formula $V = A_b h$, so the volume is $V = (150)(40) = 6{,}000$ cubic feet.

A **pyramid** is a three-dimensional object that has a polygon as one base, and instead of a matching polygon as the other, there is a point. Each of the sides of a pyramid is a triangle. Pyramids are also named for the shape of their (non-point) base.

The volume of a pyramid is determined by the formula $\frac{1}{3}A_b h$.

Example
Determine the volume of a pyramid whose base has an area of 20 square feet and stands 50 feet tall.

Because the area of the base is given to us, we only need to replace the appropriate values into the formula.

$V = \frac{1}{3}A_b h$

$V = \frac{1}{3}(20)(50)$

$V = 33\frac{1}{3}$

The pyramid has a volume of $33\frac{1}{3}$ cubic feet.

Polygons

A polygon is a closed figure with three or more sides—for example, triangles, rectangles, and pentagons.

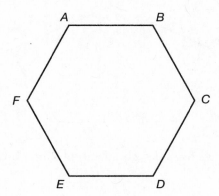

SHAPE	NUMBER OF SIDES
circle	0
triangle	3
quadrilateral (square/rectangle)	4
pentagon	5
hexagon	6
heptagon	7
octagon	8
nonagon	9
decagon	10

Terms Related to Polygons

- **Vertices** are corner points, also called **endpoints**, of a polygon. The vertices in the above polygon are A, B, C, D, E, and F, and they are always labeled with capital letters.
- A **regular polygon** has congruent sides and congruent angles.
- An **equiangular polygon** has congruent angles.

Interior Angles

To find the sum of the interior angles of any polygon, use this formula:

$S = (x - 2)180°$, where x = the number of sides of the polygon.

Example

Find the sum of the interior angles in this polygon:

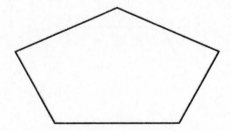

The polygon is a pentagon that has five sides, so substitute 5 for x in the formula:

$S = (5 - 2) \times 180°$

$S = 3 \times 180°$

$S = 540°$

Exterior Angles

Similar to the exterior angles of a triangle, the sum of the exterior angles of any polygon equals 360 degrees.

Similar Polygons

If two polygons are similar, their corresponding angles are congruent and the ratios of the corresponding sides are in proportion.

Example

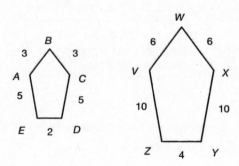

$$\angle A = \angle V = 140°$$
$$\angle B = \angle W = 60°$$
$$\angle C = \angle X = 140°$$
$$\angle D = \angle Y = 100°$$
$$\angle E = \angle Z = 100°$$

$$\frac{AB}{VW} \quad \frac{BC}{WX} \quad \frac{CD}{XY} \quad \frac{DE}{YZ} \quad \frac{EA}{ZV}$$

$$\frac{3}{6} = \frac{3}{6} = \frac{5}{10} = \frac{5}{10} = \frac{2}{4}$$

These two polygons are similar because their angles are congruent and the ratios of the corresponding sides are in proportion.

Quadrilaterals

A **quadrilateral** is a four-sided polygon. Because a quadrilateral can be divided by a diagonal into two triangles, the sum of its interior angles will equal 180 + 180 = 360°.

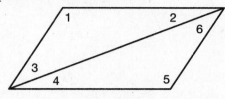

$$\angle 1 + \angle 2 + \angle 3 + \angle 4 + \angle 5 + \angle 6 = 360°$$

Parallelograms

A parallelogram is a quadrilateral with two pairs of parallel sides.

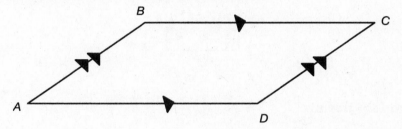

In the figure, $\overline{AB} \parallel \overline{CD}$ and $\overline{BC} \parallel \overline{AD}$. Parallel lines are symbolized with matching numbers of triangles or arrows.

A parallelogram has:

- opposite sides that are congruent ($\overline{AB} = \overline{CD}$ and $\overline{BC} = \overline{AD}$)
- opposite angles that are congruent ($\angle A = \angle C$ and $\angle B = \angle D$)
- consecutive angles that are supplementary ($\angle A + \angle B = 180°$, $\angle B + \angle C = 180°$, $\angle C + \angle D = 180°$, $\angle D + \angle A = 180°$)
- diagonals (line segments joining opposite vertices) that bisect each other (divide each other in half)

Special Types of Parallelograms

- A **rectangle** is a parallelogram that has four right angles.

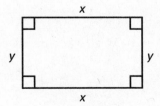

■ A **rhombus** is a parallelogram that has four equal sides.

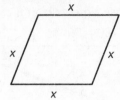

■ A **square** is a parallelogram in which all angles are equal to 90 degrees and all sides are congruent. A square is a special case of a rectangle where all the sides are congruent. A square is also a special type of rhombus where all the angles are congruent.

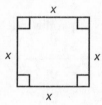

Diagonals of Parallelograms

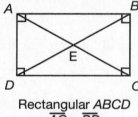

Rectangular *ABCD*
$\overline{AC} \cong \overline{BD}$

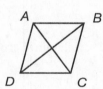

Rhombus *ABCD*
$\overline{AC} \perp \overline{BD}$

Square ABCD
$\overline{AB} \perp \overline{CD},\ \overline{AC} \cong \overline{BD}$

In this diagram, parallelogram *ABCD* has diagonals $\overline{AC}$ and $\overline{BD}$ that intersect at point *E*. The diagonals of a parallelogram bisect each other, which means that $\overline{AE} \cong \overline{EC}$ and $\overline{BE} \cong \overline{ED}$.

In addition, the following properties hold true:

■ The diagonals of a rhombus are perpendicular.
■ The diagonals of a rectangle are congruent.
■ The diagonals of a square are both perpendicular and congruent.

Example
In parallelogram *ABCD*, the diagonal $\overline{AC} = 5x + 10$ and the diagonal $\overline{BD} = 9x$. Determine the value of *x*.

Because the diagonals of a parallelogram are congruent, the lengths are equal. We can then set up and solve the equation $5x + 10 = 9x$ to determine the value of x.

$5x + 10 = 9x$	Subtract x from both sides of the equation.
$10 = 4x$	Divide 4 from both sides of the equation.
$2.5 = x$	

Area and Volume Formulas

The area of any parallelogram can be found with the formula $A = bh$, where b is the base of the parallelogram, and h is the height. The base and height of a parallelogram is defined the same as in a triangle.

Note: Sometimes b is called the length (l) and h is called the width (w) instead. If this is the case, the area formula is $A = lw$.

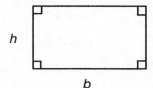 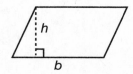

A **rectangular prism** (or **rectangular solid**) is a prism that has rectangles as bases. Recall that the formula for any prism is $V = A_b h$. Because the area of the rectangular base is $A = lw$, we can replace lw for A_b in the formula giving us the more common, easier to remember formula, $V = lwh$. If a prism has a different quadrilateral-shaped base, use the general prisms formula for volume.

Note: A cube is a special rectangular prism with six congruent squares as sides. This means that you can use the $V = lwh$ formula for it, too.

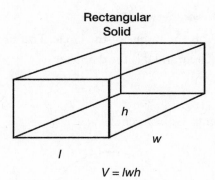

Rectangular
Solid

$V = lwh$

Circles

Terminology

A **circle** is formally defined as the set of points a fixed distance from a point. The more sides a polygon has, the more it looks like a circle. If you consider a polygon with 5,000 small sides, it will look like a circle, but a circle is not a polygon. A circle contains 360 degrees around a center point.

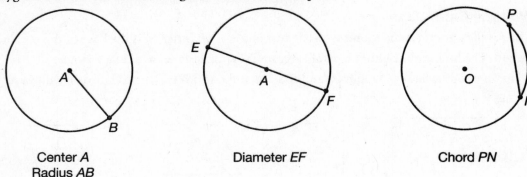

Center *A*
Radius *AB*

Diameter *EF*

Chord *PN*

- The midpoint of a circle is called the **center**.
- The distance around a circle (called **perimeter** in polygons) is called the **circumference**.
- A line segment that goes through a circle, with its endpoints on the circle, is called a **chord**.
- A chord that goes directly through the center of a circle (the longest line segment that can be drawn) in a circle is called the **diameter**.
- The line from the center of a circle to a point on the circle (half of the diameter) is called the **radius**.
- A **sector** of a circle is a fraction of the circle's area.
- An **arc** of a circle is a fraction of the circle's circumference.

Circumference, Area, and Volume Formulas

The area of a circle is $A = \pi r^2$, where r is the radius of the circle. The circumference (perimeter of a circle) is $2\pi r$, or πd, where r is the radius of the circle and d is the diameter.

Example
Determine the area and circumference of this circle:

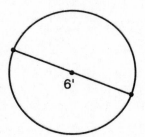

6'

We are given the diameter of the circle, so we can use the formula $C = \pi d$ to find the circumference.

$C = \pi d$

$C = \pi(6)$

$C = 6\pi = 18.85$ feet

The area formula uses the radius, so we need to divide the length of the diameter by 2 to get the length of the radius: $6 \div 2 = 3$. Then we can just use the formula.

$A = \pi(3)2$

$A = 9\pi = 28.27$ square feet.

Note: *Circumference* is a measure of length, so the answer is measured in *units*, whereas the *area* is measured in *square units*.

Area of Sectors and Lengths of Arcs

The area of a sector can be determined by figuring out what the percentage of the total area the sector is, and then multiplying by the area of the circle.

The length of an arc can be determined by figuring out what the percentage of the total circumference of the arc is, and then multiplying by the circumference of the circle.

Example

Determine the area of the shaded sector and the length of the arc *AB*.

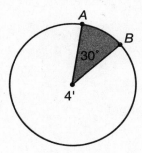

Because the angle in the sector is 30°, and we know that a circle contains a total of 360°, we can determine what fraction of the circle's area it is: $\frac{30°}{360°} = \frac{1}{12}$ of the circle.

The area of the entire circle is $A = \pi r^2$, so $A = \pi(4)^2 = 16\pi$.

So, the area of the sector is $\frac{1}{12} \times 16\pi = \frac{16\pi}{12} = \frac{4}{3}\pi \approx 4.19$ square inches.

We can also determine the length of the arc *AB*, because it is $\frac{30°}{360°} = \frac{1}{12}$ of the circle's circumference.

The circumference of the entire circle is $C = 2\pi r$, so $C = 2\pi(4) = 8\pi$.

This means that the length of the arc is $\frac{1}{12} \times 8\pi = \frac{8\pi}{12} = \frac{2}{3}\pi \approx 2.09$ inches.

A prism that has circles as bases is called a **cylinder**. Recall that the formula for the volume of any prism is $V = A_b h$. Because the area of the circular base is $A = \pi r^2$, we can replace πr^2 for A_b in the formula, giving us $V = \pi r^2 h$, where r is the radius of the circular base, and h is the height of the cylinder.

Cylinder

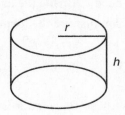

$$V = \pi r^2 h$$

A sphere is a three-dimensional object that has no sides. A basketball is a good example of a sphere. The volume of a sphere is given by the formula $V = \frac{4}{3}\pi r^3$.

Example

Determine the volume of a sphere whose radius is 1.5'.

Replace 1.5' in for r in the formula $V = \frac{4}{3}\pi r^3$.

$V = \frac{4}{3}\pi r^3$

$V = \frac{4}{3}\pi(1.5)^3$

$V = \frac{4}{3}(3.375)\pi$

$V = 4.5\pi \approx 14.14$

The answer is approximately 14.14 cubic feet.

Example

An aluminum can is 6" tall and has a base with a radius of 2". Determine the volume the can holds.

Aluminum cans are cylindrical in shape, so replace 2" for r and 6" for h in the formula $V = \pi r^2 h$.

$V = \pi r^2 h$

$V = \pi(2)^2(6)$

$V = 24\pi \approx 75.40$ cubic feet

▶ Data Analysis

Data analysis simply means reading graphs, tables, and other graphical forms. You should be able to do the following:

- read and understand scatter plots, graphs, tables, diagrams, charts, figures, and so on
- interpret scatter plots, graphs, tables, diagrams, charts, figures, and so on
- compare and interpret information presented in scatter plots, graphs, tables, diagrams, charts, figures, and so on
- draw conclusions about the information provided
- make predictions about the data

It is important to read tables, charts, and graphs very carefully. Read all of the information presented, paying special attention to headings and units of measure. This section will cover tables and graphs. The most common types of graphs are scatter plots, bar graphs, and pie graphs. What follows is an explanation of each, with examples for practice.

Tables

All tables are composed of **rows** (horizontal) and **columns** (vertical). Entries in a single row of a table usually have something in common, and so do entries in a single column. Look at the table below that shows how many cars, both new and used, were sold during the particular months.

MONTH	NEW CARS	USED CARS
June	125	65
July	155	80
August	190	100
September	220	115
October	265	140

Tables are very concise ways to convey important information without wasting time and space. Just imagine how many lines of text would be needed to convey the same information. With the table, however, it is easy to refer to a given month and quickly know how many total cars were sold. It would also be easy to compare month to month. In fact, practice by comparing the total sales of July with October.

In order to do this, first find out how many cars were sold in each month. There were 235 cars sold in July (155 + 80 = 235) and 405 cars sold in October (265 + 140 = 405). With a little bit of quick arithmetic it can quickly be determined that 170 more cars were sold during October (405 − 235 = 170).

Scatter Plots

Whenever a variable depends continuously on another variable, this dependence can be visually represented in a **scatter plot**. A scatter plot consists of the horizontal (x) axis, the vertical (y) axis, and collected data points for variable y, measured at variable x. The variable points are often connected with a line or a curve. A graph often contains a legend, especially if there is more than one data set or more than one variable. A legend is a key for interpreting the graph. Much like a legend on a map lists the symbols used to label an interstate highway, a railroad line, or a city, a legend for a graph lists the symbols used to label a particular data set. Look at the sample graph below. The essential elements of the graph—the x-axis and y-axis—are labeled. The legend to the right of the graph shows that diamonds are used to represent the variable points in data set 1, while squares are used to represent the variable points in data set 2. If only one data set exists, the use of a legend is not essential.

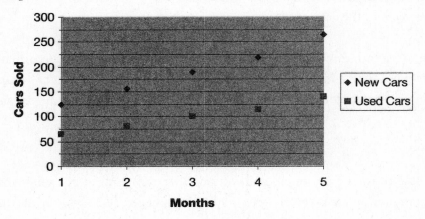

(Note: This data was used in the preceding example for tables.)

The x-axis represents the months after new management and promotions were introduced at an automobile dealership. The y-axis represents the number of cars sold in the particular month after the changes were made. The diamonds reflect the new cars sold, and the squares show the number of used cars sold. What conclusions can be drawn about the sales? Note that the new and used car sales are both increasing each month at a pretty steady rate. The graph also shows that new cars increase at a higher rate and that there are many more new cars sold per month.

Try to look for scatter plots with different trends:

- increase
- decrease
- rapid increase, followed by leveling off
- slow increase, followed by rapid increase
- rise to a maximum, followed by a decrease
- rapid decrease, followed by leveling off
- slow decrease, followed by rapid decrease
- decrease to a minimum, followed by a rise
- predictable fluctuation (periodic change)
- random fluctuation (irregular change)

Bar Graphs

Whereas scatter plots are used to show change, **bar graphs** are often used to indicate an amount or level of occurrence of a phenomenon for different categories. Consider the following bar graph. It illustrates the number of employees who were absent due to illness during a particular week in two different age groups.

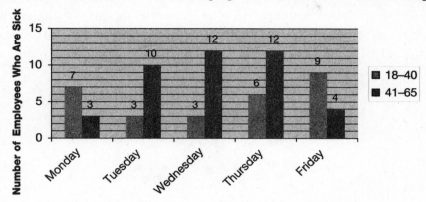

In this bar graph, the categories are the days of the week, and the frequency represents the number of employees who are sick. It can be immediately seen that younger employees are sick before and after the weekend. There is also an inconsistent trend for the younger employees with data ranging all over the place. During mid-week the older crowd tends to stay home more often.

How many people on average are sick in the 41–65 age group? To find the average, you first must find out how many illnesses occur each week in the particular age group. There are 41 illnesses in total for a five-day period ($3 + 10 + 12 + 12 + 4 = 41$). To calculate the average, just divide the total illnesses by the number of days for a total of 8.2 illnesses ($\frac{41}{5} = 8.2$) or, more realistically, 8 absences per day.

Pictographs

Pictographs are very similar to bar graphs, but instead of bars indicating frequency, small icons are assigned a key value indicating frequency.

Number of Students at the Pep Rally	
Freshmen	👤 👤 👤 👤 👤 👤 👤 👤 👤 👤 👤 👤
Sophmores	👤 👤 👤 👤 👤 👤
Juniors	👤 👤 👤 👤 👤
Seniors	👤 👤 👤

Key: 👤 indicates 10 people

In this pictograph, the key indicates that every icon represents 10 people, so it is easy to determine that there were $12 \times 10 = 120$ freshmen, $5.5 \times 10 = 55$ sophomores, $5 \times 10 = 50$ juniors, and $3 \times 10 = 30$ seniors.

Pie Charts and Circle Graphs

Pie charts and **circle graphs** are often used to show what percent of a total is taken up by different components of that whole. This type of graph is representative of a whole and is usually divided into percentages. Each section of the chart represents a portion of the whole, and all of these sections added together will equal 100% of the whole. The following chart shows the three styles of model homes in a new development and what percentage of each there is.

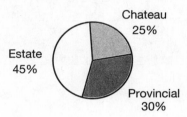

Models of Homes

The chart shows the different models of homes. The categories add up to 100% (25 + 30 + 45 = 100). To find the percentage of Estate homes, you can look at the pie chart and see that 45% of the homes are done in the Estate model.

Broken Line Graphs

Broken line graphs illustrate a measurable change over time. If a line is slanted up, it represents an increase, whereas a line sloping down represents a decrease. A flat line indicates no change.

In the broken line graph below, the number of delinquent payments is charted for the first quarter of the year. Each week the number of outstanding bills is summed and recorded.

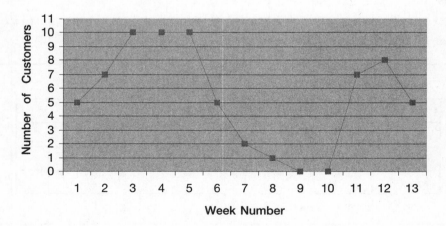

There is an increase in delinquency for the first two weeks and then the level is maintained for an additional two weeks. There is a steep decrease after week 5 (initially) until the ninth week, where it levels off again but this time at 0. The 11th week shows a radical increase followed by a little jump up at week 12, and then a decrease to week 13. It is also interesting to see that the first and last weeks have identical values.

Diagrams

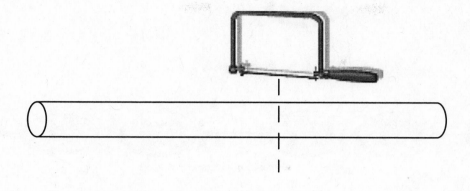

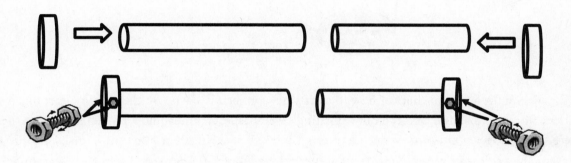

This diagram shows a sequence of events to construct two new objects out of one pipe and a few other parts. First, the instructions show that the pipe must be cut into two pieces with a saw. The next two levels show how the assembly will take place, first adding the end pieces and then bolting in those pieces.

Diagrams could be used to show a sequence of events, a process, an idea, or the relationship between different events or people.

When you see a diagram, first ask what the purpose of it is. What is it trying to illustrate? Then look at the different labeled parts of the diagram. What is the function of each part? How are they interrelated? Take a look at the following diagram:

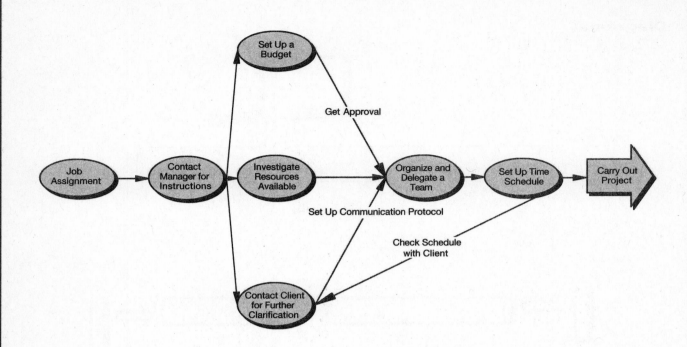

This diagram is a typical chart of how to start a new project. It starts (on the left), by learning about the assignment from the manager and then investigating several aspects of heading a project, including the client, resources, and budget. Once an overall picture is achieved you will then know how many people will be required for the project in order to create an accurate schedule for the project. There are also reminders and further protocols within the diagram in the links.

Now, take the skills you have learned or honed in this review and apply them to the next practice test.

6▶ Writing Test Review

CHAPTER SUMMARY

Good writing skills are essential to success as a teacher. To be effective both in the classroom and with your colleagues, it's important to be able to communicate ideas clearly and accurately in written English. This chapter reviews the elements of good writing: basic grammar, sentence structure, verb and pronoun agreement, and idiomatic expressions.

THE PPST WRITING TEST IS divided into two parts. Section 1 presents multiple-choice questions that measure your ability to identify errors in grammar or sentence structure, and to recognize the correct use of standard written English. Section 2 asks you to write a short essay about an assigned, general topic. The writing topics are designed so that you do not need any specialized knowledge to respond to the prompt. However, you will need to demonstrate that you can organize and support your thoughts effectively in writing. You will be given 30 minutes to create a clear, well-developed essay. The essay portion of the writing test is *not* designed to showcase creative writing; rather, it focuses on your ability to follow the rules of English grammar and avoid common errors.

The computerized writing test varies slightly from the paper-and-pencil test—these differences are outlined in the following chart.

	COMPUTER-BASED TEST	PAPER-BASED TEST
Total time	75 minutes	60 minutes
Section 1: Multiple-choice questions	38 minutes 44 multiple-choice questions	30 minutes 38 multiple-choice questions
Section 2: Essay	30 minutes 1 assigned topic	30 minutes 1 assigned topic

▶ Types of Multiple-Choice Questions

In the first part of the writing test, you will not do any writing at all. Rather, you will answer multiple-choice questions that measure your knowledge of the basics of grammar, sentence construction, and appropriate word choice, and your ability to locate errors. There are two basic types of multiple-choice questions in the writing test. To give yourself an advantage on test day, familiarize yourself with each type now.

▶ Type 1—Usage Questions

In these questions, you need to be able to identify errors and oddities in sentences. You will be presented with a sentence that has four underlined words, phrases, or punctuation marks. You will choose the underlined portion that is *incorrect*. Some sentences are correct. In that case, you would select "No error," choice **e**. None of the sentences has more than one error. Here are some examples:

1. Acid rain <u>looks</u>, feels, even tastes <u>like</u> clean rainwater, but it actually <u>contain</u> high levels <u>of pollutants</u>.
            a   **b**   **c**   **d**
   <u>No error</u>
      e

2. <u>In science fiction</u>, writers <u>have</u> the opportunity <u>to explore</u> and imagine what the world <u>will be</u> like in the
        a   **b**   **c**   **d**
   future. <u>No error</u>
          e

Answers
1. **c.** The problem in this sentence is noun and verb agreement. The pronoun *it* (referring to the subject *acid rain*) is singular, so the verb should be singular as well—*contains*.

2. e. Because this sentence contains no grammatical, idiomatic, logical, or structural errors, the correct answer is choice **e**.

On the computer-based test, the underlined words or phrases do not correspond with the answer choices **a–e**. Instead, you simply highlight your answer choice by clicking on it. To alter your highlight, click on another underlined word or phrase in the sentence. If there are no problems in the sentence, click on "No error." Here is an example of what you will see on your computer screen:

<u>Less</u> teachers attended the conference <u>this year</u>, even though <u>it offered</u> <u>more</u> workshops and seminars. <u>No error</u>

Answer

<mark>Less</mark> teachers attended the conference <u>this year</u>, even though <u>it offered</u> <u>more</u> workshops and seminars. <u>No error</u>

The first underlined choice contains a grammatical error. The modifier *less* describes singular nouns that represent a quantity or degree. The modifier *fewer* would be correct in this context—it describes plural nouns, or things that can be counted.

▶ Type 2—Sentence Correction

In these questions, you will demonstrate your ability to recognize and correct awkward sentence constructions and other grammatical elements. You will be shown a sentence with one part of it underlined. You will be asked to select one of five possible ways to rephrase the underlined part. Choice **a** always repeats the original phrasing, whereas choices **b–e** suggest changes to the underlined portion. Choose the phrasing that creates the most effective sentence with wording that is clear, exact, and without awkwardness or redundancy. If you think the original phrasing is better than the suggested alternatives, select the first answer choice. Here are some examples of this question type.

1. Lee Iacocca, the son of Italian immigrants, <u>worked arduously</u> to reach the top rungs of the Ford Motor Company corporate ladder.
   a. worked arduously
   b. worked arduous
   c. did worked arduously
   d. has work arduously
   e. had worked arduous

2. <u>As an employee, one is eligible</u> for the benefits we worked to attain, including health insurance, life insurance, and a retirement plan.

   a. As an employee, one is eligible

   b. We the employees are either eligible

   c. The employee is eligible

   d. Either the employee is eligible

   e. As employees, we are eligible

Answers

1. **a.** the sentence does not have any problems in its structure or meaning. Both the verb tense and the use of the adverb *arduously* are correct. Choices **b** and **e** incorrectly use the adjective *arduous*. Options **c** and **d** use the correct adverb, but have incorrect verb forms.

2. **e.** The problem with the original sentence is pronoun agreement. The underlined part of the sentence uses the singular pronoun *one*, which agrees with its singular antecedent *employee*. However, the plural pronoun *we* is used later in the sentence. To make a sentence with pronoun agreement, you must look for a choice that contains the pronoun *we* and the plural of *employee*.

Now that you are familiar with the format of the writing test and the two types of multiple-choice questions, you are ready to review some of the rules and patterns of English grammar, sentence structure, idioms, and word usage. This review will aid you in both parts of the writing test: the multiple-choice section and the essay section. The last part of this chapter will cover the essay portion of the test in more detail: the kinds of writing prompts that you can expect, test-taking strategies, and essential information for organizing and creating a clear, well-supported essay.

It's about Time: Tips for the Paper-Based Writing Test

You have about 30 minutes to answer 38 multiple-choice questions. Allow about ten minutes for completing the usage questions. Answering sentence-correction questions takes more time, so give yourself 20 minutes to work on these questions. If you don't know an answer, guess. There is no penalty for wrong answers on the test. Try not to get stuck on one question. If you don't know the answer, guess and move on.

► Grammatical Relationships

For the multiple-choice section of the PPST Writing test, you must be able to identify problems in the relationships between the parts of a sentence. You need to be on the lookout for the incorrect use of adjectives and adverbs, subject-verb agreement, pronoun agreement, and shifting verb tenses.

Adjectives and Adverbs

Adjectives and adverbs add spice to writing—they are words that describe, or modify, other words. However, adjectives and adverbs describe different parts of speech. Whereas adjectives modify nouns or pronouns, adverbs modify verbs, adjectives, or other adverbs.

> We enjoyed the *delicious* <u>meal</u>.
> The chef <u>prepared</u> it *perfectly*.

The first sentence uses the adjective *delicious* to modify the noun *meal*. In the second sentence, the adverb *perfectly* describes the verb *prepared*. Adverbs are easy to spot—most end in *-ly*. However, some of the trickiest adverbs do not end in the typical *-ly* form. The following are problem modifiers to look out for in the PPST Writing test:

> **Good/Well**—Writers often confuse the adverb *well* with its adjective counterpart, *good*.
> Ellie felt *good* about her test results. (*Good* describes the proper noun, *Ellie*.)
> Ruben performed *well* on the test. (*Well* modifies the verb, *performed*.)
> **Bad/Badly**—Similarly, writers confuse the function of these two modifiers. Remember to use the adverb *badly* to describe an action.
> Henry felt *bad* after staying up all night before the exam. (*Bad* describes Henry.)
> Juliet did *badly* in her first classroom presentation. (*Badly* describes the verb form, *did*.)
> **Fewer/Less**—These two adjectives are a common pitfall for writers. To distinguish between them, look carefully at the noun modified in the sentence. *Fewer* describes *plural* nouns, or things that can be counted. *Less* describes *singular* nouns that represent a quantity or a degree.
> The high school enrolls *fewer* students than it did a decade ago.
> Emilia had *less* time for studying than Maggie.

Adjectives that follow verbs can also cause confusion. Although an adjective may come after a verb in a sentence, it may describe a noun or pronoun that comes before the verb. Here is an example:

> The circumstances surrounding Shakespeare's authorship seemed strange. (The adjective, *strange*, describes the subject, *circumstances*.)

Take special note of modifiers in sentences that use verbs that deal with the senses: *touch, taste, look, smell,* and *sound*. Here are some examples of sentences that use the same verb, but different modifiers:

Sarah felt sick after her performance review. (The adjective, *sick*, modifies *Sarah*.)

The archaeologist felt carefully through the loose dirt. (The adverb, *carefully*, modifies *felt*.)

The judge looked skeptical after the witness testified. (The adjective, *skeptical*, modifies *judge*.)

The judge looked skeptically at the flamboyant lawyer. (The adverb, *skeptically*, modifies *looked*.)

Subject-Verb Agreement

They goes together, or *they go together*? You probably don't even have to think about which subject goes with which verb in this clause—your ear easily discerns that the second version is correct. Subject-verb agreement is when the subject of a clause matches the verb *in number*. Singular nouns take singular verbs; plural nouns take plural verbs. However, some instances of subject-verb agreement are tricky. Look out for the following three problem areas on the writing test:

Phrases Following the Subject—Pay close attention to the subject of the sentence. Do not be misled by phrases that may follow the subject. These phrases may confuse you into selecting a verb that does not agree with the subject. Try this practice question:

1. Betty Friedan's 1963 book, <u>an exposé</u> of domesticity <u>that challenged</u> long-held American attitudes,
   a   b

   <u>remain</u> an <u>important contribution</u> to feminism. <u>No error</u>
      c   d   e

The correct answer is choice **c**. The singular subject, *book*, needs a singular verb, *remains*. Don't be confused by the plural noun *attitudes*, which is part of a phrase that follows the subject.

Subjects Following the Verb—Be sure to locate the subject of the sentence. Test makers use subjects that come after the verb to confuse you. Sentence constructions that begin with *there is* or *there are* signal that the subject comes after the verb.

2. Although the Australian government protects the Great Barrier Reef, <u>there is environmental factors that continue to threaten</u> the world's largest coral reef ecosystem.
   a. there is environmental factors that continue to threaten
   b. there are fewer environmental factors that continue to threaten
   c. there are environmental factors that continue to threaten
   d. there are environmental factors that continued to threaten
   e. there is environmental factors that would continue to threaten

The correct answer is choice **c**. The plural subject *factors* requires a plural form of the verb, *are*. The verb *continue* is in the correct tense in the original sentence, so choices **d** and **e** are incorrect. The addition of the adjective *fewer* in choice **b** does not make sense in the sentence.

Special Singular Nouns—Some words that end in *s*, like *measles, news, checkers, economics, sports,* and *politics,* are often singular despite their plural form, because we think of them as one thing. Keep a watch out for collective nouns—nouns that refer to a number of people or things that form a single unit. These words, such as *audience, stuff, crowd, government, group,* and *orchestra,* need a singular verb.

3. That <u>rowdy</u> group of drama students <u>were</u> labeled "the anarchists," <u>because</u> they took over the university
           a   **b**   **c**

   president's office <u>in a protest</u> against the dress code. <u>No error</u>
                d   **e**

   The correct answer choice is **b.** The collective noun *group* is the singular subject of the sentence. Notice how the position of the prepositional phrase *of drama students* following the subject is misleading.

Pronoun Agreement

Pronouns are words that take the place of a noun or another pronoun, called an **antecedent.** Just as subjects and verbs must agree in number, pronouns and their antecedents must match in number. If an antecedent is singular, the pronoun must be singular. If an antecedent is plural, the pronoun must be plural.

Pronouns also need to match their antecedent in case. **Case** refers to a word's grammatical relationship to other words in a sentence. A pronoun that takes the place of the subject of a sentence should be in the nominative case (*I, we, he, she, they*), whereas a pronoun that takes the place of the object in a sentence should be in the objective case (*me, us, him, her, them*). Here are some examples.

Matteo is funny, but *he* can also be very serious. (subject)
Bernadette hired Will, and she also fired *him.* (object)

In most cases, you will automatically recognize errors in pronoun agreement. The phrase *Me worked on the project with him* is clearly incorrect. However, some instances of pronoun agreement can be tricky. Review these common pronoun problems:

- **Indefinite pronouns** like *each, everyone, anybody, no one, one,* and *either* are singular.
  <u>Each</u> of the boys presented *his* science project.
- **Two or more nouns joined by *and*** use a plural pronoun.
  <u>Andy Warhol and Roy Lichtenstein</u> engaged popular culture in *their* art.
- **Two or more singular nouns joined by *or*** use a singular pronoun.
  <u>Francis or Andrew</u> will lend you *his* book.
- **He or she?** In speech, people often use the pronoun *they* to refer to a single person of unknown gender. However, this is incorrect—a singular antecedent requires a singular pronoun.
  <u>A person</u> has the right to do whatever *he or she* wants.

The following lists some pronouns that are commonly confused with verb contractions or other words. Look out for these errors in the multiple-choice questions.

CONFUSING WORD	QUICK DEFINITION	
its	belonging to it	
it's	it is	
your	belonging to you	
you're	you are	
their	belonging to them	
they're	they are	
there	describes where an action takes place	
whose	belonging to whom	
who's	who is *or* who has	
who	refers to people	
that	refers to things	
which	introduces clauses that are not essential to the information in the sentence and do not refer to people	

Try this practice sentence-correction question:

4. A child who is eager to please will often follow <u>everything that their parents say</u>.
   a. everything that their parents say.
   b. everything which their parents say.
   c. everything that his or her parents say.
   d. most everything that their parents say.
   e. everything that their parents said.

Choice **c** is the correct answer. The antecedent, *a child*, is singular. Even though you don't know the gender of the child, the possessive pronoun should be *his or her* in order to agree in number.

Pronoun Problem—Unclear Reference

When a pronoun can refer to more than one antecedent in a sentence, it is called an unclear, or ambiguous, reference. Ambiguous pronoun reference also occurs when there is no apparent antecedent. Look carefully for this common error in the PPST Writing test—a sentence may read smoothly, but may still contain an unclear reference. Look at this practice usage question:

5. A regular feature in American newspapers <u>since</u> the early nineteenth century, <u>they</u> use satirical humor to

    a   b

visually comment <u>on</u> a current event. <u>No error</u>

    c   d   e

The answer is choice **b.** Who or what uses satirical humor? You don't know how to answer, because the pronoun *they* does not have an antecedent. If you replace *they* with *political cartoons*, the sentence makes sense.

Verbs—Action Words

A verb is the action word of a sentence. The three basic verb tenses—present, past, and future—let you know when something happens, happened, or will happen. Test makers include some of these common verb trouble spots in the PPST Writing test:

Shifting Verb Tense—Verb tense should be consistent. If a sentence describes an event in the past, its verbs should all be in the past tense.

Incorrect: When Kate visited Japan, she sees many Shinto temples.

Correct: When Kate visited Japan, she saw many Shinto temples.

Past Tense for Present Conditions—It's incorrect to describe a present condition in the past tense.

Incorrect: My sister met her husband in a cafe. He was very tall.

Correct: My sister met her husband in a cafe. He is very tall.

Incomplete Verbs—Test makers may trick you by including the *-ing* form, or progressive form, of a verb without a helping verb (*is, has, has been, was, had, had been,* etc.). Make sure that verbs are complete and make sense in the sentence.

Incorrect: The major newspapers covering the story throughout the year because of the controversy.

Correct: The major newspapers have been covering the story throughout the year because of the controversy.

Subjunctive Mood—The subjunctive mood of verbs expresses something that is imagined, wished for, or contrary to fact. The subjunctive of *was* is *were.*

Incorrect: If I was a movie star, I would buy a fleet of Rolls-Royces.

Correct: If I were a movie star, I would buy a fleet of Rolls-Royces.

Now practice answering this usage question.

6. <u>Unhappy</u> about the lack <u>of</u> parking at the old stadium, season ticket holders <u>considering</u> <u>boycotting</u> next

      a   b   c   d

week's game. <u>No error</u>

          e

The correct answer is **c**. *Considering* needs a helping verb to be complete and to make sense in this sentence. The clause should read *season ticket holders are considering boycotting next week's game.*

▶ Structural Relationships

When you speak, you may leave your sentences unfinished or run your sentences together. Written expression makes a more permanent impression than speech. In writing, sentence fragments, run-on sentences, misplaced modifiers, and dangling modifiers are structural problems that obscure the meaning of a sentence. The parts of sentences need to have a clear relationship to each other to make sense. This section reviews common errors in sentence structure that will appear on the PPST Writing test, including comparison mistakes, incorrect use of independent and subordinate clauses, double negatives, and unparallel sentence construction.

Making Comparisons

One common writing problem involves comparisons. When a sentence compares two things or activities, the form, or part of speech, of the two entities must match. A writer can compare two nouns or, alternatively, two verb phrases, but he should not compare a noun with a verb phrase.

Incorrect:	For me, watching a psychological thriller is harder than a horror film.
Correct:	For me, watching a psychological thriller is harder than sitting through a horror film.

In the correct version of the sentence, the verb phrase *watching a psychological thriller* matches the form of the verb phrase *sitting through a horror film.* Try the following practice question.

7. Even though admired by some, <u>the innovations of Lewis Carroll's later novels were</u> not as well received as his *Alice's Adventures in Wonderland.*
    a. the innovations of Lewis Carroll's later novels were
    b. Lewis Carroll's later novels were
    c. the innovations about Lewis Carroll's later novels were
    d. the innovations of Lewis Carroll were
    e. Lewis Carroll was

Choice **b** is the correct answer. The original sentence compared *the innovations* of Carroll's later novels with the book, *Alice's Adventures in Wonderland.* The comparison becomes parallel when you simply compare Lewis Carroll's later novels with his early book. Another way to make the sentence parallel would be to compare the innovations of the later novels with the innovations of the early book.

Sentence Fragments

All inventory at reduced prices! Spectacular savings for you! Although pithy and popular with advertisers, sentence fragments are incomplete sentences that do not accurately communicate an idea. To be complete, a sentence needs more than punctuation at its end—it needs a subject and an active verb. A common fragment error that you will see on the PPST Writing test is the use of the *-ing* form of a verb without a helping verb.

Incorrect:	Emily sitting on the sofa, wondering what to do next.
Correct:	Emily was sitting on the sofa, wondering what to do next.

Another common type of sentence fragment is a **subordinate clause** that stands alone. To review, clauses are groups of words that have a subject and a verb. An **independent clause** is one that stands alone and expresses a complete thought. Even though a subordinate clause has a subject and a verb, it does not express a complete thought. It needs an independent clause to support it.

To identify a sentence fragment or subordinate clause on the PPST exam, look for the following joining words, called **subordinating conjunctions**. When a clause has a subordinating conjunction, it needs an independent clause to complete an idea.

after	because	once	though	when
although	before	since	unless	where
as, as if	if	that	until	while

Examples

The Canada goose that built a nest in the pond outside our building.
As if the storm never happened, as if no damage was done.

In the first example, removing the connector *that* would make a complete sentence. In the second example, the subordinate clauses need an independent clause to make logical sense: *As if the storm never happened, as if no damage was done, Esme remained blithely optimistic.* Try to locate the sentence fragment in the following practice question.

8. <u>One participant</u> of the civil rights movement <u>explained</u> that <u>in the heated atmosphere</u> of the 1960s,
        a   **b**   **c**

<u>sit-in protests effective enough</u> to draw the attention of the nation. <u>No error</u>
        d   **e**

The correct answer choice is **d**. In this question, the independent clause has a subject (*one participant*) and a verb (*explained*). However, the subordinate clause, beginning with the connector *that* needs a verb to make sense. Adding the verb *were* completes the thought and fixes the fragment: *that in the heated atmosphere of the 1960s, sit-in protests were effective enough to draw the attention of the nation.*

Run-On Sentences

"Planning ahead and studying for a test builds confidence do you know what I mean?" In speech, you may run your sentences together, but if you do so in writing, you will confuse your reader. In a run-on sentence, two independent clauses run together as one sentence without being separated by proper punctuation.

There are four ways to correct a run-on sentence. Study how each fix listed below changes the following run-on sentence.

Example
We stopped for lunch we were starving.

1. **Add a period.** This separates the run-on sentence and makes two simple sentences.
   We stopped for lunch. We were starving.
2. **Add a semicolon.**
   We stopped for lunch; we were starving.
3. **Use a coordinating conjunction** (*and, but, or, for, nor, yet, so*) to connect the two clauses.
   We were starving, **so** we stopped for lunch.
4. **Use a subordinating conjunction** (see the preceding page for a list of subordinating conjunctions). By doing this, you turn one of the independent clauses into a subordinating clause.
   Because we were starving, we stopped for lunch.

On the PPST Writing test, be sure to look out for another common form of run-on sentence, the **comma splice**. A comma splice incorrectly uses a comma to separate two independent clauses.

Incorrect: Jacob bought the groceries, Lucy cooked dinner.

You can repair a comma splice in two ways: add a conjunction after the comma, or replace the comma with a semicolon.

Correct: Jacob bought the groceries, and Lucy cooked dinner.
                 OR
                 Jacob bought the groceries; Lucy cooked dinner.

Try this practice question.

9. *Citizen Kane*, Orson Welles's first full-length film, <u>is considered an American classic, however it did not</u> <u>manage</u> to garner the 1941 Academy Award for best picture.
   a. is considered an American classic, however it did not manage
   b. is considered an American classic. However, it did not manage
   c. is considered an American classic however it did not manage
   d. is considered an American classic however. It did not manage
   e. is considered an American classic because it did not manage

Choice **b** is correct. This original sentence is a run-on because the word *however* is used as if it were a conjunction. The words *however*, *therefore*, and *then* are not conjunctions, but rather a special kind of adverb that expresses a relationship between two clauses. Called **conjunctive adverbs**, these words cannot join two independent clauses the way a conjunction does. To repair this kind of run-on or comma splice, you can make two sentences (the way that choice **b** does). Another other option for fixing the original sentence is to separate the two main clauses with a semicolon and set the adverb off from the rest of the clause with a comma. Note that you can move the adverb around in its clause without changing the meaning of the sentence.

- *Citizen Kane*, Orson Welles's first full-length film, is considered an American classic; however, it did not manage to garner the 1941 Academy Award for best picture.
- *Citizen Kane*, Orson Welles's first full-length film, is considered an American classic; it did not manage, however, to garner the 1941 Academy Award for best picture.

More about Clauses

When a sentence contains two clauses that are linked in a logical way, they are **coordinated**. Subordinate clauses are joined by a conjunction (*as, after, although, because*) to the independent clause to complete a thought or idea. Problems occur when conjunctions are misused in a way that makes a sentence obscure and lacking in meaning. Notice below how in the first example, the conjunction *because* creates a confusing and illogical premise, whereas in the second example, the conjunction *although* sets up a contrast between the two clauses that makes sense.

Unclear: Because he was late again, the teacher let him off with just a warning.
Correct: Although he was late again, the teacher let him off with just a warning.

Another type of mistake is when a sentence has two or more subordinate clauses, but no independent clause. This is a problem with **subordination**. Here is an example:

Incorrect: Since the Industrial Revolution took place, because people have increased the concentration of carbon dioxide in the atmosphere by 30 percent by burning fossil fuels and cutting down forests.

The previous sentence contains two subordinate clauses: the first introduced by the conjunction *since*, and the second introduced by the conjunction *because.* By removing *because,* you create an independent clause, and the sentence makes sense. Try the following practice question.

10. When European settlers <u>arrived</u> in North America <u>in the fifteenth century,</u> <u>where</u> they <u>encountered</u>
                   a   **b**   **c**   **d**

    diverse Native American cultures. <u>No error</u>
                                          e

The correct answer choice is **c**. If you remove the subordinating conjunction *where*, the second subordinating clause becomes an independent clause.

Misplaced Modifiers

Modifiers are phrases that describe nouns, pronouns, and verbs. In a sentence, they must be placed as closely as possible to the words they describe. If they are misplaced, you will end up with a sentence that means something other than what you intended. The results can be comical, but the joke may be on you!

Misplaced Modifier:	My uncle told me about feeding cows in the kitchen. (Why are there cows in the kitchen?)
Correct:	In the kitchen, my uncle told me about feeding cows.

Misplaced Modifier:	A huge python followed the man that was slithering slowly through the grass. (Why was the man slithering through the grass?)
Correct:	Slithering through the grass, a huge python followed the man.
	OR
	A huge python that was slithering slowly through the grass followed the man.

Most of the misplaced modifier problems on the PPST exam are **dangling modifiers**. Dangling modifiers are phrases, located at the beginning of a sentence and set off by a comma, that mistakenly modify the wrong noun or pronoun. To be correct, modifying phrases at the beginning of a sentence should describe the noun or pronoun (the subject of the sentence) that directly follows the comma.

Dangling Modifier:	Broken and beyond repair, Grandma threw the serving dish away. (Why was Grandma broken?)
Correct:	Broken and beyond repair, the serving dish was thrown away by Grandma.
	OR
	Grandma threw away the serving dish that was broken and beyond repair.

Try the following sentence-correction question.

11. Subsidized by the federal government, <u>students can get help financing their post-secondary education through the Federal Work-Study Program.</u>

    a. students can get help financing their post-secondary education through the Federal Work-Study Program.

    b. since students finance their post-secondary education through the Federal Work-Study Program.

    c. to students who need help financing their post-secondary education.

    d. financing a post-secondary education is possible through the Federal Work-Study Program.

    e. the Federal Work-Study Program helps students finance their post-secondary education.

The correct answer is **e.** In the original sentence, the modifying phrase incorrectly describes the subject *students.* In choice **d,** the modifying phrasing incorrectly describes *financing.* Choices **b** and **c** are subordinate clauses, and, therefore, incorrect. Only choice **e** answers the question "What is subsidized by the federal government?" in a way that makes sense.

Double Negatives

When you use two negatives such as *not* or *no* in a sentence, you may think that you are emphasizing your point. In fact, you are obscuring your meaning. As in math, two negatives result in a positive. When you write, "I don't have no money," you are actually saying that you do have money. Always avoid using double negatives—they are considered grammatically incorrect. *No* and *not* are obvious negatives, but on the PPST Writing test, be on the watch for any sentence that doubles up on any of the following words:

no one	neither	nobody	scarcely
nothing	nowhere	hardly	barely

Try this usage question:

12. <u>Children</u> <u>don't hardly</u> need computers in the classroom <u>in order</u> <u>to learn</u> basic skills like math and
       a   b   c   d

reading. <u>No error</u>
       e

The correct answer choice is **b.** The negative verb *don't* and the adverb *hardly* cancel each other out. The double negative obscures the meaning of the sentence. To rewrite the sentence in a way that makes sense, you could remove either word.

Parallel Structure

When a sentence has a parallel structure, it means that its words and phrases follow the same grammatical structure. Parallel structure makes sentences easier to read and helps express ideas clearly. Parallel construction is important in sentences that make lists or describe a series of events. Each part of the list or series must be in the same form, or part of speech, as the others.

Not Parallel: Every day, I went to school, worked part-time, and was exercising.
                  (Two verbs are in the past tense; one is a past participle.)
Parallel: Every day, I went to school, worked part-time, and exercised.

Not Parallel: We are looking for a teaching assistant who is smart, reliable, and will come on time.
                  (Two characteristics are adjectives, whereas the third consists of a verb phrase.)
Parallel: We are looking for a teaching assistant who is smart, reliable, and punctual.

Parallel construction is also crucial when a sentence uses a *not only/but also* pattern. Review the following examples.

The author not only <u>raised several important questions</u>, but she also <u>made a convincing argument</u>. (Notice how the phrases following the *not only/but also* pattern are in the same form. Each has a verb in the past tense and a noun.)

The contract dispute was a result not only <u>of a breakdown in communication</u> but also <u>of the town's budgetary crisis.</u> (Here the words following the *not only/but also* pattern are in the form of prepositional phrases.)

Practice answering this sentence-correction question:

13. Expressing yourself clearly and effectively in writing means knowing the basic mechanics of language, eliminating ambiguity, choosing the right words, <u>and correct punctuation.</u>
   a. and correct punctuation.
   b. or correct punctuation
   c. and use correct punctuation.
   d. and having used correct punctuation.
   e. and using correct punctuation.

Choice **e** is correct because it follows the grammatical pattern of the sentence: a list of phrases beginning with **gerunds** (a gerund is a noun created from the *-ing* form of a verb).

► Idioms and Word Choice

Idioms—words, phrases, or expressions used in everyday language—make up a large part of English. If your native language is not English, the use of idioms may challenge you. That is because idioms often have unusual grammatical structures or have a meaning that does not make sense if you simply add up the meanings of each word. Native English speakers recognize most idioms *by ear*—the words just sound right. The PPST will require you to identify both the proper use of idiom and correct word choice.

Prepositional Idioms

Prepositions are words that express the relationship in time or space between words in a sentence. They are generally short words, such as *in, on, around, above, between, beside, by, before*, or *with*, that introduce prepositional phrases in a sentence. The PPST exam tests the idiomatic use of prepositions—word combinations that often go together. Review and familiarize yourself with this list of common prepositional idioms:

according to	depend on/upon	next to
afraid of	equal to	of the opinion
anxious about	except for	on top of
apologize for (something)	fond of	opposite of
apologize to (someone)	from now on	prior to
approve of	from time to time	proud of
ashamed of	frown on/upon	regard to
aware of	full of	related to
blame (someone) for	glance at/through	rely on/upon
blame (something) on	grateful for (something)	respect for
bored with	grateful to (someone)	responsible for
capable of	in accordance with	satisfied with
compete with	incapable of	similar to
complain about	in conflict	sorry for
composed of	inferior to	suspicious of
concentrate on	insist on/upon	take care of
concerned with	interested in	thank (someone) for
congratulate on	in the habit of	tired of
conscious of	in the near future	with regard to
consist of	knowledge of	

Keep your ear attuned to the use of prepositional idioms in this practice usage question.

14. The <u>period of</u> intellectual development known as the Renaissance <u>corresponded toward</u> a <u>time of</u> political
           a   **b**   **c**

stability <u>in western Europe</u>. <u>No error</u>
                      d   **e**

The answer is **b**. The word combination *corresponded toward* is simply not idiomatic. When followed by a thing, such as a time period, either *corresponded with* or *corresponded to* are the correct prepositional idioms. When followed by a person, use *correspond with*.

Redundancy and Wordiness

You may be asked to identify redundant or wordy language. Your ability to write concisely and clearly will also be an important part of the essay portion of the test. To eliminate unnecessary repetitions or excessive wordiness, look for words that add no new information to a sentence.

Redundant:	<u>Due to the fact that</u> the circumstances of the case were <u>sensitive in nature</u>, the proceedings were kept confidential.
Correct:	<u>Because</u> the circumstances of the case were <u>sensitive</u>, the proceedings were kept confidential.

Redundant:	Charles <u>returned back</u> to his room <u>at 10 A.M. in the morning</u>.
Correct:	Charles <u>returned</u> to his room <u>at 10 A.M.</u>

Commonly Confused Words

A misused word can significantly alter the meaning of a sentence. The following list contains some commonly confused words. If you find some that you frequently confuse, study them and practice using them correctly in a sentence.

CONFUSING WORD	QUICK DEFINITION
accept	recognize, receive
except	excluding
affect (verb)	to influence
effect (noun)	result
effect (verb)	to bring about
all ready	totally prepared
already	by this time

CONFUSING WORD	QUICK DEFINITION
allude	make indirect reference to
elude	evade
illusion	unreal appearance
all ways	every method
always	forever
among	in the middle of several
between	in an interval separating (two)
assure	to make certain (assure someone)
ensure	to make certain
insure	to make certain (financial value)
beside	next to
besides	in addition to
complement	match
compliment	praise
continual	constant
continuous	uninterrupted
disinterested	no strong opinion either way
uninterested	don't care
elicit	to stir up
illicit	illegal
eminent	well known
imminent	pending
farther	beyond
further	additional
incredible	beyond belief, astonishing
incredulous	skeptical, disbelieving
loose	not tight
lose	unable to find
may be	something could possibly be
maybe	perhaps
overdo	do too much
overdue	late
persecute	to mistreat
prosecute	to take legal action

CONFUSING WORD	QUICK DEFINITION
personal	individual
personnel	employees
precede	go before
proceed	continue
proceeds	profits
principal (adjective)	main
principal (noun)	person in charge
principle	standard
stationary	still, not moving
stationery	writing material
than	in contrast to
then	next
to	on the way to
too	also
weather	climate
whether	if

► Mechanics

Knowing the mechanics of language means getting down to basics—the rules of punctuation and capitalization. Punctuation marks are standardized marks that clarify meaning for your reader, serving as traffic signs that direct the reader to pause, connect, stop, consider, and go. Although most likely you have studied and learned many of the basic rules of punctuation and capitalization, this section will cover some common problem areas that may appear on the PPST exam, including misuse of commas, semicolons, colons, apostrophes, and capitalization.

Commas

Commas create pauses, clarify meaning, and separate different parts of a sentence. The comma splice is a common misuse of the comma—review this problem on page 234. For the PPST exam, remember the six basic rules for using commas outlined on the following page.

Use a comma:

1. **To separate independent clauses** joined by a coordinating conjunction, such as *and, but, nor, so, for,* or *or.* Use a comma before the conjunction.

    My instinct was to solve the problem slowly and deliberately, *but* we only had a week before the deadline.

2. **To set off nonessential clauses.** A nonessential clause is one that can be removed from a sentence without changing its meaning.

    My friend Rebecca, *who is active in the local labor union,* is a fifth-grade teacher.

3. **To set off words or phrases that interrupt** the flow of thought in a sentence.

    The certification program, *however,* works well for me.

    Elena Alvarez, *my adviser and mentor,* was present at the meeting.

4. **To set off an introductory element,** such as a word or phrase that comes at the beginning of a sentence.

    Thrilled by the results, Phin presented the study to his colleagues.

5. **To set apart a series of words in a list.** Usually, the last item in a list is preceded by a conjunction. Although a comma is not necessary before the conjunction, it is preferred that you use one.

    Micah, Jose, and Sam attended the conference.

    Micah, Jose and Sam attended the conference.

6. **To separate elements of dates and addresses.** Commas are used to separate dates that include the day, month, and year. Dates that include just the month and year do not need commas. When the name of a city and state are included in an address, set off both with commas.

    Margaret moved to *Portsmouth, New Hampshire,* for the job.

    Maco came to Greensboro on *June 15, 2004,* right after she graduated from the program.

    Maco came to Greensboro in *June 2004* after she graduated from the program.

Semicolons

You may be asked to recognize errors involving the use of semicolons on the PPST Writing test. Review how to use this mark correctly in the following guidelines and examples:

1. **Use a semicolon to separate independent clauses** that are not joined by a conjunction.
2. **Use a semicolon to separate independent clauses that contain commas,** even if the clauses are joined by a conjunction.
3. **Use a semicolon to separate independent clauses connected with a conjunctive adverb,** such as *however, therefore, then, thus,* or *moreover.*

Colons

Colons are used to introduce elements and to show an equivalent relationship (almost like an equal sign in math). Follow these guidelines to recognize the correct use of commas:

1. **Use a colon to introduce a list** when the clause before the colon can stand as a complete sentence.

   These are the first-year teachers: Ellen, Ben, and Eliza.

   The first-year teachers are Ellen, Ben, and Eliza. (No colon here.)

2. **Use a colon to introduce a restatement or elaboration** of the previous clause.

   James enjoys teaching *Measure for Measure* each spring: it is his favorite play.

3. **Use a colon to introduce a word, phrase, or clause** that adds emphasis to the main body of the sentence.

   Carrie framed the check: it was the first paycheck she had ever earned.

4. **Use a colon to introduce a formal quotation.**

   Writer Gurney Williams offered this advice to parents: "Teaching creativity to your child isn't like teaching good manners. No one can paint a masterpiece by bowing to another person's precepts about elbows on the table."

Use the punctuation guidelines you have reviewed to answer this practice question.

15. Alternative medicine, <u>which</u> includes a range of practices outside of conventional medicine such as
           a

   herbs, homeopathy, massage, yoga, and acupuncture; <u>holds</u> increasing appeal for Americans. <u>No error</u>
      b   **c d**   **e**

Choice **c** is the correct answer. The semicolon does not work because it does not separate two independent clauses. It should be replaced with a comma, setting off the nonessential clause that begins with the word *which*.

Apostrophes

Apostrophes are used to show possession, contractions, and so on. Consider these eight rules for using apostrophes:

1. **Add *'s* to form the singular possessive, even when the noun ends in *s*:**

   Mr. Summers's essay convinced me.

2. **Add *'s* to plural words not ending in *s* to show possession.**

   The *children's* ability to absorb foreign language is astounding.

   The workshops focus on working *women's* needs.

3. **Add *'* to plural words ending in *s* to show possession.**

   The *students'* grades improved each semester.

4. **Add *'s* to indefinite pronouns that show ownership.**

   Everyone's ability level should be considered.

5. **Never use apostrophes with possessive pronouns.**

   This experiment must be *yours.*

6. **Use *'s* to form the plurals of letters, figures, and numbers, as well as expressions of time or money.**

   Mind your *p's* and *q's.*

   The project was the result of a *year's* worth of work.

7. **Add *'s* to the last word of a compound noun, compound subject, or name of a business or institution to show possession.**

   The *president-elect's* speech riveted the audience.

   Gabbie and Michael's wedding is in October.

   The *National Science Teachers Association's* meeting will take place next week.

8. **Use apostrophes to show that letters or words are omitted in contractions.**

   Abby *doesn't* (does not) work today.

   Who's (who is) on first?

Capitalization

Capitalization is necessary both for specific words and to start sentences and quotations. The following are six instances when capitalization is needed:

1. the first word of the sentence
2. proper nouns (names of *specific* people, places, and things)
3. the first word of a complete quotation, but not a partial quotation
4. the first, last, and any other important words of a title
5. languages
6. the pronoun *I,* and any contractions made with it

Sometimes knowing when to capitalize a word is tricky. Look for these trouble spots on the PPST Writing test:

- **Compass directions**, such as *east* or *west*, are not capitalized unless they refer to a specific geographical area.
  The American Civil War was fought between the *North* and the *South.*
- **Family relationships** are not capitalized when they are preceded by a pronoun.
  I met *my mother* for lunch.
  Uncle Russ agreed to babysit, so that I could meet *Mother* for lunch.
- **Seasons and parts of the academic year** are not capitalized.
  I'll register for the course this *fall.*
- **Words modified by proper adjectives** are not capitalized, unless they are part of a proper name.
  Jacob recommended the *Italian restaurant* in his neighborhood.

Practice answering this usage question.

16. When Thomas Jefferson sent explorers Lewis and Clark into the <u>West,</u> he patterned their mission on the

                                                                              a

<u>Enlightenments'</u> scientific methods<u>:</u> to observe, collect, document, and classify. <u>No error</u>

   b   **c**   **d**   **e**

The answer is **b**. As a proper noun, *the Enlightenment* is correctly capitalized; however, the apostrophe is misplaced. To show possession, add *'s* to a singular noun. The *West* is correctly capitalized because it refers to a geographical region of the United States.

▶ Introducing the Essay

Essay tests can intimidate anyone—even prospective teachers. You know you will be asked to write an essay, but you don't know your topic beforehand. And you are under pressure: You have only 30 minutes to complete the task. Even though this sounds nerve-racking, with preparation, you will be ready to produce your best writing. The good news is that because the time limit is brief, your essay doesn't need to be long (about four to five paragraphs). Furthermore, because you are provided with a topic, you don't need to spend valuable time deciding what to write about. Also, you can be confident that you will be able to answer the question: All of the topics, or writing prompts, on the PPST Essay test are designed to be general so that you do not need any specialized knowledge or experience to write about them.

Creative, innovative writing is not the goal of the Praxis essay. Instead, it aims to measure your ability to generate ideas and support them through details and evidence in clear, concise writing. It tests how effectively and logically you organize your thoughts and it evaluates your ability to use correct grammar and appropriate word choice. Do not spend a lot of time trying to produce a masterpiece—simply express your views through precise, direct language. To learn more about the criteria on which your essay will be judged, review the rubrics provided in the answer explanations found after each practice exam.

What to Expect

All of the possible writing prompts in the PPST test present a statement and ask you to respond to it. Be ready to explain and back up your position with specific reasons and examples from your personal experience, observations, or reading. You do not need any background knowledge to respond to the prompt. **Do not write about a topic other than the one provided.** To receive a score, you must write in English. These are some examples of the general topics you might find on the PPST Essay exam:

- "We live in a culturally diverse society. In-depth study of different cultures should be mandatory for all students."
- "Celebrities are just ordinary people with high-profile jobs. They don't have more responsibility than other adults to act as role models for children."

- "Because of the prevalence of information technology in society, computer training should be required for all teachers, regardless of the subject the instructor will teach."
- "Using a grade scale of A–F creates unnecessary competition and negative stress. Colleges and universities should replace the grade scale with a pass/fail report."

Essay Prompts Online

You can find more than 70 typical writing prompts at the Educational Testing Service (ETS) website. The essay prompt you get at exam time may not be included in this list, but reviewing the list will familiarize you with common types of prompts and topics. You can follow these instructions:

- Go to www.ets.org.
- Click on "Praxis™" under "Tests."
- Click on "About the Test" under "For Test Takers."
- Click on "Praxis I®: Pre-Professional Skills Test (PPST)."
- In the top tabs, find "Test Preparation" and find "Tests at a Glance (TAAG)."
- Click on "PPST: Writing" or "Computerized PPST: Writing."

Your computer must be able to read pdf files.

Manage Your Time

You have 30 minutes to produce a clear, strong essay. Should you jump right into the writing or take time to plan your response? Even with a time limit, your ability to craft a well-organized, well-written essay improves if you take time to plan your essay. Allow time for each step of the writing process: planning, writing, and proofreading. You can break down the 30 minutes this way:

5–10 minutes	Plan (choose your thesis, brainstorm, and organize).
15–20 minutes	Write.
5 minutes	Proofread (read for errors or adjust word choice).

▶ Steps to a Strong Essay

The prewriting—or planning—process is essential to developing a clear, organized essay. Because of the time limit, you may be tempted to skip the prewriting stage. However, the 5–10 minutes that you spend planning will be worth it. Prewriting consists of some quick, basic steps: carefully reading and understanding the writing prompt, formulating a thesis, brainstorming for examples that will support your thesis, and drafting an outline or basic structure for your essay.

Step 1—Create a Clear Thesis

To begin, carefully read the statement presented in the writing prompt. Make sure that you fully understand it. Then, decide what your position is: Do you agree or disagree with the statement? Consider to what extent you agree or disagree with the position: Are you in 100% agreement or do you only partly agree with the statement? Your answer to these questions will make up the main idea or **thesis** of your essay. It will form the foundation of your essay and will determine what kind of support, or examples, you will provide.

A strong thesis does not merely repeat or rephrase the question or prompt. It does not state how *others* might respond to it. Rather, it presents *your* point of view.

A thesis statement should:

- answer the question given in the writing prompt
- tell the reader what your subject is
- inform the reader what you think and feel about the subject
- use clear, active language

Don't waste time making your thesis statement a masterpiece. You will be able to grab the reader's attention by clearly stating your purpose in simple words.

Consider the following prompt:

"Focusing on fashion and clothes can distract students from learning. School uniforms should be mandatory for all high-school students."
Discuss the extent to which you agree or disagree with this opinion. Support your views with specific reasons and examples from your own experience, observations, or reading.

The following sentences are *not* thesis statements:

- Many private schools already require school uniforms.
- Some students prefer school uniforms, while others detest them.
- Why do schools use uniforms?

The following *are* thesis statements; they relate directly to the prompt:

- School uniforms discourage high-school students from learning responsibility and developing individuality.
- School uniforms are effective in creating a positive learning environment.

Remember that you can also impose some conditions on your answer. For example, if you disagree with mandatory school uniforms, you can still qualify your answer: "I disagree that students should be required to wear school uniforms, but I believe a dress code helps create an effective learning atmosphere."

Step 2—Brainstorm for Ideas

Your answer to the question in the writing prompt will form the argument that you present in your essay. Once you have decided what your position will be, you will begin to brainstorm—think up ideas—that support your thesis. For your PPST essay, try to generate about three to five reasons that back up your main idea.

Brainstorming is a prewriting process in which you imagine or write down any ideas that come to mind. To brainstorm effectively, do not judge your ideas initially—simply put them down on paper. If you are stuck for ideas, try these brainstorming strategies:

- Try the **freewriting** technique in which you write nonstop for two minutes. Keep your pen to paper and your hand moving. Doubtlessly, your ideas will emerge.
- **List** as many ideas as you can. Don't edit for grammar or structure; just write down whatever comes to mind.
- Now get selective. Choose three to five of your strongest ideas for your essay.

For example, here's how you might brainstorm supporting ideas for the writing prompt mentioned earlier:

Thesis: Mandatory school uniforms are not effective tools for creating a positive, learning environment.

Examples
Why?
Uniforms don't give students the opportunity to make choices.
Uniforms send a message to students that they cannot be trusted.
Students find distractions in class even when they are wearing uniforms.
Teenage years are a time of self-exploration.
Learning isn't only something you read in a book—it's about finding out who you are.
Students need to learn about making good choices.

Personal experience—In my parochial high school, kids wore uniforms.
Lack of trust—We couldn't be trusted to do even a simple thing like dressing ourselves.
Found other ways to rebel—smoking, wearing makeup, dyeing our hair to attract attention
Distractions in class other than clothes—note writing, gossip, cell phones
Self-exploration—Clothes let teens try on different identities (sporty, punk, artistic).
Learning about good choices—Introduce a forum for students where they can talk about making choices? Encourage kids to talk about how they present themselves when they wear different clothes; talk about choices teens make that can be dangerous; talk about choices adults face.

Step 3—Outline Your Essay

To make sure that your essay is well developed and organized, draft an outline. An outline will help you put your ideas into a logical order and identify any gaps in your supporting details. Essays follow a basic three-part structure:

1. **Introduction:** Present your position to your readers. State your thesis.
2. **Body:** Provide specific support for your thesis.
3. **Conclusion:** Bring closure to your essay and restate your thesis.

Your PPST essay should follow this basic structure, too. Because the essay is short, plan on writing about five paragraphs, listing one point on your outline for each paragraph. The body of your essay will be broken down into three supporting ideas:

1. Introduction
2. Body: support 1
3. Body: support 2
4. Body: support 3
5. Conclusion

Although you don't have to follow this model exactly, keep in mind that developing three supporting paragraphs is a good guide for the PPST essay. By providing three supporting paragraphs, you will give enough support to make a strong case for your argument.

Essay Structure

Where you put your introduction and conclusion is obvious. However, you need a pattern, or structure, to organize the ideas in the body of your essay. The four most common patterns are **chronological order**, **comparison and contrast**, **cause and effect**, and **order of importance**. The following chart lists each organizing principle's key characteristics and effective uses in writing:

ORGANIZATIONAL PATTERN	CHARACTERISTICS	EFFECTIVE USES
chronological order	uses time as organizing principle; describes events in the order in which they happened	historical texts, personal narratives, fiction
order of importance	arranges ideas by rank instead of time	persuasive essays, newspaper articles
comparison and contrast	places two or more items side by side to show similarities and differences	comparative essays
cause and effect	explains possible reasons why something took place	historical analysis, analysis of current events

Best Bet: Order of Importance

What is the most effective way to organize your PPST essay when you don't have much time to consider the options? Because the prompts on the writing exam ask you to take a position on a subject, you are essentially developing a brief argument in your essay. A logical and effective strategy for making an argument is to organize your ideas by their importance, or rank. Using this pattern, you can arrange your ideas in two ways:

- by increasing importance (Begin with your least important idea and build up to your most important idea.)
- by decreasing importance (Start with your strongest, most persuasive, idea and end with your least important idea.)

Either arrangement works. However, if you develop your essay by the principle of increasing importance, you save your strongest idea for last, creating a greater impact in your conclusion.

Now it's time to make a detailed outline based on the writing prompt described earlier in the chapter. The outline organizes the supporting ideas by increasing importance. It includes reasons that support the thesis and examples that support each reason. Because this outline is so detailed, it offers a guide for almost every sentence in the body of the essay.

Introduction

Thesis: Mandatory school uniforms are not effective tools for creating a positive, learning environment.

Reason 1: When students feel that they are not trusted, they "live down" to expectations.

   Examples: Feel need to prove individuality through attention to makeup, hair; draw attention through risky behaviors like smoking; continue to find distractions like gossip, note passing, cell phones

Reason 2: School uniforms discourage self-discovery and individuality.

   Examples: Can't try out looks that come with different identities (sporty, punk, artistic); fashion is harmless way to find out who you are

Reason 3: Students don't learn to make good choices.

   Examples: Students aren't prepared for making decisions, simple (clothes, nutrition) or big (college, jobs, whether or not to engage in risky behaviors, friends, romantic relationships)

Conclusion:

   Robbing students of choice discourages self-discovery and does not prepare students for making decisions. Allow students to make choices about their clothes, but also provide a class or forum for discussing how to make good choices, both big and small.

Target Your Audience

Effective writing pays close attention to its *audience*. Good writers consider their readers: Who are they? What do they know about the subject? What preconceived notions do they have? What will hold their attention?

On the PPST, you will be writing to a general audience, meaning your readers are people with a variety of interests and backgrounds. Knowing your audience helps you make key writing decisions about your level of formality and detail. Your level of formality determines whether you will use slang, an informal tone, technical jargon, or formal language in your writing. A good guide for the PPST test is a balanced approach:

- Treat your readers with respect.
- Don't put off your readers with language that is too formal or pretentious. Don't try to use big, important-sounding words.
- Avoid slang (too informal) or jargon (technical or specialized language).
- Aim for a natural tone, without being too informal.

Your level of detail is also based on your audience. Because you are writing for a general audience and not for friends or family, your readers will not be familiar with your background or experiences. For example, if you are arguing against mandatory student uniforms, do not assume that your readers know whether your high school implemented such a rule. Give your readers adequate context by briefly describing your experience as it applies to your argument.

First Impression—The Introduction

Once you have completed your detailed outline, you are ready to write. Because you only have 15–20 minutes to write, you don't have time to perfect the wording of your introduction. Instead, use clear, direct language to introduce your reader to your thesis and focus. A good way to begin is to restate in your own words the quotation given in the prompt and then state your thesis. Here is an example using the prompt discussed earlier:

Although fashion and clothes can sometimes distract students, mandatory school uniforms are not the answer to creating a good learning environment.

Another useful technique for creating a strong introduction is to begin with your thesis and then give a summary of the evidence (supporting details) you will be presenting in the body of your essay. Here is an expanded version of the above thesis statement:

Although fashion and clothes can sometimes distract students, mandatory school uniforms are not the answer to creating a good learning environment. School uniforms can be a negative influence in that they send a message that students can't be trusted to make good choices. High-school students need to explore different identities through the harmless means of fashion.

Notice how this introduction outlines the first two main points of the essay's body: how mandatory school uniforms (1) send a negative message about students' ability to make decisions and (2) discourage self-discovery.

Supporting Paragraphs—The Body of the Essay

Working from your detailed outline, begin composing the body of your essay (about three paragraphs long). Treat each of your paragraphs like a mini-essay, with its own thesis (a topic sentence that expresses the main idea of the paragraph) and supporting details (examples). Follow these guidelines for creating supporting paragraphs:

- **Avoid introducing several ideas within one paragraph.** By definition, a paragraph is a group of sentences about the *same* idea.
- **Use at least one detail** or example to back up each main supporting idea.
- **Aim for about three or four sentences in each paragraph.** Your PPST essay will be short. If you write more sentences for each paragraph you may run short on time and space. If you write fewer sentences, you may not develop your idea adequately.
- **Use transitions.** Key words and phrases can help guide readers through your essay. You can use these common transitions to indicate the order of importance of your material: *first and foremost, most important, first, second, third, moreover, finally,* and *above all.* Do not use "firstly," "secondly," or "thirdly"—these forms are incorrect and awkward.

Active versus Passive Voice

For precise, direct writing, use the active voice. In English grammar, *voice* expresses a relationship between the verb and the subject of the sentence or its direct object. When you write in the *active voice*, the subject of the sentence causes, or is the source of, the action (verb). When you use the *passive voice*, the subject does not perform the action, but rather is acted upon. Sentences in the passive voice are often wordier and more difficult to understand. Here are some examples of active versus passive voice:

Active:	We suggest that you organize your ideas by importance.
Passive:	It is suggested that you organize your ideas by importance. (Note that this sentence does not say *who* performed the action.)

Active:	Her brother typed the letter.
Passive:	The letter was typed by her brother. (Here the *doer* of the action is the direct object *brother*, not the subject of the sentence, *letter.*)

Sentence Variety

A strong PPST essay will show your ability to manipulate sentence structure for effect. Sentence structure is an important element of style. If all of your sentences have the same pattern, your writing will be monotonous and dull:

School uniforms are negative. They don't boost students' confidence. They don't make students feel trustworthy. They don't let students explore different styles and personalities.

Although these sentences are simple and direct, they are unlikely to captivate a reader. Because they all have the same length and structure, they create a monotonous pattern. Here is the same paragraph, revised to show variety in sentence structure:

School uniforms are negative because they do not boost students' confidence or make them feel trustworthy. Fashion choices allow students to explore different styles and personalities.

Four sentences are reduced to two; the pronoun *they* is no longer repeated; and verb choices are active and varied. You can also create emphasis in your writing through sentence structure. The best place to put sentence elements that you want to emphasize is at the end. What comes lasts lingers longest in the reader's mind.

He is tall, dark, and handsome. (The emphasis is on *handsome.* If *tall* is the most important characteristic, then it should come last.)

You can also use a dash to set off a part of a sentence for emphasis:

He is tall, dark, handsome—and married.

The dash emphasizes the last element, heightening the sense of disappointment the writer is trying to convey.

Your Conclusion

The last paragraph of your essay should sum up your argument. Avoid introducing new ideas or topics. Instead, your concluding paragraph should restate your thesis, but in *new words*. Your conclusion should demonstrate that you covered your topic fully and should convince readers that they have learned something meaningful from your argument. Here's an example:

School uniforms might be the easy answer: They create conformity and minimize distractions in the classroom. However, in order to teach students how to make good choices when they face tough decisions, school administrators need to invest students with the responsibility to practice everyday choices—like deciding what they wear to school.

The Last Step—Proofread

On the timed essay test, you should take about five minutes to proofread—a time allowance that does not let you substantially revise or rewrite your piece. Much of what happens when you rewrite—like reorganizing your argument or making sure you present adequate support—must occur during the *prewriting* process, when you are outlining your essay. The goal of proofreading is to give your essay a final polish, by checking your spelling, correcting grammatical errors, and if needed, changing word order or word choice. To proofread, carefully read your essay, paying attention to anything that doesn't sound right. The following checklist outlines some basic grammatical problems to look out for as you proofread. (All of these grammar trouble spots are discussed earlier in the chapter.)

- **Make sure nouns and verbs agree.** The subject of the sentence must match the verb in number. If the subject is singular, the verb is singular. If the subject is plural, the verb is plural.
- **Make sure pronouns and antecedents agree.** Pronouns and the nouns they represent, antecedents, must agree in number. If the antecedent is singular, the pronoun is singular; if the antecedent is plural, the pronoun is plural.
- **Check your modifiers.** Look out for modifiers that are easy to confuse like *good/well*, *bad/badly*, *fewer/less*. Remember: adjectives modify nouns and pronouns; adverbs describe verbs, adjectives, or other adverbs.
- **Avoid double negatives.** Do not use two negative words, like *no*, *not*, *neither*, *hardly*, or *barely*, in one sentence. See page 237 for a list of other negatives.
- **Keep your verb tense consistent.** Switching tense within a sentence can change its meaning. Generally, a sentence or paragraph that begins in the present tense should continue in the present tense.
- **Review prepositional idioms.** If you have studied the list of prepositional idioms on page 239, you may be able to "hear" whether a preposition (*to*, *of*, *about*, *for*, *with*, *about*, *on*, *upon*) sounds right with a particular phrase or verb.
- **Check your sentence structure.** Keep an eye out for sentence fragments, run-on sentences, comma splices, and misplaced or dangling modifiers.

Now, take the skills you have learned or honed in this review and apply them to the next practice test.

7 ▶ Praxis I Practice Exam 2

CHAPTER SUMMARY

Here is another full-length test based on the three elements of the Praxis I, the Pre-Professional Skills Tests (PPSTs) of Reading, Mathematics, and Writing. Now that you have completed the review chapters, take this exam to see how much your score has improved.

LIKE THE REAL PRAXIS I, the exam that follows is made up of three tests: Reading (multiple-choice questions), Mathematics (multiple-choice questions), and Writing (multiple-choice questions and one essay).

With this practice exam, you should simulate the actual test-taking experience as closely as you can. Find a quiet place to work where you won't be disturbed. Use the answer sheet on the next page and write your essay on a separate piece of paper. Allow yourself an hour for the Reading test; an hour for the Mathematics test; 30 minutes for the Section 1 of the Writing test; and 30 minutes for Section 2 of the Writing test (your essay).

Set a timer or stopwatch for each part of the exam, but do not worry too much if you go over the allotted times on this practice exam. You can work more on timing when you take the third practice exam in Chapter 8.

After the exam, use the answer explanations to learn more about the questions you missed and use the scoring guide to figure out how you did.

► Answer Sheet

SKILLS TEST IN READING

1. (a) (b) (c) (d) (e)
2. (a) (b) (c) (d) (e)
3. (a) (b) (c) (d) (e)
4. (a) (b) (c) (d) (e)
5. (a) (b) (c) (d) (e)
6. (a) (b) (c) (d) (e)
7. (a) (b) (c) (d) (e)
8. (a) (b) (c) (d) (e)
9. (a) (b) (c) (d) (e)
10. (a) (b) (c) (d) (e)
11. (a) (b) (c) (d) (e)
12. (a) (b) (c) (d) (e)
13. (a) (b) (c) (d) (e)
14. (a) (b) (c) (d) (e)
15. (a) (b) (c) (d) (e)
16. (a) (b) (c) (d) (e)
17. (a) (b) (c) (d) (e)
18. (a) (b) (c) (d) (e)
19. (a) (b) (c) (d) (e)
20. (a) (b) (c) (d) (e)
21. (a) (b) (c) (d) (e)
22. (a) (b) (c) (d) (e)
23. (a) (b) (c) (d) (e)
24. (a) (b) (c) (d) (e)
25. (a) (b) (c) (d) (e)
26. (a) (b) (c) (d) (e)
27. (a) (b) (c) (d) (e)
28. (a) (b) (c) (d) (e)
29. (a) (b) (c) (d) (e)
30. (a) (b) (c) (d) (e)
31. (a) (b) (c) (d) (e)
32. (a) (b) (c) (d) (e)
33. (a) (b) (c) (d) (e)
34. (a) (b) (c) (d) (e)
35. (a) (b) (c) (d) (e)
36. (a) (b) (c) (d) (e)
37. (a) (b) (c) (d) (e)
38. (a) (b) (c) (d) (e)
39. (a) (b) (c) (d) (e)
40. (a) (b) (c) (d) (e)

SKILLS TEST IN MATHEMATICS

1. (a) (b) (c) (d) (e)
2. (a) (b) (c) (d) (e)
3. (a) (b) (c) (d) (e)
4. (a) (b) (c) (d) (e)
5. (a) (b) (c) (d) (e)
6. (a) (b) (c) (d) (e)
7. (a) (b) (c) (d) (e)
8. (a) (b) (c) (d) (e)
9. (a) (b) (c) (d) (e)
10. (a) (b) (c) (d) (e)
11. (a) (b) (c) (d) (e)
12. (a) (b) (c) (d) (e)
13. (a) (b) (c) (d) (e)
14. (a) (b) (c) (d) (e)
15. (a) (b) (c) (d) (e)
16. (a) (b) (c) (d) (e)
17. (a) (b) (c) (d) (e)
18. (a) (b) (c) (d) (e)
19. (a) (b) (c) (d) (e)
20. (a) (b) (c) (d) (e)
21. (a) (b) (c) (d) (e)
22. (a) (b) (c) (d) (e)
23. (a) (b) (c) (d) (e)
24. (a) (b) (c) (d) (e)
25. (a) (b) (c) (d) (e)
26. (a) (b) (c) (d) (e)
27. (a) (b) (c) (d) (e)
28. (a) (b) (c) (d) (e)
29. (a) (b) (c) (d) (e)
30. (a) (b) (c) (d) (e)
31. (a) (b) (c) (d) (e)
32. (a) (b) (c) (d) (e)
33. (a) (b) (c) (d) (e)
34. (a) (b) (c) (d) (e)
35. (a) (b) (c) (d) (e)
36. (a) (b) (c) (d) (e)
37. (a) (b) (c) (d) (e)
38. (a) (b) (c) (d) (e)
39. (a) (b) (c) (d) (e)
40. (a) (b) (c) (d) (e)

SKILLS TEST IN WRITING, SECTION 1

1. (a) (b) (c) (d) (e)
2. (a) (b) (c) (d) (e)
3. (a) (b) (c) (d) (e)
4. (a) (b) (c) (d) (e)
5. (a) (b) (c) (d) (e)
6. (a) (b) (c) (d) (e)
7. (a) (b) (c) (d) (e)
8. (a) (b) (c) (d) (e)
9. (a) (b) (c) (d) (e)
10. (a) (b) (c) (d) (e)
11. (a) (b) (c) (d) (e)
12. (a) (b) (c) (d) (e)
13. (a) (b) (c) (d) (e)
14. (a) (b) (c) (d) (e)
15. (a) (b) (c) (d) (e)
16. (a) (b) (c) (d) (e)
17. (a) (b) (c) (d) (e)
18. (a) (b) (c) (d) (e)
19. (a) (b) (c) (d) (e)
20. (a) (b) (c) (d) (e)
21. (a) (b) (c) (d) (e)
22. (a) (b) (c) (d) (e)
23. (a) (b) (c) (d) (e)
24. (a) (b) (c) (d) (e)
25. (a) (b) (c) (d) (e)
26. (a) (b) (c) (d) (e)
27. (a) (b) (c) (d) (e)
28. (a) (b) (c) (d) (e)
29. (a) (b) (c) (d) (e)
30. (a) (b) (c) (d) (e)
31. (a) (b) (c) (d) (e)
32. (a) (b) (c) (d) (e)
33. (a) (b) (c) (d) (e)
34. (a) (b) (c) (d) (e)
35. (a) (b) (c) (d) (e)
36. (a) (b) (c) (d) (e)
37. (a) (b) (c) (d) (e)
38. (a) (b) (c) (d) (e)

▶ Skills Test in Reading

Directions: Read the following passages and answer the questions that follow.

Use the following passage to answer question 1.

James Carruthers' recent essays attempt to redefine arts criticism as a play of critical intelligence that can take place free from the bonds of political partisanship. In Carruthers' view, this play of the mind, working itself free from constraints, is the only ethical approach to the arts.

1. What is the best definition of the word *play* as it is used in the passage?
  a. acting or conducting oneself in a specified way
  b. moving or operating freely
  c. pretense; mimicry
  d. careless or indifferent behavior
  e. a stake or wager in a game

Use the following passage to answer question 2.

Rhesus monkeys use facial expressions to communicate with each other and to enforce social order. For example, the "fear grimace," although it looks ferocious, is actually given by a subordinate monkey that is intimidated by a dominant member of the group.

2. In the passage, the word *subordinate* most nearly means
  a. playful.
  b. powerful.
  c. angry.
  d. lower in status.
  e. sick.

Use the following passage to answer questions 3–5.

O'Connell Street is the main thoroughfare of Dublin City. Although it is not a particularly long street, Dubliners will tell the visitor proudly that it is the widest street in all of Europe. This claim usually meets with protests, especially from French tourists, claiming the Champs Elysees of Paris as Europe's widest street. But the witty Dubliner will not relinquish bragging rights easily and will trump the French visitor with a fine distinction: the Champs Elysees is a boulevard; O'Connell is a street.

Divided by several important monuments running the length of its center, the street is named for Daniel O'Connell, an Irish patriot. His monument stands at the lower end of the road, that is, the end closest to the river Liffey that bisects Dublin. O'Connell stands high above the unhurried crowds of shoppers, businesspeople, and students on a sturdy column, surrounded by four serene angels seated at each corner of the monument's base. Further up the street is the famous General Post Office that the locals affectionately call "the GPO." During the 1916 rebellion, the GPO was taken over and occupied by the Irish rebels to British rule, sparking weeks of armed combat in the city's center. To this day, the angels of O'Connell's monument bear the marks of the fighting: one sits reading calmly, apparently unaware of the bullet hole dimpling her upper arm; another, reaching out to stroke the ears of a huge bronze Irish wolfhound, has survived what should be a mortal wound to her heart.

3. Which of the following would be the best title for this passage?
   a. Dublin's Famous Monuments
   b. The Irish Take Pride in Their Capital City
   c. The Widest Street in Europe
   d. Sights and History on Dublin's O'Connell Street
   e. Tourism in Dublin

4. What is the best definition for the word *trump* as it is used in the first paragraph of the passage?
   a. to trumpet loudly, to blare or drown out
   b. to trample
   c. to get the better of by using a key or hidden resource
   d. to devise a fraud, to employ trickery
   e. to use a particular suit of cards

5. With which of the following statements about the people of Dublin would the author of the passage most likely agree?
   a. They are proud of their history but lack industry.
   b. They are playful and tricky.
   c. They are rebellious and do not like tourists.
   d. They are witty and relaxed.
   e. They are unaware of their history.

Use the following passage to answer questions 6 and 7.

The fictional world of Toni Morrison's novel *Sula*—the African-American section of Medallion, Ohio, a community called "the Bottom"—is a place where people, and even natural things, are apt to go awry, to break from their prescribed boundaries, a place where bizarre and unnatural happenings and strange reversals of the ordinary are commonplace. The very name of the setting of *Sula* is significant; the Bottom is located high up in the hills. The novel is furthermore filled with images of mutilation, both psychological and physical. A great part of the lives of the characters, therefore, is taken up with making sense of the world, setting boundaries and devising methods to control what is essentially uncontrollable. One of the major devices used by the people of the Bottom is the seemingly universal one of creating a _____—in this case, the title character Sula—upon which to project both the evil they perceive outside themselves and the evil in their own hearts.

6. Which of the following words would best fit into the blank in the final sentence of the passage?
   a. victim
   b. hero
   c. leader
   d. scapegoat
   e. outcast

7. Why does the writer of this passage mention that *the Bottom is located high up in the hills*?
   a. to show that ordinary expectations are reversed in this community
   b. to tell the reader where the novel is set
   c. to explain why natural things often go wrong there
   d. to describe the weather in the Bottom
   e. to emphasize that *Sula* is a work of fiction

Use the following passage to answer question 8.

When Maria plays in a softball game for her company's team, she plays catcher. If she is unable to attend a game, either Christine or Thomas plays catcher.

8. Based only on the information in the passage, which of the following is a valid conclusion?
   a. Christine and Thomas don't like playing catcher as much as Maria does.
   b. Christine and Thomas are equally good softball players.
   c. If Maria and Thomas both play in a game, Maria plays catcher.
   d. Maria is the best catcher on the team.
   e. Maria often misses softball games.

Use the following passage to answer question 9.

Wondering what to do with that old Atari Home Video Game in the attic? It's on the wish list of the Computer Museum of America, in San Diego, California, which hopes you will donate it to their holdings. The Museum was founded in 1983 to amass and preserve historic computer equipment, such as calculators, card punches, and typewriters, and now owns one of the world's largest collections. In addition, it has archives of computer-related magazines, manuals, and books that are available to students, authors, researchers, and others for historical research.

9. All of the following are probably part of the collection of the Computer Museum of America EXCEPT
   a. adding machines.
   b. old computers.
   c. operation manuals for calculators.
   d. card punch machines.
   e. kitchen scales.

Use the following passage to answer question 10.

In 1904, the U.S. Patent Office granted a patent for a board game called "The Landlord's Game," which was invented by a Virginia Quaker named Lizzie Magie. Magie was a follower of Henry George, who started a tax movement that supported the theory that the renting of land and real estate produced an unearned increase in land values that profited a few individuals (landlords) rather than the majority of the people (tenants). George proposed a single federal tax based on land ownership; he believed this tax would weaken the ability to form monopolies, encourage equal opportunity, and narrow the gap between rich and poor.

   Lizzie Magie wanted to spread the word about George's proposal, making it more understandable to a majority of people who were basically unfamiliar with economics. As a result, she invented a board game that would serve as a teaching device. The Landlord's Game was intended to explain the evils of monopolies, showing that they repressed the possibility for equal opportunity. Her instructions read in part: "The object of this game is not only to afford amusement to players, but to illustrate to them how, under the present or prevailing system of land tenure, the landlord has an advantage over other enterprisers, and also how the single tax would discourage speculation."

10. In paragraph 2, what does *repressed the possibility for equal opportunity* mean?
   a. Monopolies led to slavery.
   b. Monopolies were responsible for the single tax problems.
   c. Monopolies made it impossible for poorer people to follow Henry George.
   d. Monopolies were responsible for Lizzie Magie's $500 payment and Charles Darrow's millions.
   e. Monopolies made it impossible for poorer people to have the same chances as the wealthy.

Use the following passage to answer questions 11–14.

The roots of the modern-day sport of lacrosse are found in tribal stick and ball games developed and played by many native North American tribes dating back as early as the fifteenth century. The Native American names for these games reflected the bellicose nature of those early contests, many of which went far beyond friendly recreational competition. For example, the Algonquin called their game Baggattaway, which meant, "they bump hips." The Cherokee Nation and the Six Tribes of the Iroquois called their sport Tewaarathon, which translated into "Little Brother of War." Rules and style of play differed from tribe to tribe and games could be played by as few as 15 to as many as 1,000 men and women at a time. These matches could last for three days, beginning at dawn each day and ending at sunset. The goals could be specific trees or rocks, and were a few hundred yards to a few miles apart.

Despite these differences, the sole object of every game was the same: to score goals by any means necessary. Serious injuries caused by blows from the heavy wooden sticks used in the games were not uncommon, and often expected. Not surprisingly, the Native Americans considered these precursors to today's lacrosse excellent battle preparation for young warriors, and games were often used to settle disputes between tribes without resorting to full-blown warfare.

11. The author translates the Native American names for their games in order to
   a. demonstrate a strong knowledge of Native American languages.
   b. highlight the differences between the various tribes.
   c. revive the use of ancient tribal languages.
   d. prove that lacrosse has existed for centuries.
   e. emphasize the warlike aspects of these games.

12. In the second sentence, *bellicose* most closely means
   a. beautiful.
   b. warlike.
   c. peaceful.
   d. family minded.
   e. clumsy.

13. Which of the following titles would be the most appropriate for this passage?
   a. Little Brother of War
   b. Lacrosse: America's Most Violent Sport
   c. The Origins of the Modern Lacrosse Stick
   d. The Six Tribes
   e. Hockey: the Little Brother of Lacrosse

14. Near the end of the passage, the author's use of the phrase *by any means necessary* emphasizes
   a. the unpredictable nature of the game.
   b. the mild nature of the game.
   c. the violent nature of the game.
   d. the fact that both women and men participated in the games.
   e. the importance of scoring goals.

Use the following passage to answer questions 15 and 16.

Among traditional societies of the Pacific Northwest—including the Haidas, Kwakiutls, Makahs, Nootkas, Tlingits, and Tsimshians—the gift-giving ceremony called potlatch was a central feature of social life. The word *potlatch*, meaning "to give," comes from a Chinook trading language that was used all along the Pacific Coast. Each nation, or tribe, had its own particular word for the ceremony, and the tribes all had different potlatch traditions. However, the function and basic features of the ceremony were universal among the tribes.

Each nation held potlatches to celebrate important life passages, such as birth, coming of age, marriage, and death. Potlatches were also held to honor ancestors and to mark the passing of leadership. A potlatch, which could last four or more days, was usually held in the winter when the tribes were not engaged in gathering and storing food. Each potlatch included the formal display of the host family's crest and masks. The hosts performed ritual dances and provided feasts for their guests. However, the most important ritual was the lavish distribution of gifts to the guests. Some hosts might give away most or all of their accumulated wealth in one potlatch. The more a host gave away, the more status was accorded him. In turn, the guests, who had to accept the proffered gifts, were then expected to host their own potlatches and give away gifts of equal value.

15. According to the passage, potlatch is best defined as a
   a. ceremony with rigid protocol to which all Pacific Northwest tribes adhered.
   b. generic term for a gift-giving ceremony celebrated in the Pacific Northwest.
   c. socialist ritual of the Pacific Northwest.
   d. lavish feast celebrated in the Pacific Northwest.
   e. wasteful ritual that was banned in the 1880s.

16. According to the passage, the gift-giving central to the potlatch can best be characterized as
   a. reciprocal.
   b. wasteful.
   c. selfless.
   d. spendthrift.
   e. commercialized.

Use the following passage to answer question 17.

Moscow has a history of chaotic periods of war that ended with the destruction of a once largely wooden city and the building of a "new" city on top of the rubble of the old. The result is a layered city, with each tier holding information about a part of Russia's past. In some areas of the city, archaeologists have reached the layer from 1147, the year of Moscow's founding. Among the findings from the various periods of Moscow's history are carved bones, metal tools, pottery, glass, jewelry, and crosses.

17. From the passage, the reader can infer that

   a. the people of Moscow are more interested in modernization than in preservation.

   b. the Soviet government destroyed many of the historic buildings in Russia.

   c. Moscow is the oldest large city in Russia, founded in 1147.

   d. Moscow has a history of invasions, with each new conqueror razing past structures.

   e. Moscow has endured many periods of uprising and revolution.

Use the following passage to answer question 18.

Beliefs are easily the most enduring and distinctive aspects of maritime culture. Common examples include beliefs about good and bad luck, signs for predicting the weather, interpretations of supernatural happenings, and remedies for sickness and injury. Commercial fishing is considered to be the most hazardous of all industrial occupations in the United States. Statistics show that fishermen are seven times more likely to die than workers in the next most dangerous occupation. Adhering to a system of beliefs most likely helps bring sense and order to a world in which natural disasters and misfortune are a part of daily life. Many fishermen also make a precarious living at best. Maritime beliefs contain the collective wisdom of generations and following these traditions may help fishermen catch more fish without taking unnecessary risks.

18. The purpose of the statistic in the passage is to

   a. qualify the statement that fishing is hazardous.

   b. prove that fishing is an undesirable occupation.

   c. illustrate the relative ease of other professions.

   d. quantify the hazardous nature of commercial fishing.

   e. demonstrate that fishermen need a system of beliefs.

Use the following poem by Alfred, Lord Tennyson to answer question 19.

The Eagle

He clasps the crag with crooked hands;
Close to the sun in lonely lands,
Ringed with the azure world he stands.
The wrinkled sea beneath him crawls;
He watches from his mountain walls,
And like a thunderbolt he falls.

19. Given the tone of the poem, and noting especially the last line, what is the eagle most likely doing in the poem?
   a. dying of old age
   b. hunting prey
   c. learning joyfully to fly
   d. keeping watch over a nest of young eagles
   e. battling another eagle

Use the following passage to answer questions 20 and 21.

Elizabeth Blackwell was the first woman to receive an M.D. degree since the Renaissance, graduating from Geneva Medical College, in New York State, in 1849. She supported women's medical education and helped many other women's careers. By establishing the New York Infirmary in 1857, she offered a practical solution to one of the problems facing women who were rejected from internships elsewhere but determined to expand their skills as physicians. She also published several important books on the issue of women in medicine, including *Address on the Medical Education of Women* in 1864 and *Medicine as a Profession for Women* in 1860.

   In her book *Pioneer Work in Opening the Medical Profession to Women*, published in 1895, Dr. Blackwell wrote that she was initially repelled by the idea of studying medicine. She said she had "hated everything connected with the body, and could not bear the sight of a medical book. . . . My favorite studies were history and metaphysics, and the very thought of dwelling on the physical structure of the body and its various ailments filled me with disgust." Instead she went into teaching, then considered more suitable for a woman. She claimed that she turned to medicine after a close friend who was dying suggested she would have been spared her worst suffering if her physician had been a woman.

20. The passage is primarily concerned with
   a. the inevitable breaking down of social barriers for women.
   b. the effect of adversity in shaping a person's life.
   c. one woman's determination to open the field of medicine to females.
   d. one woman's desire to gain prestige.
   e. the quality of healthcare available in the 1800s.

21. The passage implies that Blackwell's attitude toward studying and practicing medicine changed from
   a. tenacious to wavering.
   b. uninterested to resolute.
   c. cynical to committed.
   d. idealized to realistic.
   e. theoretical to practical.

Use the following passage to answer question 22.

Jazz, from its early roots in slave spirituals and the marching bands of New Orleans, had developed into the predominant American musical style by the 1930s. In this era, jazz musicians played a lush, orchestrated style known as *swing*. Played in large ensembles, also called *big bands*, swing filled the dance halls and nightclubs. Jazz, once considered risqué, was made more accessible to the masses with the vibrant, swinging sounds of these big bands, whose musicians improvised from the melody to create original performances. Then came *bebop*. In the mid-1940s, jazz musicians strayed from the swing style and developed a more improvisational method of playing known as bebop. Jazz was transformed from popular music to an elite art form.

22. The swing style can be most accurately characterized as
  a. complex and inaccessible.
  b. appealing to an elite audience.
  c. lively and melodic.
  d. lacking in improvisation.
  e. played in small groups.

Use the following passage to answer question 23.

The youngest member of the Greenville High School track team can run a mile in 5.2 minutes. Sarah runs a mile in 4.9 minutes.

23. Based only on the information in the passage, which of the following must be true?
  a. A runner's speed is related to his or her age.
  b. Other members of the track team can run a mile faster than Sarah.
  c. Sarah is not the youngest member of the track team.
  d. Sarah is not a member of the Greenville High School track team.
  e. Sarah is the best runner on the team.

Use the following passage to answer questions 24–26.

Cuttlefish are intriguing little animals. The cuttlefish resembles a rather large squid and is, like the octopus, a member of the order of cephalopods. Although they are not considered the most highly evolved of the cephalopods, they are extremely intelligent. While observing them, it is hard to tell who is doing the observing, you or the cuttlefish, especially since the eye of the cuttlefish is very similar in structure to the human eye. Cuttlefish are also highly mobile and fast creatures. They come equipped with a small jet located just below the tentacles that can expel water to help them move. Ribbons of flexible fin on each side of the body allow cuttlefish to hover, move, stop, and start. By far their most intriguing characteristic is their ability to change their body color and pattern.

The cuttlefish is sometimes referred to as the "chameleon of the sea" because it can change its skin color and pattern instantaneously. Masters of camouflage, cuttlefish can blend into any environment for protection, but they are also capable of the most imaginative displays of iridescent, brilliant color and intricate designs, which scientists believe they use to communicate with each other and for mating displays. However, judging from the riot of ornaments and hues cuttlefish produce, it is hard not to believe they paint themselves so beautifully just for the sheer joy of it. At the very least, cuttlefish conversation must be the most sparkling in all the sea.

24. Which of the following is correct according to the information given in the passage?
   a. Cuttlefish are a type of squid.
   b. Cuttlefish use jet-propulsion as one form of locomotion.
   c. The cuttlefish does not have an exoskeleton.
   d. Cuttlefish are the most intelligent cephalopods.
   e. Cuttlefish always imitate the patterns and colors of their environment.

25. Which of the following best outlines the main topics addressed in the passage?
   a. I. explanation of why cuttlefish are intriguing
       II. communication skills of cuttlefish
   b. I. classification and difficulties of observing cuttlefish
       II. scientific explanation of modes of cuttlefish communication
   c. I. explanation of the cuttlefish's method of locomotion
       II. description of color displays in mating behavior
   d. I. comparison of cuttlefish with other cephalopods
       II. usefulness of the cuttlefish's ability to change color
   e. I. general classification and characteristics of cuttlefish
       II. uses and beauty of the cuttlefish's ability to change color

26. Which of the following best describes the purpose of the author in the passage?
   a. to prove the intelligence of cuttlefish
   b. to explain the communication habits of cuttlefish
   c. to produce a fanciful description of the chameleon of the sea
   d. to persuade scuba divers of the interest in observing cuttlefish
   e. to describe the chameleon of the sea informatively and entertainingly

Use the following passage to answer question 27.

Public art fulfills several functions essential to the health of a city and its citizens. It educates about history and culture—of the artist, the neighborhood, the city, the nation. Public art is also a "place-making device" that instantly creates memorable, experiential landmarks, fashioning a unique identity for a public place, personalizing it and giving it a specific character. It stimulates the public, challenging viewers to interpret the art and arousing their emotions, and it promotes community by stimulating interaction among viewers. In serving these multiple and important functions, public art beautifies the area and regenerates both the place and the viewer.

27. Which sentence best sums up the main idea of the passage?
   a. Public art serves several important functions in the city.
   b. Public art is often in direct competition with private art.
   c. Public art should be created both by and for members of the community.
   d. In general, public art is more interesting than private art.
   e. Few people are aware of how much public art is around them.

Use the following passage from Jack London's The Cruise of the Snark *to answer questions 28 through 30.*

[N]ow to the particular physics of surf-riding. Get out on a flat board, six feet long, two feet wide, and roughly oval in shape. Lie down upon it like a small boy on a coaster and paddle with your hands out to deep water, where the waves begin to crest. Lie out there quietly on the board. Sea after sea breaks before, behind, and under and over you, and rushes in to shore, leaving you behind. When a wave crests, it gets steeper. Imagine yourself, on your board, on the face of that steep slope. If it stood still, you would slide down just as a boy slides down a hill on his coaster. "But," you object, "the wave doesn't stand still." Very true, but the water composing the wave stands still, and there you have the secret. If ever you start sliding down the face of that wave, you'll keep on sliding and you'll never reach the bottom. Please don't laugh. The face of that wave may be only six feet, yet you can slide down it a quarter of a mile, or half a mile, and not reach the bottom. For, see, since a wave is only a communicated agitation or impetus, and since the water that composes a wave is changing every instant, new water is rising into the wave as fast as the wave travels. You slide down this new water, and yet remain in your old position on the wave, sliding down the still newer water that is rising and forming the wave.

28. The author compares surfing to
    a. an ever-increasing hole forming in the water.
    b. a chemistry experiment gone wrong.
    c. a boy sledding down a hill on a coaster.
    d. a transformation of time and space.
    e. flying through the air like a bird.

29. As used in the passage, the word *impetus* most nearly means
    a. a moving force.
    b. a serious obstacle.
    c. a slight annoyance.
    d. a slight hindrance.
    e. an area of very warm water.

30. What is the secret referred to in the passage?
    a. why a good wave for surfing must to be at least six feet tall
    b. A six-foot wave is between a quarter mile and a half mile in length.
    c. how a surfer can slide down a six-foot wave for a quarter of a mile
    d. The smarter surfers paddle out to the deep water to catch the best waves.
    e. The water that composes a wave remains with the wave until it reaches the shore.

Use the following passage to answer question 31.

Today's shopping mall has as its antecedents historical marketplaces, such as Greek agoras, European piazzas, and Asian bazaars. The purpose of these sites, as with the shopping mall, is both economic and social. People go not simply to buy and sell wares, but also to be seen, catch up on news, and be part of the human drama. Both marketplace and its descendant, the mall, might also contain restaurants, banks, theaters, and professional offices.

31. The statement that people went to marketplaces to *be part of the human drama* suggests that people
    a. prefer to shop anonymously.
    b. like to act on stage rather than shop.
    c. seem to be more emotional in groups.
    d. like to be in community, interacting with one another.
    e. prefer to be entertained rather than shop for necessities.

Use the following passage to answer question 32.

The Great Depression, which began during the presidency of Herbert Hoover, led to the election of President Franklin D. Roosevelt in 1932. Roosevelt introduced relief measures that would revive the economy and bring needed relief to Americans who were suffering the effects of the depression. In his first hundred days in office, Roosevelt and Congress passed major legislation that saved banks from closing and regained public confidence. These measures, called the New Deal, included the Agricultural Adjustment Act, which paid farmers to slow their production in order to stabilize food prices; the Federal Deposit Insurance Corporation, which insured bank deposits in the case that banks fail; and the Securities and Exchange Commission, which regulated the stock market. Although the New Deal offered relief, it did not end the depression. The economy sagged until the nation entered World War II. However, the New Deal changed the relationship between government and American citizens, by expanding the role of the central government in regulating the economy and creating social assistance programs.

32. The content of the passage would most likely support which of the following statements?
   a. The New Deal policies were not radical enough in challenging capitalism.
   b. The economic policies of the New Deal brought about a complete business recovery.
   c. The Agricultural Adjustment Act paid farmers to produce surplus crops.
   d. The federal government became more involved in caring for needy members of society.
   e. The New Deal measures went too far in turning the country toward socialism.

Use the following passage to answer questions 33–35.

In the summer of 1919, the Cleveland Indians and the New York Yankees were two of the strongest teams in baseball's American League, but one team stood head and shoulders above the rest: the Chicago White Sox. The Chicago White Sox, called the White Stockings until 1902, were owned by an ex-ballplayer named Charles Comiskey. Between the years of 1900 and 1915, the White Sox had won the World Series only once, and Comiskey was determined to change that. In 1915, he purchased the contracts of three of the most promising stars in the league. Comiskey only had to wait two years for his plan to come to fruition; the 1917 White Sox, playing in a park named for their owner, won the World Series. Two years later they had the best record in all of baseball and were again on their way to the World Series.

Baseball players' salaries in that era were much different than the exorbitant paychecks of today's professional athletes. Often, ballplayers would have second careers in the off-season because of the mediocrity of their pay. To make matters worse, war-torn 1918 was such a horrible year for baseball attendance that many owners cut player salaries for the following season. However, it is said in all of baseball there was no owner as parsimonious as Charles Comiskey. In 1917 he reportedly promised every player on the White Sox a bonus if they won the American League Championship. After winning the championship, they returned to the clubhouse to receive their bonus—a bottle of inexpensive champagne. Unlike other owners, Comiskey also required the players to pay for the cleaning of their uniforms. The White Sox had the best record in baseball, but they were paid the least, were the most discontented, and wore the dirtiest uniforms.

33. In the fourth sentence of the second paragraph, the word *parsimonious* most nearly means
a. generous.
b. stingy.
c. powerful.
d. friendly.
e. jovial.

34. According to facts from the passage, what was the name of the White Sox's ballpark?
a. Chicago Park
b. Comiskey Park
c. Sullivan Stadium
d. White Sox Park
e. Sox Field

35. According to the passage, how many World Series did the White Sox win between 1900 and 1919?
a. none
b. one
c. two
d. three
e. four

Use the following passage from Charlotte Brontë's Jane Eyre *to answer questions 36–38.*

I went to my window, opened it, and looked out. There were the two wings of the building; there was the garden; there were the skirts of Lowood; there was the hilly horizon. My eye passed all other objects to rest on those most remote, the blue peaks: it was those I longed to surmount; all within their boundary of rock and heath seemed prison-ground, exile limits. I traced the white road winding round the base of one mountain, and vanishing in a gorge between two: how I longed to follow it further! I recalled the time when I had traveled that very road in a coach; I remembered descending that hill at twilight: an age seemed to have elapsed since the day which brought me first to Lowood, and I had never quitted it since. My vacations had all been spent at school: Mrs. Reed had never sent for me to Gateshead; neither she nor any of her family had ever been to visit me. I had had no communication by letter or message with the outer world: school-rules, school-duties, school-habits and notions, and voices, and faces, and phrases, and costumes, and preferences, and antipathies: such was what I knew of existence. And now I felt that it was not enough: I tired of the routine of eight years in one afternoon. I desired liberty; for liberty I gasped; for liberty I uttered a prayer; it seemed scattered on the wind then faintly blowing. I abandoned it and framed a humbler supplication; for change, stimulus: that petition, too, seemed swept off into vague space: "Then," I cried, half desperate, "grant me at least a new servitude!"

36. It can be inferred from the passage that life at Lowood was
   a. very unconventional and modern.
   b. very structured and isolated.
   c. harsh and demeaning.
   d. liberal and carefree.
   e. urban and sophisticated.

37. The passage suggests that the narrator
   a. will soon return to Lowood.
   b. was sent to Lowood by mistake.
   c. is entirely dependent upon the people at Lowood.
   d. has run away from Lowood before.
   e. is naturally curious and rebellious.

38. In the final lines of the passage, the narrator reduces her petition to simply *a new servitude* because she
   a. doesn't believe in prayer.
   b. is not in a free country.
   c. has been offered a position as a servant.
   d. knows so little of the real world.
   e. has been treated like a slave at Lowood.

Use the following passage to answer questions 39 and 40.

In the 1980s, I was just beginning as an internist, working in a private practice. Then in my late twenties, I felt pity for my patients who talked to me about a surgical fix for their wrinkles or other signs of aging. I felt that if they had a developed sense of self-esteem, they would not feel the need to surgically alter their appearance. I also felt a certain degree of envy for my cosmetic-surgeon colleagues, some of whom worked across the hall. To my "green" eye, they looked like slick salespeople reaping large financial rewards from others' insecurity and vanity. It was difficult for me to reconcile the fact that patients were willing to fork over thousands of dollars for cosmetic fixes, while primary care physicians struggled to keep their practices financially viable.

Since that time, my attitude has changed. Although cosmetic surgery sometimes produces negative outcomes—the media often highlights surgery disasters—for the most part, the health risk for cosmetic procedures is low and patient satisfaction is high. Often, people who have been hobbled by poor body image all of their lives walk away from cosmetic surgery with confidence and the motivation to lead healthier lives. In addition, reconstructive surgery for burn and accident victims or to those disfigured from disease restores self-esteem and well-being in a way that other therapies cannot. I believe it is time for members of the medical community to examine the benefits and results of cosmetic surgery without prejudice or jealousy.

39. The argument in the passage would be most effectively strengthened by which of the following?
   a. information about making plastic surgery more affordable
   b. anecdotes about incompetent plastic surgeons
   c. facts to support the author's claim that health risks are low for cosmetic procedures
   d. a description of the author's personal experience with patients
   e. a description of the psychological benefits of improved body image

40. Which audience is the author most likely addressing?
   a. burn or accident victims
   b. women with poor body image
   c. plastic surgeons
   d. healthcare providers
   e. baby boomers

▶ Skills Test in Mathematics

Directions: Choose the best answer to each of the following questions.

Use the following figure to answer question 1.

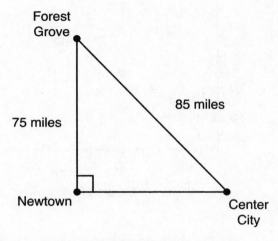

Note: Figure not drawn to scale.

1. Pierre's usual route between Center City and Forest Grove is 85 miles long, as shown in the diagram. Because of construction, he must now take a detour through Newtown first before driving the 75 miles between Newtown and Forest Grove. How much longer is the detoured route than his regular route between Center City and Forest Grove?
   a. 10 miles
   b. 30 miles
   c. 40 miles
   d. 75 miles
   e. 115 miles

Use the following information to answer question 2.

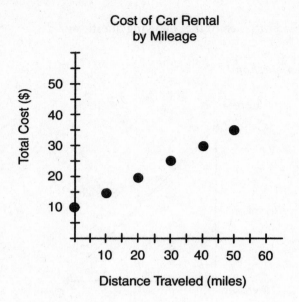

Cost of Car Rental by Mileage

2. The graph shows the cost of renting a car according to the number of miles the car is driven. Which of the following answer choices represents the equation of the line that is determined by the data in the scatter plot?

   a. $y = 2x + 10$
   b. $y = \frac{1}{2}x + 10$
   c. $y = 10x + 15$
   d. $y = 5x + 10$
   e. $y = -5x + 15$

Use the following information to answer questions 3 and 4.

The cost of tickets to the school play is $7.50 for adults and $5 for children ages 12 and under. On Saturday and Sunday afternoon, there is a special matinee price: $5.50 for adults and $3 for children ages 12 and under. Special group discounts are available for groups of 30 or more people.

3. Which of the following can be determined from the information given in the passage?
   a. how much it will cost a family of four to buy tickets for the school play on Saturday afternoon
   b. the difference between the cost of two tickets for the school play on Tuesday night and the cost of one ticket on Sunday afternoon
   c. how much tickets to the school play will cost each person if he or she is part of a group of 40 people
   d. the difference between the cost of a ticket for the school play for an adult on Friday night and a ticket for the school play for a 13-year-old on Saturday afternoon
   e. the total amount of money saved by a group of 35

4. Using the passage, how can you find the difference in price between a ticket for the school play for an adult and a ticket for a child under the age of 12 if they are attending the show on Saturday afternoon?
   a. subtract $3.00 from $7.50.
   b. subtract $3.00 from $5.50.
   c. subtract $5.00 from $7.50.
   d. subtract $7.50 from $5.50.
   e. add $5.50 and $3.00 and divide by 2.

5. There were 504 candies in a jar. Between 8 o'clock and 9 o'clock, $\frac{1}{8}$ of the candies were given out. Between 9 o'clock and 10 o'clock, $\frac{2}{9}$ of the remaining candies were handed out. If in the following hour $\frac{1}{7}$ of the remaining candies are distributed, how many candies will be left?
   a. 441
   b. 343
   c. 294
   d. 188
   e. 96

6. Joe has exactly 720 hours until his vacation begins. How many days are there before his vacation begins?
   a. 30
   b. 60
   c. 72
   d. 144
   e. 17,280

7. Which of the following is equivalent to $3 \times 5 + 3 \times 8$?
   a. $3 + 5 \times 3 + 8$
   b. $3(5 \times 8)$
   c. $(3 \times 5) + 8$
   d. $3(5 + 8)$
   e. $(3 \times 5) \times (3 \times 8)$

Use the following table to answer question 8.

Class Time Schedule

Period	Start Time	End Time
1	7:55	8:35
2	8:39	9:19
3		10:03
4	10:07	10:47
5	10:51	11:31
6	11:35	12:15
7	12:19	12:59
8	1:03	
9	1:47	2:27

8. According to the table, what is the starting time of period 3 and the ending time of period 8, respectively?
   a. 9:24, 1:43
   b. 9:23, 1:44
   c. 9:29, 1:59
   d. 9:23, 1:43
   e. 9:24, 1:44

Use the following information to answer question 9.

A grocery store has a total of 55 different varieties of candy bars. Twelve are made of milk chocolate, 5 are made of white chocolate, and 15 are made of dark chocolate. The candy bars are made by three different companies: Hometown Confections, Cocoa Inc., and Taste of Chocolate.

9. Which of the following facts can be determined from the information given?
   a. the number of candy bars made by Hometown Confections
   b. the ratio of milk chocolate candy bars to white chocolate candy bars
   c. the number of toffee candy bars
   d. the cost of a milk chocolate candy bar made by Cocoa Inc.
   e. the ratio of milk chocolate peanut butter candy bars to dark chocolate candy bars with nuts

Use the following information to answer questions 10 and 11.

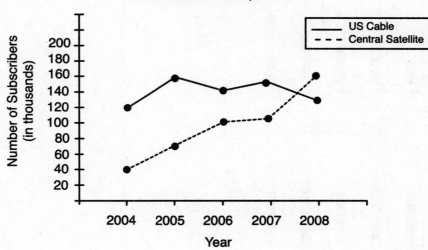

Number of Subscribers at
Two Television Companies

10. Approximately what percentage of the total subscribers to both services subscribed to US Cable in 2006?

   a. 33%

   b. 40%

   c. 58%

   d. 71%

   e. 85%

11. Which of the following most accurately depicts the information in the graph on the preceding page?

a.

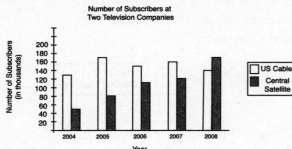

b.

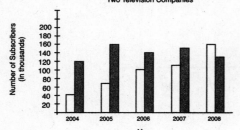

c.

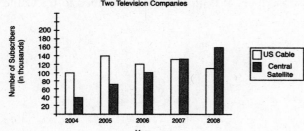

d.

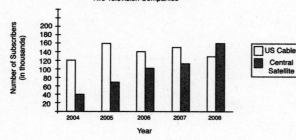

e.

12. Out of 100 students polled at a local university, 80 said they would favor being offered a course in web page development. If there are 30,000 students enrolled at this university, how many would you expect to favor being offered such a course?
   a. 2,400
   b. 6,000
   c. 16,000
   d. 22,000
   e. 24,000

13. Jacob pays a $19 flat fee for his cellular phone service each month, which includes the first 120 minutes of airtime he uses. He is then charged $0.32 per minute for each minute after that. If x represents the total airtime he uses each month, and he always uses more than 120 minutes of airtime each month, which of the following expressions can be used to calculate his monthly cellular phone bill?
   a. $19 + 0.32x$
   b. $19x + 0.32$
   c. $19(x - 120) + 0.32x$
   d. $19 + 0.32(x - 120)$
   e. $19x + 0.32(x - 120)$

14. What is 56.73647 rounded to the nearest hundredth?
   a. 57
   b. 56.7
   c. 56.73
   d. 56.74
   e. 56.736

Use the following graph to answer question 15.

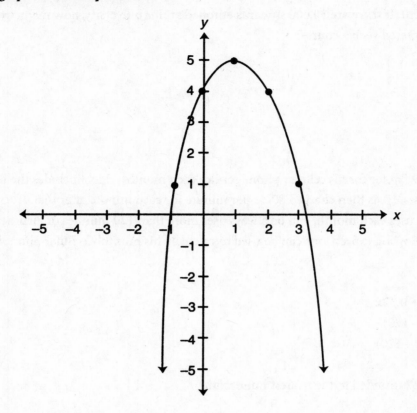

15. Which equation is best represented by the graph?

    a. $y = -x^2 + 2x + 4$

    b. $y = -x^2 + 2x - 4$

    c. $y = x^2 + 2x + 4$

    d. $y = x^2 + 2x - 4$

    e. $y = -x^2 - 2x - 4$

16. A factory operates 20 machines that make granola bars. Each machine can make between 80 and 100 granola bars per minute. Which of the following could be the number of granola bars produced per hour if all 20 machines are working at the same time?

    a. 1,800

    b. 5,000

    c. 18,000

    d. 100,000

    e. 125,000

17. Ridgefield Stadium has a total of 36,042 seats. At the first home game of the year, every seat was sold out, and 16,534 of the people in attendance were male. Approximately how many more women attended this game than men?
  a. 1,500
  b. 2,000
  c. 3,000
  d. 4,000
  e. 4,500

18. If a, b, and c represent nonzero real numbers, which of the following statements are equivalent?
  I. $a + (b + c)$
  II. $(a + b) + (a + c)$
  III. $(a + b) + c$
  a. I and II
  b. I and III
  c. II and III
  d. I, II, and III
  e. None of the statements is equivalent.

19. An aquarium has a base length of 12 inches and a width of 5 inches. If the aquarium is 10 inches tall, what is the total volume?
  a. 480 cubic inches
  b. 540 cubic inches
  c. 600 cubic inches
  d. 720 cubic inches
  e. 1,200 cubic inches

Use the following chart to answer questions 20 and 21.

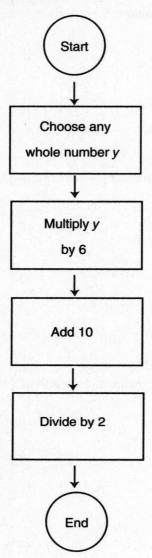

20. If *y* = 4, what is the result when steps 3 and 4 are reversed?

   a. 10

   b. 12

   c. 13

   d. 17

   e. 22

21. According to the flow chart on the preceding page, no matter what whole number is inputted, the resulting number will always be

   a. odd.

   b. even.

   c. prime.

   d. a multiple of 6.

   e. an integer.

Use the following chart to answer question 22.

Enrollment by Division

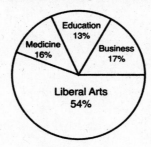

22. The pie chart shows the semester enrollment for four different divisions of a university. Which of the following combinations made up 70% of the total enrollment?

   a. Education and Business

   b. Education and Liberal Arts

   c. Business and Liberal Arts

   d. Business and Medicine

   e. Liberal Arts and Medicine

23. Mrs. Savoie noted the number of absences from her psychology class for the past six days. There were 11, 4, 0, 5, 4, and 6 students absent those six days, respectively. On those particular days, what was the average number of students absent?

   a. 4

   b. 5

   c. 6

   d. 7

   e. 8

24. Jacqueline was $\frac{1}{3}$ as young as her grandmother 15 years ago. If the sum of their ages is now 110, how old is Jacqueline's grandmother?

    a. 80

    b. 75

    c. 65

    d. 60

    e. 50

25. Which of the following is between $\frac{1}{3}$ and $\frac{1}{4}$?

    a. $\frac{1}{2}$

    b. $\frac{1}{5}$

    c. $\frac{2}{3}$

    d. $\frac{2}{5}$

    e. $\frac{2}{7}$

Use the following graph to answer question 26.

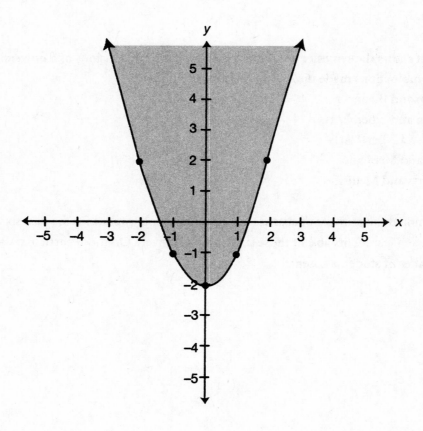

26. Which of the following inequalities is represented by the graph on the previous page?

   a. $y \geq x^2 + 2$

   b. $y \leq x^2 - 2$

   c. $y \geq x^2 + 2x$

   d. $y \geq x^2 - 2$

   e. $y \leq x^2 + 2$

27. If a function is defined as $f(x) = 3x^2 - \frac{1}{2}x + 7$, what is $f(\frac{1}{2})$?

   a. $\frac{15}{2}$

   b. $-\frac{15}{2}$

   c. 8

   d. $\frac{17}{2}$

   e. $-\frac{17}{2}$

28. Given the equation $y = 5 + 4x$, what is the value of y when $x = 3$?

   a. 6

   b. 9

   c. 12

   d. 17

   e. 20

29. At the grocery store, if Lucinda purchases a total of $30 or less, she will pay with cash. If Lucinda spends an amount between $30 and $70 she will pay with a check. If Lucinda spends $70 or more, she will use a credit card. If Lucinda recently paid for a grocery bill using a check, which of the following statements could be true?

   a. The bill was $20.

   b. The bill was $80.

   c. If the bill was $20 more, she would have paid with cash.

   d. The bill was at least $70.

   e. The bill was more than $25.

Use the following figure to answer question 30.

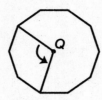

30. If the figure is a tile in the shape of a regular decagon with a center at Q, what is the measure of the indicated angle?

a. 36°

b. 45°

c. 80°

d. 90°

e. 108°

31. Solve for x in the following equation:

$2x - 3(x - 1) = -12$

a. 11

b. 15

c. −11

d. 9

e. −15

Use the following figure to answer question 32.

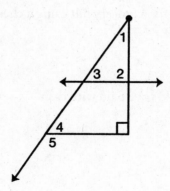

32. If angle 1 is 30°, and angle 2 is a right angle, what is the measure of angle 5?

   a. 30°

   b. 60°

   c. 120°

   d. 150°

   e. 180°

33. A circle drawn on a gymnasium floor for a basketball court has an area of 78.5 square feet. What is the length of the diameter of this circle? Use $\pi = 3.14$.

   a. 25 feet

   b. 15 feet

   c. 12.5 feet

   d. 10 feet

   e. 5 feet

34. A certain county has an annual spending budget of about $490,000. The largest area of allocation is regional transportation, in which the county spends about $98,000 per year. Which fraction most accurately portrays the portion of spending on regional transportation with respect to the total annual budget of the county?

   a. $\frac{1}{5}$

   b. $\frac{1}{4}$

   c. $\frac{2}{9}$

   d. $\frac{3}{4}$

   e. $\frac{4}{5}$

35. Which of the following is NOT equivalent to the others?

   a. $3(21 + 55) - 10$

   b. $3(55 + 21) - 10$

   c. $3 \times 55 + 3 \times 21 - 10$

   d. $(55 + 21) \times 3 - 10$

   e. $10 - 3(21 + 55)$

36. Thirty percent of the students at a middle school are involved in the vocal and instrumental music programs. If 15% of the musicians are in the choir, what percentage of the whole school is in the choir?

   a. 4.5%

   b. 9.0%

   c. 15%

   d. 30%

   e. 45%

Use the following table to answer question 37.

x	y
10	8
8	8.5
6	9
4	9.5
2	10

37. According to the information in the table, which of the following statements is true?

a. As x increases by $\frac{1}{2}$, y decreases by 2.

b. As x decreases by 2, y decreases by $\frac{1}{2}$.

c. As x increases by 1, y decreases by 2.

d. As x decreases by 2, y increases by $\frac{1}{2}$.

e. As x increases by 2, y decreases by $\frac{1}{2}$.

38. While competing in a swim meet, Jose finished three one-hundredths of a second ahead of his opponent. Which of the following is equivalent to this value?

a. 3.0

b. 0.003

c. 0.0003

d. 0.03

e. 0.3

Use the following graph to answer question 39.

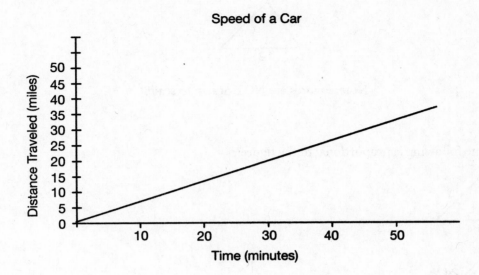

Speed of a Car

39. According to the graph, what is the approximate speed of the car in miles per hour?

  a. 10 miles per hour
  b. 20 miles per hour
  c. 33 miles per hour
  d. 40 miles per hour
  e. 50 miles per hour

Use the following figure to answer question 40.

Note: Figures are NOT drawn to scale.

40. Which of the following is proportional to the figure?

a.

b.

c.

d.

e.

▶ Skills Test in Writing—Section 1, Part A

Directions: Choose the letter for the underlined portion that contains a grammatical error. If there is no error in the sentence, choose **e**.

1. Elizabeth Blackwell, the first woman to be accepted into a medical school, she graduated from Geneva
               a   **b**   **c**   **d**

   Medical College in 1849. No error
                  e

2. The freshwater source of the Hudson River can be found in the Adirondack Mountains, at a small lake
                                                  a   **b**

   on Mount Marcy known as Lake Tear of the Clouds. No error
     c   **d**   **e**

3. Considering the principal believed in school uniforms, so he implemented a new rule in the high school.
        a   **b**   **c**   **d**

   No error
   e

4. Soon after Alison stopped to get some coffee; she realized that she had missed the ferry. No error
                   a   **b**   **c**   **d**   **e**

5. Ronald called to say that our new car had arrived and asking if we would pick it up by 6:30. No error
     a   **b**   **c**   **d**   **e**

6. Because Nick was a confident test taker, he failed horribly on the math final. No error
      a   **b**   **c**   **d**   **e**

7. Albert Einstein was a genius in the world of science and who influenced the artists of his generation
                  a   **b**   **c**

   as well. No error
     d   **e**

8. We all agreed that the quick action of the security officers' thwarted the robbery attempt yesterday at the
           a   **b**   **c**

   bank. No error
    d   **e**

9. In this travel guide, <u>you'll discover</u> great travel deals, vacation hot spots<u>, and</u> unique exotic destinations

                     a   **b**

<u>for even</u> the <u>more</u> experienced world travelers. <u>No error</u>

  c   **d**   **e**

10. The lifeguard staff at the <u>public</u> beach <u>deserve</u> recognition for <u>winning</u> the annual <u>"safest waters"</u> award.

                         a   **b**   **c**   **d**

<u>No error</u>

 e

11. <u>Any</u> player <u>who arrives</u> late to the soccer tryout will <u>give the coach</u> a bad first impression, <u>but</u> probably

  a   **b**   **c**   **d**

be cut from the team. <u>No error</u>

                     e

12. Pressed <u>sailors</u> in the time of <u>Lord Nelson</u> lived in cramped quarters, fought battles <u>on the high</u> seas,

          a   **b**   **c**

<u>and learn to</u> understand the blessings of a mariner's life. <u>No error</u>

    d   **e**

13. All <u>students</u> with an excellent GPA <u>are eligible</u> for a full <u>scholarship</u>, including tuition, housing,

   a   **b**   **c**

meals<u>, and money</u> for books. <u>No error</u>

      d   **e**

14. The <u>person who</u> sold me the laptop, owns the electronics store on Melrose <u>A</u>venue and knows all <u>there is</u>

           a   **b**   **c**   **d**

to know about computers. <u>No error</u>

                   e

15. The <u>aorta</u> is the largest artery in the <u>human body;</u> it receives <u>oxygen-rich</u> blood from the <u>heart and</u>

     a   **b**   **c**   **d**

carries it to the rest of the body. <u>No error</u>

                         e

16. Ernest Hemingway <u>and fellow</u> writer F. Scott Fitzgerald met as <u>expatriates</u> in Paris during the 1920s;
                                a   **b**

<u>he</u> was the first of the two to move <u>there,</u> in 1921. <u>No error</u>
c   **d**   **e**

17. <u>During</u> the summer season, boat owners should replace <u>their</u> oil filters at least once <u>a month; a</u> dirty filter
     a   **b**   **c**

<u>reduce</u> engine efficiency. <u>No error</u>
   d   **e**

18. In areas <u>or regions</u> of the world <u>that don't</u> get much <u>rain,</u> water-storing plants <u>dominate</u> the landscape.
           a   **b**   **c**   **d**

<u>No error</u>
  e

19. Our company <u>CEO</u> truly believes that money equals <u>happiness;</u> he's not <u>ashamed with himself</u> to admit
                  a   **b**   **c**

<u>that</u> his first love is cash. <u>No error</u>
   d   **e**

20. <u>John Glenn</u>—the first American to orbit the <u>earth</u>—returned to space in <u>1998,</u> 36 years
     a   **b**   **c**

<u>after his first</u> historic space flight. <u>No error</u>
   d   **e**

21. The archaeologists excavating the ruins <u>were</u> surprised to have <u>uncovered:</u> ancient <u>roads,</u> primitive
                                       a   **b**   **c**

<u>plumbing,</u> and personal items. <u>No error</u>
   d   **e**

► Skills Test in Writing—Section 1, Part B

Directions: Choose the best replacement for the underlined portion of the sentence. If no revision is necessary, choose **a**, which always repeats the original phrasing.

22. <u>Along with your membership to our golf club goes</u> three free personal golf lessons.
    a. Along with your membership to our golf club goes
    b. Along with your membership to our golf club go
    c. With your membership to our golf club there is
    d. In addition to your membership to our golf club there's
    e. Added to your membership to our golf club,

23. When the doorbell <u>rung, Alvaro had been feeding</u> his fish.
    a. rung, Alvaro had been feeding
    b. rung, Alvaro was feeding
    c. rang, Alvaro was feeding
    d. had rung, Alvaro was feeding
    e. rang, Alvaro had feeded

24. There are a number of skeptics who don't believe in the <u>effects of global warming upon the earths climate.</u>
    a. effects of global warming upon the earths climate.
    b. effects' of global warming upon the earth's climate.
    c. effect's of global warming upon the earths climate.
    d. effect's of global warming upon the earths' climate.
    e. effects of global warming upon the earth's climate.

25. Vitellius "the Glutton" <u>was the greediest of all of the Roman emperors.</u>
    a. was the greediest of all of the Roman emperors.
    b. was the greedliest of all of the Roman emperors.
    c. was the greedier of all of the Roman emperors.
    d. was the most greedful of all of the Roman emperors.
    e. was the greedfullest of all of the Roman emperors.

26. <u>There wasn't never a comedian that was funnier.</u>
    a. There wasn't never a comedian that was funnier.
    b. There was never a comedian more funnier.
    c. Never was there a comedian more funnier.
    d. There never was a more funnier comedian.
    e. There never was a funnier comedian.

27. <u>The Doctor in Spokane can speak Italian, French, and Urdu.</u>

    a. The Doctor in Spokane can speak Italian, French, and Urdu.

    b. The doctor in spokane can speak italian, french, and urdu.

    c. The doctor in Spokane can speak Italian, French, and Urdu.

    d. The doctor in Spokane can speak italian, french, and urdu!

    e. The Doctor in spokane can speak Italian, French, and Urdu.

28. <u>I look forward to speaking with you and having</u> the opportunity to explain my views on the subject.

    a. I look forward to speaking with you and having

    b. I will look forward to our speaking and having

    c. As I look forward to our speaking and to have

    d. I look forward to speaking with you and have

    e. Looking forward to our speaking and hoping to have

29. Of the two cars, the <u>newest model is safest than the oldest one.</u>

    a. the newest model is safest than the oldest one.

    b. the newest model is safest than the older one.

    c. the newest model is more safe than the oldest one.

    d. the newer model is safer than the older one.

    e. the newer model is more safer than the older one.

30. The lacrosse team scored <u>less goals today than they did</u> last Monday.

    a. less goals today than they did

    b. today less goals than were scored

    c. fewer goals today then on

    d. fewer goals today than they did

    e. a lesser number of goals today then they did

31. <u>When twins have the same DNA, it is said to be identical.</u>

    a. When twins have the same DNA, it is said to be identical.

    b. When twins has the same DNA, it is said to be identical.

    c. Twins with the same DNA is said to be identical.

    d. They are identical when the said twins has the same DNA.

    e. When twins have the same DNA, they are said to be identical.

32. Athletic ability depends <u>not only on hand-eye coordination, but also</u> on mental acuity and physical fitness.

    a. not only on hand-eye coordination, but also

    b. not simply on hand-eye coordination, then too

    c. only just not on hand-eye coordination, also

    d. on hand-eye coordination alone, but also

    e. not only on hand-eye coordination, however, it also depends

33. <u>It snowed; so I tried to shovel the driveway.</u>

    a. It snowed; so I tried to shovel the driveway.

    b. It snowed, so I tried to shovel the driveway.

    c. It snowed, I tried to shovel the driveway.

    d. It's snowing, I tried to shovel the driveway.

    e. It will snow, so I tried to shovel the driveway.

34. <u>The Mississippi River, it originates in Minnesota,</u> empties into the Gulf of Mexico.

    a. The Mississippi River, it originates in Minnesota,

    b. The Mississippi River, that originates in Minnesota,

    c. The Mississippi River, who originates in Minnesota,

    d. The Mississippi River, which originates in Minnesota,

    e. The Mississippi River, whose originates in Minnesota,

35. The second layer of human skin is known as the <u>dermis, which is located</u> directly below the epidermis.

    a. dermis, which is located

    b. dermis, and which is located

    c. dermis but located

    d. dermis it is located

    e. that its location is

36. My favorite subjects <u>are gym and calculus, my second semester electives are Italian and physics.</u>

    a. are gym and calculus, my second semester electives are Italian and physics.

    b. are gym, and calculus; my second semester electives are Italian, and physics.

    c. are gym and calculus; my second semester electives are Italian and physics.

    d. are gym and calculus; my second semester electives are italian and physics.

    e. are gym, and calculus, my second semester electives are Italian, and physics.

37. <u>Because the economy is improving,</u> there are still many people who are unemployed.

    a. Because the economy is improving,

    b. Because the economy was improving,

    c. The economy is improving,

    d. Although the economy is improving,

    e. Although the economy is improving;

38. Nobody on the team <u>skates more graceful than me.</u>

    a. skates more graceful than me.

    b. skates more gracefully than I do.

    c. skates gracefuller than I do.

    d. skates more graceful than I do.

    e. skates more gracefully than me.

► Skills Test in Writing—Section 2, Essay Writing

Carefully read the essay topic that follows. Plan and write an essay that addresses all points in the topic. Make sure that your essay is well organized and that you support your central argument with concrete examples. Allow 30 minutes for your essay.

There are more vegetarians in this country than ever before. Should school and workplace cafeterias accommodate these people by offering vegetarian selections? Use specific reasons and examples as support for your argument.

► Answers

Skills Test in Reading

1. b. The connotations of words like *bonds* and *constraints* in the passage suggest a confined space of criticism where the mind must be allowed to find some movement or play. None of the other choices makes sense in the context of the passage.

2. d. The passage says that the subordinate monkey grimaces when he is *intimidated by a dominant member of the group*. Because *intimidated* means *afraid*, and *dominant* means *powerful* or *in a leadership position*, one can infer that *subordinate* means *lower in status*.

3. d. The title *Sights and History on Dublin's O'Connell Street* touches on all the specific subjects of the passage—the sights to see on this particular street and the history connected to them.

4. c. The hidden or key resource mentioned in the passage is the fine distinction between the definitions of street and boulevard, which is used to win the argument with, or get the better of, tourists.

5. d. The author offers an example of Dublin wit and mentions the unhurried pace of Dublin crowds.

6. d. A *scapegoat* is one who is forced to bear the blame for others or upon whom the sins of a community are heaped.

7. a. In the beginning of the passage, the author describes *the Bottom* as a *place where bizarre and unnatural happenings and strange reversals of the ordinary are commonplace*. It is a reversal of the ordinary to name a hilltop community *the Bottom*, and the author mentions this in order to emphasize his or her point about the strangeness of this community.

8. c. This is the only conclusion that is supported by information in the passage.

9. e. The passage mentions calculators (adding machines), computers, card punches, and manuals. The only item not mentioned is kitchen scales.

10. e. Look back to the last sentence of the first paragraph, where George's single-tax proposal (the idea The Landlord's Game was meant to teach) is described as aiming to *weaken the ability to form monopolies, encourage equal opportunity, and narrow the gap between rich and poor*.

11. e. In the beginning of the passage, the author writes that these games *went far beyond friendly recreational competition*, and the end of the passage says that Native Americans viewed these games as *excellent battle preparation* for the young.

12. b. *Bellicose* most closely means *warlike*. There are two major clues in this passage to help you answer this question. The first clue lies in the translation of the name *Tewaarathon*, meaning "Little Brother of War." Another clue lies in the line where the author states that these games were *excellent battle preparation for young warriors*.

13. a. *Little Brother of War* is the best choice for the title of this passage, because the games are described as fierce and warlike. At the end of the passage, the author write that games were often used to settle disputes between tribes without resorting to full-blown warfare. Therefore, these games could be considered an alternative to war, or war's "little brother." The other choices do not fit, because they are unsupported by the passage, or describe only a small portion of the passage.

14. c. The answer can be found in the two sentences that follow the phrase. The sentences state that the games were often high-stakes substitutes for war, and it was not uncommon for players to suffer serious injuries at the hands (and sticks) of others. These statements describe the fierce nature of the games, and suggest that players would not hesitate to resort to violent tactics to score, *by any means necessary.* Choices **d** and **e** are true and mentioned in the passage, but they do not fit in context with the phrase.

15. b. The passage clearly states that potlatch is a gift-giving ceremony. The author explains that *potlatch* is a generic word for the ceremony that comes from a shared trading language, while each nation has its own specific word for potlatch.

16. a. The passage states that guests were expected to give a potlatch with gifts of equal value to what they received. This arrangement can best be described as reciprocal. The other choices are not supported by the passage.

17. d. Choice **d** is the most accurate conclusion because the first sentence speaks of periods of war. The other choices, whether true or false, are not addressed in the selection.

18. d. The statistic provides numerical evidence of (quantifies) the degree to which commercial fishing is hazardous compared to the next most dangerous occupation.

19. b. Saying that the eagle watches and then falls *like a thunderbolt* implies alertness and striking, so the most logical choice is that the eagle is hunting.

20. c. The focus of the passage is Blackwell's efforts to open the profession of medicine to women. The first paragraph states that Blackwell *supported women's medical education and helped many other women's careers.*

21. b. Initially Blackwell was interested in teaching. However, she was inspired by her dying friend, and went on to become not only the first woman doctor since the Renaissance, but also a supporter of medical education for women.

22. c. The passage describes swing as *vibrant*, a synonym for *lively*. It is also stated that the bands *improvised from the melody*, indicating that the music was *melodic*.

23. c. None of the other choices can be proven based on the information given.

24. b. The passage describes the cuttlefish's use of a water jet to move. Choice **a** is incorrect because the passage only describes cuttlefish as *resembling* squid.

25. e. This choice covers the most important ideas in the two paragraphs. All the other choices list more minor details from the paragraphs as the main subjects.

26. e. This choice includes both the informational content and light tone of the passage.

27. a. The passage discusses the many important functions of public art and its impact on the city.

28. c. In the passage, the author states a surfer should lie upon a surfboard *like a small boy on a coaster*, and then goes on to say that the surfer slides down a wave *just as a boy slides down a hill on his coaster.*

29. a. As it is used in the passage, *impetus* most nearly means *a moving force*. In this case, a wave is a moving force through the water. If you did not know the correct definition, the best way to answer this question would be to replace *impetus* in the sentence with each of the given answer choices to see which one makes the most sense in context.

30. c. The author compares surfing to sliding down a hill. But unlike a six-foot hill, a surfer can slide down a six-foot wave for more than a quarter of a mile without ever reaching the bottom. The author explains that this is possible because new water is rising into the wave as fast as the wave travels, preventing the surfer from reaching the bottom. So while a surfer is sliding along moving water, he or she is holding the same position on a wave as it moves through the water. That's the secret.

31. d. The passage explains that there was a social component to a trip to the marketplace. To be social means to be around others, suggesting that people sought out interaction with one another.

32. d. The end of the passage states that the New Deal expanded *the role of the central government in regulating the economy and creating social assistance programs.* Choices **b** and **c** are incorrect and choices **a** and **e** require an opinion; the author does not offer his or her viewpoint about the New Deal measures.

33. b. *Parsimonious* is a word used to describe someone who is frugal to the point of stinginess. Comiskey's pay cuts, bonus of cheap champagne, and refusal to launder uniforms are all clues that should help you deduce the answer from the given choices.

34. b. Answering this question involves a bit of deductive reasoning. Though the actual name of the ballpark is never given in the passage, the passage states that the 1917 White Sox won the World Series playing in a park named for their owner.

35. c. The passage states between the years of 1900 and 1915 the White Sox had won the World Series only once, and then it tells us they won it again in 1917. Be careful not to mistakenly select choice **d**, three; the question asks for the number of World Series the Sox won, not the number of World Series played.

36. b. The narrator describes the view from her window as a *prison-ground, exile limits*, and says *I had no communication . . . with the outer world.* Thus, it can be inferred that Lowood is both a structured and isolated place.

37. e. The narrator's desire for freedom and to explore the world are evident in this passage; she longs to follow the road that leads away from Lowood and she is *half desperate* in her cry for something new, something beyond Lowood and the rules and systems she *tired of . . . in one afternoon.*

38. d. Because Lowood had been the narrator's home for eight years and all she *knew of existence* was school rules, duties, habits, faces, and the like—because she had had *no communication . . . with the outer world*, it is likely that she feels her initial prayers were unrealistic. At least a *new servitude* would provide some familiar territory, and it therefore seems more realistic and attainable than *liberty* or *change.*

39. c. In the second paragraph, the author states that *the health risk for cosmetic procedures is low*, but does not give factual information to back this claim. The statement is important to the author's argument because he or she cites it as one of the reasons his or her attitude toward plastic surgery has changed.

40. d. The author directly invokes the audience he or she hopes to reach in the last sentence: *members of the medical community.*

Skills Test in Mathematics

1. b. The length of the regular route is the hypotenuse of a right triangle. The length of the detour is the sum of the legs of a right triangle. Use the Pythagorean theorem ($a^2 + b^2 = c^2$, or leg^2 + leg^2 = hypotenuse^2) to find the missing side of the triangle; $x^2 + 75^2 = 85^2$. Evaluate the exponents; $x^2 + 5,625 = 7,225$. Subtract 5,625 from each side of the equation; $x^2 + 5,625 - 5,625 = 7,225 - 5,625$; $x^2 = 1,600$. Take the square root of each side of the equation; $x = 40$. Because the distance between Center City and Newtown is 40 miles and the distance between Newtown and Forest Grove is 75 miles, then length of the detour is $40 + 75 = 115$ miles. To find how much longer the detour is, subtract $115 - 85 = 30$ miles.

2. b. The scatter plot compares the number of miles driven with the total cost of renting a car. Because the points in the scatter plot form a straight line, the equation will be in the form $y = mx + b$, where m is the slope of the line and b is the y-intercept. To find the y-intercept, look on the graph for the point at 0 miles. This value is \$10 so the y-intercept is 10. Moving from one point to another from left to right, as the cost increases by \$5, the number of miles increases by 10. Because the slope of the line equals the change in y-values over the change in x-values, the slope of the line is $\frac{5}{10}$, which reduces to $\frac{1}{2}$. Thus, the equation is $y = \frac{1}{2}x + 10$.

3. d. Choices **a**, **b**, and **e** can be ruled out because there is no way to determine how many tickets are for adults or how many are for children. Choice **c** can be ruled out because the price of group tickets is not given.

4. b. The adult price on Saturday afternoon is \$5.50; the child's price is \$3.00. By subtracting \$3.00 from \$5.50, you can find the difference in price.

5. c. Just remember that when taking a fraction *of* some number, you are actually *multiplying* that number by the fraction. Let's look at what happens hour by hour:

Time	Number of Candies
Start	504
8–9 o'clock	minus $\frac{1}{8} \cdot 504$, or $-63 = 441$
9–10 o'clock	minus $\frac{2}{9} \cdot 441$, or $-98 = 343$
10–11 o'clock	minus $\frac{1}{7} \cdot 343$, or $-49 = 294$

6. a. This problem is a straight conversion problem. Use the fact that there are 24 hours in one day to solve the problem. Remember, converting from a smaller unit to a larger unit requires division: $720 \div 24 = 30$. It is always a good idea to make sure the answer makes sense. Multiplying by 24 (instead of dividing) would result in choice **e**, which is not correct and does not make sense. If Joe had to wait 17,280 days before his vacation, that would mean he planned his vacation a little more than 47 years in advance!

7. d. This is an example of the distributive property of multiplication over addition. The number outside of the parentheses gets multiplied by each of the terms inside the parentheses. A way to solve this type of question, or to check your answer, is to simplify the expression in the question. Multiply first, then add; $3 \times 5 + 3 \times 8 = 15 + 24 = 39$. If each of the answer explanations is evaluated, the only one that also has a value of 39 is choice **d**.

8. d. First, examine the table to determine that there are 40 minutes in each class period and 4 minutes of passing time between each class. To determine the starting time of period 3, add 4 minutes to the ending time of period 2. Thus, the starting time of period 3 is 9:23. To calculate the ending time of period 8, add 40 minutes to the starting time. The ending time is 1:43. The answer choice with both of these times is choice **d**.

9. b. Because the only categories quantified are the types of chocolate in the candy bars, only the ratio of milk chocolate candy bars to white chocolate candy bars can be found. You would need additional information to determine any of the other choices.

10. c. The number of subscribers to US Cable in 2006 was 140 thousand. The number of subscribers to Central Satellite in 2006 was 100 thousand. The percent of US Cable subscribers can be found using the ratio: $\frac{\text{part}}{\text{total}} = \frac{\%}{100}$. Because the total number of subscribers in 2006 was $140 + 100 = 240$ thousand, the ratio becomes $\frac{140}{240} = \frac{x}{100}$. Cross multiply to get $240x = 14,000$. Divide each side of the equal sign by 240 to get $x \approx 58\%$.

11. d. Only answer choice **d** shows the heights of the bars at the same values for each year in the double-line graph. Choice **a** has each company's values by year increased by 10,000. Choice **b** has the values for US Cable and Central Satellite switched. Choice **c** has each of the values for US Cable decreased by 10,000. The graph in choice **e** has reversed the values for each company by starting with the amounts for 2008, instead of 2004, and sequentially going backwards for the heights of the bars.

12. e. Because 80 students out of the 100 polled would prefer this class, 80 out of 100 is 80%. To find 80% of 30,000, multiply $0.80 \times 30,000$ to get 24,000.

13. d. His total bill will include the $19 flat fee plus $0.32 \times$ the number of minutes of airtime over 120. If $x = $ total airtime minutes, then $x - 120 = $ total airtime minutes over 120. Therefore, the expression becomes $19 + 0.32(x - 120)$.

14. d. The hundredths place is two places to the right of the decimal point. In this case, the number in the hundredths place is 3. In order to round this number, look to the place directly to the right of the number to be rounded. If this number is 4 or less, keep the number and drop off the remaining numbers to the right. If this number is 5 or greater, add one to the number and drop off the remaining numbers to the right. Because the number to the right of 3 is 6, the 3 is rounded up to 4 and the entire rounded number becomes 56.74.

15. a. The standard form of a quadratic equation is $y = ax^2 + bx + c$, where a, b, and c are real numbers. Because the curve opens downward, the value of a, the number in front of the x^2 term, must be negative. Remember that $-x^2$ means $-1x^2$. This narrows down the choices to **a**, **b**, or **e**. Because the curve intercepts the y-axis at the point (0,4), the equation must have a c value of $+4$. Therefore, the answer must be choice **a**.

16. d. First, calculate the minimum number and maximum number of granola bars that the 20 machines can make per minute. Because the minimum number per machine is 80, multiply 80×20 to get 1,600 as the minimum number per minute for all 20 machines. The maximum number per machine is 100, so multiply 100×20 to get 2,000 as the maximum number per minute for all 20 machines. Be careful—although 1,800 is between 1,600 and 2,000, choice **a** is not correct. The minimum and maximum numbers found so far are per minute; the question asks for the number *per hour*. To find the minimum and maximum numbers per hour, multiply by 60, because there are 60 minutes in an hour.

$$\text{minimum per hour} = 1,600 \times 60 = 96,000$$
$$\text{maximum per hour} = 2,000 \times 60 = 120,000$$

Choice **d**, 100,000, is the only number between 96,000 and 120,000.

17. c. To estimate quickly, the numbers can be rounded to 36,000 and 16,500; 36,000 people minus 16,500 male attendees is equal to 19,500 female attendees. The difference between the number of females in attendance and males in attendance can be found by subtracting $19,500 - 16,500 = 3,000$. There were approximately 3,000 more women than men.

18. b. Statements I and III illustrate the associative property of addition. In this property the association, or grouping, of the numbers changes but the result is the same. Another way to approach this type of question is to substitute numbers for a, b, and c and look for the statements that give the same result. Try $a = 3$, $b = 4$, and $c = 5$. Statement I would then become $3 + (4 + 5) = 3 + 9 = 12$. Statement II would then become $(3 + 4) + (3 + 5) = 7 + 8 = 15$. Statement III would become $(3 + 4) + 5 = 7 + 5 = 12$. Because statements I and III both yield the same result, they are equivalent.

19. c. The volume of the aquarium can be found by using the formula $V = l \times w \times h$. Because the length is 12 inches, the width is 5 inches, and the height is 10 inches, multiply $V = 12 \times 5 \times 10$ to get a volume of 600 cubic inches.

20. e. To find the value, start with $y = 4$. Multiply 4 by 6 to get 24. Because step 3 and step 4 are switched, divide 24 by 2 to get 12. Add 10 to 12 to get a result of 22.

21. e. In this case, the only solution you are guaranteed when starting with a whole number is a value that is an integer. Remember that the set of integers is the whole numbers and their opposites. For example, if $y = 5$ the result is 20, which is even. However, if $y = 8$ the result is 29, which is odd and also prime. Each result is an integer.

22. e. In this problem, look for two sectors that when combined will add to 70%. The sector for Liberal Arts is 54% and the sector for Medicine is 16%. Because $54\% + 16\% = 70\%$, the two sectors are Liberal Arts and Medicine.

23. b. The average is found by dividing the sum of the absences by the total number of days. The sum of the absences is: $11 + 4 + 0 + 5 + 4 + 6 = 30$. Because there were six days, $\frac{30}{6} = 5$. There was an average of 5 students absent each day of the six-day period.

24. b. This uses two algebraic equations to solve for the age. Jacqueline (J) and her grandmother (G) have a sum of ages of 110 years. Therefore, $J + G = 110$. Jacqueline was $\frac{1}{3}$ as young as her grandmother 15 years ago. Therefore, $J - 15 = \frac{1}{3}(G - 15)$. Solve the first equation for J and substitute that value into the second equation; $J = 110 - G$; $(110 - G) - 15 = \frac{1}{3}(G - 15)$. This simplifies to $95 - G = \frac{1}{3}G - 5$. Add G and 5 to each side; $100 = \frac{4}{3}G$. Multiply each side of the equation by $\frac{3}{4}$ to get $G = 75$.

25. e. You can use the decimal equivalents to compare the numbers. Since $\frac{1}{3} \approx 0.33$ and $\frac{1}{4} = 0.25$, look for an answer choice that will be between those when written as a decimal; $\frac{1}{2} = 0.50$ (too large); $\frac{1}{5} = 0.20$ (too small); $\frac{2}{3} \approx 0.66$ (too large); $\frac{2}{5} = 0.40$ (too large). Because answer choice **e** is $\frac{2}{7} \approx 0.29$, it is the only answer choice between the two fractions.

26. d. This graph is in the shape of a parabola with the y-axis as the axis, or line, of symmetry. Therefore, the line is in the general form $y = x^2$. The shading of the inequality is done above the graph, making the symbol used in the inequality *greater than or equal to*, or $\geq$. This narrows down the possible choices to **a**, **c**, or **d**. Because the graph has a y-intercept of -2, the inequality is $y \geq x^2 - 2$, which is choice **d**.

27. a. Substitute the value of $\frac{1}{2}$ in each x in the function. The function then becomes $3(\frac{1}{2})^2 - \frac{1}{2}(\frac{1}{2}) + 7 = 3(\frac{1}{4}) - \frac{1}{4} + 7 = \frac{3}{4} - \frac{1}{4} + 7 = \frac{1}{2} + 7 = 7\frac{1}{2}$. This is equal to choice **a**, which is $\frac{15}{2}$.

28. d. Substitute $x = 3$ into the equation $y = 5 + 4x$. Thus, $y = 5 + 4(3)$. Multiply first and then add; $y = 5 + 12$, so $y = 17$.

29. e. The only answer choice that follows is choice **e**. Because Lucinda pays with a check only if an item costs more than $30, the item must have cost more than $25. Choice **a** is not correct because if the bill was $20, she would have paid with cash. Choice **b** is not correct because if the bill was $80, she would have used her credit card to pay. Choice **c** is not correct because she pays cash only for bills less than $30; if she has paid with a check, you can assume that the bill is already greater than this. Choice **d** is not correct because if the bill was at least $70, she would have used her credit card.

30. e. Because the figure is a regular decagon, it can be divided into ten equal triangular sections by straight lines passing through the center. The two lines that form the indicated angle also form an area equivalent to three of these ten sections. Therefore, to find the measure of the angle shown, find $\frac{3}{10}$ of 360; $\frac{3}{10} \times 360 = 0.3 \times 360 = 108°$.

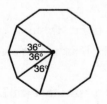

31. b. First, eliminate the parentheses on the left side of the equation using the distributive property. The equation becomes $2x - 3x + 3 = -12$. Combine like terms on the left side of the equal sign; $-1x + 3 = -12$. Subtract 3 from both sides of the equal sign; $-1x + 3 - 3 = -12 - 3$. Simplify; $-x = -15$. Divide each side of the equal sign by -1 to get an answer of $x = 15$.

32. c. Because the measure of angle 2 is a right angle, its measure is 90° and is corresponding with the indicated right angle. Therefore, the two horizontal lines in the figure must be parallel. Because angle 1 is 30° and angle 2 is 90°, angle 3 must be 60° because the angles in a triangle have a sum of 180°. Angle 3 and angle 4 are also corresponding angles formed by two parallel lines, making the measure of angle 4 also equal to 60°. Because angle 4 and angle 5 form a linear pair, subtract 180° − 60° = 120° to find the measure of angle 5.

33. d. The area of a circle can be found using the formula $A = \pi r^2$, where r is the radius of the circle. Because the area of 78.5 square feet is given, substitute $A = 78.5$ and $\pi = 3.14$ into the formula; $78.5 = 3.14r^2$. Divide each side of the equation by 3.14 to get $25 = r^2$. Take the square root of each side to get $r = 5$ feet. The diameter is twice the radius, and in this case, it is 10 feet.

34. a. Rounding to compatible numbers can help in this problem; 490,000 rounds to 500,000 and 98,000 rounds to 100,000. The question now becomes 100,000 compared to 500,000, which is equal to $\frac{100,000}{500,000}$. This reduces to $\frac{1}{5}$, which is equal to choice **a**.

35. e. In each of the answer choices, the numbers remain the same but the order changes. The commutative property changes the order but the result is the same. This property is true when used with addition or multiplication, but does not hold for subtraction. Because the terms surrounding the subtraction sign in choice **e** are switched, this expression will most likely not have the same value as the others. To check, evaluate each expression to see which one results in a different value as the others. Be sure to use the correct order of operations (PEMDAS) when evaluating expressions. When evaluated, each answer choice gives a result of 218 except for choice **e**. Choice **e** evaluated becomes $10 - 3(76) = 10 - 228 = -218$.

36. a. In this question, you need to find 15% of the 30% of students who are in the music program. To find 15% of 30%, change the percents to decimal form and multiply. Because 30% = 0.30 and 15% = 0.15, multiply $(0.30)(0.15) = 0.045$. As a decimal, this is equivalent to 4.5%, which is choice **a**.

37. d. Examine the x column of the table. As the table is read downward, each value of x decreases by 2. At the same time, the y-values increase by 0.5, or $\frac{1}{2}$. Therefore, the answer is choice **d**.

38. d. The hundredths place in a decimal is two places to the right of the decimal point. Three one-hundredths of a second is written as a decimal with the number 3 in the hundredths place, or 0.03.

39. d. Because the graph has the unit of time in minutes, to convert to hours find a value that will be easy to work with. By reading the graph, in 30 minutes the car has traveled a total of 20 miles. The line in the graph is a straight line, so it can be assumed that the slope, or speed, is constant. Therefore, because the distance in $\frac{1}{2}$ hour is 20 miles, the distance in 1 hour will be double that, or 40 miles. Thus, the car is traveling at a speed of 40 miles per hour.

40. e. The answer choice that is proportional to the given triangle will have sides that can be multiplied or divided by the same number in order to change to the values of the original triangle. In choice **e**, each of the sides from the original triangle of 12, 16, and 20 can be divided by 4 to get the sides 3, 4, and 5.

Skills Test in Writing—Section 1, Part A

1. c. There are two subjects, *Elizabeth Blackwell* and *she*, that mean the same thing. To correct this problem, the word *she* should be deleted from the sentence.

2. e. Because there are no grammatical, idiomatic, logical, or structural errors in this sentence, choice **e** is the best answer.

3. a. Starting the sentence with the conjunction *considering* is a subordination error because it creates two dependent clauses in this sentence. It should be deleted to make the sentence grammatically correct.

4. b. The semicolon should be replaced by a comma. This is a complex sentence; the first clause is dependent and the second clause is independent. A semicolon should be used only when both clauses are independent.

5. d. In this sentence there is faulty parallelism. The word *asking* should be replaced by the verb *asked*. This sentence is in the past tense, so the two verbs *asked* and *called* should both be in the past tense.

6. a. The word *because* creates a coordination error between the two clauses in this sentence. Replacing *because* with another conjunction such as *although* or *even though* would make this sentence grammatically correct.

7. c. The use of *and who* in this sentence creates faulty parallelism between the two clauses. Deleting *and* would make the sentence parallel.

8. b. The apostrophe at the end of the word *officers* is incorrect and should be deleted. In this sentence *officers* is not possessive.

9. d. This sentence makes a comparison. The comparative *more* is incorrect because the situation requires the superlative *most*. *More* is used only to compare two things.

10. b. The singular collective noun *staff* requires a singular verb form. Therefore, the plural form *deserve* should be replaced with the singular *deserves*.

11. d. The use of the word *but* makes this sentence illogical. The word *but* should be replaced by the word *and*.

12. d. There are three items in a series in this sentence: *lived in cramped quarters*, *fought battles*, and *learn to understand the blessings*. To make these three items parallel, the word *learn* in the underlined portion represented by choice **d** should be changed to *learned*.

13. e. Because there are no grammatical, idiomatic, logical, or structural errors in this sentence, choice **e** is the best answer.

14. b. The comma between the words *laptop* and *owns* is unnecessary and should be deleted. The clause *who sold me the laptop* is restrictive (essential) and should not be set off by commas.

15. e. Because there are no grammatical, idiomatic, logical, or structural errors in this sentence, choice **e** is the best answer.

16. c. The pronoun *he* does not have a definitive antecedent; it could be referring to either writer. Replacing *he* with *Hemingway* would make this sentence grammatically (and factually) correct.

17. d. The subject of the second independent clause is *dirty filter*, a singular noun. Therefore, the singular form of the verb should be used. The verb *reduce* should be replaced by the verb *reduces*.

18. a. Because the words *areas* and *regions* mean the same thing, this sentence contains a redundancy. To eliminate this redundancy, *or regions* should be deleted.

19. c. The phrase *ashamed with himself* is not idiomatic. The word *with* should be replaced by *of* to create the appropriate idiomatic phrase *ashamed of himself*.

20. e. Because there are no grammatical, idiomatic, logical, or structural errors in this sentence, choice **e** is the best answer.

21. b. This sentence contains a punctuation error. When using a colon, it is important to note that the preceding clause should have a subject and a predicate; in other words, it should be able to function as an independent clause. In this sentence, no colon is necessary.

Skills Test in Writing—Section 1, Part B

22. b. This is the correct choice because it is the only one where the subject and verb are in agreement. The subject *three months of free golf lessons* is plural and therefore agrees with the plural *go*.

23. c. The verbs *ring* and *feed* are irregular verbs, and this is the only choice to use correct verb formation and the appropriate verb tense.

24. e. This is the only choice that contains the correct plural form of *effect* and the correct possessive form of *the earth*. To form the possessive case of a singular noun, add *'s*.

25. a. This is the only correct choice because the sentence makes a comparison among many things (Roman emperors), and therefore requires the superlative, *greediest*. Do not be fooled by choices **b** and **e**; *greedliest* and *greedfullest* are in superlative form, but *greedly* and *greedful* (also in choice **d**) are not real words.

26. e. This is the correct choice because the sentence does not contain a double negative or a double comparison.

27. c. This is the only sentence with correct capitalization. A title (such as *doctor*) is capitalized only when it precedes a person's name or is used as a direct address. The names of cities and the names of languages should always be capitalized.

28. a. This sentence requires parallelism between the verbs *speak* and *have*, and choice **a** is the only choice that does this (*speaking* and *having*).

29. d. This is the only choice that uses the correct comparative form for the words *new, safe,* and *old*. When comparing two things (in this case, cars), use the comparative form (*-er*) for short modifiers of one or two syllables. Choice **e** uses the correct comparative form for the three modifiers, but the use of *more* before *safer* creates a double comparison, and is therefore incorrect.

30. d. When a comparison is made, the word *fewer* is used with nouns that can be counted; the word *less* is used with quantities that cannot be counted.

31. e. This is the only choice to have agreement between the subject and verb and between the pronoun and its antecedent.

32. a. This sentence requires the comparison to be completed by *not only . . . but also.* The other choices create sentences that are ambiguous, unclear, and idiomatically incorrect.

33. b. The most common way to join two independent clauses is with a comma and a coordinating conjunction. The only sentence that correctly does both is choice **b.** Two closely related independent clauses can also be linked by a semicolon, but for choice **a** to be correct the coordinating conjunction *so* needs to be deleted. Choice **d** lacks a proper coordinating conjunction, and has faulty parallelism. Choice **e** contains a verb tense error.

34. d. This is the only sentence that uses the correct pronoun, *which.* Use *which* when introducing clauses that are not essential to the information in the sentence, unless they refer to people (then use *who*). The second clause in choice **c** is referring to a river, not a person, so the use of *who* is incorrect.

35. a. This is the only choice that does not have faulty subordination. The first part of the sentence is an independent clause; the second part is a dependent clause. Choice **a** is correct because the dependent clause is correctly introduced by the relative pronoun *which.*

36. c. This is the only choice that uses correct punctuation and contains no capitalization errors. Choice **d** uses correct punctuation, but *Italian* should be capitalized. Two independent clauses should be joined by a semicolon or a coordinating conjunction, not a comma, so choice **a** is incorrect. Choices **b** and **e** are incorrect because no commas are necessary when two items are linked by a conjunction (*gym and calculus; Italian and physics*).

37. d. This is the only choice that employs the correct conjunction *although* and uses the proper punctuation between the two clauses. The use of the conjunction *because* in choices **a** and **b** sets up faulty coordination between the two clauses. In addition, the use of *was* in choice **b** is a verb-tense error that creates a nonparallel sentence. Choice **c** lacks a proper conjunction, and is incorrect. Choice **e** is properly coordinated, but the incorrect use of a semicolon instead of a comma creates a punctuation error.

38. b. This is the only choice that uses the adverb correctly and establishes the appropriate comparison. Choices **a, c,** and **d** are incorrect because an adverb (*gracefully*) is required to modify the verb *skates.* Choice **e** correctly uses the adverb, but contains a comparison error: When the conjunction *than* is used to indicate a comparison, it should be followed by the nominative case, *I.*

Skills Test in Writing—Section 2, Essay Writing

Following are sample criteria for scoring a PPST essay.

A score "6" writer will

- create an exceptional composition that appropriately addresses the audience and given task
- organize ideas effectively, include very strong supporting details, and use smooth transitions
- present a definitive, focused thesis and clearly support it throughout the composition
- include vivid details, clear examples, and strong supporting text to enhance the themes of the composition
- exhibit an exceptional level of skill in the usage of the English language and the capacity to employ an assortment of sentence structures
- build essentially error-free sentences that accurately convey intended meaning

A score "5" writer will

- create a commendable composition that appropriately addresses the audience and given task
- organize ideas, include supporting details, and use smooth transitions
- present a thesis and support it throughout the composition
- include details, examples, and supporting text to enhance the themes of the composition
- generally exhibit a high level of skill in the usage of the English language and the capacity to employ an assortment of sentence structures
- build mostly error-free sentences that accurately convey intended meaning

A score "4" writer will

- create a composition that satisfactorily addresses the audience and given task
- display satisfactory organization of ideas, include adequate supporting details, and generally use smooth transitions
- present a thesis and mostly support it throughout the composition
- include some details, examples, and supporting text that typically enhance most themes of the composition
- exhibit a competent level of skill in the usage of the English language and the general capacity to employ an assortment of sentence structures
- build sentences with several minor errors that generally do not confuse the intended meaning

A score "3" writer will

- create an adequate composition that basically addresses the audience and given task
- display some organization of ideas, include some supporting details, and use mostly logical transitions
- present a somewhat underdeveloped thesis but attempt to support it throughout the composition
- display limited organization of ideas, have some inconsistent supporting details, and use few transitions
- exhibit an adequate level of skill in the usage of the English language and a basic capacity to employ an assortment of sentence structures
- build sentences with some minor and major errors that may obscure the intended meaning

A score "2" writer will
- create a composition that restrictedly addresses the audience and given task
- display little organization of ideas, have inconsistent supporting details, and use very few transitions
- present an unclear or confusing thesis with little support throughout the composition
- include very few details, examples, and supporting text
- exhibit a less than adequate level of skill in the usage of the English language and a limited capacity to employ a basic assortment of sentence structures
- build sentences with a few major errors that may confuse the intended meaning

A score "1" writer will
- create a composition that has a limited sense of the audience and given task
- display illogical organization of ideas, include confusing or no supporting details, and lack the ability to effectively use transitions
- present a minimal or unclear thesis
- include confusing or irrelevant details and examples, and little or no supporting text
- exhibit a limited level of skill in the usage of the English language and little or no capacity to employ basic sentence structure
- build sentences with many major errors that obscure or confuse the intended meaning

Sample 6 Essay

It's a fact: more and more people across the United States are vegetarian, and school and workplace cafeterias should be required to provide vegetarian lunch options for them. There are many reasons why vegetarians choose this diet. Health concerns, moral issues, and religion are among them. Schools and workplaces should honor these reasons by making it easier for vegetarians to purchase healthful, meat-free lunches.

Some vegetarians are responding to the generally unhealthy American diet, which consists of plenty of fast food. They prefer more healthful choices, such as simply prepared salads, vegetables, and protein sources such as beans, soy-based products, and dairy products. However, this is not what may be found in most cafeterias. Cafeterias, both in schools and in businesses, tend to resemble fast food restaurants, offering such items as hamburgers, fried chicken, pizza, French fries, and sodas. If they also stocked more healthful, meat-free choices, not only would the vegetarians be served, but also perhaps some of the overweight students and employees would eat them also. This could improve the health of many people.

It would not be difficult to transform the typical school or workplace cafeteria into a vegetarian-friendly one. Many of the lunch selections currently offered could be made vegetarian, and therefore more healthy, with a few simple and inexpensive substitutions. Veggie burgers, for example, offered alongside beef burgers, would give vegetarians a satisfactory option. Tacos, burritos, and other Mexican entrees could be made with beans rather than ground beef. A salad bar would serve the dual purpose of providing both vegetarians and others concerned about the health and weight the opportunity for a satisfying meal. These changes, while relatively simple for cafeterias to incorporate, would provide vegetarians with acceptable lunch selections, and in the process, provide all the students or employees they serve with more healthful alternatives.

Sample 4 Essay

In the United States there are many people who are vegetarian. Many of these people are students or workers who eat lunch at their cafeterias on a daily basis. Surprisingly though, school and workplace cafeterias are not required to provide vegetarian options. That means that most often they don't. That means that vegetarians may be limited to lunches comprised of french fries, or pizza loaded with cheese. While these are vegetarian (non-meat), they are not healthy, especially if they are eaten every day.

Schools and businesses should have a wider variety of vegetarian options. Such as a salad bar, or perhaps even something with tofu. Entrees that use beans or soy-based products instead of meat would also be good. It wouldn't cost cafeterias more money to provide vegetarian lunches. In fact, the ingredients used to make them (like beans) are typically much cheaper than their carnivorous counterparts (like ground beef). Salads require little preparation in comparison with French fries, which could save money on payroll. Also, cafeterias could buy premade vegetarian selections in bulk, just as they do non-vegetarian dishes. These premade foods are becoming more and more popular, and are not more expensive.

While cafeterias can't meet all the demands of those they serve, it is important to offer those committed to a vegetarian lifestyle the choice to eat healthfully and meat-free. Schools should create a menu that offers these options for all students.

Sample 1 Essay

Many people are vegetarian and don't eat meat. This may be because they are afraid of diseases found in meat, such as mad cow disease, salmanella, or avian influenza. Or, they may not eat meat because of their religion. Some care about animal rites, and others are vegetarian because they are concerned about their health. They believe a vegetarian diet will help them lose wieght and in general improve their health. But this is not necessarily the case. You could just eat French fries, cold cereal, and pizza every day and be a vegetarian. Vegetarians need to learn about how to eat this diet and make it healthy too. School and workplace cafeterias could help by offering them good selections at lunch.

▶ Praxis I Scoring

Once again, in order to evaluate how you did on this practice exam, start by scoring the three parts of the PPST—Reading, Mathematics, and Writing—separately. You will recall that your scores on the PPST multiple-choice segments of the exam are based on the number of questions you answered correctly; there is no "guessing penalty" or penalty for unanswered questions. You will also recall that the Educational Testing Service has not set passing scores for these tests; this is left up to the institutions, state agencies, and associations that utilize the tests. Therefore, the interpretation of your score depends on the purpose for which you are taking the test.

If you are unsure of the passing score you will need, you can set yourself a goal of at least 70% of the answers right on each test of the Praxis I. To find the percent you answered correctly, add up the number of correct answers, and then divide by the total number of questions to find your percentage.

Even if you have scored well on the Reading test, the Mathematics test, and the multiple-choice subsections of the Writing test, don't forget that you must receive a passing score on the essay portion of the PPST Writing test. On this portion, your essay will be scored by at least two writing experts, and their combined score will be used to evaluate how you did. The scoring criteria are outlined in detail in the answer explanations. The best way to see how you did on the essay portion of the exam is to give your essay and the scoring criteria to a teacher or other reader whom you trust to see what scores he or she would assign.

You have probably seen improvement between your first practice exam score and this one; but if you didn't improve as much as you would like, ask yourself the following: Did I run out of time before I could answer all the questions? Did I go back and change my answers from right to wrong? Did I get flustered and sit staring at a difficult question for what seemed like hours? If you had any of these problems, once again, be sure to go over the LearningExpress Test Preparation guide in Chapter 2 again to learn how to avoid them.

Once you have honed your test-taking skills, go back to the review chapters and study again the areas that gave you the most trouble. After working on your reading, writing, and math skills, take the third practice exam that follows in Chapter 8 to see how much you have improved.

8 ▶ Praxis I Practice Exam 3

CHAPTER SUMMARY

This is the last of the three practice exams in this book based on the three elements of the Praxis I, the Pre-Professional Skills Tests (PPST) of Reading, Mathematics, and Writing. This exam gives you another chance to master your test-taking skills and get ready for your exam.

LIKE THE PREVIOUS PRACTICE exams in this book, this one is made up of three tests: a Reading test (multiple-choice questions), a Mathematics test (multiple-choice questions), and a Writing test (multiple-choice questions and an essay).

Once again, you should pretend you are taking a real exam. Work in a quiet place, away from interruptions. Use a timer or stopwatch and allow yourself an hour for the Reading test, an hour for the Mathematics test, 30 minutes for the Section 1 of the Writing test, and 30 minutes to write your essay.

After the exam, use the answer explanations to learn about why you missed certain questions. Then, use the scoring section at the end of the exam to see how you did overall.

► Answer Sheet

SKILLS TEST IN READING	SKILLS TEST IN MATHEMATICS	SKILLS TEST IN WRITING, SECTION 1

SKILLS TEST IN READING

1. ⓐ ⓑ ⓒ ⓓ ⓔ
2. ⓐ ⓑ ⓒ ⓓ ⓔ
3. ⓐ ⓑ ⓒ ⓓ ⓔ
4. ⓐ ⓑ ⓒ ⓓ ⓔ
5. ⓐ ⓑ ⓒ ⓓ ⓔ
6. ⓐ ⓑ ⓒ ⓓ ⓔ
7. ⓐ ⓑ ⓒ ⓓ ⓔ
8. ⓐ ⓑ ⓒ ⓓ ⓔ
9. ⓐ ⓑ ⓒ ⓓ ⓔ
10. ⓐ ⓑ ⓒ ⓓ ⓔ
11. ⓐ ⓑ ⓒ ⓓ ⓔ
12. ⓐ ⓑ ⓒ ⓓ ⓔ
13. ⓐ ⓑ ⓒ ⓓ ⓔ
14. ⓐ ⓑ ⓒ ⓓ ⓔ
15. ⓐ ⓑ ⓒ ⓓ ⓔ
16. ⓐ ⓑ ⓒ ⓓ ⓔ
17. ⓐ ⓑ ⓒ ⓓ ⓔ
18. ⓐ ⓑ ⓒ ⓓ ⓔ
19. ⓐ ⓑ ⓒ ⓓ ⓔ
20. ⓐ ⓑ ⓒ ⓓ ⓔ
21. ⓐ ⓑ ⓒ ⓓ ⓔ
22. ⓐ ⓑ ⓒ ⓓ ⓔ
23. ⓐ ⓑ ⓒ ⓓ ⓔ
24. ⓐ ⓑ ⓒ ⓓ ⓔ
25. ⓐ ⓑ ⓒ ⓓ ⓔ
26. ⓐ ⓑ ⓒ ⓓ ⓔ
27. ⓐ ⓑ ⓒ ⓓ ⓔ
28. ⓐ ⓑ ⓒ ⓓ ⓔ
29. ⓐ ⓑ ⓒ ⓓ ⓔ
30. ⓐ ⓑ ⓒ ⓓ ⓔ
31. ⓐ ⓑ ⓒ ⓓ ⓔ
32. ⓐ ⓑ ⓒ ⓓ ⓔ
33. ⓐ ⓑ ⓒ ⓓ ⓔ
34. ⓐ ⓑ ⓒ ⓓ ⓔ
35. ⓐ ⓑ ⓒ ⓓ ⓔ
36. ⓐ ⓑ ⓒ ⓓ ⓔ
37. ⓐ ⓑ ⓒ ⓓ ⓔ
38. ⓐ ⓑ ⓒ ⓓ ⓔ
39. ⓐ ⓑ ⓒ ⓓ ⓔ
40. ⓐ ⓑ ⓒ ⓓ ⓔ

SKILLS TEST IN MATHEMATICS

1. ⓐ ⓑ ⓒ ⓓ ⓔ
2. ⓐ ⓑ ⓒ ⓓ ⓔ
3. ⓐ ⓑ ⓒ ⓓ ⓔ
4. ⓐ ⓑ ⓒ ⓓ ⓔ
5. ⓐ ⓑ ⓒ ⓓ ⓔ
6. ⓐ ⓑ ⓒ ⓓ ⓔ
7. ⓐ ⓑ ⓒ ⓓ ⓔ
8. ⓐ ⓑ ⓒ ⓓ ⓔ
9. ⓐ ⓑ ⓒ ⓓ ⓔ
10. ⓐ ⓑ ⓒ ⓓ ⓔ
11. ⓐ ⓑ ⓒ ⓓ ⓔ
12. ⓐ ⓑ ⓒ ⓓ ⓔ
13. ⓐ ⓑ ⓒ ⓓ ⓔ
14. ⓐ ⓑ ⓒ ⓓ ⓔ
15. ⓐ ⓑ ⓒ ⓓ ⓔ
16. ⓐ ⓑ ⓒ ⓓ ⓔ
17. ⓐ ⓑ ⓒ ⓓ ⓔ
18. ⓐ ⓑ ⓒ ⓓ ⓔ
19. ⓐ ⓑ ⓒ ⓓ ⓔ
20. ⓐ ⓑ ⓒ ⓓ ⓔ
21. ⓐ ⓑ ⓒ ⓓ ⓔ
22. ⓐ ⓑ ⓒ ⓓ ⓔ
23. ⓐ ⓑ ⓒ ⓓ ⓔ
24. ⓐ ⓑ ⓒ ⓓ ⓔ
25. ⓐ ⓑ ⓒ ⓓ ⓔ
26. ⓐ ⓑ ⓒ ⓓ ⓔ
27. ⓐ ⓑ ⓒ ⓓ ⓔ
28. ⓐ ⓑ ⓒ ⓓ ⓔ
29. ⓐ ⓑ ⓒ ⓓ ⓔ
30. ⓐ ⓑ ⓒ ⓓ ⓔ
31. ⓐ ⓑ ⓒ ⓓ ⓔ
32. ⓐ ⓑ ⓒ ⓓ ⓔ
33. ⓐ ⓑ ⓒ ⓓ ⓔ
34. ⓐ ⓑ ⓒ ⓓ ⓔ
35. ⓐ ⓑ ⓒ ⓓ ⓔ
36. ⓐ ⓑ ⓒ ⓓ ⓔ
37. ⓐ ⓑ ⓒ ⓓ ⓔ
38. ⓐ ⓑ ⓒ ⓓ ⓔ
39. ⓐ ⓑ ⓒ ⓓ ⓔ
40. ⓐ ⓑ ⓒ ⓓ ⓔ

SKILLS TEST IN WRITING, SECTION 1

1. ⓐ ⓑ ⓒ ⓓ ⓔ
2. ⓐ ⓑ ⓒ ⓓ ⓔ
3. ⓐ ⓑ ⓒ ⓓ ⓔ
4. ⓐ ⓑ ⓒ ⓓ ⓔ
5. ⓐ ⓑ ⓒ ⓓ ⓔ
6. ⓐ ⓑ ⓒ ⓓ ⓔ
7. ⓐ ⓑ ⓒ ⓓ ⓔ
8. ⓐ ⓑ ⓒ ⓓ ⓔ
9. ⓐ ⓑ ⓒ ⓓ ⓔ
10. ⓐ ⓑ ⓒ ⓓ ⓔ
11. ⓐ ⓑ ⓒ ⓓ ⓔ
12. ⓐ ⓑ ⓒ ⓓ ⓔ
13. ⓐ ⓑ ⓒ ⓓ ⓔ
14. ⓐ ⓑ ⓒ ⓓ ⓔ
15. ⓐ ⓑ ⓒ ⓓ ⓔ
16. ⓐ ⓑ ⓒ ⓓ ⓔ
17. ⓐ ⓑ ⓒ ⓓ ⓔ
18. ⓐ ⓑ ⓒ ⓓ ⓔ
19. ⓐ ⓑ ⓒ ⓓ ⓔ
20. ⓐ ⓑ ⓒ ⓓ ⓔ
21. ⓐ ⓑ ⓒ ⓓ ⓔ
22. ⓐ ⓑ ⓒ ⓓ ⓔ
23. ⓐ ⓑ ⓒ ⓓ ⓔ
24. ⓐ ⓑ ⓒ ⓓ ⓔ
25. ⓐ ⓑ ⓒ ⓓ ⓔ
26. ⓐ ⓑ ⓒ ⓓ ⓔ
27. ⓐ ⓑ ⓒ ⓓ ⓔ
28. ⓐ ⓑ ⓒ ⓓ ⓔ
29. ⓐ ⓑ ⓒ ⓓ ⓔ
30. ⓐ ⓑ ⓒ ⓓ ⓔ
31. ⓐ ⓑ ⓒ ⓓ ⓔ
32. ⓐ ⓑ ⓒ ⓓ ⓔ
33. ⓐ ⓑ ⓒ ⓓ ⓔ
34. ⓐ ⓑ ⓒ ⓓ ⓔ
35. ⓐ ⓑ ⓒ ⓓ ⓔ
36. ⓐ ⓑ ⓒ ⓓ ⓔ
37. ⓐ ⓑ ⓒ ⓓ ⓔ
38. ⓐ ⓑ ⓒ ⓓ ⓔ

► Skills Test in Reading

Directions: Read the following passages and answer the questions that follow.

Use the following passage to answer questions 1 and 2.

In 1899, Czar Nicholas II of Russia invited the nations of the world to a conference at The Hague. This conference—and a follow-up organized by Theodore Roosevelt in 1907—ushered in a period of vigorous growth in international law. This growth was in response to several factors, not the least of which was the increasing potential for destruction of modern warfare. The recently concluded Civil War in the United States made this potential clear.

During this growth, the subjects of international law were almost exclusively restricted to the relationships that countries had with one another. Issues of trade and warfare dominated both the disputes and the agreements of the period. _____, the developments of this period paved the way for further expansion of international law, which has occurred in the last several years. _____, organizations such as the United Nations and the International Court of Justice are greatly concerned not only with the way countries deal with one another, but the ways in which they treat their own citizens.

1. Which words or phrases, if inserted in order into the blanks in the passage, would help the reader understand the sequence of the author's ideas?
   a. Therefore; In addition
   b. However; Now
   c. Furthermore; Yet
   d. Even if; On the other hand
   e. As a result; Meanwhile

2. Which of the following is the best meaning of the phrase *ushered in* as it is used in the beginning of the passage?
   a. escorted
   b. progressed
   c. guarded
   d. heralded
   e. conducted

Use the following passage to answer question 3.

The 1964 report on smoking and health issued by the Surgeon General's office had a significant impact on public attitudes and policy. A Gallup Survey conducted in 1958 found that only 44% of Americans believed smoking caused cancer, while 78% believed so by 1968. In the course of a decade, it had become common knowledge that smoking damaged health, and mounting evidence of health risks gave the 1964 report public resonance. Yet, while the report proclaimed that "cigarette smoking is a health hazard of sufficient importance in the United States to warrant appropriate remedial action," it remained silent on concrete remedies. That challenge fell to politicians. In 1965, Congress required all cigarette packages distributed in the United States to carry a health warning, and since 1970 this warning is made in the name of the Surgeon General. In 1969, cigarette advertising on television and radio was banned, effective September 1970.

3. The statement that the 1964 Surgeon General's report *remained silent on concrete remedies* implies that it
   a. served primarily as a manifesto that declared the views of the Surgeon General.
   b. would have recommended banning cigarette advertising if it were not for political pressure.
   c. was ignorant of possible remedial actions.
   d. maintained its objectivity by abstaining from making policy recommendations.
   e. did not deem it necessary to recommend specific actions that would confront the health problem of smoking.

Use the following passage to answer question 4.

Time is running out for the old-growth forests of Finland. The vast majority of Finland's valuable old-growth forest is owned by the state and logged by the state-owned company Metsähallitus. Metsähallitus' logging practices include clearcutting, logging in habitats of threatened and vulnerable species, and logging in areas of special scenic or cultural value—including in areas that are critical for the reindeer herding of the indigenous people.

4. According to the passage, which is NOT a logging practice engaged in by Metsähallitus?
   a. employing the clearcutting method
   b. logging in the habitat of reindeer
   c. logging near scenic Finnish vistas
   d. logging within in the boundaries of the indigenous people
   e. logging in traditional Norwegian fjords

Use the following passage to answer questions 5–7.

By using tiny probes as neural prostheses, scientists may be able to restore nerve function in quadriplegics and make the blind see or the deaf hear. Thanks to advanced techniques, a single, small, implanted probe can stimulate individual neurons electrically or chemically and then record responses. Preliminary results suggest that the microprobe telemetry systems can be permanently implanted and replace damaged or missing nerves.

The tissue-compatible microprobes represent an advance over the typical aluminum wire electrodes used in studies of the cortex and other brain structures. Researchers accumulate much data using traditional electrodes, but there is a question of how much damage they cause to the nervous system. Microprobes, which are about as thin as a human hair, cause minimal damage and disruption of neurons when inserted into the brain.

In addition to recording nervous system impulses, the microprobes have minuscule channels that open the way for delivery of drugs, cellular growth factors, neurotransmitters, and other neuroactive compounds to a single neuron or to groups of neurons. Also, patients who lack certain biochemicals could receive doses via prostheses. The probes can have up to four channels, each with its own recording/stimulating electrode.

5. As it is used in the passage, *prostheses* most closely means
   a. medications.
   b. electrodes.
   c. artificial body parts.
   d. wires.
   e. brain cells.

6. Which of the following best expresses the main idea of the passage?
   a. Microprobes require further technological advances before they can be used in humans.
   b. Wire electrodes are antiquated as a means for delivering neuroactive compounds to the brain.
   c. Microprobes have great potential to help counteract neural damage.
   d. Technology now exists that may counteract the nervous system.
   e. Use of wire electrodes is being replaced by use of wire electrodes.

7. All of the following are mentioned in the passage as potential uses for prostheses EXCEPT
   a. transportation of medication.
   b. induction of physical movement.
   c. compensation for damaged nerves.
   d. transportation of growth factor.
   e. removal of biochemicals from the cortex.

Use the following passage to answer question 8.

In a recent Senate race, the Republican candidate dropped out because an illness made it difficult for him to campaign. The candidate who replaced him lost the election to the opposing Democrat.

8. According to the information given, which statement must be true?
   a. The first Republican candidate would have been elected if he had stayed in the race.
   b. It is unusual for Senate candidates to withdraw from a race.
   c. The first Republican candidate will never run for office again.
   d. Senate candidates may withdraw from a race due to illness.
   e. The Democratic candidate was the best choice for senator.

Use the following passage to answer question 9.

The U.S. population is going gray. A rising demographic tide of aging baby boomers—those born between 1946 and 1964—and increased longevity have made adults age 85 and older the fastest-growing segment of today's population. This unprecedented "elder boom" will have a profound effect on American society, particularly the field of healthcare. Is the U.S. health system equipped to deal with the demands of an aging population? Although we have adequate physicians and nurses, many of them are not trained to handle the multiple needs of older patients. Only about 230 new geriatricians (physicians who are experts in aging-related issues) are certified each year. Some studies estimate a need for about 26,000 more geriatricians than are likely to be available by 2030.

9. The author uses the phrase *going gray* in order to
   a. maintain that everyone's hair loses its color eventually.
   b. suggest the social phenomenon of an aging population.
   c. depict older Americans in a positive light.
   d. demonstrate the normal changes of aging.
   e. highlight the tendency of American culture to emphasize youth.

Use the following passage to answer questions 10–12.

The history of microbiology begins with a Dutch haberdasher named Antoni van Leeuwenhoek, a man of no formal scientific education. In the late 1600s, Leeuwenhoek, inspired by the magnifying lenses used by drapers to examine cloth, assembled some of the first microscopes. He developed a technique for grinding and polishing tiny, convex lenses, some of which could magnify an object up to 270 times. After scraping some plaque from between his teeth and examining it under a lens, Leeuwenhoek found tiny squirming creatures, which he called "animalcules." His observations, which he reported to the Royal Society of London, are among the first descriptions of living bacteria. Leeuwenhoek discovered an entire universe invisible to the naked eye. He found more animalcules—protozoa and bacteria—in samples of pond water, rainwater, and human saliva. He gave the first description of red corpuscles, observed plant tissue, examined muscle, and investigated the life cycles of insects.

Nearly 200 years later, Leeuwenhoek's discovery of microbes aided French chemist and biologist Louis Pasteur to develop his "germ theory of disease." This concept suggested that disease derives from tiny organisms attacking and weakening the body. The germ theory later helped doctors to fight infectious diseases, including anthrax, diphtheria, polio, smallpox, tetanus, and typhoid.

10. According to the passage, Leeuwenhoek would be best described as a
   a. bored haberdasher who stumbled upon scientific discovery.
   b. trained researcher with an interest in microbiology.
   c. proficient hobbyist who made microscopic lenses for entertainment.
   d. inquisitive amateur who made pioneer studies of microbes.
   e. talented scientist interested in finding a cure for disease.

11. In the second sentence of the passage, *inspired* most nearly means
   a. introduced.
   b. invested.
   c. influenced.
   d. indulged.
   e. inclined.

12. The author's attitude toward Leeuwenhoek's contribution to medicine is one of
   a. ecstatic reverence.
   b. genuine admiration.
   c. tepid approval.
   d. courteous opposition.
   e. antagonistic incredulity.

Use the following passage to answer question 13.

According to a poll of Smithtown residents, the number of adults who belong to a health club or gym is 25% higher than it was five years ago. This higher level of physical fitness among Smithtown adults must account for the reduced rate of heart disease during the same period.

13. Which of the following, if true, most weakens the author's argument?
   a. All of the health clubs and gyms in Smithtown offer information on improving cardiac health.
   b. Smithtown has always had a relatively low rate of heart disease.
   c. Not all adults participated in the poll.
   d. A new cardiac clinic was established in Smithtown ten years ago.
   e. Most of the adults who have joined gyms in the past five years only work out a few times a month.

Use the following passage to answer question 14.

A book proposal has three major functions. First, it should sell a publisher on the commercial potential of the as-yet-to-be-written book. Second, the writing in the proposal itself should convince the publisher that the author has the ability to write the book. Finally, the proposal should show that the author has the background necessary to write the book.

14. Which of the following is the best meaning of the word *background* as it is used in the passage?
   a. something behind the main event
   b. something in a subordinated position
   c. one's ability to do something
   d. events leading up to something
   e. facts to help explain something

Use the following passage to answer question 15.

In the mid-1800s, the art world in England was rattled by the initials PRB. The PRB (or Pre-Raphaelite Brotherhood) was founded by William Holman Hunt, John Everett Millais, and Dante Gabriel Rossetti. These three burgeoning artists (the oldest of whom was 21) and their disdain for the artistic conventions of the time would have a dramatic influence on the art world for generations to come. During the era leading up to the PRB, the Royal Academy dominated British art. The Royal Academy advocated a style that was typically staid and relied heavily upon the use of dark amber and brown tones to depict overly idealized landscapes, carefully arranged family portraits and still lifes, and overly dramatic nature scenes such as boats caught in stormy seas. By contrast, the PRB believed that art should present subjects that, by their very nature, had greater meaning and more accurately depicted reality.

15. The author's main purpose in this passage is to
   a. describe the lives of the founders of the PRB.
   b. describe the artistic principles of the PRB.
   c. compare and contrast revolutions in art.
   d. describe the controversy created by the PRB.
   e. describe how the PRB influenced future artists.

Use the following passage to answer questions 16 and 17.

(1) The Woodstock Music and Art Fair—better known to its participants and to history simply as "Woodstock"—should have been a colossal failure. (2) Just a month prior to its August 15, 1969, opening, the fair's organizers were informed by the council of Wallkill, New York, that permission to hold the festival was withdrawn. (3) Amazingly, not only was a new site found, but word also got out to the public of the fair's new location.

(4) At the new site, fences that were supposed to facilitate ticket collection never materialized, and all attempts at gathering tickets were abandoned. (5) Crowd estimates of 30,000 kept rising; by the end of the three days, some estimated the crowd at 500,000. (6) And then, on opening night, it began to rain. (7) Off and on, throughout all three days, huge summer storms rolled over the gathering. (8) In spite of these problems, most people think of Woodstock not only as a fond memory but also as the defining moment for an entire generation.

16. Which of the following would be the most appropriate title for this passage?
   a. Woodstock as Metaphor
   b. Backstage at Woodstock
   c. Woodstock: From The Band to The Who
   d. Remembering Woodstock
   e. Woodstock: The Untold Story

17. Which of the numbered sentences of the passage best represents an opinion rather than a fact?
   a. sentence 1
   b. sentence 2
   c. sentence 3
   d. sentence 4
   e. sentence 5

Use the following passage to answer question 18.

The Sami are an indigenous people living in the northern parts of Norway, Sweden, Finland, and Russia's Kola peninsula. Originally, the Sami religion was animistic; that is, for them, nature and natural objects had a conscious life, a spirit. One was expected to move quietly in the wilderness and avoid making a disturbance out of courtesy to these spirits. Ghengis Khan is said to have declared that the Sami were one people he would never try to fight again. Since the Sami were not warriors and did not believe in war, they simply disappeared in times of conflict. They were known as peaceful retreaters.

18. Based on the tone of the passage, which of the following words best describes the author's attitude toward the Sami people?
   a. admiring
   b. pitying
   c. contemptuous
   d. patronizing
   e. perplexed

Use the following passage to answer question 19.

From its beginnings in the 1920s, the modeling industry has provided beautiful people to help sell everything from magazines to computers to vacation destinations. John Robert Powers, who opened the first modeling agency in 1923, was a former actor who hired his actor friends to model for magazine advertisements. Cary Grant, Lucille Ball, and Princess Grace of Monaco were clients. However, for many models, "great-looking" was where their resumes began and ended. The height of popularity for them was in the 1980s and 1990s, the era of the supermodel. A handful of "perfect" women commanded salaries of up to $25,000 a day to walk catwalks at fashion shows, appear in print ads, and pose their way through commercials. They were celebrities, treated with all of the lavish attention usually paid to heads of state or rock stars.

19. The clause *"great-looking" was where their resumes began and ended* is
   a. a description of the models' work experience.
   b. meant to be taken literally.
   c. meant to be taken figuratively.
   d. a truthful statement.
   e. an example of pathos.

Use the following passage by Edith Wharton to answer question 20.

There are at least two reasons why a subject should find expression in novel-form rather than as a tale; but neither is based on the number of what may be conveniently called incidents, or external happenings, which the narrative contains. There are novels of action which might be condensed into short stories without the loss of their distinguishing qualities. The marks of the subject requiring a longer development are, first, the gradual unfolding of the inner life of its characters, and secondly the need of producing in the reader's mind the sense of the lapse of time. Outward events of the most varied and exciting nature may without loss of probability be crowded into a few hours, but moral dramas usually have their roots deep in the soul, their rise far back in time; and the suddenest-seeming clash in which they culminate should be led up to step by step if it is to explain and justify itself.

20. The author's main purpose in this passage is to
   a. provide guidelines for choosing the narrator in a novel.
   b. provide tips for making short stories and novels more realistic.
   c. debunk several myths about writing novels.
   d. explain why some tales are better for novels than short stories.
   e. explain why novels are better than stories.

Use the following passage to answer questions 21–23.

Heat reactions usually occur when large amounts of water and/or salt are lost through excessive sweating following strenuous exercise. When the body becomes overheated and cannot eliminate this excess heat, heat exhaustion and heat stroke are possible.

Heat exhaustion is generally characterized by clammy skin, fatigue, nausea, dizziness, profuse perspiration, and sometimes fainting, resulting from an inadequate intake of water and the loss of fluids. First aid treatment for this condition includes having the victim lie down, raising the feet 8–12 inches, applying cool, wet cloths to the skin, and giving the victim sips of salt water (1 teaspoon per glass, half a glass every 15 minutes), over the period of an hour.

Heat stroke is much more serious; it is an immediately life-threatening situation. The characteristics of heat stroke are a high body temperature (which may reach 106° F or more); a rapid pulse; hot, dry skin; and a blocked sweating mechanism. Victims of this condition may be unconscious, and first aid measures should be directed at cooling the body quickly. The victim should be placed in a tub of cold water or repeatedly sponged with cool water until his or her temperature is lowered sufficiently. Fans or air conditioners will also help with the cooling process. Care should be taken, however, not to overchill the victim once the temperature is below 102° F.

21. The most immediate concern of a person tending a victim of heat stroke should be to

    a. get salt into the victim's body.

    b. raise the victim's feet.

    c. lower the victim's pulse rate.

    d. have the victim lie down.

    e. lower the victim's temperature.

22. Heat stroke is more serious than heat exhaustion because heat stroke victims

    a. have too little salt in their bodies.

    b. cannot take in water.

    c. do not sweat.

    d. have frequent fainting spells.

    e. may have convulsions.

23. On the basis of the information in the passage, symptoms such as nausea and dizziness in a heat exhaustion victim indicate that the person most likely needs to

    a. be immediately taken to a hospital.

    b. be immersed in a tub of water.

    c. be given more salt water.

    d. sweat more.

    e. go to an air-conditioned place.

Use the following passage to answer question 24.

After rock and roll exploded on the music scene in the 1950s, many rock artists began covering blues songs, thus bringing the blues to a mainstream audience and giving it true national and international exposure. In the early 1960s, the Rolling Stones, Yardbirds, Cream, and others remade blues songs such as Robert Johnson's "Crossroads" and Big Joe Williams' "Baby Please Don't Go" to wide popularity. People all across America listened to songs with lyrics that were intensely honest and personal, songs that told about any number of things that give us the blues: loneliness, betrayal, unrequited love, a run of bad luck, being out of work or away from home or broke or brokenhearted.

24. In the sentence, "People all across America listened to songs with lyrics that were intensely honest and personal, songs that told about any number of things that give us the blues: loneliness, betrayal, unrequited love, a run of bad luck, being out of work or away from home or broke or brokenhearted," the author is

 a. defining blues music.

 b. identifying the origin of the blues.

 c. describing the lyrics of a famous blues song.

 d. explaining why blues cover songs were so popular.

 e. making a connection between the blues and the Civil Rights movement.

Use the following passage from Aristotle's Nicomachean Ethics *to answer questions 25 and 26.*

Good things are commonly divided into three classes: (1) external goods, (2) goods of the soul, and (3) goods of the body. Of these, we call the goods pertaining to the soul goods in the highest and fullest sense. But in speaking of "soul," we refer to our soul's actions and activities. Thus, our definition [of good] tallies with this opinion which has been current for a long time and to which philosophers subscribe. We are also right in defining the end as consisting of actions and activities; for in this way the end is included among the goods of the soul and not among external goods.

Also the view that a happy man lives well and fares well fits in with our definition: for we have all but defined happiness as a kind of good life and well-being.

Moreover, the characteristics which one looks for in happiness are all included in our definition. For some people think that happiness is a virtue, others that it is practical wisdom, others that it is some kind of theoretical wisdom; others again believe it to be all or some of these accompanied by, or not devoid of, pleasure; and some people also include external prosperity in its definition.

25. As it is used in the first paragraph of the passage, the word *tallies* means

 a. keeps count.

 b. records.

 c. labels.

 d. corresponds.

 e. scores.

26. The author's definition of happiness in the second paragraph of the passage is related to the definition of good in that

 a. living a good life will bring you happiness.

 b. happiness is the same as goodness.

 c. happiness is often sacrificed to attain the good.

 d. all things that create happiness are good things.

 e. happiness is a virtue.

Use the following passage to answer questions 27 and 28.

The inhabitants of the Trobriand Islands, an archipelago off the coast of Papua New Guinea in the South Pacific, are united by a ceremonial trading system called the *kula ring*. Kula traders sail to neighboring islands in large ocean-going canoes to offer either shell necklaces or shell armbands. The necklaces, made of red shells called *bagi*, travel around the trading ring clockwise, and the armbands, made of white shells called *mwali*, travel counterclockwise.

Each man in the kula ring has two kula trading partners—one partner to whom he gives a necklace for an armband of equal value, although the exchanges are made on separate occasions, and one partner with whom he makes the reverse exchange. Each partner has one other partner with whom he trades, thus linking all the men around the kula ring. For example, if A trades with B and C, B trades with A and D, and C trades with A and E, and so on. A man may have only met his own specific kula partners, but he will know by reputation all the men in his kula ring. It can take anywhere from two to ten years for a particular object to complete a journey around the ring. The more times an object has made the trip around the ring, the more value it accrues. Particularly beautiful necklaces and armbands are also prized. Some famous kula objects are known by special names and through elaborate stories. Objects also gain fame through ownership by powerful men, and, likewise, men can gain status by possessing particularly prized kula objects.

27. What is the best definition for *accrues* as it is used in the second paragraph of the passage?
   a. increases over time
   b. decreases over time
   c. becomes worthless
   d. steals
   e. exchanges

28. According to the passage, necklaces and armbands gain value through all the following means EXCEPT
   a. being in circulation for a long time.
   b. being especially attractive.
   c. being owned by a powerful man.
   d. being made of special shells.
   e. being known by a special name.

Use the following passage adapted from Ian Johnston's My Body the Billboard *to answer questions 29–32.*

Traditional body signage seems largely to have disappeared. Well, many of the old symbols and names are still around, of course, but they are part of the commercial range of options. Seeing someone in a Harvard or Oxford sweatshirt or a kilt or a military tie now communicates nothing at all significant about that person's life other than the personal choice of a particular consumer. Religious signs are still evocative, to be sure, but are far less common than they used to be. Why should this be? I suspect one reason may be that we have lost a sense of significant connection to the various things indicated by such signs. Proclaiming our high school or university or our athletic team or our community has a much lower priority nowadays, in part because we live such rapidly changing lives in a society marked by constant motion that the stability essential to confer significance on such signs has largely gone.

But we still must attach ourselves to something. Lacking the conviction that the traditional things matter, we turn to the last resort of the modern world: the market. Here there is a vast array of options, all equally meaningless in terms of traditional values, all equally important in identifying the one thing left to us for declaring our identity publicly, our fashion sense and disposable income. The market naturally manipulates the labels, making sure we keep purchasing what will most quickly declare us excellent consumers. If this year a Chicago Bulls jacket or Air Jordan shoes are so popular that we are prepared to spend our way into a trendy identity, then next year there will be something else.

29. The main purpose of the passage is to
   a. discuss basketball's importance in today's fashions.
   b. relate the tribal history of tattoos.
   c. tell a story about the good old days.
   d. help the reader discover his or her own true identity.
   e. discuss commercialism's powerful influence upon personal identity.

30. The author would agree with all the following statements EXCEPT which one?
   a. A person wearing a New York Yankees baseball hat is not necessarily a fan or resident of New York.
   b. Pride in our school or community is not as strong today as it was years ago.
   c. In today's society, being trendy is more important than keeping tradition.
   d. You can tell a lot about somebody by what he or she is wearing.
   e. The last resort of the modern world is the marketplace.

31. Which statement best simplifies the author's point of view of today's society, as stated in the last sentence of paragraph 1?
   a. Times have changed.
   b. People's lives today are very similar to those of a generation ago.
   c. Fashion is very important in today's world.
   d. People today don't have proper nutrition.
   e. Life is short.

32. In the second paragraph, *disposable income* refers to
   a. recyclable goods.
   b. spending money.
   c. life savings.
   d. a donation to charity.
   e. garbage.

Use the following passage to answer question 33.

Emperor Charlemagne of the Franks was crowned in 800 A.D. The Frankish Empire at that time extended over what is now Germany, Italy, and France. Charlemagne died in the year 814, but his brief reign marked the dawn of a distinctly European culture. The artists and thinkers who helped create this European civilization drew on the ancient texts of the Germanic, Celtic, Greek, Roman, Hebrew, and Christian worlds. Many of the traditions of these cultures remained active in Frankish society for centuries. These mores in turn laid the groundwork for the laws, customs, and even attitudes of today's Europeans.

33. Which of the following is the best meaning of the word *culture* as it is used in the passage?
   a. the fashionable class
   b. a community of interrelated individuals
   c. a partnership
   d. a group of loosely associated outsiders
   e. an organized group with a common goal

Use the following passage to answer question 34.

Sir Isaac Newton, English mathematician, philosopher, and physicist, was born in 1642 in Woolsthorpe-by-Colsterworth, a hamlet in the county of Lincolnshire, England. Newton was educated at Grantham Grammar School. In 1661 he joined Trinity College, Cambridge, and continued there as Lucasian professor of mathematics from 1669 to 1701. In 1665 he originated the binomial theorem and began to develop a mathematical theory that would later become calculus. However, his most important discoveries were made during the two-year period from 1664 to 1666, when the university was closed due to the Great Plague. Newton retreated to his hometown and set to work on developing calculus, as well as advanced studies on optics and gravitation. It was at this time that he formulated the Law of Universal Gravitation and discovered that white light is composed of all the colors of the spectrum. These findings enabled him to make fundamental contributions to mathematics, astronomy, and theoretical and experimental physics.

34. Which statement best summarizes the life of Sir Isaac Newton?
   a. distinguished inventor, mathematician, physicist, and great thinker of the seventeenth century.
   b. eminent mathematician, physicist, and scholar of the Renaissance
   c. noteworthy physicist, astronomer, mathematician, and British lord
   d. Lord Isaac Newton: from Woolsthorpe to Cambridge
   e. Isaac Newton: founder of calculus and father of gravity

Use the following passage to answer question 35.

Through the years, the U.S. Department of Transportation conducted polls concerning Daylight Saving Time and found that many Americans were in favor of it because of the extended hours of daylight and the freedom to do more in the evening hours. In further studies, the Department of Transportation also found that DST conserves energy by cutting the electricity usage in the morning and evening for lights and particular appliances. During the darkest winter months (November through February), the advantage of conserving energy in afternoon Daylight Saving Time is outweighed by needing more light in the morning because of late sunrise. In Britain, studies showed that there were fewer accidents on the road because of the increased visibility resulting from additional hours of daylight.

35. In which month does the need for more energy in the morning offset the afternoon conservation of energy by DST?
   a. June
   b. July
   c. October
   d. January
   e. March

Use the following passage to answer questions 36 and 37.

An estimated 75 million Americans suffer from an allergic disease, which results from the immune system reacting to a normally innocuous substance, such as pollen or dust. An allergic response begins with a process called *sensitization*. When a foreign substance—an allergen such as pollen, for example—first enters the body of an allergic person, cells called *macrophages* engulf the invader, chop it into pieces and display the pieces on their surfaces. T-helper cells recognize certain allergen fragments and bind to the macrophages. This process causes the T-helper cells to secrete signaling molecules, including interleukin-4 (IL-4). IL-4, in turn, spurs nearby B cells to mature into plasma cells. Plasma cells produce Y-shaped antibody proteins.

36. An allergic disease occurs when the body's immune system reacts to a substance that is usually
   a. common.
   b. toxic.
   c. irritating.
   d. airborne.
   e. harmless.

37. Cells that surround allergens within the body are known as
   a. T-helper cells.
   b. macrophage cells.
   c. B cells.
   d. plasma cells.
   e. IL-4.

Use the following poem by Emily Dickinson to answer questions 38 and 39.

A Narrow Fellow in the Grass

A narrow fellow in the grass
Occasionally rides;
You may have met him did you not?
His notice sudden is.
The grass divides as with a comb,
A spotted shaft is seen,
And then it closes at your feet
And opens further on.
He likes a boggy acre,
A floor too cool for corn,
Yet when a boy, and barefoot,
I more than once at noon
Have passed, I thought, a whip-lash
Unbraiding in the sun,
When, stooping to secure it,
It wrinkled, and was gone.

Several of nature's people
I know and they know me;
I feel for them a transport
Of cordiality;

But never met this fellow,
Attended or alone,
Without a tighter breathing
And zero at the bone.

38. Who or what is the *fellow* in this poem?
    a. a whip-lash
    b. a weed
    c. a snake
    d. a gust of wind
    e. a boy

39. The lines *Without a tighter breathing / And zero at the bone* most nearly indicate
    a. fright.
    b. cold.
    c. grief.
    d. awe.
    e. relief.

Use the following passage to answer question 40.

Do you sing in the shower while dreaming of getting your own record deal? There are a couple of "reality" shows made just for you. Audition, and make the cut, so some British guy who has never sung a note can rip you to pieces on live television. At least you can take comfort in the knowledge that the winner probably wouldn't have been able to get a record deal in real life without the votes of a supportive audience. Or maybe you're lonely and fiscally challenged, and dream of walking down the aisle with a millionaire? Real marriage doesn't involve contestants who know each other for a couple of days. The people on these shows seem to be more interested in how they look on camera than in the character of the person they might spend the rest of their life with. Let's hope that reality TV isn't reality.

40. What does the author find most troublesome about reality TV?
    a. It isn't original.
    b. It can humiliate people.
    c. It invades people's privacy.
    d. It doesn't accurately show reality.
    e. It shows how shallow people are.

▶ Skills Test in Mathematics

Directions: Choose the best answer to each of the following questions.

Use the following figure to answer question 1.

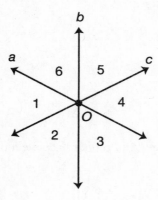

1. In the diagram, lines *a*, *b*, and *c* intersect at point *O*. Which of the following are NOT adjacent angles?
   a. ∠1 and ∠6
   b. ∠1 and ∠4
   c. ∠4 and ∠5
   d. ∠2 and ∠3
   e. All of the angles are adjacent.

2. A middle school cafeteria has three different options for lunch.
   For $2, a student can get either a sandwich or two cookies.
   For $3, a student can get a sandwich and one cookie.
   For $4, a student can get either two sandwiches, or a sandwich and two cookies.
   If Jimae has $6 to pay for lunch for her and her brother, which of the following is NOT a possible combination?
   a. three sandwiches and one cookie
   b. two sandwiches and two cookies
   c. one sandwich and four cookies
   d. three sandwiches and no cookies
   e. one sandwich and three cookies

3. The sequence of numbers 0, 2, 2, 4, 6, 10, 16 follows a pattern. Using this pattern, which of the following is the next number in the sequence?

  a. 16

  b. 20

  c. 22

  d. 26

  e. 32

4. A model of the ancient city of Rome uses a scale of 1 foot:100 yards. The Coliseum, a stadium built nearly two thousand years ago, is about 617 feet long. Which is the length, in feet, of the Coliseum in the model, rounded to the nearest tenth?

  a. 1.5 feet

  b. 2.1 feet

  c. 6.2 feet

  d. 24.7 feet

  e. 60 feet

Use the following figure to answer question 5.

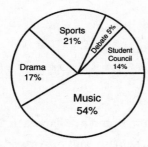

5. According to the graph, if 105 students at the school are involved in sports, how many are involved in the drama club?

  a. 17

  b. 35

  c. 85

  d. 105

  e. 175

6. The average high temperature for the first five days in July was 90°. If the temperature the first four days was 95°, 85°, 88°, and 84°, respectively, what was the temperature on the fifth day?

  a. 90°

  b. 92°

  c. 94°

  d. 96°

  e. 98°

7. A jar of coins contains 8 dimes, 10 quarters, 3 nickels, and 9 pennies. What is the probability of selecting either a nickel or a penny if drawing one coin from the jar?

  a. $\frac{1}{10}$

  b. $\frac{2}{5}$

  c. $\frac{4}{15}$

  d. $\frac{3}{10}$

  e. $\frac{1}{3}$

8. What is the perimeter of a pentagon with three sides of 3 inches, and the remaining sides 5 inches long?

  a. 24 inches

  b. 19 inches

  c. 14 inches

  d. 12 inches

  e. 9 inches

9. What is the product when 11 is multiplied by 0.032?

  a. 0.032

  b. 0.0352

  c. 0.32

  d. 0.352

  e. 3.20

10. Amanda buys three T-shirts on sale at a, b, and c dollars each. If she gets a discount of 90%, which expression would determine the average price paid by Amanda for each T-shirt?

  a. $\frac{a+b+c}{0.9}$

  b. $(a+b+c) \times 0.9$

  c. $\frac{a+b+c}{3}$

  d. $3 \times \frac{a+b+c}{0.9}$

  e. $\frac{0.9(a+b+c)}{3}$

11. Garth wants to know if he has enough money to purchase several items at the grocery store. He needs three cans of soup, which cost $.99 each, and two boxes of rice, which cost $3.49 each. He uses the expression $(3 \times \$0.99) + (2 \times \$3.49)$ to calculate how much the items will cost. Which of the following expressions could also be used?

   a. $3 \times (\$3.49 + \$.99) - \$3.49$

   b. $3 \times (\$3.49 + \$.99)$

   c. $(2 + 3) \times (\$3.49 + \$.99)$

   d. $(2 \times 3) + (\$3.49 \times \$.99)$

   e. $3 \times (\$3.49 + \$.99) + \$3.49$

12. Tess finds the average of her three most recent history quiz scores by using the following expression, where a, b, and c are the three scores: $\frac{a+b+c}{3}$. Which of the following would also determine the average of her scores?

   a. $\left(\frac{a}{3} + \frac{b}{3} + \frac{c}{3}\right)$

   b. $\frac{\frac{a+b+c}{3}}{100}$

   c. $(a + b + c) \times 3$

   d. $\frac{a \times b \times c}{3}$

   e. $\frac{a+b+c}{3+100}$

13. What is $\frac{2}{3}$ divided by $\frac{5}{12}$?

   a. $1\frac{3}{5}$

   b. $1\frac{5}{18}$

   c. $1\frac{7}{36}$

   d. $1\frac{5}{6}$

   e. $1\frac{2}{3}$

Use the following table to answer question 14.

Train Schedule

Train	Arrival Time	Departure Time
A	6:42 A.M.	6:53 A.M.
B	7:24 A.M.	7:34 A.M.
C	7:55 A.M.	8:06 A.M.
D	8:13 A.M.	8:24 A.M.
E	9:03 A.M.	9:11 A.M.
F	9:31 A.M.	9:42 A.M.

14. What is the difference between the arrival time for Train A and the departure time for Train D?
   a. 1 hour, 18 minutes
   b. 1 hour, 24 minutes
   c. 1 hour, 42 minutes
   d. 2 hours, 6 minutes
   e. 2 hours, 18 minutes

15. Which of the following represents the solution to the inequality $-4x - 1 \geq 11$?
   a. $x \leq 3$
   b. $x \geq 3$
   c. $x \geq -3$
   d. $x \leq -3$
   e. $x \geq 2\frac{1}{2}$

16. Given a polygon with four congruent sides, which of the following does NOT contradict the statement: "If a polygon has four congruent sides, then the polygon is a square"?
   a. The polygon has five congruent sides.
   b. The polygon does not have four congruent sides.
   c. The polygon has exactly one pair of parallel sides.
   d. The polygon is a triangle.
   e. The polygon is also a rhombus.

17. Of the 6,251 teachers in a study of certification areas, 312 have dual certification in two subject areas. What is a reasonable estimate of the percentage of teachers in the study who have dual certification?

   a. 0.5%

   b. 2%

   c. 5%

   d. 20%

   e. 50%

Use the following chart to answer questions 18–20.

Major Causes of Home Fires in the Previous Four-Year Period

CAUSE	FIRES (% OF TOTAL)	CIVILIAN DEATHS (% OF TOTAL)
heating equipment	161,500 (27.5%)	770 (16.8%)
cooking equipment	104,800 (17.8%)	350 (7.7%)
incendiary, suspicious	65,400 (11.1%)	620 (13.6%)
electrical equipment	45,700 (7.8%)	440 (9.6%)
other equipment	43,000 (7.3%)	240 (5.3%)
smoking materials	39,300 (6.7%)	1,320 (28.9%)
appliances, air-conditioning	36,200 (6.2%)	120 (2.7%)
exposure and other heat	28,600 (4.8%)	191 (4.2%)
open flame	27,200 (4.6%)	130 (2.9%)
child play	26,900 (4.6%)	370 (8.1%)
natural causes	9,200 (1.6%)	10 (0.2%)

18. What is the percentage of the total fires caused by both electrical equipment and other equipment combined?

   a. 7.8%

   b. 14.9%

   c. 15.1%

   d. 29.9%

   e. 30.0%

19. Of the causes listed in the table, which one has the highest ratio of the percentage of deaths to the percentage of total fires?

   a. heating equipment
   b. smoking materials
   c. exposure and other heat
   d. child play
   e. natural causes

20. Which of the following answer choices would most accurately show the percentages from the "Fires" column in the table?

   a.

   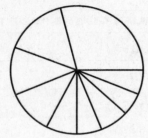

   b.

   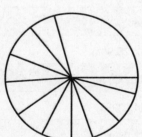

   c.

   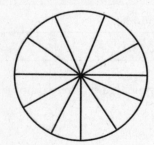

   d.

   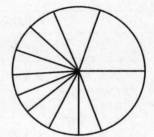

   e.

   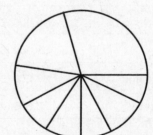

21. All of the rooms on the main floor of an office building are rectangular, with 8-foot-high ceilings. Keira's office is 9 feet wide by 11 feet long. What is the combined surface area of the four walls of her office, including any windows and doors?

   a. 99 square feet

   b. 160 square feet

   c. 320 square feet

   d. 729 square feet

   e. 288 square feet

22. A springtime day had a temperature of 40° C. What was the temperature in degrees Fahrenheit? The formula for converting Celsius to Fahrenheit is $F = \frac{9}{5}C + 32$.

   a. 100° F

   b. 101° F

   c. 102° F

   d. 103° F

   e. 104° F

23. Which of the following fractions are in order from greatest to least?

   a. $\frac{1}{2}, \frac{6}{11}, \frac{3}{5}, \frac{5}{8}$

   b. $\frac{3}{5}, \frac{6}{11}, \frac{1}{2}, \frac{5}{8}$

   c. $\frac{5}{8}, \frac{6}{11}, \frac{3}{5}, \frac{1}{2}$

   d. $\frac{5}{8}, \frac{3}{5}, \frac{6}{11}, \frac{1}{2}$

   e. $\frac{3}{5}, \frac{1}{2}, \frac{5}{8}, \frac{6}{11}$

Use the following chart to answer question 24.

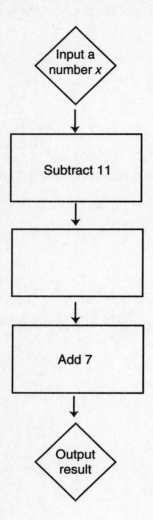

24. When the input is 63, the result is 11. What is the missing step?

    a. Divide by 4.

    b. Subtract 31.

    c. Subtract 41.

    d. Divide by 13.

    e. Divide by 2.

25. How much is one-eighth of one-sixth?

 a. $\frac{1}{48}$

 b. $\frac{1}{2}$

 c. $\frac{6}{8}$

 d. $\frac{1}{12}$

 e. $\frac{1}{6}$

26. Given the equation $14x + 2(x + 1) = 34$, each of the following steps would most likely be used to solve the problem EXCEPT

 a. subtract 2 from each side of the equation.

 b. divide each side of the equation by 16.

 c. combine $14x$ and $2x$.

 d. add 2 to each side of the equation.

 e. use the distributive property to multiply $2 \times (x + 1)$.

27. During her shift at a busy restaurant, a chef uses $2\frac{1}{4}$ pounds of flour the first hour, $4\frac{5}{8}$ pounds of flour the second hour, and $\frac{1}{2}$ pound of flour the third hour. How many pounds of flour does the chef use during these three hours?

 a. $6\frac{3}{8}$

 b. $6\frac{7}{8}$

 c. $7\frac{1}{4}$

 d. $7\frac{3}{8}$

 e. $7\frac{3}{4}$

28. A floor rug in the shape of a circle has a diameter of 152 cm. What is the approximate area of the rug?
 1 cm = 0.39 inches

 a. 878.53π in.^{2}

 b. 360π in.^{2}

 c. $3{,}514.12\pi$ in.^{2}

 d. $2{,}252.64\pi$ in.^{2}

 e. $5{,}776\pi$ in.^{2}

29. First year members of an auto club have to purchase the membership at the full price of $84.50, but those who were also members last year get a 15% discount. Those who have been members for at least three years get an additional 10% off the discounted price. How much does a person who has been a member at least three years have to pay for the membership?

   a. $63.38

   b. $64.64

   c. $65.78

   d. $71.83

   e. $72.05

Use the following table to answer question 30.

h	k
3	4
6	5
9	6
12	7
15	8

30. Which of the following equations expresses the relationship between h and k in the table?

   a. $k = 3h + 3$

   b. $k = \frac{1}{3}h + 3$

   c. $h = \frac{1}{3}k + 3$

   d. $h = 3k + 3$

   e. $k = \frac{2}{3}h + 3$

Use the following table to answer question 31.

Distance Traveled from Chicago with Respect to Time

TIME (HOURS)	DISTANCE FROM CHICAGO (MILES)
1	60
2	120
3	180
4	240

31. A train moving at a constant speed of 60 miles per hour leaves Chicago for Los Angeles at time $t = 0$. If Los Angeles is 2,000 miles from Chicago, which of the following equations describes the distance from Los Angeles at any time t?

    a. $D(t) = 60t - 2,000$

    b. $D(t) = 60t$

    c. $D(t) = 2,000 - 60t$

    d. $D(t) = -2,000 - 60t$

    e. $D(t) = 2,000 + 60t$

32. At a baseball game, Deanna bought food for herself and her sister Jamie: one jumbo box of popcorn to share at $7 a box, two hot dogs for each of them (four total) at $3 a dog, and one soda for each at $4 apiece. Jamie paid for their tickets at $13 a ticket. Who spent more money and by how much?

    a. Deanna, by $1

    b. Deanna, by $3

    c. Jamie, by $1

    d. Jamie, by $2

    e. Jamie, by $4

Use the following figure to answer questions 33 and 34.

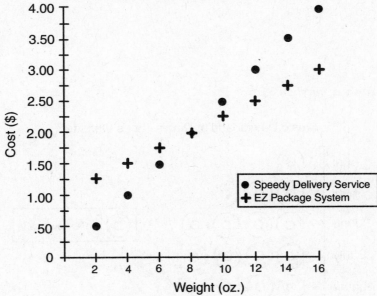

This double scatter plot compares the rates for different-weight packages for two companies.

33. Using the company with the better rate for each weight, which of the following combinations of packages would be the least expensive to ship?

a. 8 oz. and 2 oz.

b. 2 oz. and 6 oz.

c. 2 oz. and 10 oz.

d. one 12 oz. package

e. 6 oz. and 8 oz.

34. At what weight is the cost for shipping at Speedy Delivery Service 20% more than the cost for the same-weight package at EZ Package System?

a. 2 oz.

b. 4 oz.

c. 6 oz.

d. 10 oz.

e. 12 oz.

35. Felicia spent $5,618 on rent this year, and $5,085 the year before. She predicts she will be paying approximately $6,163 next year. To the nearest ten, what is the best estimate of the total amount she will spend on rent during this three-year span?

a. $16,800

b. $16,860

c. $16,870

d. $16,900

e. $17,000

Use the following figure to answer question 36.

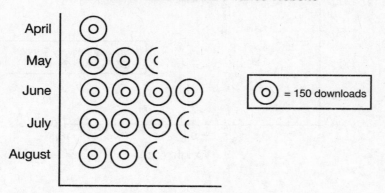

Music Downloads at Dina's Tunes Website

36. According to the figure, what is the average number of music downloads sold per month over the five-month period?

   a. 150

   b. 375

   c. 390

   d. 405

   e. 2,025

37. A triangle has two sides that measure 14 cm and 17 cm, respectively. Which of the following could be the length of the triangle's third side?

   a. 33 cm

   b. 31 cm

   c. 25 cm

   d. 44 cm

   e. 3 cm

38. One thousand students are participating in the regional math competition. Teams of five students are placed in equal amounts into four different gymnasiums. Each team has one adult coach. To find the total number of people (students and coaches) in each gymnasium you could

   a. divide 1,000 by 4, divide that result by 5, and then add that result and 1,000.

   b. divide 1,000 by 5, add that result to 1,000, and then divide that result by 4.

   c. divide 1,000 by 4, divide that result by 4, and then add that result and 1,000.

   d. divide 1,000 by 5, divide that result by 4, and then add that result and 50.

   e. divide 1,000 by 4, add 50 to that result, and then divide that result by 5.

39. Harold has two containers that he has filled with water. One is a rectangular plastic box with a base of 16 square inches, and the other is a cylindrical container with a base radius of 2 inches and a height of 11 inches. If the rectangular box is filled with water 9 inches from the bottom, and Harold pours the water into the cylinder without spilling, which of the following will be true?

a. The cylinder will overflow.

b. The cylinder will be exactly full.

c. The cylinder will be filled to an approximate level of 10 inches.

d. The cylinder will be filled to an approximate level of 8 inches.

e. The cylinder will be filled to an approximate level of 6 inches.

40. Robert, Linda, Miguel, and Sonja are friends. They all practice unique sports: One enjoys skiing, one enjoys fishing, one enjoys tennis, and one enjoys volleyball. The friend who fishes is Miguel's neighbor. Robert and Linda dislike sports that use balls. Sonja is older than both Robert and the friend who fishes. Who likes to fish?

a. Robert

b. Miguel

c. Sonja

d. Linda

e. The answer cannot be determined from the information given.

▶ Skills Test in Writing—Section 1, Part A

Directions: Choose the letter for the underlined portion that contains a grammatical error. If there is no error in the sentence, choose **e**.

1. <u>As soon as</u> we stepped off of the water taxi, <u>which</u> pulled away from the <u>dock, leaving</u> both of us standing
      a   **b**   **c**

    <u>in a puddle of</u> river water. <u>No error</u>
      d   **e**

2. <u>As the popularity</u> of professional lacrosse <u>continues</u> to grow, more and more companies <u>are investing</u>
     a   **b**   **c**

    thousands of <u>dollars</u> to become primary sponsors so they can get their brand names in front of
              d

    television viewers. <u>No error</u>
                e

3. <u>When</u> the casting agent called out her name, <u>she walked</u> rather <u>hesitant</u> to the front of the stage and
    a   **b**   **c**

    stood <u>there</u> shaking. <u>No error</u>
         d   **e**

4. In John F. <u>Kennedy's</u> famous inaugural address in <u>1961, he</u> implored his fellow <u>Americans</u> to "<u>ask not</u>
             a   **b**   **c**   **d**

    what your country can do for you, ask what you can do for your country." <u>No error</u>
                                                  e

5. Corporate educators will often <u>use</u> analogies and metaphors <u>from</u> sports <u>describing</u> business
                              a   **b**   **c**

    decision<u>s and</u> goals. <u>No error</u>
        d   **e**

6. I am looking for <u>an</u> assistant <u>who is</u> smart, <u>reliable,</u> and <u>will come on time</u>. <u>No error</u>
                  a   **b**   **c**   **d**   **e**

7. The famous <u>composer</u> Igor Stravinsky <u>was born</u> in <u>Russia, his</u> father was a <u>well-established</u> opera singer.
             a   **b**   **c**   **d**

    <u>No error</u>
     e

8. My <u>mother</u> <u>is</u> a teacher <u>and who</u> also has <u>been a principal</u>. <u>No error</u>
         a   **b**   **c**   **d**   **e**

9. <u>During</u> the first act of the play, I <u>begun</u> to ask <u>myself</u> why I spent my hard-earned money on tickets <u>to</u>
    a   **b**   **c**   **d**
such a flop. <u>No error</u>
         e

10. A <u>captain</u> sailing a ship from <u>New York Harbor</u> to <u>San Francisco Bay</u> can shave 7,872 miles off his <u>or</u> her
     a   **b**   **c**   **d**
trip by cutting through the Panama Canal. <u>No error</u>
                                    e

11. We <u>couldn't</u> barely hear the <u>Spanish</u> <u>lesson;</u> the teacher <u>spoke</u> in a very soft voice. <u>No error</u>
         a   **b**   **c**   **d**   **e**

12. The used car had been treated <u>bad</u> by <u>its</u> previous <u>owner, but</u> the people at the car dealership
                               a   **b**   **c**
<u>worked hard</u> to fix it up like new. <u>No error</u>
  d   **e**

13. After <u>Pele's</u> final soccer <u>game, in</u> which he played for both <u>teams, players</u> from both squads carried him
       a   **b**   **c**
off the field on <u>their</u> shoulders. <u>No error</u>
           d   **e**

14. The harsh <u>Winter</u> of <u>1777</u> tested the <u>endurance and</u> spirit of the American <u>revolutionaries, but</u> it did not
            a   **b**   **c**   **d**
break them. <u>No error</u>
         e

15. The <u>principal's</u> decision at last <u>Monday's</u> teacher conference is sure to have an <u>affect</u> on all of the
       a   **b**   **c**
<u>students</u> in the junior high school. <u>No error</u>
  d   **e**

16. The <u>b</u>iologist <u>spoke at length</u> about his discovery of a new <u>species</u> of bacteria and <u>its</u> possible uses in
       a   b   c   d

medicine. <u>No error</u>
       e

17. <u>Although</u> the owner of the theater <u>acknowledged</u> that the ticket prices of $15.00 for adults and $8.50 for
      a   b

children are too expensive for some, <u>also noted</u> that many moviegoers <u>can take advantage of</u> the matinee
                                 c   d

discounts. <u>No error</u>
        e

18. By mixing sounds from the <u>Jazz Age</u> with the beats of <u>contemporary modern</u> dance music, the DJ will
                     a   b

show how twentieth-century musicians <u>can be influenced</u> by the <u>sound and style</u> of early styles of music.
                                  c   d

<u>No error</u>
  e

19. Wolfgang <u>A</u>madeus Mozart <u>began playing</u> music <u>on</u> a piano-like instrument called a <u>c</u>lavier. <u>No error</u>
            a   b   c   d   e

20. As you read <u>them</u>, remember that this story <u>is intended to be</u> a source of entertainment and that <u>nothing</u>
               a   b   c

in it is <u>factual</u>. <u>No error</u>
      d   e

21. <u>Neither</u> the soldiers <u>nor</u> the sergeant <u>was</u> sure of <u>their</u> location. <u>No error</u>
      a   b   c   d   e

▶ Skills Test in Writing—Section 1, Part B

Directions: Choose the best replacement for the underlined portion of the sentence. If no revision is necessary, choose **a**, which always repeats the original phrasing.

22. <u>To determine the speed of pitches, radar is often used by baseball scouts.</u>
    a. To determine the speed of pitches, radar is often used by baseball scouts.
    b. To determine the speed of pitches, it is often necessary for baseball scouts to use radar.
    c. In determining the speed of pitches, the use of radar by baseball scouts is often employed.
    d. To determine the speed of pitches, baseball scouts often use radar.
    e. Radar by baseball scouts in determining the speed of pitches is often used.

23. The entire class signed the homework petition before <u>we submit it</u> to the teacher.
    a. we submit it
    b. one submits them
    c. you submit them
    d. we will submit it
    e. we submitted it

24. At 13 years old, Keisha Castle-Hughes was the <u>younger</u> nominee ever for the Academy Award for Best Actress.
    a. younger
    b. more young
    c. most youngest
    d. youngest
    e. most youngly

25. Gloria has a multifaceted fitness regimen: <u>she swims laps, plays basketball, the weight machines, and surfing.</u>
    a. she swim laps, plays basketball, the weight machines, and surfing.
    b. she swims laps, plays basketball, lifts weights, and surfs.
    c. she swim laps, plays basketball, she lift weights, and surfs.
    d. swimming laps, basketball, lifting weights, and surfing.
    e. swims laps, plays basketball, lifting weights, and surfing.

26. Miles Davis, <u>a twentieth-century American trumpeter, is well known and renowned for creating</u> important improvisational jazz techniques.

    a. a twentieth-century American trumpeter, is well known and renowned for creating

    b. an American trumpeter who lived and played in the twentieth century, is well known for the creation of

    c. renowned and prominent, was known as a twentieth-century American trumpeter for creating

    d. he is an American trumpeter well known and renowned for creating

    e. a twentieth-century American trumpeter, is well known for creating

27. NASA scientists confirmed <u>that the Mars rover's signal was lost for more than 24 hours.</u>

    a. that the Mars rover's signal was lost for more than 24 hours.

    b. that the Mars rover's signal were lost for more than 24 hours.

    c. that the Mars rovers' signal were lost for more than 24 hours.

    d. that the Mars rovers' signal was lost for more than 24 hours.

    e. for more than 24 hours that the Mars rover's lost its signal.

28. Reverend Martin Luther King, Jr. helped organize the famous 1963 March on Washington, <u>which drew</u> hundreds of thousands of civil rights supporters from all over the United States.

    a. which drew

    b. it drew

    c. but it drew

    d. that it drew

    e. and drawing

29. Please remember that I am <u>older than him and have</u> more experience in these matters.

    a. older than him and have

    b. oldest than him and have

    c. older than he and have

    d. more older than he and have

    e. less older than him and have

30. <u>In 1978 the year I was born</u> the average price of a new car was about $14,000.

    a. In 1978 the year I was born

    b. In 1978, the year I was born

    c. In 1978, the year I was born:

    d. In 1978, the year I was born,

    e. In 1978, the year I was born;

31. The likenesses of Washington, Jefferson, Lincoln, and Roosevelt <u>is carved</u> into the side of Mount Rushmore.
   a. is carved
   b. carved
   c. is been carved
   d. been carved
   e. are carved

32. A relationship <u>between two dissimilar organisms that mutually benefits</u> both organisms is called symbiosis.
   a. between two dissimilar organisms that mutually benefits
   b. among two dissimilar organisms that mutually benefits
   c. among two dissimilar organisms that mutually benefit
   d. between two dissimilar organisms that mutually benefit
   e. with two dissimilar organisms that mutually benefit

33. The CEO wished <u>to insure the stockholders that their investment would be spent wisely.</u>
   a. to insure the stockholders that their investment would be spent wisely.
   b. that the stockholders would be insured of investment wisely spent.
   c. in assuring the stockholders, that their investment would be wisely spent.
   d. to assure the stockholders that he would spend their investment wisely.
   e. to assure and promise the stockholders of his intentions to spend their investment wisely.

34. <u>Beside their use in jewelry,</u> silver has many uses in photography and electronics.
   a. Beside their use in jewelry,
   b. Beside jewelry,
   c. In addition also to its jewelry applications,
   d. Besides its use in jewelry,
   e. Besides your using it in jewelry,

35. <u>It poured; so I tried to run for cover.</u>
   a. It poured; so I tried to run for cover.
   b. It poured, so I tried to run for cover.
   c. It poured, I tried to run for cover.
   d. It's poured, I tried to run for cover
   e. It will pour, so I tried to run for cover.

36. The Beatles were <u>a big hit in America like England.</u>
   a. a big hit in America like England.
   b. as well a big hit in England as they were in America.
   c. as big a hit in America as they were in England.
   d. just as big a hit in America than in England.
   e. a big hit as well as in both England and America.

37. <u>The novel *The Grapes of Wrath* written by John Steinbeck in 1939 won the Pulitzer Prize in 1940.</u>
   a. The novel *The Grapes of Wrath* written by John Steinbeck in 1939 won the Pulitzer Prize, in 1940.
   b. The novel *The Grapes of Wrath,* written by John Steinbeck, in 1939 won the Pulitzer Prize, in 1940.
   c. The novel *The Grapes of Wrath* written by John Steinbeck, in 1939 won the Pulitzer Prize, in 1940.
   d. The novel, *The Grapes of Wrath*, written by John Steinbeck in 1939, won the Pulitzer Prize in 1940.
   e. The novel *The Grapes of Wrath*, written by John Steinbeck in 1939, won the Pulitzer Prize in 1940.

38. <u>Running toward the gate as the plane took off, leaving Aramis and I standing helplessly in the terminal.</u>
   a. Running toward the gate as the plane took off, leaving Aramis and I standing helplessly in the terminal.
   b. While running toward the gate and watching the plane take off, which left Aramis and me standing helplessly in the terminal.
   c. Left helplessly standing in the terminal after Aramis and me ran toward the gate and watched the plane take off.
   d. As we ran toward the gate, the plane took off, leaving Aramis and me standing helplessly in the terminal.
   e. After having run toward it, the plane taking off and leaving Aramis and me in the terminal, watching helplessly.

▶ Skills Test in Writing—Section 2, Essay Writing

Carefully read the essay-writing topic that follows. Plan and write an essay that addresses all points in the topic. Make sure that your essay is well organized and that you support your central argument with concrete examples. Allow 30 minutes for your essay.

Many people would say that the Internet has become an indispensable aspect of our lives, affecting our work, our school, and our modes of communication. Write an essay in which you show how important or not the Internet is to modern life.

► Answer Explanations

Skills Test in Reading

1. b. The context of the passage indicates that the sentences in question are pointing out an unforeseen consequence (*however*) and the current situation (*now*).

2. d. To *herald* means to give an indication of things to come; this choice best fits the meaning of the sentence.

3. b. The author's statement implies that the report could have suggested specific actions to confront the health problem of smoking but that it did not.

4. e. Answer choices **a–d** are all unauthorized logging practices performed by Metsähallitus in Finland. Choice **e** is incorrect because it refers to another country.

5. c. The passage states that neural prostheses could *replace damaged or missing nerves.* Therefore, it can be inferred that prostheses are artificial body parts—in this case, artificial nerves.

6. c. The tone throughout the passage suggests the potential for microprobes. They can be permanently implanted, they have advantages over electrodes, they are promising candidates for neural prostheses, they will have great accuracy, and they are flexible.

7. e. According to the third paragraph, people who lack biochemicals could receive doses via prostheses. However, there is no suggestion that removing biochemicals would be possible.

8. d. None of the other choices is supported by the information given in the passage.

9. b. The author uses the phrase *going gray* as a metaphor for growing older. It describes the phenomenon of a large segment of a population growing older.

10. d. Although he was a man of no formal scientific education, Leeuwenhoek demonstrated a craving after knowledge. The phrase *stumbled upon* in choice **a** is too accidental to describe Leeuwenhoek's perseverance. The words *hobbyist* and *entertainment* in choice **c** do not accurately describe Leeuwenhoek's skill and drive depicted in the passage. Choices **b** and **e** are incorrect; Leeuwenhoek was not trained as a researcher, nor did he know that his discoveries would later help to cure disease.

11. c. *Inspired* means to exert an animating or enlivening influence on. In the context of the passage, Leeuwenhoek's creation of microscope lenses was influenced by the lenses used by drapers.

12. b. The tone of the passage is positive. However, ecstatic reverence (choice **a**) is too positive, and tepid approval (choice **c**) is not positive enough.

13. e. This is the answer choice that most significantly weakens the author's first assumption: that Smithtown adults are more physically fit overall than they were five years ago. If most of the new members do not work out regularly, it cannot be assumed that they are in better shape than they were before, and therefore, increased gym membership is not necessarily a reason for the decline in heart disease. Choice **a** would strengthen, not weaken, the author's argument. Choice **b** is irrelevant to the argument, which focuses on the *decline* in heart disease in Smithtown. Choice **c** does not weaken the author's contention; it is not necessary to poll every adult in order for the survey to be accurate. While the establishment of a cardiac clinic may have contributed to the drop in heart disease, this occurred prior to the five-year period the author mentions.

14. c. Any of the choices may be a definition of *background*; however, the context of the passage indicates that the word refers to the education and training of the proposed author—that is, the author's ability to write the book.

15. b. In the passage, the author describes the principles of the PRB—why the group was formed and how the group defined itself in opposition to the dominant Royal Academy. There is little or no information offered about the other answer choices.

16. d. This is the most accurate choice because the passage deals mainly with remembering the fair.

17. a. Sentence 1 contains the phrase *should have been a colossal failure,* which is an opinion of the author. The other choices are sentences that provide factual information about Woodstock.

18. a. To depict the Sami, the author uses words that point to their gentleness, which is an admirable quality: they move quietly, display courtesy to the spirits of the wilderness, and were known as peaceful retreaters.

19. c. A resume is literally the summary of one's job experience, education, and skills. The author is saying that there is nothing one can say about these models except that they look great; their figurative resume has only one item on it. Being great-looking isn't work experience (choice **a**), one would not literally list "great-looking" alone on a resume (choices **b** and **d**), and pathos is a feeling of pity or sorrow (choice **e**).

20. d. After making it clear that subjects are not equally suitable for short stories and novels, Wharton explains what makes a particular subject suitable for the novel form and how the elements of time and character development are different in the short story.

21. e. This is stated in the last paragraph: *first aid measures should be directed at cooling the body quickly.*

22. c. Heat stroke victims have a blocked sweating mechanism, as stated in the third paragraph.

23. c. The second paragraph states that for the symptoms of heat exhaustion, which include nausea and dizziness, first aid treatment includes giving the victim sips of salt water. The other choices relate to heat stroke.

24. d. This sentence stating that the blues remakes were enjoyed by people all across America suggests why the songs were so popular by describing how the lyrics touched a common emotional chord in listeners, all of whom have had the blues from one or more of the sources listed in the sentence.

25. d. At the beginning of the passage, Aristotle notes that the definition of good *corresponds* with the current opinion about the nature of the soul.

26. a. In the second paragraph, Aristotle states that *we have all but defined happiness as a kind of good life and well-being.* Thus, the definitions of happiness and goodness are intertwined; living a good life will bring happiness.

27. a. If an object *accrues* value, it *increases* in value. This can be inferred from the next sentence, which says that beautiful objects are also *prized,* suggesting that an object that has made many trips around the ring is considered very valuable.

28. d. At the end of the passage, the author states the ways in which a kula object gains value; special shells are not mentioned.

29. e. The author's primary purpose in writing this passage is to discuss his belief that commercialism's strong presence in today's society strongly influences a person's view of his or her personal identity. A good illustration of this can be found in the second paragraph, where the author states: *we are prepared to spend our way into a trendy identity.*

30. d. The statement that one *can tell a lot about somebody by what he or she is wearing* is directly contradicted by the claim the author makes in the first paragraph: *Seeing someone in a Harvard or Oxford sweatshirt or a kilt or a military tie now communicates nothing at all significant about that person's life other than the personal choice of a particular consumer.*

31. a. The author's point of view of today's society is that today's world is much smaller and more hectic than it used be, which makes it harder for people to put down solid roots and identify with a singular way of life. In short, *times have changed.*

32. b. The term *disposable income* refers to the specific amount of a person's income that is allotted as spending money. This is the only choice that makes sense in the context of the passage.

33. b. Although all of the choices are possible definitions of culture, the passage is speaking of a community of interrelated individuals—Europeans.

34. a. Choice **a** is correct because it lists the proper accolades and the proper timeframe in which he lived. Choice **b** is incorrect because he did not live during the Renaissance; choices **c** and **d** are incorrect because he was not a lord, but a knight (indicated by the title *Sir*); and choice **e** is incorrect because it is not the best summary of his vast accomplishments.

35. d. Of all the choices, January is the only month that falls within the darkest period (November through February) mentioned in the passage.

36. e. The first sentence notes that an allergic disease results from the immune system *reacting to a normally innocuous substance.* Choices **b** and **c** are contradicted in the passage by this statement. Choices **a** and **d** are not reflected in the passage.

37. b. See the third sentence, which says that cells called macrophages engulf the invader (that is, the allergen).

38. c. The fellow frightens the speaker. Choices **a**, **b**, **d**, and **e** would not be frightening.

39. a. *Tighter breathing* indicates fear, as does *zero at the bone* (one is sometimes said to be cold with fear). Also, the subject is a snake, which is an animal that is commonly feared.

40. d. While there is evidence for the other choices, they are not most troublesome. Throughout the passage, beginning with the first mention of "reality," in quotation marks, the author emphasizes the fact that reality TV is not an accurate portrait of real life.

Skills Test in Mathematics

1. b. Adjacent angles share a vertex and a common side, but do not overlap. Angles 1 and 4 are the only ones not adjacent, or next to, each other.

2. a. It will cost $3 for a sandwich and a cookie. To get two additional sandwiches, it would cost another $4. Therefore, it would cost $7 to get three sandwiches and a cookie. Because she has only $6 to spend, this combination is not possible.

3. d. After the first two terms, each term is obtained by adding the preceding two terms in the sequence: $10 + 16 = 26$.

4. b. One foot in the model represents 100 yards, or 300 feet. So you can use a proportion involving feet to solve this problem. Let l represent the actual length of the Coliseum in feet:

$$\frac{1 \text{ foot}}{300 \text{ feet}} = \frac{l}{617} \text{ feet}$$
$$300 \times l = 1 \times 617$$
$$l \approx 2.06$$

So, when rounded to the nearest tenth, the length of the Coliseum in the model is about 2.1 feet.

5. c. Because there are a total of 105 students involved in sports and this makes up 21% of the students involved in extracurricular activities, find the total number of students by using the proportion $\frac{105}{x} = \frac{21}{100}$. Cross multiply to get $21x = 10,500$. Divide each side of the equal sign by 21 to get $x = 500$. There are 500 students in extracurricular activities, so find 17% of 500 to find the number of students involved in drama; 17% of $500 = 0.17 \times 500 = 85$.

6. e. To find the average of the numbers, divide the sum of the numbers by the number of terms being averaged. In this case, let x represent the temperature on the fifth day and set the expression equal to the average temperature for the five days, which was 90; $\frac{95 + 85 + 88 + 84 + x}{5} = 90$. Simplify the expression to $\frac{352 + x}{5} = 90$, because the total sum of the first four days is 352. Cross multiply to get $352 + x = 450$. By subtracting 352 from each side, x is equal to 98. If unsure about this type of question, this problem could also be solved by trying each of the answer choices to see which one results in an average of 90°. When 98 is added to the temperatures for the first four days, the sum is 450; 450 divided by 5 is 90.

7. b. The probability of selecting a nickel or a penny is equal to the number of nickels and pennies in the jar divided by the total number of coins in the jar. In other words, $\frac{\text{nickels} + \text{pennies}}{\text{total coins}}$. Because there are 3 nickels and 9 pennies, the number in the numerator (or top) of the fraction is 12. There are a total of 30 coins in the jar, so the probability becomes $\frac{12}{30}$, which reduces to $\frac{2}{5}$.

8. b. The perimeter of an object is the distance around the object. This can be found by finding the sum of the sides of the object. Because this figure is a pentagon, it has five sides. Three of the sides measure 3 inches and the remaining two sides measure 5 inches. Therefore, the sum of the sides is equal to $3 + 3 + 3 + 5 + 5 = 19$ inches.

9. d. When multiplied together, 11×0.032 is equal to 0.352. A quick way to solve a question that contains a number of decimal places is to first multiply the numbers as whole numbers; $11 \times 32 = 352$. Then count the number of decimal places in the numbers being multiplied and apply the same number of places to the answer. Because there are three decimal places in the number 0.032, the result of 352 becomes 0.352.

10. e. The 90% discount is applied to all three of the items. Therefore the total cost of the three T-shirts is equal to the sum of the items multiplied by 0.9. This is equal to $0.9 \times (a + b + c)$. To find the average cost of one T-shirt, divide the total cost of all three by 3. Therefore, the expression would become $\frac{0.9(a + b + c)}{3}$.

11. a. The expression in choice **a** uses the distributive property of multiplication over addition to find the total of purchasing three of each item, and then subtracts the cost of one box of rice because he is actually purchasing only two. Another way to solve this question is to find the total cost of the five items that are purchased ($9.95) and see that only choice **a** also results in this total when evaluated.

12. a. In the expression in the question, the terms a, b, and c are written over a common denominator of 3. Another way this can be expressed is to write each term individually over this common denominator of 3, as in choice **a**. Since the sum of the terms is still being divided by 3, choice **a** is equivalent to the original expression.

13. a. In order to divide two fractions, multiply the fraction being divided into by the reciprocal of the fraction being divided by. The expression $\frac{2}{3} \div \frac{5}{12}$ then becomes $\frac{2}{3} \times \frac{12}{5} = \frac{24}{15}$. This reduces to $\frac{8}{5}$, which is equal to $1\frac{3}{5}$ as a mixed number.

14. c. The arrival time of Train A is 6:42 A.M. and the departure time of Train D is 8:24 A.M. There are 18 minutes between 6:42 A.M. and 7:00 A.M., and there is one hour between 7:00 A.M. and 8:00 A.M. There are an additional 24 minutes between 8:00 A.M. and the departure time of 8:24 A.M. To find the difference of the times, add these values: 18 minutes + 1 hour + 24 minutes = 1 hour, 42 minutes.

15. d. To solve the inequality for x, first add 1 to each side of the inequality; $-4x - 1 + 1 \geq 11 + 1$ becomes $-4x \geq 12$. Next, divide each side of the inequality by -4. Note that when you divide or multiply each side of an inequality by a negative number, the inequality symbol reverses; $\frac{-4x}{-4} \geq \frac{12}{-4}$ simplifies to $x \leq -3$.

16. e. The only statement that does not contradict the original statement is choice **e**, because a square is a special rhombus.

17. c. In order to look for a reasonable answer, use rounding to make the numbers in the question compatible; 6,251 can be rounded to 6,000 and 312 can be rounded to 300. To find the percentage of teachers that have dual certification, divide 300 by 6,000. This can also be thought of as $\frac{3}{60}$. Since 3 out of 50 would be equal to 6 out of 100, or 6%, the most reasonable answer choice is 5%. This answer can be checked by dividing 3 by 60 to get 0.05, which is equal to 5%.

18. c. To find the total percentage, add the percent for electrical equipment and the percent for other equipment together. Adding 7.8% (electrical equipment) and 7.3% (other equipment) results in a total of 15.1% for both causes.

19. b. To answer this question, you are looking for the greatest difference in percentage between the percentage of deaths and total fires. Because smoking materials account for only 6.7% of the fires but for 28.9% of the deaths, this area has the greatest discrepancy in the percentages. It therefore has the highest ratio of percentage of deaths to total fires.

20. d. There are 11 different causes listed in the table, so look for the answer choices that have 11 sections within the circle graphs. Answer choices **a** and **e** do not contain 11 sections, so they can be eliminated immediately. Multiply the decimal form of each percentage from column 1 of the table by 360° to find the total degrees in each sector of the circle graph. Because the largest section is 27.5% of the circle, $0.275 \times 360 = 99$, so the largest sector of the graph should be about 100°. In answer choice **b**, the largest sector appears to be too large in relation to the next largest sector, and in answer choice **c** the largest sector appears to be smaller than 90°. The answer choice that has sectors that most reasonably represent the information in the table is choice **d**.

21. c. Each 9-foot wall has an area of 9×8 or 72 square feet. There are two such walls, so those two walls combined have an area of 72×2 or 144 square feet. Each 11-foot wall has an area of 11×8 or 88 square feet, and again there are two such walls: $88 \times 2 = 176$. To find the total surface area, add 144 and 176 to get 320 square feet.

22. e. Substitute the value of 40 in for C into the given formula: $\frac{9}{5}(40) + 32 = 72 + 32 = 104$. Therefore, 40° Celsius is equal to 104° Fahrenheit.

23. d. A way to order the fractions is to change each to its decimal form and compare the values. Change a fraction to a decimal by dividing the numerator (top number) by the denominator (bottom number); $\frac{1}{2} = 0.50$, $\frac{6}{11} = 0.54$, $\frac{3}{5} = 0.60$, and $\frac{5}{8} = 0.625$. These four fractions are in order from least to greatest. Because the question asked for the fractions in order from greatest to least, the correct order is choice **d**.

24. d. If the input is 63, the first step of the flow chart is $63 - 11 = 52$. Because the next step is missing, take a look at the third step and the final result that is obtained. The third step will add 7 to the answer of the missing step and get a result of 11. Therefore, the result of the missing step must be $11 - 7 = 4$. To get an answer of 4 from 52, you must divide 52 by 13. Thus, the missing step is to divide by 13.

25. a. Write out the equation. Remember *is* means equals and *of* means times. To find the answer, you first write one-eighth and one-sixth as fractions, and then you multiply straight across: $\frac{1}{8} \times \frac{1}{6} = \frac{1}{48}$.

26. d. In order to solve the equation $14x + 2(x + 1) = 34$, first use the distributive property to eliminate the parentheses. The equation then becomes $14x + 2x + 2 = 34$. Then, combine the like terms of $14x$ and $2x$ to get $16x + 2 = 34$. Subtract 2 from each side of the equation: $16x + 2 - 2 = 34 - 2$; $16x = 32$. Divide each side of the equation by 16 to get a result of $x = 2$. The only step not useful in solving this equation was choice **d**, add 2 to each side of the equation.

27. d. First convert the two mixed numbers to improper fractions; $2\frac{1}{4}$ becomes $\frac{9}{4}$ and $4\frac{5}{8}$ becomes $\frac{37}{8}$. Use a common denominator of 8 in order to add the three fractions together; $\frac{1}{2} = \frac{4}{8}$ and $\frac{9}{4} = \frac{18}{8} \cdot \frac{18}{8} + \frac{37}{8} + \frac{4}{8}$ $= \frac{59}{8}$. This is equal to $7\frac{3}{8}$ as a mixed number, which is choice **d**.

28. a. In order to solve this problem, first calculate the area of the rug. Then convert the answer to square inches, because each answer choice uses square inches as a label. The formula for the area of a circle is $A = \pi r^2$, where $r =$ the radius of the circle. Because each answer choice is left in terms of π, do not bother to substitute 3.14 for this symbol. The diameter of the rug is 152 cm so the radius, which is half of this measure, must be 76 cm. Substitute into the area formula: $A = \pi(76)^2 = 5{,}776\pi$ cm². Because each answer choice is in square inches and 1 cm = 0.39 in., then 1 cm² = 0.1521 in.². Multiply the area by 0.1521 to convert cm² to in.²; $5{,}776\pi \times 0.1521 = 878.53\pi$ in.².

29. b. Take caution in percent problems, especially when the percent taken is off of two different amounts. Figure the problem in two steps: first find 15% of $84.50 and then find 10% of the membership price *after* the 15% discount; 15% of $84.50 = 0.15 × 84.50 = 12.68; $84.50 − 12.68 = $71.82. Now, calculate 90% of $71.82 (remember, if you save 10%, you need to pay 90%); 0.90 × 71.82 = $64.64.

30. b. Notice that each value in the first column (h) is a multiple of three. If a multiple of three is multiplied by $\frac{1}{3}$, the result will be an integer. Because each number in the second column is an integer, try choice **b** first. If $h = 3$, then $k = \frac{1}{3} \times 3 + 3 = 1 + 3 = 4$. If $h = 6$, then $k = \frac{1}{3} \times 6 + 3 = 2 + 3 = 5$. If $h = 9$, then $k = \frac{1}{3} \times 9 + 3 = 3 + 3 = 6$. If $h = 12$, then $k = \frac{1}{3} \times 12 + 3 = 4 + 3 = 7$. If $h = 15$, then $k = \frac{1}{3} \times 15 + 3 = 5 + 3 = 8$. Each pair of values in the table satisfies the equation in choice **b**.

31. c. The speed of the train is 60 miles per hour, so as each hour increases by 1 the number of miles increase by 60. Therefore, the distance from Chicago would be equal to $60t$, because distance = rate × time. However, as the train moves on, the distance decreases from Los Angeles, so there must be a function of $-60t$ in the equation. At time $t = 0$, the distance is 2,000 miles, so the function is $2,000 - 60t$.

32. a. This problem has multiple steps. First, figure out what Deanna spent: $7 for popcorn, 2 hot dogs × 2 girls × $3 each = $12, 2 sodas × $4 = $8. Then add them up: $7 + $12 + $8 = $27. Next, figure out what Jamie spent: $13 × 2 = $26. Last, subtract the two numbers: $27 − $26 = $1. Deanna spent $1 more.

33. b. Because you are looking for the best rate for each weight, use the lesser amount in each weight category. The cost for a 2 oz. and a 6 oz. is $0.50 + $1.50, respectively, which is equal to a total of $2.00. The total cost for choice **a** is $2.50, choice **c** is $2.75, choice **d** is $2.50, and choice **e** is $3.50. Because choice **b** has the lowest cost, it is the least expensive.

34. e. The cost for 12 ounces at Speedy Delivery Service is $3.00 and the cost for 12 ounces at EZ Package System is $2.50. The difference between these amounts is $0.50. To find the percent of the difference, substitute these amounts into the proportion: $\frac{\text{change}}{\text{original amount}} = \frac{\%}{100}$. The proportion becomes $\frac{.50}{2.50} = \frac{x}{100}$. Cross multiply to get $2.5x = 50$. Divide 50 by 2.5 to get $x = 20\%$.

35. c. One way to solve this problem is to round each of the amounts to the nearest ten and then add the rounded amounts together; 5,618 rounds to 5,620, 5,085 rounds to 5,090, and 6,163 rounds to 6,160. The sum of 5,620 + 5,090 + 6,160 is equal to 16,870. Another approach would be to add the unrounded numbers first, and then round the answer to the nearest ten. When added, the sum of the numbers before rounding is 16,866. This number is also equal to 16,870 when rounded to the nearest ten.

36. d. Recall that to find an average (arithmetic mean), divide the sum of the terms by the total number of terms in the situation. To find the average number sold per month for the five-month period, first find the total number of music downloads sold and divide this number by 5. To find the total downloads represented, count the total number of symbols in the figure. There are 12 whole symbols and three half-symbols, making a total of 13.5 symbols in the figure. Because each symbol represents 150 downloads sold, multiply 13.5 × 150 = 2,025. Divide this amount by 5 to get an average of 405 downloads sold per month.

37. c. The third side of the triangle must be less than the sum of the other two sides (17 + 14) and greater than their difference (17 − 14). This means that the third side must be less than 31 and greater than 3. Only choice **c** fits these criteria.

38. b. Because there are 1,000 students and there are five students on a team, $1,000 \div 5 = 200$ teams. Therefore, there are a total of $1,000 + 200 = 1,200$ people involved; $1,200 \div 4$ gymnasiums is equal to 300 in each gym.

39. a. First determine the amount of water held in each container by finding the volume of each. The volume of water held by the rectangular box is found by multiplying the area of the base by the height of the water; $16 \text{ in.}^2 \times 9 \text{ in.} = 144 \text{ in.}^3$. The total volume of the cylindrical container can be found by using the formula $V = \pi r^2 h$, where r = the radius of the base, h = the height of the container, and $\pi = 3.14$; $V = (3.14)(2)^2(11) = (3.14)(4)(11) = 138.16 \text{ in.}^3$. Because there is more water in the rectangular box to begin with, the cylinder will overflow.

40. d. Keep in mind that in this question you are only looking for the person who likes to fish. Because it is stated that the friend who fishes is Miguel's neighbor, the person who fishes is not Miguel. Robert and Linda dislike sports that use balls, so the person who fishes must be one of them (it must be Sonja and Miguel who like tennis and volleyball). The statement *Sonja is older than both Robert and the friend who fishes* allows you to conclude that Robert is not the person who fishes. Therefore, the person who likes to fish must be Linda.

Skills Test in Writing—Section 1, Part A

1. b. This is not a complete sentence, because it has no subject. To correct this problem, the word *which* should be replaced by the word *it*, which becomes the subject of the sentence.

2. e. Because there are no grammatical, idiomatic, logical, or structural errors in this sentence, choice **e** is the best answer.

3. c. The verb *walked* should be modified by an adverb, not an adjective. The adverb *hesitantly* should replace the incorrect adjective *hesitant*.

4. e. Because there are no grammatical, idiomatic, logical, or structural errors in this sentence, choice **e** is the best answer.

5. c. The gerund *describing* is incorrect in this sentence. The infinitive *to describe* should be used.

6. d. This sentence has faulty parallelism. Two of the assistant's characteristics are adjectives (*smart, reliable*), while the third characteristic consists of a verb phrase and prepositional phrase (*will come on time*). To create proper parallelism, make all three characteristics adjectives by changing *will come on time* to *punctual* or *timely*.

7. c. The error is in punctuation. The two clauses in this compound sentence are independent and should be separated by a semicolon, not a comma.

8. c. This sentence contains faulty coordination. Using the conjunction *and* in this sentence creates an illogical link between the dependent and independent clauses. To make the sentence grammatically correct, you must delete *and*.

9. b. The error is in verb formation. The sentence requires the past tense of the verb *begin*. To correct this error, the past participle *begun* should be replaced with the past tense *began*.

10. e. Because there are no grammatical, idiomatic, logical, or structural errors in this sentence, choice **e** is the best answer.

11. a. When a negative word such as *no* or *not* is added to a sentence that already contains a negative, a double negative results. Because *barely* is a negative word, the use of *not* in this sentence creates a double negative. To correct this, change *couldn't* to *could*.

12. a. The verb *treated* should be modified by an adverb. *Bad* is an adjective and is used incorrectly; it should be replaced by the adverb *badly*.

13. e. Because there are no grammatical, idiomatic, logical, or structural errors in this sentence, choice **e** is the best answer.

14. a. This sentence contains a capitalization error. The names of seasons are not capitalized, so *Winter* should be lowercase (*winter*).

15. c. Here, the word *affect* is used incorrectly as a noun. *Affect* is a verb meaning to influence. As a noun, *effect* means result, which is how it is used in this sentence.

16. e. Because there are no grammatical, idiomatic, logical, or structural errors in this sentence, choice **e** is the best answer.

17. c. This is a sentence fragment; the independent clause does not have a subject. The first clause in the sentence is dependent and therefore does not stand alone. The subject must occur in the second clause. To correct this structural problem, a subject (*she*, *he*, or a person's name) should be added before the underlined *also noted*.

18. b. *Contemporary* and *modern* mean the same thing, so one of those words should be deleted to avoid a redundancy.

19. e. Because there are no grammatical, idiomatic, logical, or structural errors in this sentence, choice **e** is the best answer.

20. a. This sentence has an agreement problem. The plural pronoun *them* does not agree with the singular noun *story*. Therefore, *them* should be replaced by the singular pronoun *it*.

21. d. This sentence contains a pronoun error. When antecedents are connected with a *neither . . . nor* phrase, the pronoun should agree with the closer antecedent. In this sentence, the two antecedents are *soldiers* and *sergeant*. Because *sergeant* is the antecedent closer to the pronoun, the pronoun should be singular—either *his* or *her*—not the plural *their*. However, because *their location* makes more sense, a better solution would be to reverse the two antecedents.

Skills Test in Writing—Section 1, Part B

22. d. This choice is best because it is written in the active voice, and the sentence is constructed so that all modifiers are appropriately placed.

23. e. This is the correct choice because there is no shift in verb tense, and there is agreement between the noun *petition* and the pronoun *it*.

24. d. This is the only correct choice because the sentence makes a comparison among many things (every Best Actress nominee ever), and therefore requires the superlative, *youngest.* Do not be fooled by choice **c**, *most youngest.* Using *most* before *youngest* creates a double comparison, and therefore the makes the sentence grammatically incorrect. In choice **e**, *youngly* is not a real word.

25. b. The second clause of this sentence requires a parallel construction. Choice **b** is the only one in which all four elements are parallel.

26. e. This is the only choice that maintains the structure and meaning of the sentence and does not contain a redundancy.

27. a. This is the only choice that uses correct possession and the correct verb tense. Because *signal* is a singular noun, it needs a singular verb (*was*). Choice **e** implies that the scientists were in the act of confirming for 24 hours.

28. a. The other choices create either faulty subordination or a comma splice.

29. c. This is the only choice that contains both the correct pronoun and comparative form. The verb *is* is understood, so the sentence requires the subject pronoun *he*, not the object pronoun *him*. Because the comparison in this sentence is between only two people, the comparative form (*-er*) is required, not the superlative form (*-est.*) The use of *more* in choice **d** creates a double comparison, and is therefore incorrect. Besides containing the incorrect pronoun, choice **e** is incorrect because *less older* makes no sense.

30. d. Commas should be used to avoid ambiguity and to separate parenthetical elements. The phrase *the year I was born* is parenthetical.

31. e. The verb *are carved* in choice **e** is in agreement with the plural noun *likenesses*.

32. a. There are two possible errors in this sentence: One is subject-verb agreement and the other is the use of the words *between* and *among. Between* is used to compare two things; *among* is used to compare more than two. In this sentence *between* is correct, so choices **b** and **c** can be ruled out. Choices **d** and **e** are wrong because the verb *benefit* does not agree with the subject relationship.

33. d. The word *insure* in incorrect in this sentence. The word that should be used here to make the sentence clear and logical is *assure*.

34. d. The word *beside* means *at the side of*; the word *besides* means *other than* or *together with*. Choice **d** also corrects the subject-verb agreement error.

35. b. The most common way to join two independent clauses is with a comma and a coordinating conjunction. The only sentence that correctly does both is choice **b**. For choice **a** to be correct, the coordinating conjunction *so* needs to be deleted. Choice **d** lacks a proper coordinating conjunction, and has faulty parallelism. Choice **e** contains a verb tense error.

36. c. The comparison in this sentence between the America and England requires *as . . . as.* Choice **c** establishes the proper comparison and creates the only sentence that is clear and logical.

37. e. This is the only choice that properly places the commas between the three clauses in the sentence.

38. d. In this complex sentence, choice **d** is the only choice that results in a complete sentence.

Skills Test in Writing—Section 2, Essay Writing

Following are sample criteria for scoring a PPST essay.

A score "6" writer will

- create an exceptional composition that appropriately addresses the audience and given task
- organize ideas effectively, include very strong supporting details, and use smooth transitions
- present a definitive, focused thesis and clearly support it throughout the composition
- include vivid details, clear examples, and strong supporting text to enhance the themes of the composition
- exhibit an exceptional level of skill in the usage of the English language and the capacity to employ an assortment of sentence structures
- build essentially error-free sentences that accurately convey intended meaning

A score "5" writer will

- create a commendable composition that appropriately addresses the audience and given task
- organize ideas, include supporting details, and use smooth transitions
- present a thesis and support it throughout the composition
- include details, examples, and supporting text to enhance the themes of the composition
- generally exhibit a high level of skill in the usage of the English language and the capacity to employ an assortment of sentence structures
- build mostly error-free sentences that accurately convey intended meaning

A score "4" writer will

- create a composition that satisfactorily addresses the audience and given task
- display satisfactory organization of ideas, include adequate supporting details, and generally use smooth transitions
- present a thesis and mostly support it throughout the composition
- include some details, examples, and supporting text that typically enhance most themes of the composition
- exhibit a competent level of skill in the usage of the English language and the general capacity to employ an assortment of sentence structures
- build sentences with several minor errors that generally do not confuse the intended meaning

A score "3" writer will

- create an adequate composition that basically addresses the audience and given task
- display some organization of ideas, include some supporting details, and use mostly logical transitions
- present a somewhat underdeveloped thesis but attempt to support it throughout the composition
- display limited organization of ideas, have some inconsistent supporting details, and use few transitions

- exhibit an adequate level of skill in the usage of the English language and a basic capacity to employ an assortment of sentence structures
- build sentences with some minor and major errors that may obscure the intended meaning

A score "2" writer will
- create a composition that restrictedly addresses the audience and given task
- display little organization of ideas, have inconsistent supporting details, and use very few transitions
- present an unclear or confusing thesis with little support throughout the composition
- include very few details, examples, and supporting text
- exhibit a less than adequate level of skill in the usage of the English language and a limited capacity to employ a basic assortment of sentence structures
- build sentences with a few major errors that may confuse the intended meaning

A score "1" writer will
- create a composition that has a limited sense of the audience and given task
- display illogical organization of ideas, include confusing or no supporting details, and lack the ability to effectively use transitions
- present a minimal or unclear thesis
- include confusing or irrelevant details and examples, and little or no supporting text
- exhibit a limited level of skill in the usage of the English language and little or no capacity to employ basic sentence structure
- build sentences with many major errors that obscure or confuse the intended meaning

Sample 6 Essay

In the twenty-first century, the first place people turn to when there is a question to be answered, information to be located, or people to be contacted, is often the Internet. The Internet has supplanted the traditional encyclopedia, as well as a number of other reference sources, such as telephone books, and travel agents. On it, one can make reservations, plan vacations, play interactive games, learn a language, listen to music or radio programs, read the newspaper, and find out about a medical condition, without coming face-to-face with another person. Clearly, the Internet is an invaluable tool in modern life.

There is no limit to the subject matter that can be researched on the Internet. Search engines such as Yahoo! or Google, with a few keywords or Web addresses, can summon links to more sources than one could imagine. The Internet allows those at home in front of their computers to shop no matter what they wish to purchase. If that happens to be a bargain or an unusual item, popular auction sites are available with millions of unique items for sale.

If, however, one wishes to speak directly to another person, there are chat rooms and e-mail on the Internet that enable such dialogue. On almost any given topic, groups of people converse with one other. They may be giving opinions about a perfect travel itinerary, a book, or even a political party. Chat rooms can be a place to meet people, exchange ideas, or learn a new skill. The most prevalent use of the Internet, however, is the sending and receiving of e-mail messages. It is possible through e-mail to communicate instantly with anyone, anywhere, as long as there is an Internet connection. In a world where people frequently travel, and where family members do not necessarily live in the same state, e-mail is a means of making simple, inexpensive, immediate contact. In addition to verbal messages, digital cameras allow pictures to be taken and instantly transmitted on the Internet.

Unfortunately, there are individuals who subvert the opportunities offered by this technology. They are less than honest, disguise their identity, bilk people in financial scams, and entice unsuspecting people, including children, into giving them personal information. Caveats about these problems are currently being publicized so Internet users will not be victimized.

Of course, Internet providers, such as AOL, Microsoft, and Earthlink, are in business to make a profit, so there is usually a monthly fee for access. To increase profits, these providers sell advertising space. Some is easy to ignore, such as banners at the top and bottom of the screen. However, some advertising comes in the form of pop-ups that appear on the subscriber's screen and require the user to stop and respond, either positively or negatively, to the ads.

When one considers that, among other things, you can hear a concert, read a book, visit a museum and view its contents, visit the websites of numerous individuals and organizations, play a game with one or more people, and pay your bills, it becomes obvious that the uses of the Internet are too vast for a short list. Most would agree that much has been added to people's lives by connecting them to the Internet, and that we probably cannot anticipate what new purposes will be explored in the future.

Sample 4 Essay

The Internet has many important purposes. It has connected people all over the world in a way that has never been done before. You can send and receive e-mail from friends and colleagues whenever you want. You can also meet people through the Internet, and make friends. These facts prove the importance of the Internet in people's daily lives.

The internet is also good for research. If you want to get information about just about any topic, you can look it up. You don't have to go to the library. You can also use the Internet for recreation purposes. There are also good games and music that you can download, often for free.

Shopping may also be done on the Internet. You can buy things at home, without having to go the store.

For providers, the internet is a way for them to make money. They sell subscriptions, and also sell advertising space. Some provide good service, while others seem to want to make the most profit, and don't hire many technical people to help when there is a problem.

While the internet has its downside, such as identity theft problems and stalkers, these problems are found off the internet, too. You just have to be careful when using the internet, and you can enjoy the countless ways in which it has improved our lives.

Sample 1 Essay

The Internet has lots of purposes. It has been around for about ten years and it has really taken off. Most people have at least one computer in their house. Most of them have an internet connection. If you ask them why they have it, they will probably tell you about the useful purposes.

One of the best things you can do on the Internet is play games, such as chess and backgammon, with people you don't even know. Sometimes you have to pay for the games, and sometimes they are free. Sometimes you play against a really tough opponent, and sometimes you can win every game. I prefer the latter. It's also fun to listen to music on the internet. You can find just about any kind you like. These are some purposes of the Internet.

▶ Praxis I Scoring

Again, evaluate how you did on this practice exam by scoring the three tests of the Praxis I—Reading, Mathematics, and Writing—separately. First, find the number of questions you got right in each section. Questions you skipped or got wrong don't count; just add up the number of correct answers, and then divide by the number of questions in the section to come up with a percentage. Remember, if you don't know the score you need, try to aim for at least 70%.

You must also receive a passing score on the essay portion of the PPST Writing test. On this portion, the combined score of at least two writing experts will be used to evaluate how you did. The scoring criteria are outlined in detail in the answer explanations. Once again, take your essay and the scoring criteria to a teacher or a trusted friend and ask that person to assign a score to your essay.

You have probably seen improvement between your second practice exam score and this one; but if you didn't improve as much as you had hoped for, here are some options you may wish to consider.

- If you scored below 60%, you should seriously consider whether you are ready for the Praxis I at this time. A good idea would be to take some brush-up courses, either at a university or community college nearby or through correspondence, in the areas you feel less sure of. If you don't have time for a course, you might try private tutoring.
- If your score is in the 60–70% range, you need to work as hard as you can to improve your skills. Also, reread and pay close attention to all the advice in Chapters 2, 4, 5, and 6 of this book in order to improve your score. It might also be helpful to ask friends and family to make up mock test questions and quiz you on them.
- If your score is between 70% and 90%, you could still benefit from additional work by going back to chapters 4, 5, and 6 and brushing up your reading, writing, and general math skills before the exam.
- If you scored above 90%, that's great! This kind of score should make you a success in the academic program of your choice or in a teaching position. Don't lose your edge, though; keep studying right up to the day before the exam.

The key to success in almost any pursuit is to prepare for all you are worth. By taking the practice exams in this book, you have made yourself better prepared than other people who may be taking the exam with you. You have diagnosed where your strengths and weaknesses lie and learned how to deal with the various kinds of questions that will appear on the test. So go into the exam with confidence, knowing that you're ready and equipped to do your best.

Appendix A: Praxis II

THE PRAXIS II: SUBJECT ASSESSMENTS measure your knowledge of specific subjects that K–12 educators teach, as well as general and subject-specific teaching skills and knowledge.

Praxis II: Principles of Learning and Teaching (PLT)

TEST CODE	NAME OF TEST
0521	Principles of Learning and Teaching: Early Childhood
0522	Principles of Learning and Teaching: Grades K–6
0523	Principles of Learning and Teaching: Grades 5–9
0524	Principles of Learning and Teaching: Grades 7–12

Praxis II: Subject Assessments

TEST CODE	NAME OF TEST
0700	Agriculture
0900	Agriculture (CA)
0780	Agriculture (PA)
0133	Art: Content Knowledge
0132	Art: Content, Traditions, Criticism, and Aesthetics
0131	Art Making

TEST CODE	NAME OF TEST
0340	Audiology
0030	Biology and General Science
0233	Biology: Content Essays
0231	Biology: Content Knowledge, Part 1
0232	Biology: Content Knowledge, Part 2
0235	Biology: Content Knowledge
0100	Business Education
0242	Chemistry: Content Essays
0241	Chemistry: Content Knowledge
0245	Chemistry: Content Knowledge
0070	Chemistry, Physics, and General Science
0087	Citizenship Education: Content Knowledge
0800	Communication (PA)
0810	Cooperative Education
0867	Driver Education
0022	Early Childhood: Content Knowledge
0020	Early Childhood Education
0571	Earth and Space Sciences: Content Knowledge
0910	Economics
0271	Education of Deaf and Hard-of-Hearing Students
0353	Education of Exceptional Students: Core Content Knowledge
0382	Education of Exceptional Students: Learning Disabilities
0542	Education of Exceptional Students: Mild to Moderate Disabilities
0544	Education of Exceptional Students: Severe to Profound Disabilities
0021	Education of Young Children
0410	Educational Leadership: Administration and Supervision
0012	Elementary Education: Content Area Exercises
0014	Elementary Education: Content Knowledge

TEST CODE	NAME OF TEST
0011	Elementary Education: Curriculum, Instruction, and Assessment
0041	English Language, Literature, and Composition: Content Knowledge
0042	English Language, Literature, and Composition: Essays
0043	English Language, Literature, and Composition: Pedagogy
0360	English to Speakers of Other Languages
0830	Environmental Education
0120	Family and Consumer Sciences
0840	Foreign Language Pedagogy
0173	French: Content Knowledge
0171	French: Productive Language Skills
0511	Fundamental Subjects: Content Knowledge
0433	General Science: Content Essays
0431	General Science: Content Knowledge, Part 1
0432	General Science: Content Knowledge, Part 2
0435	General Science: Content Knowledge
0920	Geography
0181	German: Content Knowledge
0182	German: Productive Language Skills
0357	Gifted Education
0930	Government/Political Science
0856	Health and Physical Education: Content Knowledge
0550	Health Education
0200	Introduction to the Teaching of Reading
0600	Latin
0310	Library Media Specialist
0234	Life Science: Pedagogy
0560	Marketing Education
0061	Mathematics: Content Knowledge

TEST CODE	NAME OF TEST
0065	Mathematics: Pedagogy
0063	Mathematics: Proofs, Models, and Problems, Part 1
0146	Middle School: Content Knowledge
0049	Middle School English Language Arts
0069	Middle School Mathematics
0439	Middle School Science
0089	Middle School Social Studies
0112	Music: Analysis
0111	Music: Concepts and Processes
0113	Music: Content Knowledge
0091	Physical Education: Content Knowledge
0092	Physical Education: Movement Forms—Analysis and Design
0093	Physical Education: Movement Forms—Video Evaluation
0481	Physical Science: Content Knowledge
0483	Physical Science: Pedagogy
0262	Physics: Content Essays
0261	Physics: Content Knowledge
0265	Physics: Content Knowledge
0530	Pre-Kindergarten Education
0390	Psychology
0201	Reading Across the Curriculum: Elementary
0202	Reading Across the Curriculum: Secondary
0300	Reading Specialist
0860	Safety/Driver Education
0420	School Guidance and Counseling
0400	School Psychologist
0211	School Social Worker: Content Knowledge
0951	Social Sciences: Content Knowledge

TEST CODE	NAME OF TEST
0082	Social Studies: Analytical Essays
0081	Social Studies: Content Knowledge
0085	Social Studies: Interpretation and Analysis
0083	Social Studies: Interpretation of Materials
0084	Social Studies: Pedagogy
0950	Sociology
0191	Spanish: Content Knowledge
0194	Spanish: Pedagogy
0192	Spanish: Productive Language Skills
0352	Special Education: Application of Core Principles across Categories of Disability
0351	Special Education: Knowledge-Based Core Principles
0690	Special Education: Preschool/Early Childhood
0371	Special Education: Teaching Students with Behavioral Disorders/Emotional Disturbances
0381	Special Education: Teaching Students with Learning Disabilities
0321	Special Education: Teaching Students with Mental Retardation
0220	Speech Communication
0330	Speech-Language Pathology
0048	Teaching Foundations: English
0068	Teaching Foundations: Mathematics
0528	Teaching Foundations: Multiple Subjects
0438	Teaching Foundations: Science
0880	Teaching Speech to Students with Language Impairments
0280	Teaching Students with Visual Impairments
0050	Technology Education
0640	Theatre
0890	Vocational General Knowledge
0940	World and U.S. History
0941	World and U.S. History: Content Knowledge

Appendix B: How to Use the CD-ROM

HOW PREPARED ARE you for the official Praxis Exam? Here's a great way to build confidence and know you are ready: Use LearningExpress's Academic Skills Tester AutoExam™ CD-ROM software developed by PEARSoft Corporation. The disk, included inside the back cover of this book, can be used with any PC running Windows XP SP2 or Vista. (Currently, this CD-ROM does not work with Macintosh.) If installing on Windows XP SP2, your PC will need Microsoft.NET Framework 3.0, but if it doesn't have this software, the CD-ROM software will automatically install it.

The following description represents a typical "walk through" of the software. To install the program:

1. Insert the CD-ROM into your CD-ROM drive. The CD should run automatically. If it does not, proceed to Step 2.
2. From Windows XP or Vista, Select **Start** and then choose **Run**; from Windows, select **File**.
3. Type D:\Setup (assuming your CD-ROM is drive D).
4. Click OK.

The screens that follow will walk you through the installation procedure and basic usage.

For in-depth instructions and information on all of the Academic Skills Tester's unique features, click the blue "?" button found on the top-right corner of the main sign-in screen to access the User's Guide. Here, you can learn everything you need to know about creating a user account, configuring and taking a practice exam, and even how to review your results.

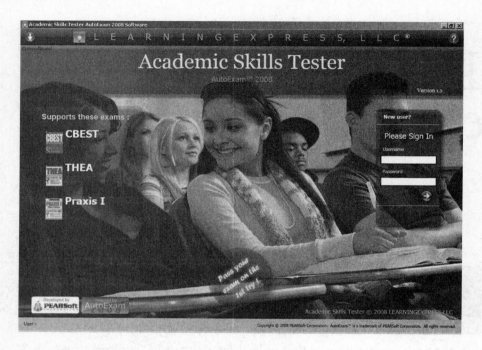

From the sign-in screen, click the **New User? <u>Click here</u>** link.

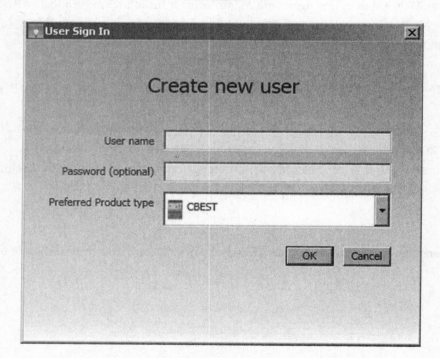

Now enter whatever username you would like to use. You also have the option of using a password. This allows you to record your progress and review your performance for as many simulated exams as you would like.

Now, because this CD-ROM supports 3 different academic exams, you need to select your exam of interest—Praxis I—under the Preferred Product type pull-down.

Click **OK.**

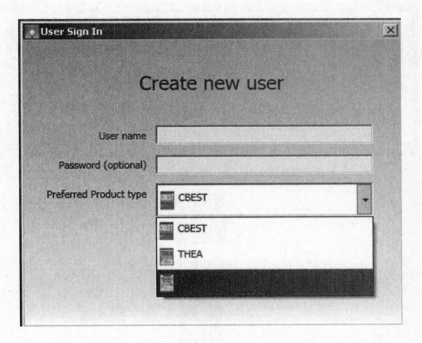

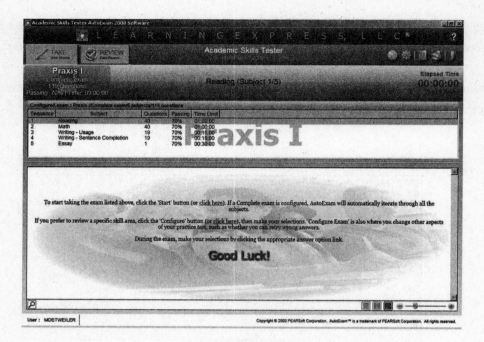

Figure 1

Figure 2

Now you are into the **Take New Exams/Review Past Exams** section, as shown above.

You can choose **Start Exam** button (Figure 1 above) to start taking your test, or the **Configure Options** button (Figure 2 above). The next screenshot shows you what your configuration options are.

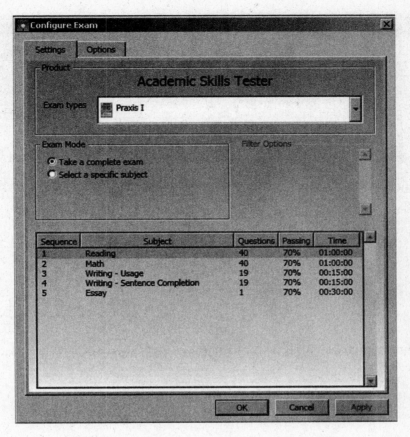

Pressing the **Configure Options** button gives you plenty of options to help you fine-tune your rough spots. How about warming up with questions about math? Click **Select a specific subject**, and then the **Math** option. Choose the number of questions you want to review right now. By clicking the **Options** tab, you can choose whether to wait until you have finished to see how you did (**Final Review & Score**) or have the computer tell you after each questions whether your answer is right (**Continuous Review & Score**). Choose **Retry Incorrect Responses** to get a second chance at questions you answer wrong. (This option works best with the setting **Select a specific subject** rather than the setting **Take a complete test**.) If you have chosen the wrong academic exam, you can change that in the **Exam types** pull-down menu. When you finish choosing your settings and options, click **Apply** to apply those settings and options and **OK** to start. Then click the **Start Exam** button (illustrated in Figure 1 on the previous page) on the main exam screen. Your screen will look like the one shown next.

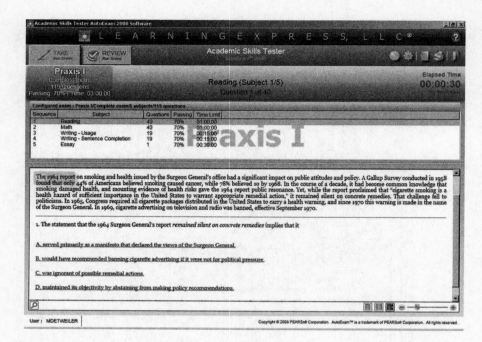

Questions come up one at a time, just as they will on the real exam, and you click on the desired choice to answer.

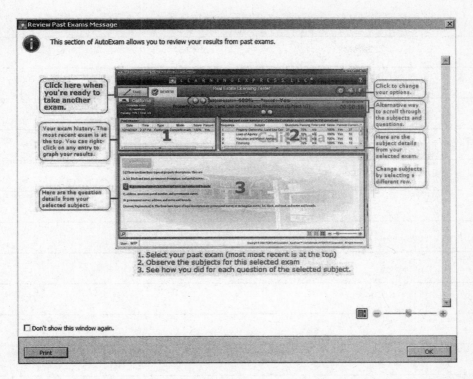

When you have finished your exam or subject area, you will receive the **Review Past Exams Message**, which contains detailed instructions that you can print out for how you can proceed. Click **OK** on the **Review Past Exams** screen to view your results. If you don't want to review your results now, you can always do it later by clicking on the **Review Past Exams** tab on the toolbar on the main screen. When you use **Review Results**, you will see your score and whether you passed. The questions come up one at a time. By clicking the **Configure Options** button from this screen, you can choose whether to look at all the questions or just the ones you missed. You can also choose whether you want an explanation of the correct answer displayed automatically under the question.

Again, to take full advantage of all of the Academic Skills Tester's features, be sure to review the User's Guide, which you can access clicking the blue "**?**" button found on the top-right corner of the CD-ROM's main sign-in screen.

For technical support, call 800-295-9556.

NOTES

NOTES

NOTES